INCOMPARABLE

In Remembrance
Capitaine Léon Charles Émile Auguste Loÿ
(1873–1915)
Mort pour la France

INCOMPARABLE

NAPOLEON'S 9TH LIGHT INFANTRY REGIMENT

T.E. CROWDY

First published in Great Britain in 2012 by Osprey Publishing,
Midland House, West Way, Botley, Oxford OX2 0PH, United Kingdom.
443 Park Avenue South, New York, NY 10016, USA.
Email: info@ospreypublishing.com

OSPREY PUBLISHING IS PART OF THE OSPREY GROUP

ISBN: 978 1 84908 332 4
E-pub ISBN: 978 1 78200 184 3
PDF ISBN: 978 1 78200 183 6

Page design by Ken Vail Graphic Design, Cambridge UK
Index by Alan Thatcher
Typeset in Minion Pro
Originated by PDQ Digital Media Solutions Ltd., Suffolk UK
Printed in China through Worldprint

12 13 14 15 16   10 9 8 7 6 5 4 3 2 1

Osprey Publishing is supporting the Woodland Trust, the UK's leading woodland conservation
charity, by funding the dedication of trees.

www.ospreypublishing.com

Front cover: The 9th Light Infantry turn the field at Marengo. (akg-images)

CONTENTS

ACKNOWLEDGEMENTS

A t the outset it would be remiss not to acknowledge the work of two French soldier-historians in centuries past. Firstly Captain L. Dubois of a later incarnation of the 9th Light Infantry, who in 1839 compiled the surviving documentation of the corps in the French Army's archives. After completing his work, Dubois penned a short history of the 9th Light. This manuscript contains a number of anecdotes which he attributed to officers of Napoleonic vintage whom he had interviewed, or corresponded with. I have therefore classed Dubois' account as part of the oral history of the regiment. The second great chronicler of the regiment's history was Captain Léon Loÿ to whom this work is respectfully dedicated. Loÿ was killed in action during the Great War, but he left us with a monumental regimental history of the 84th Line, completed in 1905, which incorporates a detailed summary of the Ninth's many campaigns. My own work builds on these two sources and incorporates several key accounts which only came to light after Loÿ's work.

This book is the product of more than a decade and a half of research, travel and debate. In that time a great number of friends and colleagues have inspired and advised me. I am deeply indebted to Martin Lancaster and Pierre-Yves Chauvin for their advice and valuable contributions; also to Gerd Hoad, who kindly commented on my early draft. I also wish to express my thanks to Professor Alan Forrest, director of the Centre for Eighteenth Century Studies and Colonel Dr Frédéric Guelton, former head of department of the French Army's Service Historique de la Défense (SHD), both of whom were generous with their time and advice. Personal thanks go to Ian Edwards, Ron Greatorex, Bernard Coppens, Carlo Demuth, Todd Fisher, Yves Martin, Hans-Karl Weiss, Robert Ouvrard, Alfred Umhey, Oliver Schmidt, David Hollins, Steve Vickers, Ian Castle, Anthony 'Louis' Lofts, Ashley Kane and the late Graeme Harrison-Jones.

I wish to express my gratitude to the staff at the Service Historique de l'Armée de Terre (Vincennes); the British Library (London); Agathe Formery of the Photographic Service at the Musée de l'Armée (Paris); Pierre Lierneux at the Musée Royal de l'Armée (Brussels); Peter Harrington at the Anne S. K. Brown Military Collection; and Emmanuel Bodart, president of Société Archéologique de Namur for his gracious permission to reproduce excerpts from the Cardron letters.

At Osprey I would like to thank Kate Moore, Emily Holmes, John Tintera and Mike Ramalho for their advice and support. My special thanks also go to Ruth Sheppard who commissioned and edited this project. Of course, none of this would have been possible without the constant support, patience and understanding of my dear wife, Sarah.

GLOSSARY

In part of the era when this book is set, France had adopted the Revolutionary Calendar. For clarity all dates have been converted to the Gregorian calendar. Place names have been given in the form most familiar to English-speaking readers. Where place names have changed significantly, the modern name is also noted. Wherever possible, technical terminology and military ranks have been translated into their nearest English-language equivalent. Several words are not in common use, or require clarification, including:

Cantineer	Licensed female sutler attached to army (from Fr. *cantinière*)
Carabineer	An early term for French rifleman. During the Napoleonic period the term carabineer was synonymous with grenadier
Chasseur	A French light infantryman or light cavalryman (literally huntsman)
Cheval-de-frise	Temporary defensive obstacle; commonly formed by a log with spikes inserted (literally Frisian horse)
Fathom	In old French there was no equivalent measurement of a yard (3ft), but fathoms (Fr. *toise*) were used on land; a fathom equalled six French feet or 1.949cm
Foot	Unit of measurement; a French foot (Fr. *pied*) was 32.484cm
Gendarme	Military policeman
Inch	Unit of measurement; a French inch was 2.707cm

Jaeger	A German light infantryman; the term was also used by the Russian army
League	Unit of distance approximately 4km; as a rule of thumb, one league equated to the distance infantry could march in an hour
Pound	Unit of mass; a French pound (Fr. *livre*) was 489.5g; in 1812 the French pound was rationalized at 500g
Sapper	A pioneer soldier equipped with an axe and leather apron
Sub-officer	A non-commissioned officer with the rank of sergeant, or above; French corporals are not classed as NCOs

LIST OF IMAGES

Between pages 128 and 129

Colonel Meunier is standing on his father-in-law's left. (akg-images)

9. Distribution of the Eagles by Napoleon on the Champ de Mars, Paris 5 December 1804. (Mary Evans Picture Library)

10. Detail: the Ninth's Eagle is held above all others. (Mary Evans Picture Library)

11. Presentation of the Legion of Honour at the Camp of Boulogne, 15 August 1804. (The Bridgeman Art Library)

12. Colourful depiction of French light infantry on the march near Jena in 1806. By Johann-Martin-Friedrich Geissler. (The Art Archive)

13. Detail of Marshal Michel Ney (1769–1815), the Ninth's inspirational corps commander in 1804–05. By Charles Meynier. (The Art Archive)

Between pages 272 and 273

14. Military hospital at Marienburg, Poland, June 1807. French and Russian wounded receive treatment in the crowded, ancient hall of the Knights of the Teutonic Order. By Adolphe Roehn. (The Art Archive)

15. The departure ceremony of French conscripts in 1807 (detail); by Louis Leopold Boilly. The Ninth received something like 15,000 recruits in the Napoleonic era. (The Art Archive)

16. Carabineer officer of the 9th Light Infantry believed to be by Weiland (1808). (Anne S.K. Brown Military Collection)

17. Carabineer and chasseur of the 9th Light Infantry in 1808. These soldiers are wearing the classic full dress light infantry uniform of the early empire period. (Anne S.K. Brown Military Collection)

18. The turning point of the war. Dupont surrenders at Bailen on 23 July 1808, (detail) by Jose Casado del Alisal. (The Bridgeman Art Library)

19. In response to Bailen, Napoleon took an army to Madrid. They met the Spanish at the pass of Somosierra on 30 November 1808. Painting by Louis Lejeune. (The Bridgeman Art Library)

20 and 21. Two interpretations of the brutality in Spain. (Top) Goya's *The 3rd of May 1808*. Spanish rebels are executed by a French firing squad. Compare this to detail of a painting by Lejeune showing a guerrilla attack on a French convoy near Salinas. A French captive is brutally put to death. (akg-images/Erich Lessing and The Art Archive)

PROLOGUE: AUTUMN 1799

On the left bank of the Seine, at the edge of the Faubourg Saint-Germain, the army pensioners in the Hôtel des Invalides snored contentedly in their bunks. The Champ de Mars was quiet and the sentinels outside the École Militaire looked up into the autumnal night, waiting forlornly for a first glimpse of dawn. A little to the east, through leafy gardens and along the Rue de Babylone, two drummers marched under lantern light into the forecourt of the barracks and began to beat the reveille. The drumbeats echoed off the courtyard walls and into the sleeping chambers behind them. Hundreds of pairs of eyes blinked open followed by a universal groan and a chorus of spluttering coughs.

The building was soon a hive of activity by smoky candlelight as the men of the 9th Light Infantry put themselves to work. While some beat and folded heavy woollen blankets, others opened the shutters to allow the morning air to circulate. The corporals took roll-call and then went scampering off looking for their sergeants. From everywhere came the hollow clanking of hobnailed shoes on bare wooden floors and stairs; above, below and on the cobblestones in the yard, a perpetual stomp, stomp, stomp.

The Babylone Casern was a functional, five-storey barrack building. As dawn broke and the first rays of light peeked through the attic windows, the routines of garrison life were in full swing. Inside each room the veterans smoked pipes and reminisced over their latest exploits while their younger bunkmates swept the floors.

The men spanned a broad range of ages. Although most were in their early to mid-20s, some had been in uniform since before the Revolution and had served in the King's army. A precious few, men like Corporal Guillaume Lombars and Sergeant François Brunot, could still remember going to the American Revolution with Rochambeau 20 years before. The veterans had rude complexions; weather beaten and prematurely wrinkled by privation and alcohol. Their cheeks were ruddy, pockmarked with powder burns and slow-roasted by countless open fires and summer suns. In comparison the younger men looked pale and soft.

Perched on the ends of their bunks men sewed patches onto their coats or mended their gaiters with needle, thread and awl. Others brushed their coats and a newly appointed corporal cursed after jabbing his finger sewing his chevrons onto the sleeve of his coat. Smoke billowed from the chimneys as the soldier cooks prepared fires for the daily soup. While some fetched water, others rubbed grease into their mess pans to keep them clean. An old hand nuzzled slabs of ammunition bread, smelling if it was fresh or taken with mould.

Meanwhile the sergeant-majors gathered outside the duty commandant's office with their notebooks and pencils to receive the daily orders. On his way to check the guardhouse, an adjutant asked if there had been deserters overnight – more to add to his list. Beyond the sergeant-majors stood a motley assembly of soldiers, anxiously waiting to speak to the same duty officer; each with petitions for compassionate leave, pleas to be excused duty and troubles galore.

In the forecourt, just inside the main gate, some of the sergeants were joking with the cantineers who were preparing to set off into town to replenish their stocks of brandy, vinegar, tobacco and non-rationed delicacies such as sausage and cheese. As the cantineers set off, the sharp-eyed sentinels on the gatehouse snapped to attention as the chief passed on the way back from his morning ride. Auguste Caffarelli acknowledged their coming to attention with a polite nod and continued past the barracks to his lodgings at No. 10 Rue de Babylone. The residence was a fairly grand affair. It had been the town house of Prince de Conti before the Revolution and had passed in ownership to Caffarelli's eldest brother, Max. Taking coffee in the study, he shuffled his papers and committed his brain to the particulars of the forthcoming Council of Administration.

Across the Seine and to the east of the city, beyond the site of the Bastille and into the Faubourg Saint Antoine, the depot was quartered in the Rue de

Charonne. Captain Pierre Gros went into the fresh morning air smoking his pipe. He looked down at his paralysed left hand and remembered the feeling of strength he'd once had there. Gros' contemplation was interrupted by the children of the corps racing past to their morning lessons. These young scamps were the sons of officers, or army orphans, taught to read, write and schooled in the soldierly arts. Both of Captain Gros' sons had been pupils and the eldest, Pierre, had recently graduated, signing up for active service at the age of 16.

Around the yard the craftsmen prepared their workshops for a busy day. Dressed in a thick apron, Master Cobbler Antoine Kastner assembled the tools on his bench to re-sole his brother-in-law's boots. The air in the shop was heavy with the acrid smell of animal glue, waxes, stains and dyes. While Master Kastner arranged his hammer, nails and threads, the tailor, Master Fontaine, prepared for another day of miracle working. With a concerned expression he inspected the precious and dwindling bolts of serge, linen and heavy woollen cloth. Meanwhile his subordinates sat on stools and made forage caps from the recycled cloth from the slop chests. The apprentices cut white woollen hunting horn badges and sewed them onto the turn-backs of the newly made coats. Among the apprentices was Master Fontaine's son, François.

Downstairs in the workshop below the tailors, the armourer, Master Regnier, prepared for a delivery of muskets while his son worked the bellows on the forge. Regnier had his work cut out ensuring the soldiers' 'five-foot clarinets' were in the best working order. There were many different models of flintlock musket in use, a long-running problem created by successive unit amalgamations and a vogue among light infantrymen for shorter-barrelled muskets. In a time before precision machine tooling, Regnier's workshop was stacked with boxes of spare springs, screws, ramrod heads and files. For cleaning and polishing there were stocks of brick dust, vinegar for use on brass fittings, lubricating oils and everywhere lay bundles of rags donated by the tailors. Stacked in the corner were barrels of knapped flints and lead wrappers for holding them in the jaws of a musket lock. Outside his shed, a rickety, mud-splattered cart containing boxes of new muskets came juddering to a halt. Each musket would have to be stripped down, inspected, cleaned and oiled before being numbered and issued to one of the new recruits exercising in the yard.

Such was a typical morning for these men in the Paris garrison. Little did they know their fate was being shaped in sleepy Saint-Raphaël on France's Mediterranean coast. On 9 October 1799 General Napoleon Bonaparte stepped off a boat from Egypt to a tumultuous welcome. As Bonaparte climbed into a carriage and set off for Paris he did not have a plan as such, only an infinite sense of destiny and ambition. France was ready for change and General Bonaparte was the man to lead it. The great Napoleonic drama had begun and the 9th Light Infantry were to be cast in a leading role.

ESPRIT DE CORPS

T he year 1799 was a sombre ending to a century illuminated by enlightenment and revolutionary optimism. Europe was ablaze with a seemingly interminable war. Ten summers on from the storming of the Bastille, a second coalition of the Great Powers had been formed against republican France. Desperate to stop French expansion and the spread of revolutionary ideologies, the forces of Great Britain, Russia, Austria and the Ottoman Empire were embroiled in a bitter conflict raging from India to Egypt; Palestine and Syria; up through Naples into northern Italy; Switzerland, along the Rhine into Holland; and across the globe's oceans. Hundreds of thousands of young men were in uniforms of every hue, all sullied by dirt, sweat and blood. Villages and country lanes resounded to the crunch of hobnailed boots and the clanking and creaking of military vehicles and horse teams. In the year Frenchmen first adopted the metric system and discovered the Rosetta Stone in Egypt, there was scant cause for optimism.

In 1799 the 9th Light Infantry (hereafter, simply 'the Ninth') was commanded by Auguste Caffarelli. At this time the rank of colonel was suppressed as it was considered a reminder of the despotic times before the storming of the Bastille. For the same reason the term 'regiment' was not used by the French army. In republican parlance, the Ninth was a half-brigade of light infantry. Instead of 'colonel', Citizen Caffarelli bore the rank of 'brigade commander'.

By all accounts a tall man, Caffarelli had just celebrated his thirty-third birthday. Like many of his generation, he could already reflect on a life rich in experience. He had been born as François-Auguste de Caffarelli du Falga in 1766 at the family seat not far from Toulouse. His was a large noble family of Italian descent, made rich by the building of the Canal du Midi. Showing an aptitude for military subjects at a young age, Caffarelli enrolled in the army of the King of Sardinia with the rank of sub-lieutenant and remained in service until the Wars of the Revolution broke out in 1792. With his native south-west France threatened by Spanish invasion, Caffarelli quit Italy and patriotically enrolled as a trooper in the 15th Dragoons, in the Army of the Eastern Pyrenees. Before long he was employed in various staff appointments, rising to the rank of brigade commander in the Army of the Sambre and Meuse.

Caffarelli's appointment to the Ninth came at the tail-end of the War of the First Coalition (1792–97). General Bonaparte's victories in Italy had forced Austria into a peace settlement and so the Ninth was withdrawn from the Rhine frontier to Paris and earmarked for the proposed invasion of England. This expedition never sailed. In 1799 hostilities with Great Britain, Austria and Russia were renewed and the War of the Second Coalition began. As this war raged, the Ninth remained in Paris, seemingly forgotten. While reputations were being made on the field of honour, Caffarelli's chief opponents were the bureaucrats at the Ministry of War who were seemingly intent on condemning his command to abject poverty and cannibalizing it to populate other units.

In an inspection report prepared by the commander of the 17th Military Division (the military administrative district of the Paris area), General Lestrange described the Ninth's esprit de corps as excellent and noted the men were well disciplined. Despite the predominance of youth, General Lestrange found the men to be very clean, keeping themselves quiet and constantly busy with things to do around the barracks and sheds. Lestrange described the men's appearance as excellent, despite the poor quality of the uniforms he saw. He remarked he could say nothing about the soldiers' linen as it was in such poor condition.[1]

The rank and file of the light infantry were called chasseurs (huntsmen). When correctly attired, a chasseur's uniform consisted of a short-tailed, dark blue coat, with red collar, cuff flaps and white trimmings; tight blue pantaloons; gaiters cut to resemble ornate hussar boots; a felt bicorne hat with a tricolour cockade; green epaulettes and a short sword which bestowed a certain status on them. The badge of the chasseur was the hunting horn. This device was worn on the turn-backs of the coattails and stamped onto their buttons. The elite troops of the Ninth were the carabineers; a name derived from the rifled carbines with which they were originally armed. As elite troops, the carabineers wore red epaulettes and the flaming-grenade badge of the grenadiers. Their shakos were fitted with tumbling, red horsehair plumes. Originally the unit's sharpshooters, the carabineers had become shock troops. Sometimes a commander did not need a brigade or a battalion, just a handful of men who would flinch at nothing. The carabineers were these men and their special uniforms were an important part of their esprit de corps. A man smartly dressed in military uniform demanded respect; one dressed like a vagrant merited only pity or scorn.

Retaining a good standard of uniform was all a question of finance and, like the rest of France in 1799, the Ninth's coffers were empty. Financial management was the responsibility of the half-brigade's Council of Administration. As the title suggests, this body was responsible for all the details relating to the appointment of officers, to the pay of the troops, the bookkeeping and so on.[2] The council met at a member's lodgings weekly or extraordinarily, if the commander thought necessary. The council had seven members: the brigade commander, three captains, a lieutenant or sub-lieutenant, one sub-officer and one corporal or volunteer. It was chaired by Caffarelli and each member had an equal vote. The quartermaster treasurer also attended the council, sitting opposite the chairman. He made a financial report and acted as secretary for the council, but he did not have a vote.

At the best of times, managing the finances of an organization with over 3,000 employees requires skilful administration; but to manage the accounts of a half-brigade in the latter half of the 1790s required someone better versed in the rites of alchemy than bookkeeping. In 1799 the Ninth's alchemist was a former pharmacy student named Etienne Saÿvé. A veteran from the Royal Army, Saÿvé had volunteered in 1784 at the age of 20. His first taste of military administration came in 1788 when appointed quartermaster corporal, the useful soul who organized a company's food and lodgings on the march. After the Revolution, Saÿvé became an officer and then quartermaster treasurer. He performed his duties with distinction and was duly rewarded with a set of captain's epaulettes. General Lestrange was clearly taken by Saÿvé, commenting he 'fulfils his duties with zeal and exactitude.' He noted Saÿvé to be 'a very good citizen,' displaying 'probity and integrity' along with, 'wise conduct.'[3]

Captain Saÿvé's duties were manifold, but foremost he was an executor of the decisions made by the Council of Administration and the unit's accountant. His records kept track of exactly how much (or little) money came in from the Ministry of War and its subsequent allocation towards uniforms, provisions and pay. He also oversaw the management of a complicated series of deductions from the men's pay that covered items such as the men's 'petty equipment' (their shirts, collars, shoes, buckles and haversack). There were further deductions for food, heating fuel and separate accounts that provided for the laundry, barbers, tailors and upkeep of the leather equipment. Saÿvé supplemented these funds from the pay deductions of men in the guardroom, prison and from those on leave. Saÿvé could also raise money by auctioning the personal effects of deserters and the dead. It was an enormous task, further complicated by reckless hyperinflation and drastic changes in government fiscal policy.

To maintain their uniforms, the Ninth needed an injection of cash. At the time of General Lestrange's inspection, the Ninth's pay chest was full of worthless *assignats*, a type of government bond long since devalued. The council wrote a letter to the Ministry of War explaining their financial plight. The reply? It was unpatriotic to ask for what the government did not have. Rendered impotent, Caffarelli ordered the Ninth's clothing officer to buy the cheapest cloth possible and to scrimp, cutting every corner while endeavouring to retain a semblance of the proud uniform. It was hard enough keeping the existing men dressed, so when the conscripts began flooding in to meet the demands of the escalating conflict, they found themselves in a wretched state. According to one account, instead of coats they were issued jackets made of calico, sometimes blue, sometimes white. Instead of gaiters, they tore strips of cloth and made puttees, binding their ill-fitting shoes or wooden clogs.[4]

The man entrusted with the thankless task of 'clothing officer' was Captain Pierre Gros, the Ninth's depot commander. Like many of the senior officers in the corps, Pierre Gros' history with the Ninth stretched back to the Royal Army. He had served with the unit from the beginning, since September 1784 when the Ninth bore the title of Chasseurs of Cévennes. In that year, Pierre Gros had been employed in the cloth trade in the city of Carcassonne. He had only just quit the army having served in the Regiment of Angoumois. He was married, had sired a son and was looking to settle down. Unfortunately there was a recession in the textile industry and the enlistment bounties being paid by the new Cévennes battalion were too good for an old soldier to ignore. Gros accepted a substantial bounty and was immediately promoted to sergeant. As a further incentive, his two-year-old son Pierre Gros Jr was added to the quota of 'children of the corps,' ensuring the infant was fed at the battalion's expense.[5]

After the fall of the Bastille, Gros climbed towards his captaincy, each promotion facilitated by the emigration of officers opposed to the Revolution or enemy gunfire. Towards the end of the War of the First Coalition, on 18 April 1797, Captain Gros was asked to lead an attack near Neuwied where the French army was forcing a crossing of the Rhine. To resist their passage the Austrians built a redoubt protected by five guns. Twice the Ninth attacked, and twice they were beaten back. Desperate to clear a path for the army behind them, the Ninth's carabineer companies were combined into an assault force. Gros put himself at their head and led them forward, seizing the position and two hundred prisoners.[6] In the assault Gros was struck in the left forearm by a ball which shattered the bone. He was left with a deep scar and the permanent paralysis of his wrist and hand. Given the medical knowledge of the age, he was lucky not to lose the arm completely.

When peace was made in 1797, Gros was in his late forties and by rights should have been invalided out of service. However, with a lame arm, work would be very hard to come by at his age. His brother officers conspired to keep him gainfully employed. During his inspection General Lestrange recommended Gros for a garrison command. The recommendation was never fulfilled. Instead, in October 1798, Gros was put in charge of the depot and made clothing officer. This was a role to which he was theoretically well suited given his background in the cloth trade.

Prior to Gros' appointment, command of the depot (or auxiliary company as it was known before 1797) had been entrusted to Captain Robert Marthe, a freckle-faced former timber merchant from Versailles. Like Gros, Marthe had joined the Cévennes battalion at its creation, transferring from the Regiment of Soissonois in return for a promotion to sergeant. While Gros had made a name for himself in combat, Marthe excelled in the administrative aspects of service. Working his way up from quartermaster corporal to the officer corps, Marthe was the battalion's quartermaster treasurer before Saÿvé took over. In 1793 Marthe helped organize the finances of the Army of the Ardennes and received high praise for his skills. At the end of the war General Lestrange reported Marthe to be 'a very good citizen, wise in conduct and proven in honesty.' He praised his 'good administration, great intelligence and integrity.' Lauding his praises, Lestrange recommended Marthe for a superior administrative role. However, instead of a summons to the Ministry of War, Marthe found himself back in charge of a company, as his position was freed up for Pierre Gros. Was Marthe pleased to make way for an old comrade, or was he privately irked to have gone back into the line after years of administrative work? Finding him a suitable desk job would become something of a cause célèbre for successive commanders.

While it was stationed in Paris the Ministry of War expected the Ninth to reach its full complement of 3,169 men, organized into three 'field battalions' and a depot. The Ninth had returned from the previous war with fewer than 800 men fit for service. It therefore required a dramatic influx of recruits.

During the previous war recruitment had been a fairly haphazard affair relying on voluntary enlistments and a series of emergency levies. To make recruitment more reliable, a formal system of military conscription was introduced in France on 5 September 1798. Any man between the ages of 20 and 25 on the first day of Vendémiaire[7] was assigned to one of five annual conscription 'classes'. The lists of those eligible were provided by the birth registers held in each 'commune' (local municipality). The candidates were required to take a medical and if found fit they were entered into a lottery. The draw began with the first (youngest) class and moved up through the others as required.

The first ballot called up 200,000 men on 28 September 1798. All over France, young men resorted to desperate measures to avoid service. The roads were full of young men off to visit distant relations on the west coast or up in the mountains. There was an epidemic of 'accidents' resulting in severed trigger fingers; mysterious, previously unheard of sicknesses struck at the very age group in question; birth registers went missing; and the average age of marriage among males plummeted, bachelors being called up first.

At the time these unhappy conscripts began arriving in the Ninth's depot for training, the Ministry of War delivered a bombshell to Caffarelli. It demanded 175 fully trained sub-officers and corporals to act as a cadre for the revitalized 11th Light Infantry, which had previously been disbanded for insubordination. Caffarelli wrote to the government on 17 November 1798 and explained his predicament. When they arrived in Paris the previous year, there had been fewer than 1,000 men in the Ninth. This number was quickly reduced to 800 by those discharged for wounds, infirmities, on compassionate grounds and by the death of some in hospital. Since then the unit had expanded and there were now 2,000 men under arms, the majority inexperienced conscripts. There was absolutely no way he could spare 200 of his best men for the 11th Light.

The government pressed the issue again and on 19 November Caffarelli relented. He had been asked to supply 13 sergeant-majors, 12 quartermaster corporals, 50 sergeants and 100 corporals. Instead he sent seven sergeant-majors, six quartermaster corporals, 30 sergeants and 60 corporals; in total 103 men, many of whom Caffarelli admitted were ignorant of their duties. It is hard to imagine Caffarelli sent his best; more likely the most promising new arrivals were rapidly promoted and shown the door.

This still left many conscripts to train. Training a chasseur was a gradual process ideally requiring four months of continual exercise. Not only did the conscript have to learn the arms drill, loading and basic platoon manoeuvres, they had to be physically hardened as well. To hone the body, the light infantry used to embark on route marches which became progressively longer as the legs were broken in. If a conscript buckled under the weight of the musket, or failed to appreciate the gallows humour, there was a good chance he would try to desert into the backstreets of Paris.

The problem of supervision and training was eased slightly by the formation of 'auxiliary battalions' in the summer of 1799. The conscripts of each of France's administriative divisions, or 'departments' were herded into battalions under the command of retired officers and trained locally. Every battalion formed its own light infantry company, with one-ninth of the conscripts selected as chasseurs. These men were generally the most energetic and likely to survive the fast, fatiguing marches undertaken by light infantry. Between August and September 1799, six of these chasseur companies joined the Ninth, pushing its strength up to 2,643 men by mid-October 1799.[8]

These reinforcements arrived in the nick of time. There was fierce fighting in the Black Forest and the Army of the Upper Rhine, under General Lecourbe, was hard-pressed by the Austrians. Caffarelli was ordered to detach one of his three field battalions to assist.

Caffarelli chose the 3rd Battalion for this mission. This battalion was commanded by a tremendous specimen named Christian Kuhmann. Aged 55, Kuhmann was the old adjutant from the Cévennes days. He was not a Frenchmen, but a native of Rohrbach, a Bavarian village near Gochsheim. The son of a common labourer, Kuhmann started life as an apprentice weaver. Travelling to work in Strasbourg in 1764 he saw the Regiment of Alsace march past on parade and realized he was in the wrong profession. Abandoning his loom, he enlisted in the regiment at a time when army life was very strict and seldom rewarded. Despite this, Kuhmann came to the attention of the regiment's proprietor, Prince Max, the future king of Bavaria. Eight years Kuhmann's junior, the prince promised Kuhmann promotion if he learned to read and count. Spurred by this, Kuhmann took private lessons and, true to his word, Prince Max made him a corporal.[9]

After a stint in the cavalry, in 1784 Kuhmann was lured to the Cévennes battalion with the rank of adjutant. For a commoner, Kuhmann had reached the summit of his career. Before the Revolution, the vast majority of commoners were disqualified from entering the officer corps by the 1781 Edict of Ségur. This piece of legislation barred entry to the officer corps for anyone unable to demonstrate four generations of nobility. The Revolution swept this legislation away and men like Kuhmann, Pierre Gros, Marthe and Saÿvé were able to profit from an unparalleled boom in social mobility.

The highlight of Kuhmann's military career came on 7 December 1795 when an Austrian counter-attack near Messenheim left him cut off with a detachment of four weakened chasseur companies. In dense forest Kuhmann's force came into contact with 800 Austrian hussars. The hussars surrounded the Frenchmen and fired on them with their carbines from the shelter of the trees. Above the rattle of musketry Kuhmann's Germanic tone rose up and bawled his men into holding their ranks. By the sheer force of character Kuhmann kept them united and led them all out of the encirclement to the safety of their own lines.

His career was not without setbacks. While the Revolution opened doors to Kuhmann, it also posed new dangers. By the end of 1793, France was in the middle of a violent, turbulent period known as 'The Terror' where it was governed by an increasingly paranoid and bloodthirsty body inappropriately titled 'the Committee of Public Safety'. All over France actual and suspected counter-revolutionaries were rounded up and arrested. Despite 30 years' distinguished service for France, 'the foreigner' Kuhmann was suspended from duty and sent from the front line to 'the interior' on 24 December 1793.

By the end of July 1794, the period of Terror came to an end and Kuhmann was allowed to return to service along with his brother-in-law, Kastner the master cobbler, another 'foreigner' suspended from service. At the end of the war, General Lestrange made the following notes about Kuhmann's personal characteristics: 'A proven civic sense; great self control; sangfroid; intrepid; correct; honest and a father of a worthy family; very attached to his duties.'[10] Kuhmann married Master Kastner's sister, Françoise, and had several children. When Kuhmann's first son, Pierre, was born at Longwy on 27 January 1797, the godparents were Captain Pierre Gros and Kastner's wife Elisabeth. When Kuhmann went off to Switzerland in 1799 he left his wife expecting their third child.

With Kuhmann headed east, Caffarelli took the remaining two battalions west. On 15 October 1799 a Royalist insurrection had engulfed the west of France and plunged the countryside into chaos. The causes of this revolt are typically complex. This was the third Royalist uprising in the west since the execution of Louis XVI on 21 January 1793. The Bretons were a fiercely independent people, conservative and ultra religious. Supposedly known as *Chouans* after the owl calls they communicated with, they were ruthless guerrilla fighters. In the marshes of the Vendée, the primeval forests of Brittany and the hedgerow country of Normandy, they ambushed and terrorized at will. This third outbreak of *Chouannerie* was partly in response to the conscription laws, which were perceived as unjust and partly opportunistic. In 1799 the war had gone badly for France; with the armies hard-pressed to maintain the frontiers, the Chouans sensed the time was ripe for an uprising. The insurrectionists captured Le Mans. Nantes and Vannes fell soon after along with countless villages in Brittany and Lower Normandy. In most cases the gains were not held for more than a matter of hours; but in those few hours, the prisons were opened, refractory conscripts released and the papers used for drawing up the conscription ballots were destroyed.

This civil war in the west conjured unhappy memories for Caffarelli. In 1792, when Louis XVI was deposed, Caffarelli family's loyalties were split. While he embraced the Revolution, two of his brothers went to England. In 1795 Philippe de Caffarelli took part in the British-backed expedition to Quiberon. This windswept and savage peninsula on the Breton coast became the rallying point for an uprising of royalist counter-revolutionaries. Over the course of July 1795 a series of battles took place from which the republican forces emerged victorious. Philippe de Caffarelli was captured wearing a British uniform and shot.

On the same expedition was a veteran of the American Revolutionary War, Count Louis-Charles d'Hervilly. Such was the complexity of this era, d'Hervilly fought *against* the British to achieve American liberty, but then fought *with* the British to prevent the same liberties coming to France. Mortally wounded at Quiberon, d'Hervilly was shipped to London where he died in exile at the end of 1795. Less than four years later, on 26 April 1799, his daughter Julienne was married to Auguste Caffarelli. Had the old man survived, his loyalties would have been surely torn to see his estates pass through marriage into the hands of a republican soldier, even one of good birth.

With such thoughts to dwell on, Caffarelli started out for the west on 8 November. Having sat idle in Paris for two years, the Ninth left for Le Mans just as things became interesting. Napoleon Bonaparte had arrived in the French capital on 16 October. With the backing of the Paris garrison, Bonaparte made his move for power on 9 November. By the following evening he found himself the first of three consuls governing France. One of his first acts was to calm the Chouans. Bonaparte promised freedom of worship and offered to stop the conscription levies in the west in exchange for an immediate submission by the insurgents. With 30,000 government troops descending upon them, the majority of Chouan leaders submitted. There were a few skirmishes while patrolling the country lanes and some casualties, but nothing like the scale of the fighting seen in 1795. The Ninth was thus spared the worst horrors of a civil war.

Other than family connections to the civil war, there had been something else on Caffarelli's mind since Bonaparte's return. When Bonaparte went to Egypt in 1798, Caffarelli's eldest brother Maximilian had gone along as the expedition's chief engineer. On 24 April 1799 Max was surveying the siege lines at Acre when his right elbow was smashed by a ball. An amputation was necessary and gangrene set in, followed by fever. Such an infection was beyond the ken of the expedition's surgeons and he died. A few hours before he passed away on 27 April, Bonaparte came to visit the engineer. Max begged Bonaparte to take care of his brothers' careers. Overcome with grief, Bonaparte agreed. Once the dust settled after the coup, Bonaparte created the Consular Guard, a force which would act as his personal escort and bodyguard, and filled the ranks with men devoted to his cause. General Joachim Murat was put in command and Caffarelli was offered the role of adjutant-general. Caffarelli accepted and from that moment he was elevated into the inner circle of Bonaparte's most trusted men.

On 29 December 1799 command of the Ninth passed to the senior battalion commander, Mathieu Labassée. The son of a veteran of the Seven Years War (1756–63), Labassée was the sole survivor of the Ninth's pre-revolutionary officer corps. His military career had had unorthodox beginnings, starting at sea at the age of eleven in 1775. He served on a succession of frigates and took part in the War of the American Revolution, seeing action off the Channel Islands and Gibraltar. By the end of his teenage years Labassée had been shot through his torso, neck and knee. He also bore scars from a boarding action when a British 'Tar' took a cutlass to his face and hands. If Labassée had any sense of destiny in his twentieth year it was to become a captain of corsairs and make his fortune plundering British merchantmen on the high seas. Such buccaneering pretensions came to a premature end in 1784 when Labassée received orders to travel to the south-western city of Carcassonne to take a commission as sub-lieutenant in the newly raised Chasseurs of Cévennes regiment.

His father was behind this timely transfer. During the Seven Years War Hubert de la Bassée had served in the Condé Legion, a mixed legion of dragoons and light infantry.[11] Although light troops had proved their value in wartime, they were seen as an unnecessary peacetime expense. The legion was axed in 1776 and the officers were distributed among the regular regiments or became increasingly bored supernumerary officers. With such an apparent dearth of opportunities on land, Labassée's father had sent his boy to sea. But brotherhoods formed in war are not easily broken, so despite being scattered to the four winds, Labassée's father remained in contact with the legion's officers. In 1779 six regiments of horse chasseurs were formed. The fourth of these regiments was formed from personnel who had served in the Condé Legion. In 1784 a battalion of light infantry was added to the chasseur regiment (now titled the Chasseurs of Cévennes) and Hubert grasped the opportunity to obtain his son a commission. With so many noble officers unemployed and facing financial ruin, competition for officer postings was fierce; more so for Labassée as his father was a commoner promoted to the officer corps in wartime. However, unlike Kuhmann, Labassée was exempt from the Edict of Ségur's nobility qualification because his father had been awarded the Cross of St Louis in 1778.[12]

With priority given to ex-legionnaire officers, Hubert put his own name on the register, making it appear as if he was taking the position himself. On 24 September 1784, the 'Marshal of the Camps'[13] Baron de Livron came to Carcassonne to preside over the inauguration of the new battalion. The ceremony took place on the parade ground between the Royal Casern and the southern gate to the Bastide.[14] His report on the ceremony described Labassée as a 'former officer of the Legion of Condé' not yet present with the corps.[15] Satisfied with this, the inspector departed and once he was safely on his way, young Sub-Lieutenant Labassée packed his sea trunk in Boulogne and made the long journey south to the Languedoc.

Arriving in Carcassonne, Labassée found himself in the company of some truly venerable men. Although almost exclusively drawn from the nobility, the officers were not beribboned dandies, but professional soldiers with long family traditions of military service. Of the battalion's 21 officers, 16 had been drawn from the 4th Chasseurs or the Condé Legion. Of the others, at least two were related to serving, or former, officers in these corps.[16] Labassée would surely have been welcomed and mentored by his father's former comrades. Whatever he lacked in social status he made up for with his battle scars.

The commander of the battalion was Chevalier Joseph de Barroussel, a 55-year-old veteran of two wars.[17] De Barroussel had intimate knowledge of light infantry operations, having commanded a motley detachment charged with scouting and reporting on enemy movements in the previous war.[18] With no formal regulations defining the role of light infantry, de Barroussel's experience was vital for training the younger officers.

De Barroussel's deputy was an equally talented and experienced officer. Major Pierre Justin Marchand de Villionne was aged 44, and had served as a grenadier officer in the Seven Years War. He then vanished on a secret mission to India between 1770 and 1773 before reappearing as a captain in the 1st Horse

Chasseurs.[19] As de Barroussel's deputy, Major de Villionne's primary function was to oversee the training of the battalion, its policing and discipline. He was ably assisted in this by his adjutant, Christian Kuhmann. Between them, de Barroussel and de Villionne poached a cadre of experienced sub-officers for the new battalion; men like Pierre Gros, Robert Marthe and Etienne Saÿvé. What is more, de Barroussel had no qualms about spending the king's money to entice the best recruits with excessive enlistment bounties.

Despite the unpopularity of a poorly paid, harshly disciplined, peacetime army, with promotion hard to come by, in a country bankrupted by its pursuit of costly foreign policies and unwittingly on the verge of a cataclysmic revolution, de Barroussel was highly successful in attracting good recruits. They were not the usual misfits, vagrants, drunkards and thieves that the army attracted, but young men captivated by a spirit of adventure. The very title of the corps invoked this spirit: the 'huntsmen' of Cévennes. The provincial title referred to a sparsely populated mountain region over a hundred miles to the north-east of Carcassonne. It was a region inhabited by toothless hermits, deluded mystics, bandits and wolves. However, the battalion was fairly cosmopolitan in composition.

By 1789 the Cévennes battalion was composed of men from all over France. Of the 327 men in service, just 74 came from the Languedoc. The remainder heralded from Alsace, Lorraine, Champagne, Franche-Comté, Bourgogne and other areas. There were Bretons, Normans, Parisians, Picards, German speakers, Flemish – a rich tapestry of brogues. The majority of them were simple labourers, pioneers and other 'workers of the land', some held trades like baker, cobbler, mason, blacksmith, locksmith, tailor, barber and carpenter. Seventy of them were listed as townsfolk and included those working in the manufacture of luxury goods and artists. Of these men, 64 had more than eight years' service in the army and 23 had seen active wartime service, 12 of them at sea.

The initial recruits were fine physical specimens. The inspector, the Marquis de Frimont, noted the 169 chasseurs recruited between September 1784 and July 1785 were 'of a good size for the infantry. The foot chasseurs are young and should gain in size … and will be in a condition to make war next year.' From this we can see de Barroussel targeted youths not fully physically developed, but bursting with vigour. A year later we find Frimont confirming his prediction.

The men had 'gained in size since last year, they have strengthened and are in a condition to make war.'[20]

Frimont also made an interesting comment on the musketry practice carried out by the battalion at this time. In addition to physical fitness, chasseurs were expected to be marksmen. In an earlier experiment with light infantry, in 1759, each infantry regiment had been ordered to select the three chasseurs per company who would be drawn together and charged with scouting the march of their corps, searching woods and skirmishing.[21] The selection process for chasseurs was simple: they were to be the best marksmen. This important credential appears to have applied to the new chasseur regiments. Frimont ordered the regiment to begin target shooting in the summer of 1785[22] and to continue 'as long as the season permits it.' In the following year's inspection we read, '… This regiment fires at the target very well. One will continue to fire at the target as long as munitions permit it.'

In 1788 the commitment to marksmanship was reaffirmed in a new reorganization.[23] The mixed regiments of foot and horse chasseurs were broken up. Twelve independent light infantry battalions were created, the Cévennes battalion being ranked ninth in seniority.[24] The ordinance of 12 March 1788 described the role and type of men required for service in the chasseurs. They were to be trained in the 'services external and in advance' of the king's armies. By this the regulation was describing a species of warfare called *petit guerre* (petty war); the service of advanced guards, reconnaissance missions, raids and the protection of camps.

The ordinance was quite specific on the type of recruits required for the new battalions: 'The service of light infantry battalions particularly demands robust men and good marchers, the commanders of these battalions will take care to procure recruits of this type, not prizing them by the greatness of height.'[25] Each company would select 12 'chasseur-carabineers'. Unlike grenadiers, these elite troops were chosen 'without a single regard for their height, from among the best soldiers in the battalion, giving equal preference to the most skilful shooters and never admitting recruits.'

Returning to the career of Mathieu Labassée, at the epoch of the storming of the Bastille on 14 July 1789 he was still a junior sub-lieutenant. As a commoner he was not affected by the abolition of aristocratic privileges following the

Revolution and there is no indication that the Cévennes battalion was involved in any of the mutinies that rocked the army through the course of 1790. For Labassée the impact of the Revolution would prove to be more of a slow-burning fuse.

De Barroussel died in April 1790 and command passed to de Villionne. The battalion moved to garrison the fortress of Longwy in Lorraine, where its provincial title of Cévennes was suppressed. Henceforth the battalion was only identified as the 9th Chasseurs, albeit that many officers continued to refer to it as 'Cévennes' informally.[26] While everything appeared calm in the Ninth, the rest of the army was falling to pieces. A number of noble officers had begun to emigrate from France fearing the Revolution would rage out of control. These fears appeared to be confirmed when King Louis XVI also attempted to flee France, only to be arrested at Varennes on the night of 20/21 June 1791. This event acted as a spur to many nobles and on 1 July 1791 the Ninth lost its first émigré officer, Lieutenant de Châteauville.

As more nobles began to emigrate, there were excellent promotion opportunities in other regiments. The Ninth therefore began to lose a significant number of officers to other corps. Captains from the Ninth took command of the 1st, 5th and 10th chasseur battalions while de Villionne accepted the colonelcy of the 55th Infantry Regiment in February 1792. These departures began to create vacancies within the Ninth for junior officers like Labassée and many sub-officers of long service.

The real challenges to the battalion came after the declaration of war against Austria on 20 April 1792. Six officers deserted on 4 May 1792. Within a fortnight another captain had gone over to the enemy. When the battalion received its baptism of fire at Philippeville on 23 May 1792, two officers were killed in action. In the remainder of 1792, another officer deserted, one died of natural causes and a third transferred to another regiment. In total 18 officers had been lost in 18 months from a single battalion. Labassée quickly rose to the rank of captain.

By April 1793 the battalion was commanded by Lieutenant-Colonel Jacques-Marie-Blaise Segond, a 35-year-old noble and classic 18th-century mercenary. Segond had been a soldier since 1776 and had served with the Americans at Brandywine, Germantown, Valley Forge and Charlestown. Leaving American service with the rank of major in 1784, Segond served in Holland with the Legion of Maillebois, a corps of French volunteers serving in the Dutch Patriot Revolution (1780–87). He then entered Russian service in 1788, with the rank of major in the Elsin Light Horse. Having led such an adventurous life, Segond was intoxicated by the possibilities thrown up by the Revolution and so returned home and obtained a posting in the Ninth.[27]

Following the execution of Louis XVI, France found itself at war with Austria, Prussia, Great Britain, Holland, Spain and Naples. Serving under General Charles Dumouriez, the Ninth was posted to the Belgian front. After losing the battle of Neerwinden (18 March 1793), Dumouriez entered into secret negotiations with the Austrians in which he offered to evacuate Belgium if the Austrians did not impede his retreat. These clandestine talks materialized into a secret plot where Dumouriez offered to march on Paris and overthrow the revolutionary government. In return, Dumouriez believed he would be rewarded with a suitably prominent post.

By now Lieutenant-Colonel Segond had become an ardent ally of Dumouriez and was provisionally promoted by him to the rank of marshal of the camp. Learning of the plot, Segond threw his support behind Dumouriez, also in expectation of future rewards. It is unclear how many colleagues Segond confided in, but the Ninth began to play an active role in the plot when they were sent to the village of Fresnes with orders to guard the army's treasury containing some 'two millions in cash'.

On 2 April 1793 Dumouriez had the visiting French minister of war and four government deputies arrested and handed to the Austrians as hostages against the safety of the surviving members of the French royal family. Thinking his troops would remain loyal to him, Dumouriez's plans were thwarted when they refused to support his coup. Realizing the jig was up, Dumouriez made a dash for the frontier and went into exile on 5 April.

As he dashed for the frontier, Dumouriez urged Segond to join him and to bring the army's treasury. However, before Segond could make off with the loot, the grenadiers of the 47th Line arrived at Fresnes and demanded the Ninth hand the treasury over to them. Much to Segond's horror his men complied, and the grenadiers trudged off to Valenciennes with his retirement fund. The plot had been a disaster. Segond must have guessed the consequences of supporting the coup and so announced he was going into exile.[28] Segond's deputy, Lieutenant-Colonel Blondeau, and Lieutenant Dupin followed him as did a number of the men. As the most senior officer remaining, Captain Labassée took command and led the remainder of the battalion to army headquarters at Valenciennes where he gave an account of the previous days' events. He was congratulated on his loyalty and promoted to lieutenant-colonel on the spot.[29]

By 1793 the French army was in something of a quandary. On one hand were the regular regiments, stigmatized by their links to the old order, but provided with depots containing cobblers and tailors, armourers and surgeons, and the means and know-how to recruit and train the next generation of soldiers. On the other hand were swarms of battalions of National Guard volunteers; militiamen who had been called up to defend France's frontiers and supplement the regular army. As patriotic and ideologically inspired as these volunteers were, they lacked the necessary support services to remain in the field indefinitely.

The government's solution was to create a single unified national army by amalgamating a single battalion of regulars with two battalions of volunteers and forming entirely new formations called half-brigades. On 21 February 1793, a law determined the organization of the half-brigades. Besides 196 half-brigades of the line, there would be 14 light half-brigades.[30] With the campaign season underway, the decision to enact the formation of light infantry half-brigades was postponed until the following year.

On 5 March 1794, near the town of Bouillon, the 9th Light Half-Brigade was formed by the amalgamation of the 9th Chasseurs, 28th (b) Battalion of Chasseurs[31] and the Battalion of Meuse Scouts. The two volunteer battalions were fairly recent creations, formed from a number of small, independent light infantry companies which had seen active service over the previous year.[32] Gathered together, the parent battalions were broken up and three entirely new battalions created. The officers were allocated by seniority and did not always command men from their parent battalion. In some cases individual companies were mixed to ensure an equal number of men in each. For example, the chasseur companies of 3rd Battalion comprised officers and men drawn from the following formations:

	Officers	**Men**
1st company	9th Chasseurs	9th Chasseurs
2nd	9th Chasseurs	9th Chasseurs and Meuse Scouts
3rd	9th Chasseurs	9th Chasseurs
4th	Meuse Scouts	Meuse Scouts
5th	9th Chasseurs	9th Chasseurs and Meuse Scouts
6th	28th (b) and Meuse Scouts	28th (b) Battalion
7th	28th (b) and Meuse Scouts	Meuse Scouts
8th	Meuse Scouts	9th Chasseurs and Meuse Scouts

Once the officers and companies had been assigned to their new battalions, a touching ceremony took place. The patchwork half-brigade formed up in front of the commander in chief, General Charbonnié and Citizen Gillet, a political commissar or 'Representative of the People' who proclaimed the importance of their role in the war against tyranny. His final words called on the men to swear an oath:

> Officers, sub-officers, soldiers. Swear and promise obedience to the laws and to military discipline. Swear to maintain freedom, equality, the constitution, the unity and indivisibility of the French Republic, or to die![33]

At the end of this speech there was a drum roll and Gillet ordered the men to ground arms. When the men recovered their positions, Gillet ordered the men to break ranks about him. Officers and men mixed together and embraced one another fraternally as equals before the law. Patriotic hymns were sung and tears flowed down many a battle-hardened cheek. It was an outpouring of emotion Gillet found difficult to express when he recounted the scene many years later in life. The Ninth had been reborn.[34]

Unfortunately for Labassée he did not enjoy the privilege of commanding this new corps. This honour went to Michel Eirisch, the battalion commander of the Meuse Scouts. At the age of 33 Eirisch was an experienced soldier who had been in service since 1778. Holding the rank of adjutant in 1789, Eirisch took advantage of the Revolution and quickly made his way up to the rank of captain. On 2 December 1793 Eirisch became aide-de-camp to General Michaud, who became something of a mentor to him. Inspectors were full of praise for Eirisch: 'a very good citizen attached to the government … Very good in the administration of a corps and for all details of instruction … Very firm disciplinarian … Good manoeuvrer.'[35] In contrast Labassée, a former officer in the King's army, was described on 12 January 1794 as 'very moderate, conservatively principled' by Citizen Poulet, the *agent superieur* of the Executive Council for the Army of the Ardennes.[36]

The old officer corps of the Ninth did at least retain control of the battalion commander positions. Labassée took 1st Battalion and Kuhmann the third. The 2nd Battalion initially went to Charles Léopold Sirejean, a colourful adventurer 20 years Labassée's senior. Sirejean had first seen action in 1760 when he received a sabre blow to the head and a stint as a prisoner of war. For a time he served the King of Poland as a gentleman cadet, before taking up a career in the artillery. In 1784 Sirejean suffered an unspecified '*injustice of the heart*' and left France bound for service for Holland where he became an infantry captain. At the time the Netherlands was embroiled in a revolutionary conflict in which Sirejean embraced the cause of the democrats. On their defeat, Sirejean returned to France and served as an infantry captain before his posting to the Ninth.

Despite his many excellent qualities and democratic leanings, Sirejean was suspended from duty because he was a noble. It was not until 1797 that he was allowed to return to service having missed a great deal of the war. In his absence, Jean-Baptiste Verger took command of the battalion. Verger had joined the Chasseurs of Cévennes in 1785 and was one of the better recruits the battalion attracted. He was a pleasant enough young man but felt burdened by his parents' desire for him to study and make something decent of himself in the world of business. On the day he finished his studies at the college of Castelnaudary, Verger made a fateful decision. As his parents Nicolas and Margrette awaited his return at the family home, Verger ran off down the Canal du Midi to Carcassonne and enrolled in the battalion. It must have been the ultimate horror to a family who had just invested so much in their son's education.

The campaigns they endured as part of the Army of the Sambre and Meuse took their toll on Eirisch, who fell sick. Although not formally recorded, it is clear that by 13 January 1797 Labassée was signing letters as commander of the half-brigade. With no sign of Eirisch returning to active service, Labassée may have hoped to be rewarded with command, but he was again thwarted, this time by Caffarelli who joined the Ninth on 4 June 1797. It was only with Lestrange's inspection that Labassée was at last mentioned as a candidate worthy of advancement. Lestrange described Labassée as having a 'great sense of civic duty, great bravery, honesty, a rare frankness, excellent qualities.' He also noted Labassée was 'a good father and good husband'; a virtue the young Republic considered very highly.

As Labassée took over the Ninth he knew the corps and its officers intimately. In contrast to many other half-brigades, the Ninth had enjoyed a great deal of stability since the early calamities of the war. The core of the half-brigade, its heartbeat, remained true to the principles set down by de Barroussel. The officer corps had been augmented by an intake of fresh blood during the amalgamations, drawing in officers with little formal instruction, but great charisma and dash. The epitome of the new intake was the baker's son, Captain Pierre Barrois, from Ligny en Barrois. Aged just 25 in 1799, Barrois had shown such drive that he was elected as an officer a month after enrolling as a volunteer at the age of 19. When his unit was amalgamated with the Ninth, Barrois' great leadership potential was realized and he received a fast-track promotion. He was given a stint with the carabineers and then raised to the rank of adjutant-major, putting him in a prime position for further advancement.

Of course, there were a few exceptions to the rule. Sub-Lieutenant Hermand was described as 'a villain', only promoted because he was next in line. Caffarelli had him locked up for five months on an insubordination charge, but he was still on the books. Another dubious specimen was Lieutenant Auffremand, labelled as 'addicted to wine' and 'disruptive'; but in the main the Ninth's officer corps was experienced and hungry for action after two years in Paris. Although the Ninth had been in plenty of scrapes, it had yet to experience a real *moment*. For 16 years they had trained and toiled hard. As the spring of 1800 approached they stood on the cusp of greatness, ready to follow a new leader into battle for the first time.

THE ARMY OF
THE RESERVE

Having secured political control of France at the end of 1799, First Consul Napoleon Bonaparte began planning a military campaign that would secure the country's borders and re-establish the reputation of the French army after the previous year's defeats. More than anything, Bonaparte needed a great victory; something that would cement his political position and unify the country behind him.

As he began formulating his plans in early 1800, Bonaparte reflected on the changes of fortune since he had left Europe for Egypt in the spring of 1798. The territories Bonaparte had won in Northern Italy had been lost to a combined Austro-Russian force under General Baron Michael von Melas. The only remaining foothold in that part of Italy was the narrow enclave of Liguria and the port of Genoa, and this was under threat if Melas resumed his offensive with the arrival of spring. Although Melas had been weakened by the withdrawal of Russian forces from Europe, he still posed a grave danger, threatening to invade southern France. At the same time, the Austrians had considerable forces in Germany, poised along the Rhine under General Baron Paul Kray.

The one saving grace of the previous year's campaigns was that Switzerland had remained in French hands. This mountainous country drove a wedge between the Austrian forces in Germany and those in Italy. This could be the key to victory. Poring over his charts, Bonaparte hatched a daring plan. While his existing armies in Italy and on the Rhine remained on the defensive, Bonaparte would advance through Switzerland with a new army, repeating Hannibal's feat of marching across the Alps, then seize Milan. In so doing he would cut Melas' communications with Vienna. Melas would be forced to turn around and Bonaparte would be waiting for him on ground of his own choosing.

To achieve this strategy the first consul created a new army from units which had not seen action in 1799, but had been scattered around France on various missions. On 20 March Bonaparte recalled six half-brigades from western France and ordered them to Dijon. The Ninth was selected for this new mission and quit Nantes, arriving in Dijon on 20 April. Once there Labassée was notified that the Ninth would form a part of General Jean Boudet's infantry division, along with the 59th and 30th Line half-brigades from the Paris garrison.

The first and second battalions of the Ninth spent a single night in Dijon, where they found themselves held up as an object of ridicule. Dijon was filled with foreign spies sent to observe the Army of the Reserve. So far they had amused themselves observing poorly trained conscripts and old soldiers brought out of retirement. The Ninth was now held up to these foreign agents as a crack front-line unit. Unsupplied with uniforms for over two years, and fresh out of winter quarters, they looked somewhat dishevelled. Boudet paraded the unit and was told by the inspecting general, 'You present me with troops covered in rags; how can I ask the men of the Ninth to cross the eternal ice of the Alps?'[1]

After the parade the Ninth was sent off to nearby Poligny, where their depot was now situated. The march was completed in three stages through the towns of Auxonne, Dôle, Mont-sous-Vaudrey and Salins, arriving in Poligny on the night of 24 April with 1,200 men. They were billeted on the local population, who were somewhat less than enthusiastic in their reception. The morning after their arrival, the municipal authorities sent an urgent letter of complaint to General Alexandre Berthier at Dijon asking for food and money. Despite the inhospitable welcome, the storerooms at Poligny were overflowing with new uniforms and equipment. For the next three days the first two battalions outfitted themselves. New shoes were handed out along with new linen shirts and drawers. Coats were issued to many for the first time. Worn-out belts were exchanged; bayonets and sabres issued or mended; and muskets fiddled with and tuned. At least now they looked like soldiers.

They did not know it, but the Ninth had played an important part in a deception tactic of Napoleon's. He wanted the world to focus on the conscripts at Dijon. He wanted the world to see the pitiful condition of his soldiers. He didn't want the foreign spies to see his men *after* they had been re-equipped and drilled. More than anything else, he wanted to divert attention away from Geneva and Lake Leman where the army's stores were being gathered. In Vienna there were cartoons depicting Bonaparte's new army as old men mounted on mules. If the spies had seen the Ninth after Poligny, they would have realized the truth.

The Ninth stayed at Poligny until the morning of 27 April, completing their refit. Labassée was then ordered on to Nyon on the north-western edge of Lake Leman. Captain Gros and the depot remained at Poligny to train and equip the next batch of conscripts. Labassée's route took the Ninth through Lons-le-Saunier, Clairvaux, Saint-Lupicin, Gex and finally to Nyon where they arrived on 1 May. At Nyon there was more trouble with the natives over supplies. The town municipality wrote to Berthier, explaining 'the brave defenders of our liberty' were ruining the town by their requisitions.[2] The war commissariat attached to Boudet's division had made multiple demands for supplies and, following similar requests for the divisions of generals François Watrin, Jacques-Antoine de Chambarlhac, Louis Henri Loison and others, Nyon was empty. It would be four months before any more grain could be harvested; there was no straw, no livestock, nothing.

The Ninth quit Nyon on 7 May and set out destined for Vevey. On 8 May Labassée was reunited with Christian Kuhmann and the 3rd Battalion at Chexbres. The indomitable Kuhmann had been sent from his winter quarters down into the region known as the Valais several weeks before. Here his battalion helped maintain the security of the mountain passes while Bonaparte's engineers and geographers scouted the passage over the St Bernard Pass and decided if it was practicable. With all three battalions reunited, the Ninth's strength was over 2,500 men.[3]

The Ninth arrived at Vevey on 9 May and remained there for five days. The day before departing, on 13 May, Bonaparte was scheduled to inspect Boudet's division at 11am. An inevitable panic descended upon everybody in the scramble to prepare. The process of inspection began with the humblest corporal fidgeting with his squad, to the battalion commanders bawling at their captains to hurry up. Finally, after hours of preparation, 5,118 men stood satisfactorily assembled in the market square of Vevey at 11am expecting the first consul's imminent arrival. The clock struck the hour, but there was no sign of him. Word arrived that the first consul had been delayed. This left the assembled troops in somewhat of a quandary. To dismiss the men now would cause the whole process of inspection to start again and nobody wanted that. After a little hurrying around by Boudet's staff, the kind citizens of Vevey were persuaded to donate a glass of wine to each of the assembled troops. The distribution of this eagerly anticipated refreshment kept every one occupied. Not wishing to be caught napping, Boudet sent a couple of artillery crews with their guns to keep watch for Bonaparte. They had instructions to begin firing the minute his carriage came into sight. At 2.45pm, the guns began pounding away, announcing the imminent arrival of the first consul. To Bonaparte this continuous salute was a fitting recognition of his status. To the soldiers in the square it was a warning to put out their pipes, break the stacks of arms and re-form their ranks.

A short time later Bonaparte stood before them in the town square, his eye seeing every last detail. With him in the entourage were the new army's commander in chief, General Berthier, alongside General Victor, both of whom were surrounded by splendidly dressed aides.[4] Bonaparte made his inspection, riding past the opened ranks, with drums beating, alternating by battalion. One of Brigadier General Louis Charles Guénand's half-brigades had brought along a band and they struck up, playing the martial and patriotic airs then so well known to French soldiers stationed everywhere from Paris to Cairo.

While extremely satisfied with the Ninth, the inspection of Guénand's men depressed Bonaparte.[5] He was outraged by the 30th Line. This half-brigade had been severely depleted in combat and had been quickly rebuilt around a cadre of just 300 men. In the haste to rebuild the unit, many conscripts had gone missing. Bonaparte was angry at the desertion rate and the loss of equipment he had provided for them. A sharp letter to the military commander at Paris, General Mortier, would follow the inspection after which the Gendarmes would be sent scouring the roads for deserters.

The next part of the review was an exercise in loading and firing. One by one the captains cried out the words of command and a thunder of musketry let rip, filling the square with sulphurous smoke. This was Bonaparte's way of ensuring all his conscripts had tasted powder before the real shooting began. After the drama of the live firing, Bonaparte now wished to see the men parade before him. Boudet's division formed in a long column of companies at the head of which rode Boudet and his staff. Following quickly behind came Brigadier General Louis François Félix Musnier at the head of his brigade. Labassée rode next. Behind him, with drummers at the head, came the three companies of carabineers, one behind the other. This phalanx was a particularly splendid sight, with their red plumes cascading from their shakos and their bayonets held aloft like spear-points. Behind these warriors came the battalions of chasseurs, Sirejean's first, then Verger and Kuhmann bringing up the rear. As each company reached Bonaparte they brought their arms to the port. Guénand's brigade followed suite, still attempting an air of pomp despite their earlier dressing down.

After the parade, the officers and sub-officers were called together to receive one of Bonaparte's customary harangues. 'I have offered peace to the Emperor,' he told them. 'He doesn't want it. He will not let us rest until we take it [peace] by the throat.'[6] More interesting was news of a trunk containing 8,233 francs and 10 centimes that was waiting to be doled out to the Ninth in the form of back-pay. First uniforms, then pay; Bonaparte certainly knew the hearts of soldiers. Just for the briefest of instances everyone would be solvent; then the debts from games of chance and credits would be called in, plunging the majority back into a familiar state of bankruptcy. Of course someone was always willing to offer loans … at a price.

On 14 May Boudet's division set out on its journey to the Rhone valley. The Ninth quit Vevey and headed for Villeneuve, two hours' march along the edge of Lake Leman. What had once been a small village of 500 souls had been turned into a great depot; a veritable city of boxes, barrels and crates. Hundreds of thousands of rations of brandy, corn and biscuits were piled there along with cartridges, flints, shells and balls. Four cargo ships lay moored to the jetties, having shipped these supplies from Geneva.

The men were each issued four days' biscuit ration, 50 rounds of ammunition and two good flints. The cartridges came in packets of 15 rounds. Two of these packets could be stored inside the cartridge pouch while the third packet was kept in the haversack. The leather cartridge pouch contained a wooden box with two sections divided by a block into which were sunk six holes. A packet of cartridges could be inserted into each of the larger sections, with five loose cartridges inserted into the middle block. The sixth hole contained a phial of oil for cleaning the musket. The box was closed by two flaps, the larger of which was made of stiff leather and was fastened by a buckle underneath. Under the main flap, stitched to the open face of the box, was a wallet containing the spare flints and the gun tools. These included a three-pronged screwdriver and a 'worm' attachment which attached to the musket's ramrod and could be used for removing fouled cartridges from the barrel. In addition to the spare packet of cartridges, their haversacks would typically contain a spare pair of shoes; a spare shirt; rations; and a repair kit. Carried externally were important items that had to be shared among the members of each mess: cooking pot, pan and water cans. A soldier's valuables would be found stashed in his waistcoat pockets or in the inside pockets of the coattail.

While the Ninth took on provisions, Boudet was joined by Battalion Commander Duport from the 2nd Light Artillery. Duport had eight four-pounders and two six-inch howitzers limbered up and ready to ride. The Ninth quit Villeneuve and passed into the Rhone valley, marching southwards with the river on their right and the new sound of the guns bouncing and clattering alongside them. Spring was very much in evidence. The wide valley floor looked particularly fertile. They passed through several small villages on the way, once apparently prosperous but mostly deserted since the arrival of the army. After four leagues (16km) on the wide flat road, they reached the village of Bex where they spent the night.

Next morning, the march continued towards the mountain peaks. Marching to war was a slow process in 1800. A division would normally move at a speed of one league an hour. This included a short break in which the men could refill their pipes and take a swig of water. When the march resumed, the men could spend their time singing favourite songs, reinventing the lyrics to suit their mood. There would be idle chatter, the same old yarns and perhaps even a remark about the spectacular scenery around them. Naturally there was speculation about their destination; but as the old soldiers would say, it did not really matter in the end. There would be little sleep, hardly any food and some nasty Croats taking pot shots at them. Would there be women? Of course; but there'd be husbands and fathers too. Sometimes the ranks would fall silent as the day drew on and the gradient intensified. Occasional curses would ring out, cursing the weather or the stony route, but mostly it was a time of contemplation, when one developed comradeship with the men either side. These same men you marched with, you would fight and die alongside too; a certain amount of attachment naturally grew.

After an hour they crossed the stone bridge across the Rhone at St Maurice. Here the mountains came very close to the river, forming a kind of gate to the Valais region. On the other side of the bridge was an old, decrepit castle; a monument to a forgotten age. The fertile plain steadily became less cultivated and the villages poorer. At the sight of the army most of the locals had packed up their belongings and fled to relations higher up in the mountains. Several hours after leaving St Maurice, the column passed the stunning waterfall at Pissevache. They crossed the Trient by a large stone bridge and followed the eastward bend of the Rhone. After crossing the river Drance the column turned south, entering the valley leading to the mountain pass.

They entered the town of Martigny, which was swamped by workmen drafted in to repair the roads and bridges up to the pass. At Martigny, Boudet was joined by a squadron from the 11th Hussars under Battalion Commander Ismert. Their uniform, or rather their 'costume', was a flamboyant concoction of light green, crimson and iron grey. The Army of the Reserve was short of cavalry so Boudet only received a single, weak squadron of hussars with about 80 men. Their role in the division was to work primarily as a reconnaissance force. In addition to their sabres the hussars were armed with carbines and pistols, allowing them some short-range firepower. For any serious skirmishes the hussars would be reliant on the swift-marching light infantry catching them up and bringing their muskets to bear.

Boudet's division was now fully assembled. As a force the division was capable of functioning independently or in conjunction with the rest of the army in a pitched battle. It comprised five elements: the headquarters staff; artillery and train; light cavalry; a light infantry half-brigade; and a line infantry brigade.

The headquarters staff were responsible for commanding the division, dealing with all aspects of administration, including supplies, distribution, and communication with army headquarters. The staff included Adjutant-General Dalton who fulfilled the role of Boudet's chief of staff. There would also be several aides-de-camp and adjuncts assisting Boudet by keeping his paperwork in order, delivering messages, and occasionally leading troops on semi-independent missions.

Boudet had six guns: four eight-pounders and two six-inch howitzers. The eight-pounders were capable of firing solid spherical shot for long-range bombardment and penetration, or canister for closer range, anti-personnel work. This latter consisted of a bag filled with small shot that would burst after leaving the barrel of the gun. Used correctly, canister could be devastatingly effective at bringing down lines of infantry before they could get within effective musket range. The howitzers, which were able to lob a shell over a high wall, could fire explosive shells for use against static defences. In combat the howitzers could also be loaded with canister. The artillery commander was also responsible for organizing the division's supply wagons and baggage train. There were normally two caissons (ammunition wagons) per gun and several more holding a reserve of 30,000 infantry cartridges.

The largest element of the division was its infantry component. There were two brigades, one formed by the Ninth under Brigadier General Musnier and the other composed of the 30th and 59th under Brigadier General Guénand. Musnier was the younger of the two, and he knew northern Italy well; while Guénand was an old soldier who, like Battalion Commander Sirejean, had been suspended as a noble for most of the previous war.

By 1800 there was little difference between light and line infantry on the battlefield. Both were organized in the same manner and both followed the same set of instructions for firing and manoeuvring. During the War of the First Coalition, all types of French infantry had become adept at battlefield skirmishing, something that had traditionally been the preserve of light infantry. Their armament was identical and there were only minor differences in the cut of the uniform. One difference was the cut of gaiters, which for line infantry extended above the knee and were considered to constrict the march. Light infantry gaiters were cut mid-calf and allowed the knee more flexibility. In another nod to practicality, the light infantry coats were short-tailed making them less likely to snag in undergrowth. The principal difference between light and line was found off the battlefield. Light infantry always marched at the head of the division in the advanced guard and were required to move quickly in support of cavalry and to hold ground while the line infantry came up and deployed.

The basic infantry formation of the period was the battalion. Each half-brigade was usually composed of three battalions, but for the coming campaign the 30th Line only had two.[7] Each battalion was composed of eight companies of chasseurs (or fusiliers in the line) and a single company of carabineers (grenadiers in the line). Each company had 104 chasseurs or 64 carabineers divided into eight squads, each under a corporal. There were four sergeants, each in charge of two corporals; the most senior non-commissioned soldier would be the sergeant-major. Each company would also have a quartermaster corporal, who ranked as a sub-officer. The company was commanded by a captain, deputized by a lieutenant and a sub-lieutenant. The first company in each battalion was theoretically commanded by the longest-serving captain, the eighth by the most junior.

Following the infantry regulations of 1 August 1791, when the battalion was formed, the companies were grouped into 'divisions' (not to be confused with the larger formation of the same name) in order to spread the most experienced captains along the line. The most senior captain would be on the right of the line, paired with the fifth most senior company commander on his immediate left. Next to this division would come the second captain with the sixth captain; the third would be paired with the seventh; and finally, the fourth with the eighth. As it was impractical to refer to each company by its administrative designation, the companies were instead renumbered 1 to 8 from right to left and referred to as platoons.[8]

The carabineers/grenadiers were numbered 1 to 3 independently of the other companies, and within the Ninth were referred to as the 1st, 2nd or 3rd carabineers respectively. The carabineers could fight with their parent battalion, but were usually grouped together and formed a small composite battalion. It is highly likely Guénand combined his grenadier platoons in the same manner.

When the company was formed as a platoon, the men would line up in three ranks of equal length: the tallest men at the front, the shortest in the middle rank and the middling men in the rear rank. The men stood shoulder to shoulder with a gap of one foot between the haversack and chest of the men in each file. The platoon was divided into two equal sections and the eight corporals were assigned in height order to the four extremities of each section (i.e. in the front and rear ranks in the first and last files). The captain would ordinarily stand to the right of the first corporal in the front rank. Behind him, in the third rank would be the senior sergeant. The second sergeant stood behind the left section, except in the 8th platoon when the sergeant stood to the left of the front rank – in effect being the left-hand guide of the entire battalion. In theory at least, the quartermaster corporals were assigned as guards for the battalion standard-bearer who was chosen from one of the sergeant-majors and placed at the centre of the battalion.[9]

The battalion commander was mounted on a horse. He would place himself 20 paces behind the centre of the battalion when it was formed in line. On his right the adjutant-major would stand eight paces behind the file-closers at the centre of the right half of the battalion. The adjutant sub-officer would stand on the left of the battalion commander in a similar manner. It is important to remember that the battalion commander's voice would have to be audible to the whole battalion – in battle or high winds this would have been extremely difficult. In these circumstances, the words of command were repeated by the adjutant-major and adjutant. To assist with transmitting orders, the drummers of each battalion would be gathered together in two ranks standing 15 paces behind the centre of the fifth company. If a band was present, the musicians would stand behind the drum corps of the first battalion where it would play military airs to encourage the men.

The primary weapon of the infantry was the flintlock musket. This was a cumbersome firearm, weighing 4.5kg and measuring 1.51m in length. Military doctrine of the period favoured infantry to be massed in closely packed ranks from where they could deliver devastating volleys in a variety of firing patterns. The infantry commander could order his battalions to fire either by platoon, half-battalion, battalion or by brigade. These complex firing patterns meant the volleys would roll along the line, emitting a constant hail of shot. Volleys would be delivered by all three ranks simultaneously, the front rank kneeling, the other two standing. The men could achieve a rate of fire of two to three rounds a minute. The three-rank firing system was not a popular method of delivering shot. The first problem came from the front rank's reluctance to kneel and – once down – get back up again. Commentators complained that the act of kneeling broke the fluidity of the loading process. There was also the fear of men in the third rank firing into the backs of the heads of the men in the front rank, especially when fatigue prevented them from holding the barrel horizontally. It was almost impossible to aim when all the barrels were levelled together; and with so many weapons discharging in close proximity, the smoke was often so dense after a few volleys that there was little chance of judging the result.

The infantry regulation of 1 August 1791 provided an alternative species of fire to counter these concerns. This was a form of independent fire called 'two-rank firing'. On the command 'commence firing' the front two ranks of the first file of each company would level their muskets and shoot. The fire would then ripple down the line by files to the left. As the front two ranks fired, the third-rank man would pass his loaded musket forward to the second-ranker who would fire it immediately. By the time the ripple reached the left of the platoon, the right-hand file ought to be loaded and ready to fire their next shot, thus starting another ripple. If this system was performed correctly, a unit could emit a constant hail of fire; something especially useful against cavalry. Detractors of this system claimed the third rank were often reluctant to swap guns with the second rank in case they ended up with a defective firearm. For this reason some commanders preferred the third rank to remain passive as a reserve during firing, even though it reduced the rate of fire.

The preferred method of firing for infantry was to deploy into a loose skirmish formation and fire independently. Unencumbered by their fellows, they had time to select their targets and take careful aim. This system was described in French as fighting *en tirailleur*. This species of fighting was common to all types of infantry and was a tactic born out of necessity. The rapid expansion of the French army saw a decline in the technical ability of infantry to manoeuvre and fire disciplined volleys in the traditional way. Instead, swarms of skirmishers would rush up to the enemy line, using the terrain to cover themselves and they would shoot away, goading the enemy to waste volleys on them and destroying their cohesion. Again there were detractors to this system. Skirmishers were very vulnerable to sudden cavalry charges. Untrained skirmishers would wander forwards, find the first convenient resting spot, fire off all their ammunition and then retreat from the field, their obligations supposedly fulfilled.

There were no regulations describing how to fight in this manner but a common practice developed. A portion of the force would be sent forward to skirmish while others remained in formation ready to act as a support. Communications were normally given by the beat of a drum and were kept very basic – advance, retire, move left, move right, open fire. There was not much else that a skirmisher needed know. The skirmishers would advance quickly in extended order until within musket range of the enemy. The system relied very much on the intelligence and motivation of the individual skirmisher and the French soldiers responded well to this independence. An important benefit of this extended order was to lessen the effect of enemy artillery fire. If a cannon ball struck a company in line, it could easily maim half a dozen men. If it struck a column, it had enough kinetic energy to plough through dozens of men. Skirmishers were a more difficult target and there was no dishonour in skirmishers using their intelligence and ducking to avoid enemy volleys. Such pragmatism was strictly forbidden in the line lest the cohesion of the ranks collapsed.

While the skirmishers kept the enemy occupied, the main force would manoeuvre for an attack behind them. The 'line of battle' formation was very long and impractical to manoeuvre. The line would bend and contort; obstacles like hedgerows and walls could break up the formation. To move the brigade, it was common to first re-deploy each battalion in a stack or column of single or double companies. This greatly reduced the frontage of each battalion and enabled the brigade to cross broken ground. When moving, the brigade could either re-deploy into line and open fire, or attempt to punch a hole through the enemy line by weight of numbers and sheer brute force.

This type of action rarely happened in combat. A formation receiving a charge of a column would continue to fire until the last possible moment, then present an unbroken hedge of bayonets through which the attacker had to plunge. If the defending troops remained steady, then the attack would likely fail. If, however, the artillery had been concentrated at a single point and perhaps one or two enemy companies had been wrecked and further shot up by skirmishers, then the column had a chance of success. If the enemy volleys did not stop the column, the bayonets of the attackers would come down and a blood-curdling cry would go up. Their momentum would by now have become unstoppable. The defending force would probably buckle and run before the attack was actually pressed home.

The bayonet had become something of a cult in the French army. A triangular steel spike, 57cm in length, bayonets were first and foremost a psychological weapon. Charges where bayonets crossed were very much the exception. It is difficult to imagine the carnage of two lines of men running into one another, with the file-closers pushing their men forwards onto the enemy bayonets in an attempt to force a way through; but such things did occur. As a weapon bayonets were perhaps more useful in independent actions, man against man in single combat when there was no chance to reload.

After passing through Martigny, the division moved off towards the looming mountains. From that point on, although the gradient was still fairly gentle, the ascent now began in earnest. The steady deterioration seen in the landscape since St Maurice took a further plunge here. There was little vegetation and few trees. A birdless sky loomed overhead. The greens of springtime still lay locked beneath a mantle of ice and snow, broken only in places by black rocks that cast shadows hauntingly upon the road. It was as if spring dared not follow them on their journey, that in some way this barrenness was a prelude to suffering ahead. Reaching Orsières, a bivouac was prepared for the night. It was a wonder anybody lived in these mountains, there was a total lack of luxury. Officers looking for a little extra wine were charged a small fortune for it.

The march of 16 May took the Ninth to St Pierre, a small village from where the final track to the summit was joined. The division camped down for the night in huge barns and barrack-like buildings dotted about the place. The division received three more days' ration of biscuit. On the morning of 17 May the Ninth was scheduled for a 4am departure towards the St Bernard Pass. It was important they reached St Remy on the other side of the pass before nightfall because no shelter existed before that point. The monastery at the summit of the pass was too small to shelter more than a few companies, and there would not be enough wood for their cookfires. In the darkness, the Ninth passed through a gate and left St Pierre for the track to the pass. They crossed a deep ravine and entered a narrow gorge less than a metre wide. One wrong step would be fatal as the path was flanked by a precipice, with a raging torrent below. The men snaked nervously forwards, sometimes in single file, sometimes double. Labassée, Kuhmann, Verger and Sirejean had to lead their horses by their bridles. Fortunately the weather held out. If there had been gusts, snow or rain, many would surely have plunged to their doom. After an hour or so the head of the file came into the small plain of Proz. Although the climb thus far had been strenuous, from that point on it became remorseless, with the steep path zigzagging its way to the summit nearly 2,500 metres above sea level.

Three hours after leaving St Pierre, the Ninth reached the summit. It was now 7am. To reward his men, Bonaparte had organized a welcome surprise for those reaching the summit. The St Bernard monks stood waiting in the pass. They issued every man with a beaker of wine, some Gruyere cheese and a slab of rye bread. The ranks were broken and the men were permitted to take a short rest around the monastery. Some of the officers had the opportunity to go inside and warm themselves next to the fire, while the men played with the monks' large dogs.

The subject of avalanches was very much a topic of conversation among the men. One of the reasons the Ninth had set off so early was to avoid avalanches, which were more common in the afternoon. The weather on the mountains had been unusually fine and the cold, crisp nights secured the snow drifts. One avalanche had hit Lannes' advanced guard and several men and a gun had been lost. By the time this news filtered its way down the pass, the rumourmongers told of a whole half-brigade being swallowed by the snow.

Although the climb had been tough, the Ninth had had things comparatively easy. Back down the track a battalion of the 59th had been assigned to assist with the artillery. In order to get the guns over the pass, they first had to be dismantled. The barrels had been put in hollowed-out tree trunks, which were harnessed to ropes, each pulled by a company of men. The ammunition chests, limbers, wheels, carriages and equipment were shared out between the remainder to manhandle over the narrow paths as best they could. In the original plan a large number of peasants and their mules had been assembled to assist the soldiers. However, the work of transporting the advanced guard had proved so back-breaking that the pay was not considered compensation enough and the peasants quit. Matters were made worse by Lannes' troops, who had found the assistance of the mules so invaluable they 'forgot' to return them. By the time the 59th reached the summit, the artillery commander, General Marmont, recalled they were 'tired, harassed and annoyed' despite being given brandy by their officers.[10]

Meanwhile the Ninth moved off the summit to catch up with Lannes' advanced guard. They found themselves confronted by a very difficult descent.

In places there was nothing resembling a track. It took two hours for the men to climb down to St Remy and on to Étroubles. As they scrambled down the mountain, Lannes had pushed ahead and captured Aosta. A Croat battalion had been surprised by the attack and had fallen back after a dozen casualties. Now that the first shots of the campaign had been fired, the mood of the army changed accordingly. Berthier's chief of staff, General Pierre Dupont, put out an order of the day on 18 May warning the conscripts not to fire their muskets in camp and not to commit pillage. *'Pillage what?'* they might have asked.

The Ninth made the short journey to Aosta and rested for the remainder of the day, spending the time making running repairs to their equipment. The next morning they were set a target of 42km to reach Arnatz. They set out at 7am and marched down the Aosta Valley following the course of the Dora Baltea's left bank. A marked and welcome change in the environment was felt in this new valley. For the first time since Martigny, spring was in evidence. The sun felt warm on the men's faces; vegetation was in abundance, even colourful butterflies. It was not long before the tell-tale signs of human conflict were evident. The forests were felled or, like the many cottages they saw, burned. The fields had been left uncultivated and only a few animals remained. The inhabitants of the Aosta Valley had traditionally produced only enough to guarantee their own survival, therefore the constant intrusion of requisitioning armies over the past few years had ruined them. Many had been forced into exile; the empty shells of their dwellings left to rot. The march continued for 11 long hours, through Châtillon, which had fallen to Lannes the day before. Here the Dora Baltea bent to the south and headed down towards Fort Bard, an impregnable-looking fortress barring access from the valley into the plains beyond.

Early on 20 May, Boudet and his staff rode ahead to look at Bard. Built on a pyramidal rock, where two mountains came close together, Bard dominated the exit from the mountain passes. On one side was the sheer face of the Porcil Mountain, at the base of which rushed the Dora Baltea flowing in a semicircular course around the rock. On the other side, between the fort and the Albard Mountain, was a gorge less than 50m wide. The Aosta–Ivrea road passed between a double line of houses which made up Bard village. The village was closed by walls which could only be passed by a series of gates and drawbridges. Above the village was a gully channelling mountain flood waters away from the village.

The fort itself was no real major structural feat. It did not need to be. Around the rock were two concentric perimeter walls, overlooked by two levels of gun emplacements on the summit. The first level had 12 guns; the second six. They dominated the village below and the approaches on all sides. The attacker was extremely restricted in sighting batteries to open a breach in the walls and roofed casemates prevented any effective howitzer bombardment.

Lannes had placed some sharpshooters up into a water gully overlooking the village. These had managed to force the defenders to take cover inside the fort. He then sent his advanced guard back up the valley to try and find a passage around the fort. As he did so, General Watrin planned to assault the works. With Boudet in support and Lannes moving to outflank them, Watrin hoped the Austrian defenders might lose heart and give up.

To support the attack, Boudet sent a detachment of the Ninth up into the rocks to give supporting fire. Their first shots of the campaign rang out, splintering the fresh morning air. Unfortunately for Watrin's men, the Austrians had no intention of giving up their perch so easily. The fort's guns thundered into action stopping the assault dead in its tracks. There was simply no way to breach the outer wall and the assault force scampered back. With the Ninth's first shots came the first casualty – an officer, Sub-Lieutenant Tesson, slightly wounded.

Watrin was ordered back up to Arnatz where Lannes had found a path outflanking the fort. The following morning, on 21 May, Boudet also was ordered back up to Arnatz to follow the new path. The route crossed the Albard Mountain by means of a track from Arnatz to Donnaz. Until two days before, the locals had considered the path too dangerous even for mules. Made of stouter stuff, Lannes proved it was possible for a division to cross. The army desperately needed to get round Bard. Rations were on the verge of being cut in half and the army needed to break out on to fertile ground to find food. General Berthier ordered 1,500 men to work on making the pathway safe for the army to cross. In the steepest places steps were cut into the rock, while at the narrowest, walls had been constructed to prevent men falling over the edge. This time however the artillery would not be following. Marmont told Berthier the artillery had suffered so badly after being dismantled at St Pierre he would not allow it to be broken up again. Boudet was therefore obliged to leave his artillery behind.

Despite the engineers' work the pathway was as bad as the St Bernard Pass. The ascent took two hours. On the summit, the men could overlook Bard. The Austrians could see them too and fired a few shots in their direction. The descent to Donnaz was relatively gentle. A good track existed and took just two hours to complete. At the foot of this path the division rejoined the Ivrea road and found Watrin's men waiting for them. Boudet was sent towards the rear of Bard to prevent any Austrian breakout.

The greater part of 22 May was spent idly watching the fort for any sign of action. Some of the Ninth's soldiers got into position to snipe at any Austrians imprudent enough to surface. Occasionally the odd crack of musketry would cause people to look up momentarily, but nothing serious developed. In the evening, as the darkness had taken hold, the night watch was sent forwards to place a line of pickets near to the fort. As they waited for the night to pass all seemed quiet. Then, in the dead of night, several shots were heard and voices cried out from within the walls of the village; the pickets stood to and readied themselves. There was a tremendous explosion from the far side of Bard, which dazzled them. An assault was being delivered by the French troops on the other side of the fort. The Ivrea Gate was thrown open and several figures appeared to be coming out; the chasseurs nearest the gate opened fire and the newcomers were forced to the ground. A voice called out to cease fire: they were French grenadiers. After realizing their mistake the chasseurs helped break into the houses and loop-holed them on the fort side. By now the fort's guns were firing off blindly in every direction.

When the dust and smoke settled and morning broke, Boudet was ordered to move ahead and support Lannes who was moving against the Austrians at Ivrea. By the time they arrived, Lannes had already carried the place by storm. There had been a garrison of about 6,000 Austrians here, but they had retreated as far back as the Chiusella River on Lannes' approach. Boudet was ordered to bivouac along the banks of the Dora Baltea. Rations had been reduced by half, and storm clouds gathered overhead, releasing a deluge of rain. For the next two days the division remained static, resting and making repairs in the wet.

Shortly before sunrise on 26 May all the French troops around Ivrea were ordered to stand under arms. Lannes had been authorized to force a passage over the Chiusella in order to convince the Austrians they were destined for Turin and Genoa, rather than Milan. Daylight revealed the Austrian camp and a swarm of cavalry. A number of Austrian guns were placed to cover the approach to a long, stone bridge over the Chiusella which Watrin's troops were about to force. The Ninth was drawn up in reserve on the right of the division. They watched as the attack began with a direct assault on the bridge by the 6th Light. The Austrian artillery murdered them. Formed in a deep column, each shot ploughed its way through rank upon rank of Frenchmen. Despite this they began to get a foothold on the bridge, but then they became obscured by smoke and it was impossible to see how the attack was progressing. Several regiments of Austrian infantry could be seen moving into the smoke, marching just as if they were on parade. The Austrians charged onto the bridge and beat the French back at bayonet point.

Lannes had foreseen this check and now played his trump card; the 6th Light were redeployed and sent over a ford in the river while the 28th Line stood poised to rush the bridge. Two more half-brigades began to cross further upriver. Fearing envelopment, the Austrians began to falter and retreated from the bridge and riverbank. Boudet received the order to advance. For the novices seeing action for the first time, the march down to the bridge must have been a sobering experience. Through the intervals in the column they caught glimpses of the victims of the attack. They saw what cannon balls did to young men like themselves. To their left and right they could hear wounded men crying out in pain. Then as they crossed the bridge they saw their first Austrians close up. The uniforms were different, but the faces were the same and the blood just as red.

They climbed over a hill and halted at the village of Romano where they were confronted with a spectacular sight. Four thousand Austrian horsemen were charging Lannes' men. They passed with incredible speed through the intervals of the French battalions and continued onwards, some heading straight for Boudet's men. As the infantry quickly closed up, Boudet and his staff drew their sabres. In order to protect their general, the 80 troopers of the 11th Hussars charged the Austrians and drove them off, losing 36 of their number in the process.

As the Austrian cavalry peeled away, the general advance resumed but by now the Austrian infantry had moved too far away. The Austrian cavalry had bought them the time they needed. For the price of a single wounded chasseur, the Ninth had witnessed its first battle of the campaign. Next time the price was sure to be higher.

THE ROAD TO
PIACENZA

While Bonaparte had been forming his new army and directing it over the Alps, the Austrians had began an offensive of their own on 6 April, attacking the Ligurian Riviera with 50,000 men. Within a month the French had been pushed out of Liguria and behind the River Var into France. The only remaining French foothold was the port of Genoa, commanded by the wily General André Massena. He was in a precarious position with the Austrians besieging the city from the landward side and the British Royal Navy blockading the sea. Now Bonaparte had arrived in northern Italy, the Austrians assumed he would march to Massena's relief. They were wrong. It had always been the first consul's intention to take Milan and cut the Austrian lines of communication. This would draw the Austrians out of Liguria without Bonaparte having to fight in the difficult, mountainous terrain around Genoa.

On the morning of 27 May, General Lannes was sent towards Chivasso, seemingly in pursuit of the retreating Austrians. To the Austrians, this move confirmed their belief that Genoa was Bonaparte's intended target. Meanwhile Murat raced eastwards towards Milan with General Jean Charles Monnier's infantry division and the cavalry brigades of generals Etienne Kellermann and Pierre Champeaux. At the same time, Boudet's division was sent to Santhia to rendezvous with Loison's division and General Duhesme, who assumed direct command over both divisions.[1]

Next morning the Ninth trudged off to Vercelli on the coattails of Murat's advanced guard, arriving in the evening. Beyond the town was the River Sesia. The Austrians had burnt the bridge and positioned a battery of guns on the far bank. With a frontal attack likely to prove costly, generals Murat and Duhesme went on a reconnaissance looking for fords to outflank the Austrians. After completing their tour, the two generals formulated a plan of attack. The French would construct two artillery batteries opposite the Austrian position to pin them down while Murat led the Ninth a league and a half (6km) downstream to a ford opposite Palestro. Meanwhile, Boudet would take Guénand's brigade north to cross the river opposite Borgo Vercelli. Both prongs would be supported by light cavalry. Duhesme would wait in the centre, keeping Monnier's infantry as a reserve.

As preparations got underway, the Austrians on the far bank became inquisitive. At 3am on 29 May, the Austrians opened fire on the French batteries. Illuminated by the muzzle flashes, the Austrians saw boats moored on the French side of the river. They also saw the bayonets and muzzles of French infantry in large numbers. Convinced the French were preparing to make a frontal assault, the Austrian infantry was brought up and ordered to fire volleys blindly into the night.

Meanwhile, Murat set off with the Ninth just before daybreak, making the journey to the ford discovered the evening before. The carabineers were the first to enter the snow-chilled waters of the Sesia, gingerly placing their feet on slippery, submerged rocks. The Sesia was in full torrent. The carabineers could feel the current tugging at their legs. Someone slipped. He collided with three others and all four were swept away, never to be seen again. Fearing more casualties, Murat ordered his horse chasseurs to file into the water and form a breakwater behind which the Ninth could cross. Previous to the campaign the Ninth had formed a company of swimmers under the command of sub-lieutenants Pierre Donot and Paul Vivenot. They were called together and lined the riverbank ready to dive in and rescue anyone who lost their footing. By 7am the Ninth was across the river and advancing against the Austrian flank. At the same time Guénand crossed to the north.

Opposite Vercelli the Austrians realized they had been duped. When scouts learned about the two prongs coming in on the flanks, they retreated. When Duhesme saw they were pulling out, he ordered two companies of grenadiers into the boats and sent them in pursuit. At 8am the Ninth clashed with the Austrian rearguard. Sporadic fighting continued as far as Novara, as the Ninth harried the retreating Austrians. In the meantime a 'flying bridge' was constructed over the Sesia allowing the rest of the army to cross.[2] At Novara the Ninth was ordered to halt lest they get too far ahead of support. Making a bivouac on the edge of the town's defences, they called a halt for the following day.

On 31 May, the French resumed the pursuit. The Austrians had fallen back and taken up position behind the River Ticino at Turbigo. The area was well suited for defence. At this point the Ticino was quite deep with steep banks and meandering rivulets ideal for breaking up large troop formations. Several islands were formed by these different courses, many of which were heavily wooded. Murat concentrated his main force opposite Turbigo. Two companies of grenadiers from the 59th were ferried to a wooded island on boats which had been hidden from the retreating Austrians by local French sympathizers. A fusillade soon developed. Artillery was brought up and French soldiers were directed into the scrub and brushwood to fire on the opposing force. As the fighting intensified, Duhesme took the Ninth to find a crossing further downstream. There had been another bridge across the Ticino near Boffalora, but when Duhesme arrived he found it destroyed. However, on the opposite bank there were several boats that the Austrians had neglected to sink. These boats offered the only viable means of crossing the river, but someone would have to swim across and get them.

The water was straight off the mountains, fast moving and ice cold. To complicate matters further, the far bank was protected by Austrian soldiers. The Ninth's swimmers were called forward and told to prepare while carabineers lined the riverbank to give covering fire. Once the swimmers got into the icy water they came under fire. The temperature was freezing and the current so strong one of the swimmers floundered. Out of reach of his comrades he was sucked under and drowned. The others hesitated.

Watching the action was 26-year-old Charles Vanderbach, one of the Ninth's three surgeon-majors. The son of a doctor in the old province of Champagne, Vanderbach had been dragged away from his studies at Paris' Broussais Hospital and sent to the front line with a musket in 1793. With a shortage of medical staff at the front it was not long before he swapped his flintlock for a surgeon's saw.

It had been a bloody apprenticeship, covering everything from lancing boils and treating blistered feet to probing battlefield wounds. He watched the floundering swimmers with a growing sense of impatience. Throwing caution to the wind, Vanderbach stripped off and leapt into the freezing water, heading for the Austrians with a determined stroke. The Austrians saw him heading for the boats and opened fire. As the balls plopped into the water around him, Vanderbach pressed on. The carabineers concentrated their fire to protect him. Excited by his bravery, eight carabineers threw down their muskets and leapt in after him. Before long they had reached the far bank and seized a craft which they towed back. The remainder of the swimmers were spurred into action and a wave of them headed for the opposing bank. The carabineers' covering fire prevented the Austrians from stopping the swimmers collecting the boats. Knowing those same boats would soon be returning full of the red-plumed soldiers on the far bank, the Austrians retired with good sense. After the boats were collected, the remaining carabineers rowed themselves across. Two companies were sent in pursuit of the Austrians who were chased as far as Boffalora. Meanwhile Charles Vanderbach was heralded as a hero. This was the first of many daring feats the surgeon would perform.

Next morning, Duhesme's priority was to support the carabineers at Boffalora. The remainder of the Ninth was sent across the Ticino and told to bring back the necessary materials to rebuild the bridge. The local houses were broken up for their timbers and a bridge was soon thrown across. Over the remainder of the day, the Ninth moved up to Corbetta in readiness for the next day's push into the capital of Lombardy.

At 8am on 2 June, the army marched on Milan. At 4pm Murat entered the city unopposed at the head of the cavalry. The Ninth arrived an hour later. While Monnier's division blockaded the Austrian garrison in the Sforza Castle, Murat ordered Duhesme to march through the city and secure the Romana Gate on the south-eastern side of Milan before the first consul arrived in an hour's time. Leaving the 30th Line to support Monnier, Boudet marched through the city with the rest of his division. Crowds began to gather, stunned into silence at the sudden appearance of French troops. Passing through the large cathedral square, the Ninth quickly traversed the city, exiting via the Romana Gate and taking up position in the fields outside the city around the Via Emilia.

That night, Duhesme was ordered to push on to the town of Lodi and seize the important bridge over the Adda. It was at Lodi in 1796 that Bonaparte had begun building his career in earnest. Its recapture would be especially poignant to headquarters. Setting off, the Ninth and the 11th Hussars formed the advanced guard of Duhesme's two divisions.

The hussars rode off ahead of the column looking for the Austrians. They searched the side roads and the houses along the main road, questioning the locals, and looking for tell-tale signs of the enemy, such as musket barrels and bayonets glinting in the distance. Four hours later they finally made contact with the Austrians, in front of the village of Melegano. As soon as Sirejean's battalion arrived, the French chasseurs began advancing into the outskirts of the town. There was a brief fire-fight after which the Austrians retired over a bridge across the River Lambro. The chasseurs now infiltrated the buildings overlooking the river and began a fusillade against those on the opposite bank.

Boudet calculated the enemy's strength at this crossing point at about 1,200 infantry and 800 cavalry with two guns. The bridge needed to be stormed and the route opened as swiftly as possible so as not to detain the march on Lodi. Coming up behind Sirejean's battalion were the carabineers. While the chasseurs fired from the flanks, the carabineers were ordered to force a crossing. Duhesme's adjutant-general, Marc Gaspard Abraham Paulet, watched this attack and recalled the results in his journal later in the evening: '... our troops' attack was most audacious. The 9th Light, long accustomed to know little of obstacles, beat the charge, officers at the head, forcing the Lambro bridge.'[3]

The carabineers rushed at the guns. Austrian resistance quickly crumbled around the bridge, but rallied again on the crest of a nearby hill. Behind the carabineers came the 11th Hussars, ready for the pursuit. Austrian cavalry came up to protect their infantry and presented themselves to the hussars. This cavalry was from the De Bussy Legion, an Austrian regiment infamously officered by aristocratic French émigrés. The 11th took up the gauntlet; both sides squared up to the other and put their horses to the gallop, clattering into one another and clashing with swords.

By now the chasseur battalions were across the bridge and formed up behind the carabineers. They presented their bayonets to the Austrian infantry and advanced. With their cavalry being chased from the field by the French hussars, the Austrian infantry broke contact and sped off down the main road. Boudet gave chase for an hour, but was ordered to halt by Duhesme lest he draw too far from Loison's division behind. Boudet therefore ordered a halt and set up headquarters in Tavazzano for the evening. It had been a good day. For a dozen casualties Boudet's division had taken 150 prisoners, including five aristocratic officers from the De Bussy Legion. Duhesme's chief of staff summed up his journal entry for that day with the words, 'Boudet's division has merited the greatest eulogies.'[4]

Glorious though the day had been, Adjutant-General Dalton brought everyone back down to earth with sobering news. Since crossing the Sesia, the Ninth had expended nearly all its cartridges. The 59th had been passing cartridges up the line to the Ninth and were likewise running very low. In the morning Boudet's soldiers would have to take a bridge that had held up the whole army four years before. There was every chance the enemy encountered at Melegano had only been a rearguard to a much larger force, which might be at Lodi. Dalton wrote an urgent letter to army headquarters in Milan asking for 50,000 cartridges to be dispatched immediately. This total would bring the two half-brigades with Boudet up to 40 shots per man. He understood the army had been having difficulty with its ammunition supply since crossing the Alps, but the division's need was vital. He sent the letter with three hussars to escort the ammunition caissons he hoped would be forthcoming.

Next morning the march resumed. At about 9am the Ninth began infiltrating the outskirts of Lodi. No enemy troops were encountered, so they pushed on for the long wooden bridge across the Adda. The bridge had been cut, but the Austrians had made a poor job of it. Although they had left a strong rearguard to observe the French, they had neglected to leave any artillery with which to contest a crossing.

While Adjutant-General Paulet examined the bridge, the leading chasseurs opened fire on the enemy observation point with their last few cartridges. Duhesme arrived with the artillery and ordered it to lob a few shells at the Austrians. The carabineers were formed up ready to storm the bridge as soon as it was repaired. At the sight of this the Austrians melted away, trying to put as much distance as possible between themselves and their inevitable pursuers. When the repairs were made, the carabineers went over and secured the far bank.

The hussars followed them and galloped off towards Crema in hot pursuit of the enemy rearguard. Meanwhile a search of the town was made which gave up extensive stores of flour, tobacco, salt and a chest of paper money and gold coin.[5]

The hussars soon returned with 15 prisoners who were sent for interrogation. Furthermore a deserter revealed that the Austrians had abandoned Crema and were in a state of panic. Duhesme had performed his primary objective; the bridge was in his hands. His secondary objective was to defend it. Although the Austrians appeared to be in headlong retreat, Duhesme was cautious. Retaining the 59th on the west bank as a reserve, he ordered Boudet to position the Ninth on the far bank and to establish a network of pickets in front of the bridge.

On the east bank the Ninth was positioned in the following manner: Verger and Kuhmann's battalions bivouacked in reserve with the carabineers. Sirejean's battalion formed a semicircular cordon with a radius of half a mile.[6] The perimeter of this cordon was formed by a continuous chain of sentinels, each man within sight of the men either side of him. Behind the chain were a series of posts where a small reserve was placed under the command of a sub-officer. Behind these 'little posts' were the pickets, where the bulk of the platoon remained in reserve, mainly in concealed positions. The sentinels were replaced every hour or two by men from the pickets so that everyone was able to grab a few hours' sleep.

Small patrols would have been sent out beyond the line of sentinels looking for information or to set ambushes on the main road. If the Austrians had attacked, they would first encounter these patrols, then the sentinels. The sentinels would have fallen back on the little posts, which would then have fallen back on the pickets. The pickets would have put up some resistance and then withdrawn onto the main reserve. With such precautions an enemy attack would have been unlikely to gain the element of surprise. It would also have prevented spies from infiltrating Lodi.[7]

With Milan and Lodi in French hands, Bonaparte predicted the Austrian commander Melas would attempt to recover his communications with Vienna. With all the territory north of the Po River now in French hands, Melas' best escape route was the main road from Alessandria to Mantua via the city of

Piacenza. Bonaparte ordered Murat to race south, cross the River Po, capture Piacenza, and block Melas' escape route to Mantua. Along with the cavalry brigades of Kellermann and Champeaux, Murat was given Boudet's division.

On 4 June General Berthier at Milan ordered his chief of staff to send the Ninth 40,000 cartridges. Murat arrived at Lodi the following day and collected Boudet in the early hours of the morning. Boudet's division marched first, with his hussars scouting ahead and the infantry coming up quickly behind. Just after midday the scouts ran into Austrian forward posts near Pizzighettone. The Austrian horse jaeger fell back to their picket at the village of San Rocco where there was a bridge across a small stream. With speed essential, Boudet ordered the Ninth to clear the road. It was over in a matter of a few minutes. A pursuit was mounted and it appeared there was nothing to stop the French. Shortly before 2pm the walled city of Piacenza came into view on the other side of the Po. With the objective in sight, the Ninth pressed forward only to find themselves thwarted at the river's edge.

The commander of Piacenza, General Mosel, had been warned that the French were coming. The city's garrison was desperately under strength, so Mosel's best hope of denying the French control of the bridge was by holding a dilapidated fortification on the threatened north bank. He had the ditches widened, built up the ramparts and blocked the gateway with a cheval-de-frise. Mosel placed six guns, a company of infantry and 30 jaeger inside the fort. On the other bank he retained the rest of his infantry and positioned 18 guns which, with those inside the bridgehead, created an enfilading fire. If he could hold the French up long enough, a reinforcement under General Andreas O'Reilly was on his way, with further reinforcements expected soon after. Forewarned of Boudet's arrival by the horse jaeger, the Austrian gunners in the fort loaded their guns with canister. As the Ninth came into view they opened fire, forcing the light infantrymen to take cover.

Murat and Boudet gathered their forces and reviewed the situation. The fort was a formidable obstacle. The French had insufficient artillery to batter the place into submission and time was a factor. Boudet had dealt with similar situations before, breaking into British forts in the Caribbean. His experience and temperament told him the only way to deal with this situation was a head-on assault. Murat concurred. The Ninth was divided in half, one part commanded by General Musnier, the other by Adjutant-General Dalton. These two wings would advance on the flanks of the fort and draw fire. Boudet would then personally lead the grenadiers of the 59th Line against the main gate.

An advance against a fortified position was a terrifying prospect. The two parts of the Ninth set off on their long walks, advancing quickly against the two sides of the fort. A brisk fire erupted from the fort. Each ball or burst of canister that struck the Ninth caused a moan to rise up from the unfortunate victims. As the Ninth pressed forward, the guns that Mosel had placed on the other bank now came into play. The Ninth was under fire for 15 minutes until they reached the outer defence works. Sensing the time was right, Boudet launched his grenadiers at the gate, but they were met with a hail of fire and the attack petered out almost at once.

Although Boudet's attack had failed, the Ninth took cover around the earthworks and commenced a vengeful fusillade against the defenders. The enemy gunners were subjected to a hail of musket balls fired blindly through the embrasures as they served their pieces. One young conscript, perched calmly on a rock, fired off more than 100 rounds while exposed to continual fire; the mechanical routines of loading having replaced any sense of fear.[8] Eventually the firing died down as both sides accepted a temporary stalemate. In order to rest their men and secure their wounded, Boudet asked Murat for a reprieve until nightfall when they would try again. Murat agreed and set the assault time for 10pm.

The Austrians inside the fort guessed the French would attempt to break in under the cover of night. They had already suffered 120 casualties and would be hard-pressed to withstand a second attack. After nightfall Mosel ordered his artillery to be withdrawn back across the Po. To cover this operation, Mosel had all the artillery on the far bank of the Po open fire. This occurred just as Boudet was about to launch his second attack. Instead of assailing the fort, the Ninth found themselves pinned down by heavy fire. Meanwhile the Austrians rescued their guns and removed a section from the centre of the bridge. Inside the fort was left a rearguard of 80 men.

Once the bridge was cut, the artillery fire abruptly ceased. Captain Hippolyte Cazaux of 2nd Battalion became suspicious and decided to see if there were any Austrians left inside the fort. Accompanied only by Sergeant Lambert and four chasseurs he climbed from the ditch up into one of the embrasures. Cazaux edged his way forward through the darkness and walked straight into the 80-strong rearguard waiting for boats to transport them to safety. Cazaux looked at them; they looked at him. Thoughts of captivity must have gone through Cazaux's mind. He had previously spent two years in Austrian captivity after being wounded and captured on a previous campaign. Whatever inward reservations he may have had, without showing the slightest surprise or fear, Cazaux began to lecture the Austrians on the hopelessness of their position and how things were about to get very nasty unless they laid down their arms. The Austrians were stunned. Strained eyes looked out into the darkness. Surely this officer had not come alone? There was some movement behind the Frenchman, but they could only count a handful of men backing him up. Were there more in the darkness? Just as some of the more sceptical Austrians were about to call Cazaux's bluff, another group of Frenchmen appeared out of the darkness. A group from the 59th had become equally suspicious and had entered the fort from a different side. Their arrival did enough to convince the Austrians, who threw their weapons on the floor and surrendered to Cazaux.

Back at Murat's headquarters, the French generals were in raptures at Cazaux's action. Boudet could hardly believe the man's sangfroid and noted the action in his journal. Celebrations were tempered by some of the casualty reports coming in. The Ninth had lost 15 men, including Sub-Lieutenant Voeglin, an old soldier of long service who had been killed in a hail of canister. There were 56 more wounded, including Captain Simon Paul Bruyère who had been struck in the head. It was a heavy toll for the unit. The 59th had lost eight killed and 22 wounded besides. An inspection of the bridge revealed the damage inflicted on it by the Austrians. A direct assault against the city was now impossible. It was disappointing news; they had failed in their task and as far as they knew Piacenza could be receiving reinforcements as they spoke. There was nothing more to do that night; the men had been awake nearly 24 hours. It was time for rest.

Next morning Murat went to have a look at the bridge, wondering whether an assault could be mounted over it after repairs. Boudet also looked at it, but thought it extremely unlikely this tactic would succeed. The Po was swollen by recent heavy rains and its course was very fast. To rebuild the bridge, men would have to work in the water where they would be exposed to the strong current and enemy fire. Instead the two generals made a reconnaissance left and right of their position looking for boats or a ford. One detachment was led by Adjutant-General Berthier, the commander-in-chief's brother; the other by Adjutant-General Dalton. Other detachments were sent out to scour the area for information. On the left they reached as far as the Adda near to Maccastorno where patrols from Loison's division were encountered. On the right they reached as far as the Ticino. No enemy was reported in either case.

The troops not on patrol had other work to do. The dead had to be buried. The final resting place of a Napoleonic soldier was very humble. A sufficiently large hole was dug, the bodies were piled in one on top of another, then the hole was filled. There was no headstone, no notice of the names of those who had died. Before burial the corpses were stripped naked and their equipment recycled. What could not be distributed immediately was placed into the baggage train until a new home could be found for it. Uniforms too badly torn or bloodied could be washed and used for patches by the other troops – nothing was wasted. All the elaborate rituals of burial observed in peacetime could not be allowed to interfere with the tasks at hand. If time permitted, a detail of men from the same squads as the deceased would attend the burial and fire a few shots over the grave to mark their passing. The Revolution had de-Christianized the French army and any prayers would have been muttered under the breath. Perhaps Captain Gabriel and a few friends came to pay their last respects to Sub-Lieutenant Voeglin, say a few words and share a tot of something warming to remember him by.

Dalton's journey downstream continued for about ten miles. Having noted their usefulness, Dalton had taken the Ninth's swimmers. Together they rounded up about 15 craft of various descriptions and gathered them near the village of Nocetto. Leaving the swimmers on guard, Dalton rode back to Boudet. It was now too late in the day to attempt a river crossing, so Boudet made plans for the morrow. He would take the Ninth, the hussars and most of the 59th down to Nocetto and force a crossing before attacking Piacenza from the east.

At 2am on 7 June, Boudet took his force to Nocetto and the waiting boats. General Musnier led the Ninth and the hussars while Boudet followed with the artillery, the grenadiers and first two battalions of the 59th Line. With minimum fuss, the Ninth crossed the Po. A few Austrian scouts were perceived in the distance, counting the Frenchmen before making a speedy return to Piacenza.

Musnier sent the hussars out to scout ahead while he took the Ninth along the Cremona road to a small village about two miles east of Piacenza. When the hussars returned they reported an artillery convoy of about 1,500 vehicles leaving Piacenza by the Parma road. They were moving at a good speed and were protected by a small cavalry detachment. A column of infantry was coming up the same road heading towards Piacenza. Without hesitation, Musnier decided to act. He informed Boudet he was going to press ahead to take Piacenza with the Ninth before the Austrian reinforcements arrived. Boudet would have to catch him up later. At the same time, Musnier asked Kuhmann to try and intercept the convoy with his battalion.

There was a state of chaos inside Piacenza. Earlier that day, just before daybreak, General O'Reilly had arrived to take command of the city with two squadrons of the Nauendorf hussars. His situation appeared desperate. He had to send one squadron to protect the artillery convoy and the scouts had reported Boudet's force crossing at Nocetto. Reports confirmed that the French had also crossed the Po further west near the town of Belgiojoso. A strong reinforcement was supposed to have arrived from Genoa, but this had been delayed leaving the city. The only good news was the arrival of 600 men of the Klebeck infantry regiment. O'Reilly directed these troops to the Stradella road to the west of the city and ordered the two batteries of guns on the riverbank to limber up and follow. The remaining squadron of Nauendorf hussars was ordered to intercept the French forces landing downstream and buy time for the organization of the city's defences.

Two battalions of the Ninth were moving at speed along the road towards Piacenza when the Austrian hussars appeared before them. At the sight of cavalry the two battalions formed closed columns to prevent the cavalry from penetrating their formation. At the head of the column several of the more belligerent carabineers called out for vengeance for the day before. They had suffered heavily during their attack on the fort and wanted reprisals. Bowing to their fury, General Musnier gave the carabineers the order to attack.[9]

Opposite them, the squadron of enemy hussars began trotting forward to attack. Doubt began to creep into their minds as they watched the carabineers preparing for what looked like a bayonet charge. This was most irregular. It was one of the accepted facts of warfare – when cavalry approached infantry, the infantry would form a square or closed column and open fire. A stand-off would ensue until either the cavalry brought up artillery or the infantry received cavalry support. Faced with an advancing wall of bayonets, the Austrian cavalry lost its nerve and broke off, flowing left and right of the Ninth. As their buglers called out the rally, the Ninth raced for the unmanned city gate. Musnier rode into the city at the head of the carabineers. The general directed Labassée to mop up the streets while he took the carabineers to secure the far gate on the Stradella road. Moving through streets in a combat situation was nerve-wracking for a commander. In the narrow medieval streets he was not able to retain control of his men. Even the company captains would have difficulty retaining control. Each doorway had to be opened or kicked in and the houses examined; men needed to get onto the roof-tops, up the church towers, down in the cellars, everywhere the enemy might be hiding. The nervousness and tension was heightened by encounters with civilians who would excitedly gesture and point, talking hurriedly in Italian. Every time a gun fired, the narrow streets would amplify its blast making distances hard to judge.

Labassée directed his men to chase the fleeing Austrian troops who were heading towards the citadel. He hoped to prevent the Austrians from taking up a position there and so avoid any long drawn-out siege. Musnier meanwhile doubled his men through the main streets of Piacenza hoping to bar the gate. The danger and tension of the moment was exhilarating. Just as the carabineers reached the gate, a column of Austrian infantry began entering the city. The two sides looked at each other momentarily before Musnier ordered his men to charge. Their fury still up, the carabineers went to work on the head of the Austrian column.

Meanwhile, Kuhmann had given up trying to catch the convoy, it had too good a start. He turned his men around and skirted south of the city to approach the town from a different side and cut off any Austrians trying to escape. As he approached, he perceived the Austrians fighting at the Stradella gate. As the Austrians were assailed by the carabineers in front, Kuhmann wheeled his battalion into their flank. They did not see him until it was too late. The Austrian regiment simply disintegrated. While some threw down their guns and surrendered others made a dash for Piacenza's citadel. Lieutenant Joseph Etienne led a dozen men in pursuit through the streets and caught a party of 74 Austrians before they could reach safety. Despite the numbers stacked in their favour, the Austrians surrendered when they saw the way ahead barred. With a reputation for fearless bravery and a military career stretching back to 1784, Captain Pierre Leblanc arguably outdid Cazaux in terms of audacity. He led a handful of skirmishers into one of the Austrian redoubts and came out with 196 Austrian prisoners, including a major.[10]

As the Ninth continued mopping up, Boudet arrived with the 59th Line. He was more than happy to find the city in his hands with a large quantity of prisoners and stores awaiting his inspection. There was still some musketry around the citadel where a handful of Austrians had holed themselves up but that was all. Murat's engineers had finally got a flying bridge set up over the Po and the remaining battalion of the 59th was brought across.

Murat reported to Bonaparte that they had taken around 2,000 prisoners, killed 50 more and taken 13 pieces of artillery. Considerable stores were retrieved from the magazines and 30 large boats filled with provisions had been seized. Flying bridges had been established over the Po and the cavalry had crossed and was ready to support the next action. That night Boudet completed his journal entry for the day. He praised the Ninth in particular for their displays over the past few days, noting it would be 'difficult to find more audacity and intrepidity.'[11] They had lost another 20 men that day, bringing their total casualties to 91 men over the past three days. This was one of the highest losses in action the Ninth had ever suffered.[12]

For two days the Ninth blockaded Piacenza's citadel. Although few in number, the defenders had plenty of ammunition and there was a constant hail of bullets and shot coming from the citadel, making movement in view of the guns extremely risky. When Loison's division came up on 9 June to relieve them, Boudet chose a circuitous route for his division along the edge of the Po in order to skirt round the citadel's guns. Even under the cover of night they lost three men and two horses to the incessant Austrian fire. They were then held up trying to cross the River Trebbia. The constant rain had caused a dramatic rise in water levels so the ford they had hoped to use was impassable. A search was made for boats but only a single small craft could be found; it took the whole night and some of the following morning for the division to cross the river.

The division set off for Stradella. On the way they learned there had been a battle the day before at Casteggio. While Boudet's men had tried to force a cross at Piacenza, Lannes had spearheaded a crossing over the Po at Belgiojoso on the night of 6–7 June. On 9 June a sharp battle had been fought against an Austrian column heading for Piacenza. Because of this, Boudet was ordered to force his march and not stop until he reached the rear of Casteggio. Boudet ordered Musnier to send out patrols as far as two miles to the left of his bivouacs that evening. The patrols returned later after having encountered nothing more than a group of six deserters whom they brought back in.

The division spent the whole of 11 June waiting for new orders. Boudet was impatiently waiting for the arrival of General Guénand and the 30th Line, which had remained in Milan. He was also waiting for news on the imminent arrival of his artillery, which had only recently been able to pass Fort Bard following its surrender. Adjutant-General Dalton was ordered to write to General Marmont, commander of the army's artillery, to ask when the guns could be expected. Dalton also audited the division's strength. Only half of the cartridges ordered by Berthier had arrived. Dalton calculated the division still had a deficiency of more than 80,000 rounds:[13]

Corps	Present under arms	Existing cartridges	Cartridges needed to complete 50 shots per man
9th Light	1,745	39,578	47,672
59th Line	1,670	50,830	32,670
11th Hussars	145	1,070	3,280 (for 30 shots per man)
Total	3,560	91,478	83,622 [14]

On 12 June at 7am, the division was ordered off down the road as far as Ponte-Curone. Since arriving in Italy the weather had been fairly wet and the whole army was suffering from fits of coughing and sneezing. They trudged past the battlefield at Casteggio. The fields and hedges around the road were trampled flat. They were told that by the village of Montebello there were huge burial pits where several thousand of the slaughtered were in the process of being interred.

A while into the march the Ninth was ordered off the road to let a brigade of cavalry pass by. It was Duvignau's light cavalry, fresh from a good time whoring in Milan.[15] Duvignau ordered his brigade to 'the trot' in order to get Boudet's men back on the road as quickly as possible. The march continued through Voghera, which was a hive of excitement. Bonaparte had set up headquarters there and the streets were clogged with his beribboned lackeys. In headquarters the news of the day was that General Louis Charles Antoine Desaix had joined the army. Desaix was one of the leading generals who had risen in rank through the Revolution. Having risen to prominence in the campaigns along the Rhine, Desaix had ridden down to Italy and become one of Napoleon's most trusted lieutenants. Trusted with an independent mission to Upper Egypt, Desaix had been unable to return to Europe with Bonaparte in 1799 and had only returned to France after the present campaign had commenced. After putting his family affairs in order, he travelled to Italy with an entourage that included his two trusted aides-de-camp, Jean Rapp and Anne Jean-Marie René Savary. Bonaparte had actually sent Desaix a letter offering him the chance to sit out the campaign and wait for him in Paris; but Desaix wanted to be where the action was. In recognition of his status as a senior general he was given command of Boudet and Monnier's divisions, which would form the army's reserve.

The Ninth marched through Voghera and arrived at Ponte-Curone. A portion of the division's cattle were butchered and portioned into individual meat rations. There was no time to hang the meat as a modern butcher might. Once the carcass was cleaned and cool, portions were distributed, there being enough for the next three days.[16] While the men boiled up their broth, some wagons arrived carrying bread. Dalton inspected the delivery and found the bread had turned mouldy in the damp weather. He wanted to reject it outright, but the wagon drivers told him no more would be forthcoming. Dalton decided mouldy bread was preferable to no bread at all and reluctantly accepted it.

Late in the evening, Guénand and the 30th Line at last rejoined Boudet along with his six guns. For the first time since Fort Bard, Boudet had his complete division together again. Thirty thousand cartridges also arrived, but Dalton's pleasure was tempered by the continuing deficiency of 53,622 rounds. Learning that he and Monnier now formed the army's reserve, Boudet offered Monnier the two guns he had brought from Piacenza, as Monnier had none of his own.

There was an air of expectation now. Having been broken into detachments since the battle of Chiusella 17 days before, the French army was concentrating in preparation for the decisive battle. Lannes had over 5,000 infantry; Victor commanded just under 9,000 men; Desaix another 9,400 bayonets. There were just under 5,000 under the command of General Lapoype and 800 grenadiers of the Consular Guard. In total Bonaparte had 28,700 infantrymen ready to commit to battle with 3,500 cavalry. All he needed was news of the enemy. Spy reports said the Austrians were concentrating all their forces around the city of Alessandria. What were they going to do next?

4

MARENGO

For over a month Bonaparte had aggressively manoeuvred his army behind the enemy's lines of communication, fighting detachment after detachment without meeting the Austrians in strength. Even at Casteggio, only a small portion of Melas' army had been engaged. Bonaparte had cast his net wide and now it was being dragged in. It was only a question of time before the deciding battle came.

On 13 June Bonaparte advanced towards the great plain between Tortona and Alessandria. The first consul believed the Austrians would meet him here in order to utilize their greater strength in artillery and cavalry. The French scouts went onto the plain, but apart from the occasional picket there was no sign of the enemy army. Bonaparte was perplexed. If Melas had not prepared to meet him in open battle, where had he gone? Perhaps he was waiting for reinforcements coming up from Genoa before offering battle?

Late in the morning a spy arrived in the French camp and sought an interview with the first consul. This spy was known to Bonaparte from his first campaigns in Italy four years before. Bonaparte had confidence in him, but knew the spy was also taking money from the Austrians. His paymaster was Melas' chief of staff, Major-General Anton Zach, who presumed the spy's first loyalty was to him. Bonaparte was under no such illusion. On this occasion the spy arrived with what he touted as stolen documents. The documents provided detailed orders for 7,000 men in Genoa to march to Alessandria. Once reunited, the documents claimed, the Austrian army would head north from Alessandria, crossing the Po at Casale and then marching east to Pavia, where their lines of communication with Austria would be recovered. The documents had been fabricated by Zach as a ruse.[1]

Fortunately for Bonaparte, he displayed his true genius as a general by not relying on a single source of uncorroborated intelligence. He had General Joseph Chabran placed in observation on the left bank of the Po towards Chivasso and Crescentino. Chabran's scouts had not indicated any great escalation in activity in that direction. Retaining the possibility the spy might have been given false intelligence, the first consul's attention remained fixed on the plain around San Giuliano.

As General Victor began probing the plain, Bonaparte had a nagging doubt. What if the spy had been correct after all? Perhaps the stolen plan had been genuine? As an insurance policy Bonaparte directed Lapoype's division north to cross the Po and directed Boudet's division south to block the Alessandria–Genoa road at Serravalle. If the Austrians did come up from Genoa with 7,000 men, Boudet's division was strong enough to delay their march. It was potentially a very important mission, so Bonaparte asked Desaix to go in person with Boudet's division.

Boudet received his orders at midday and immediately gave word for the division to prepare to march. Despite a deficiency of 20,000 cartridges, the force was one of the strongest French divisions, with 5,316 infantry, around 200 cavalry (the 1st Hussars were joined with a squadron from the 3rd Cavalry) and six guns (four eight-pounders and two six-inch howitzers). Their route would take them south to Ponte-Curone, following the right bank of the River Grue. This would keep them out of sight from the fort at Tortona, which was still in Austrian hands. The division would then cross the Grue and march over the hills in the direction of Sarezzano. They would then reach the Scrivia Torrent which could be forded opposite Rivalta where the road to Novi and Serravalle was joined.

Desaix rode with the cavalry at the head of the column, the Ninth following close behind. Almost as soon as the order to march was given, the heavens opened and it began to rain. Most of the route was over hilly, dirt tracks or swampy flats. The cavalry at the front churned up the ground for those on foot behind. The gunners had to dismount and help the horse teams pull the guns through the mud. They were not enough. Reaching the hills around Sarezzano, Guénand's infantry were pressed into service. It was back-breaking and miserable work. The gunners even tried harnessing the division's cattle to the guns, but it was soon clear that the guns were going nowhere. Boudet called a halt until the rain passed.

Meanwhile, Desaix pressed on to the Scrivia with the cavalry and the Ninth. Opposite the village of Rivalta should have been a ford, but the rains had swollen the torrent. Desaix led some of the hussars over the torrent on their horses and made it to the other bank, but it was impossible for infantry to follow. Desaix felt extremely frustrated at the elements conspiring against him. While he set up headquarters at Rivalta, he ordered his trusted aide-de-camp, Savary, to scout as far upriver as Serravalle. Savary led a detachment of 50 hussars over the Scrivia and galloped off into the distance.

Watching the cavalry cross the swollen torrent put an idea into the heads of the Ninth's carabineers. They thought it might be possible for a man to be dragged across the Scrivia behind a horse by holding onto its tail. A group plucked up the courage to try and each paired off with a rider. The horses walked into the river dragging the carabineers behind. Some of these were strong swimmers and helped kick their way against the strong current. A few made it across before the inevitable happened. The current was very strong and, for some, their grip on the horse was not as firm as they would have liked. In total 12 men were swept off, forcing their comrades to run down the bank as fast as they could offering their hands and muskets for the carabineers to cling on to. Eventually they were all fished out uninjured but greatly fatigued. More importantly they had lost their muskets in the process. The effort gone into saving these men was so great no further attempts to cross were made.[2]

At Rivalta Desaix was visited by a local priest called Giuseppe Guasone. Although a man of the cloth, Guasone was a *giacobino* – an Italian who supported the ideals of the French Revolution. He told Desaix that the local Castellani-Merlani family had lost a son at the battle of Novi the year before and would therefore be willing to offer the French any assistance they could to avenge his death. In practical terms, they could mobilize the local peasants to help ferry the French over the Scrivia on boats. Desaix readily agreed to the offer and before long a gaggle of fishermen arrived. They took a detachment of the Ninth downstream towards Tortona where they had a boat hidden.[3] In the meantime Savary returned from his mission. The road was quiet. There were Imperial forces in Serravalle but Novi was empty. This meant the two Austrian forces had not yet achieved a junction. A messenger was immediately dispatched to inform Bonaparte.

Bonaparte's reply to this report came during the early hours of the morning. He could not believe Novi was empty and reiterated his order to push on at daybreak. Wondering where the Austrians might be, Desaix ordered Boudet to make a reconnaissance with Guénand's brigade to the south. Unknown to Desaix, Boudet had already sent his aide, Captain Samuel l'Héritier, with a detachment of 30 cavalrymen in that direction looking for the Austrians and a different ford. When Desaix learned of this patrol he agreed to wait for its return before committing any infantry.

In due course Captain l'Héritier reported Austrian troops in Serravalle and French cavalry in Novi, the latter presumably Savary's patrol. This at least confirmed there were Austrians on the Genoa road, but did nothing to indicate their intentions. Of more immediate concern was the apparent lack of a ford anywhere else upstream. The heavy rain had stopped during the early hours so Desaix could do nothing but sit at Rivalta and wait for the torrent to subside.

Daybreak came shortly after 4.30am on 14 June. The Ninth began to cross the Scrivia with the boat they had secured during the night. For the first time in weeks there was a clear sky and the orb of the rising sun promised a truly warm day. The crossing continued at a snail's pace, a boatload at a time, the waters still being too deep to wade. As they arrived on the opposite bank, they re-formed their companies and went off to join the carabineers already at Rivalta.

At 8.30am a cannonade was heard from the north-west, in the direction of Alessandria. Wisps of white smoke could be seen on the horizon, rising into the bright-blue sky before dissipating. Desaix became agitated. What did it mean? He weighed up the various possibilities in his mind and concluded only two things were likely. The first was that Melas had given battle, but this was unlikely else he would never have surrendered the great plain if he intended to fight. More likely then, Melas was breaking out of Alessandria as Bonaparte had suspected. The guns they now heard might only be a rearguard. On the other hand, could this be an attempt to buy time for the Austrians to come up from Genoa? It was highly likely Desaix would encounter a large Austrian force; and then what could he do? His artillery was still marooned in a sea of mud on the mountainside and he had a swollen river to his back. Desaix ordered Savary to take a cavalry patrol back to Novi and retrace his steps from the night before. Were the Austrians coming up from Genoa or not?

As Savary set out, the cannonade to the north-east redoubled. Guénand at last arrived with his mud-splattered brigade. They had spent a terrible night up by Sarezzano with nowhere to bivouac except in the churned-up mud. While the infantry began crossing in the boat, the artillery crews reckoned on their chances of getting the guns across. Fortunately the torrent was fast subsiding. At 10am the waters were low enough to take the guns across and shortly after, even the infantry could wade across. Savary returned with the same news as before: Novi was empty. Desaix sent Savary north, back to Bonaparte, to tell him he was going to remain at Rivalta until he heard differently. The sound of battle was now unmistakable.

Not long after Savary's departure, a messenger arrived with new orders for Desaix. The orders were unexpected in the circumstances. Desaix was to go to Pozzolo Formigaro, a town on the main Alessandria–Genoa road a league and a half (6km) away to the south-west. From here Desaix could march on either city, or block the road if the Austrians were trying to unite. Desaix looked at the time of the message. It had been written after 9am, so Bonaparte would have been aware of the artillery bombardment before its dispatch. Desaix gave the order to march as soon as Boudet's men were ready. It took another hour to get the division organized into a column of march and they did not set off until midday.[4]

A mile beyond Rivalta, another messenger caught up with the division. This time it was Captain Jean Pierre Bruyères of Berthier's staff. He had been given this dispatch around 11am by the first consul. The message revealed it was not a rearguard action but an attack by the whole Austrian army.[5] The message explained at 9am Victor had been engaged by the enemy but only at 10am had it become apparent Melas was attacking with his full force. Desaix was ordered to march north towards San Giuliano and then take the main road west to Marengo where battle was engaged. Desaix ordered the division to counter-march and for a reconnaissance to be made in the direction of San Guiliano. Boudet allowed the detachment from the 3rd Cavalry to ride off ahead, but Desaix retained the hussars to serve as scouts.

Having led the column, the Ninth now had the pleasure of wheeling around. Soldiers accepted marching without complaint, but counter-marches were a constant source of grumbling. It took nearly an hour to turn everyone round and to get back to where they had started from. It would take them three hours to march to San Giuliano and from there Marengo was still at least another hour and a half distant. Would the battle be over by the time they arrived? Through the hot afternoon they marched in their damp, steaming uniforms. Did the impending fight weigh heavily on their minds? All these men had now been under fire. By now they had come to accept the inevitabilities of army life, be it the lack of sleep, the scarcity of food or the random fall of shot. Every day was a lottery. They probably just wanted to get the damned thing over with.

The battle of Marengo was fought beneath a blazing Italian sun. The Austrian army had concentrated in the city of Alessandria. Melas' chief of staff, General Zach, had formulated the Imperial battle plan based largely on the deception which the spy had delivered to Bonaparte. From information provided by the same spy, Zach assumed the French would be found at Salle on the northern side of the great plain. With 30,000 men and 100 guns available, Zach's plan was to split the Imperial army into three columns. The first would head directly towards Salle and pin the French army. The main column would march out onto the plain as far as San Giuliano, then execute a left wheel and fall on the left and rear of the French. A third column would head south-east on the Genoa road looking for Desaix.

No sooner had the ink dried on Zach's plan than it began to go wrong. Finding the plain unoccupied, Victor's troops pressed on across the centre of the plain unopposed. They attacked and captured the small village of Marengo on the evening of 13 June. Zach was stupefied. In the face of Victor's attack the Austrian advanced guard had fallen back to the edge of the plain, right up to the banks of the River Bormida near Alessandria itself. They had surrendered all the ground necessary for the complex deployment planned for the next day. Despite this, Zach refused to change his plan and went to bed.

The loss of Marengo ultimately proved fatal for the Austrians. A stone's throw east of the village was the Fontanone brook, snaking its way perpendicular to the main Alessandria–Piacenza road, down which the Austrian advanced guard was scheduled to march. Although not very wide, the recent rains had swollen the Fontanone to bursting point. Its steep muddy banks waited like a snare for the Imperial forces. On 14 June at 8.30am, the Austrian attack began. The lead elements immediately ran into Gardanne's division positioned at the farm of Pedra Bona. Firing battalion and platoon volleys, Gardanne slowly retreated behind the bridge over the Fontanone and blunted the Austrian advance. Time after time the Austrians probed for a way round this obstacle, but Victor gave a master-class in defensive tactics. Each time the Austrians appeared to have outflanked him, Victor would throw in another battalion from Chambarlhac's division, which he had kept in reserve. Lannes hurried to Victor's aid, just in time to prevent the envelopment of the French right.

At 1pm Rivaud's brigade was attacked by a brigade of Austrian grenadiers. There was a toe-to-toe fire-fight lasting a full 15 minutes, in which Rivaud lost half his line and was wounded himself. On the right Lannes began to fall back and the Austrians finally broke into the grange which was piled with wounded Frenchmen. Rivaud rallied his men for one last push and retook Marengo. Lannes followed suit and retook the lost ground. By 2pm the situation had stabilized.

Half an hour later 2,000 Austrian horsemen appeared, preceded by artillery.[6] Commanding a weakened heavy cavalry brigade, General Kellermann placed his troopers in support of Gardanne's troops; but the French infantry were out of ammunition. Gardanne was forced to take shelter in the vineyards behind Marengo. This withdrawal was covered by a sharp cavalry action. The French 8th Dragoons were roughly handled by the Austrian cavalry, who were themselves broken by a charge of the French heavies. This bought enough time for Gardanne to reach safety, falling back for 15 minutes until reaching a new defensive position level with Spinetta.[7]

Also running low on ammunition, Lannes' right was being continually pressed by a column under General Carl Peter Ott. Fortunately for Lannes, reserves arrived on the scene at 3pm from Monnier's division. The 70th Line and 19th Light were directed against Ott and drove him back. Lannes was disengaged and took this advantage to fall back in line with Gardanne. The two half-brigades then took possession of the town of Castel Ceriolo, on the northern edge of the battlefield. On the main road, Bonaparte's foot guards handed out precious musket cartridges to Victor's troops. It was now approaching 4pm. The fighting around the main road was particularly heavy. The high ground either side of the road formed a defile, with trees on one side and tall, bushy vines on the other.[8] Bonaparte rode forward to sustain Lannes with a battalion of the 72nd Line and the horse grenadiers of the Guard.

At 4pm, the Austrian column under General Ott resumed its advance on the French right. There was a large hole in the French right between Lannes and Castel Ceriolo. While Ott prepared to assault the town, General Friedrich Baron Gottesheim's brigade moved into this gap.[9] Bonaparte had one last reserve with which to try and plug the hole in his line. Playing for time, he sent the infantry of the Consular Guard into action. There was a temporary reprieve as the Guard marched forward and stemmed the Austrian advance; but fusilladed from the front and charged by cavalry from the rear its resistance was eventually broken and the Austrian advance resumed.[10]

As the French grenadiers rallied around their colours and made their way back to safety, Bonaparte stared the awful prospect of failure in the face. He had never lost a battle before and momentarily lost his calm in the face of defeat. He put himself at the head of the 72nd Line and exhorted them to follow him, staking everything on one last charge. They refused, calling out, 'We do not want the First Consul to expose himself!'[11] Seeing the Guard fall back, Victor ordered his troops to retreat in the direction of the open plain. His troops marched slowly in columns ready to close up if the Austrian cavalry appeared. Kellermann rallied the remnants of his brigade and shielded the retreat. Lannes ordered Watrin to retreat and to remain in contact with Victor. They maintained their closed columns under heavy artillery fire. At that moment there were no more than 6,000 men still beneath the colours facing the might of the Austrian army. Then, just as all appeared lost, a messenger arrived and told Bonaparte Desaix had been sighted at San Giuliano. A wave of jubilation spread through the ranks.[12]

Shortly before 4pm, just prior to the Guard going into action, a messenger reached Desaix near San Giuliano. It was Captain Louis François Lejeune from Berthier's staff, imploring Desaix to press on. Lejeune later recorded the demeanour of Desaix's infantry, noting that the soldiers of the Ninth were 'marching along gaily as if attending a ball.'[13]

Their enthusiasm may have been somewhat curbed on arrival at the little village. Looking at the field hospitals and the wounded men sitting in the hot sun, it looked as if a disaster had befallen Bonaparte's army. Most of the wounded had been assisted to the rear by comrades who were reluctant to return to the fighting, instead sitting about with their unfortunate friends, comforting them and fetching water. As more wounded arrived the talk was only of disaster and retreat. The throng was swelled by the camp followers, whose wagons blocked the already congested road. Their chatter was noisy and pessimistic.

Boudet ordered the Ninth off the road lest they get caught up in the throng heading east from the battlefield. Savary returned with a new order from Bonaparte: Desaix was to take up a position level with the village of Cascina Grossa where there was a junction between a track leading directly to Marengo and the main road to Alessandria which first passed through Spinetta. This was the point at which the French army was converging and where the open plain began. If the Austrians could not be held here and their cavalry was able to deploy, it spelled doom for the army.[14]

Arriving at the indicated point just before 5pm, Boudet ordered the Ninth to form up on the left of the main road. They formed a line perpendicular with the road facing westwards; carabineers on the right and the battalions of Sirejean and Verger deployed to their left. Kuhmann's battalion remained in reserve, forming a closed column two hundred paces behind the first line. The ground ahead was obscured from view by a large hedgerow lining the side of the track to Cascina Grossa. Somewhere beyond it were the Austrians.

While the army continued to retreat, the Ninth was afforded a few minutes' rest behind the hedgerow, allowing time for their stragglers to catch up. In the meantime Boudet and Desaix formulated a plan. In front of them, just a few hundred paces ahead, was the rest of the French army, extending out to the right, north of the road. The ranks looked very thin but they were not disordered. These men had been promised reserves would arrive and the sight of the Ninth advancing up behind them had caused considerable excitement. What the French army needed was time: time to regroup and time for Guénand's brigade and the artillery to get in position.

Boudet decided he would do something to galvanize the army's spirit. He would take the fight back to the Austrians. He predicted a show of strength and courage would bring the rest of the army back to its sense of duty. Of course it was a gamble. If the Ninth were broken by the Austrians it would be the final blow to the army's morale; but the gain outweighed the risk. Agreeing to the course of action, Desaix took leave of Boudet and went to join Bonaparte and Berthier.

Noticing a rider coming towards him, Bonaparte raised his riding crop over his brow to shield his eyes from the bright sun and recognized Desaix. 'Well, well, General Desaix, quite a skirmish!' Desaix reined in his horse and dismounted, responding in his usual calm manner, 'Well General, I have arrived, we are all fresh and if we must, we will go and get killed!'[15]

The general consensus at this impromptu council of war was one of pessimism. The majority saw the battle as completely lost and the only question was how to break off contact and retreat without inviting further disaster. Bonaparte had different ideas. He refused to concede defeat. What would they say in Paris? What would his political enemies do? He had staked his reputation on this battle and he needed a victory. Moreover, he had seen a way to achieve it. Bonaparte's spirits had been raised enormously by the appearance of the confident troops at the head of Desaix's column. Napoleon would later reflect on this moment: 'I truly never had with me better troops than the 9th Legion [sic] … One saw them pass, with their determined air; the calm of brave men, their resolution. I judged they looked certain of victory and presumed the enemy would be stopped and thrown back.'[16]

Bonaparte had noted a weakness in the Austrian deployment. In order to force the French out of their position at Marengo and Spinetta, the Austrians had extended their wings in a wide pincer movement. At the same time, the French army had grouped on its centre. If the French could advance and overwhelm the weakened Austrian centre, both Austrian wings would be cut off. It was a bold plan and Desaix supported it, telling Bonaparte forcibly, 'You must recommence the battle.'[17]

Desaix now took a pivotal role in the planning of the counter-offensive. 'We must have a rapid artillery fire imposed on the enemy before we attempt a new charge; without which we shall fail. That General, is how one loses a battle.' He told Bonaparte: 'We absolutely must have a good bombardment.'[18] He then turned to Marmont and asked after the state of the artillery. Marmont told him he had established a battery with the remaining five guns the army still had and there were five more coming up in reserve. 'That's good,' replied Desaix and as the artillery of Boudet's division passed by them he continued, 'Look my dear Marmont, some guns, some guns and make the best possible use of them. If there isn't an artillery bombardment made which lasts quarter of an hour, we will lose.'[19] Suitably focused, Marmont rode off to concentrate all the remaining artillery in one battery covering the road.

Desaix left the council to check on Boudet's progress with the Ninth. Bonaparte asked his aide-de-camp, Captain Alexandre Lauriston, to accompany Desaix. In the meantime the other generals of the army rode off and began rounding up as many fit men as they could, urging them to return to their ranks in support of the new attack. Bonaparte also set about gathering as many good troops to the centre as possible, haranguing them as he went: 'Children, you know that my custom is always to sleep on the battlefield.'[20]

In Desaix's absence, Boudet had been busy. Before advancing with the Ninth, Boudet ordered Captain de Juniac to clear the ground ahead in preparation. The hussars advanced in their usual swaggering manner: heads up, sabres drawn. They rushed forward and swooped upon isolated groups of Austrian skirmishers who were pressing the retreating French. Having pushed too far forward in their enthusiasm, these skirmishers were easy prey to de Juniac's sabres. Twenty-six were put to the sword and many more surrendered.[21]

This small action, forgotten in most accounts of the battle, played a significant role in what was to occur next. Behind the retreating French battalions, the Austrian commander Melas considered the battle won and handed over pursuit of the French to his chief of staff, General Zach. Melas was old and had been injured in a fall from his horse, so retired to Alessandria to rest. Zach was giddy with victory and loudly took the credit for defeating Bonaparte, conveniently ignoring the faults in his planning.

Zach was not expecting the arrival of any significant French reserves. Forces had been sent out looking for Desaix, expecting him to be coming up from the direction of Pozzolo Formigaro. What Zach did not know was how badly Desaix had been delayed the night before, that he was much closer to the battlefield than expected and had travelled to it by a different route. Desaix's reserve was obscured by a slight elevation in the ground and a tall hedge. Many observers thought the Ninth had been concealed from the Austrians behind the hedgerows deliberately.[22] When the skirmishers were neutralized by de Juniac's hussars, Zach was rendered blind.

With a false sense of security, Zach formed an advanced guard made up of the Wallis infantry regiment and the debris of General Cristoph Baron von Lattermann's grenadier brigade. Both units had been mauled fighting their way over the Fontanone. In their joy at having overcome such danger, the men relaxed. Even the officers considered the battle over. Several had quit their positions to find friends further down the column to congratulate one another and to see who had survived the morning's engagement. Behind Zach's column, General Konrad Valentin von Kaim's infantry was in an even worse state. The men were exhausted by the day's battle and had gone looking for water; whole battalions were laid out on the ground resting. Zach's advanced guard moved forward too quickly for Kaim to keep up.

There was considerable surprise then as the Ninth suddenly burst through the hedgerow 'like rabbits' and came into view, stamping their way through a field of freshly planted vines.[23] They formed a dark blue line, 260 metres long. The red plumes of the carabineers on the right; felt bicornes of the chasseurs on the left – muskets at the shoulder, bayonets glinting in the sunlight. Having gained the element of surprise the Ninth did not immediately rush headlong in attack. Their mission was to buy time and slow the Austrians down. They halted just within musket shot of the head of the Austrian column on the road and stood in full view of the enemy, boldly laying down a challenge. If the Austrians wanted to continue their advance, they would have to reckon with them first.

The Wallis Regiment had just debouched from a thick belt of vines. The Austrian officers frantically called out for their men to deploy into some kind of line to meet the new threat. As the Wallis Regiment began to deploy, Boudet ordered skirmishers to go forward. Around 200 skirmishers leapt out of the ranks and ran forwards in extended order to begin peppering the head of the Austrian column with musket balls. The more the Austrians tried to deploy, the larger a target they presented for these marksmen. Officers caught out of position ran to rejoin their men and tell them what to do, but were picked off. There were several loud 'booms' as the five French guns deployed on the road began hurling canister rounds into the Austrian column. Boudet's artillery deployed alongside the first five guns. As soon as their crews were in position they added to the bombardment. Before long there were 16 guns in battery firing on the road.

The hail of canister and musket balls caused utter carnage. Unable to complete their deployment and sustaining terrible casualties with little hope of response, the commander of the Wallis Regiment did the only thing he could to save his men: he ordered them to run for their lives. Any jubilation felt by the light infantrymen was short-lived. Behind the Wallis Regiment, Lattermann's grenadier brigade had deployed out of musket range. As the first wave of infantry fled, intervals were opened in the grenadier battalions to let them pass. The grenadiers then resumed the advance, entering a cornfield adjacent to the vineyards. Behind the grenadiers, artillery had been brought up to bombard the Ninth and the French battery to the north of the road. Behind the artillery came a massive force of cavalry which started to deploy north of the road.

The Ninth had advanced well ahead of where the army was re-forming. They had been instructed to buy time for Guénand's brigade to deploy and for the army to regain its composure. The only currency they had to offer in return for this was their lives. The enterprising skirmishers did what they could, trying to disrupt the advancing bearskins. To their great credit, the Austrian grenadiers ignored the shots and continued forward, supported by a growing artillery fire.

Boudet looked around him and watched as files of chasseurs were cut down every instant. The survivors did not seem perturbed by this bombardment, only impatient to come to close quarters. Solid shot and canister smashed into their ranks, clattering off their bayonets, breaking, disfiguring, dismembering and decapitating the soldiers still in line. Bodies lay strewn around the floor grotesquely distorted. Those not deployed in the skirmish line stood motionless awaiting death. A light breeze blew into their faces from the west, bringing with it the first signs of storm clouds off the distant mountains. Their view was soon obscured by a dense sulphurous smog of black powder smoke, which drew in like a veil. There was nothing to take their minds off the ordeal except the shouts of their officers and sergeants ordering them to close ranks; yelling at them, urging them to weather the storm. Each time a ball struck home the line would shudder; the terrible cries of the wounded would rise up, only to be drowned out by new detonations. The survivors anaesthetized themselves with a welling rage that waited to explode, to be unleashed, but still they stood motionless in support of the skirmish screen in front. Every man who fell would have to be revenged and the Austrian gunners would certainly be brought to account.

Arranged in five small battalions, the grenadiers advanced, firing volleys at the Ninth in a chequerboard manner. With their skirmishers deployed in front, the main body of the Ninth was unable to return fire. Boudet was becoming very worried that sooner rather than later something would have to give before his whole line was engaged. Where was Desaix?

Desaix returned from the council of war to oversee the progress of Boudet's troops. The guns were firing as planned and Guénand was almost in place with his troops. Guénand had taken position behind the artillery, placing the 30th in line formation, with the 59th in close columns behind. To the right of Guénand, General Monnier stationed two battalions of the 72nd Line that had been held in reserve at San Giuliano. The remains of Gardanne's division rallied behind them. Lannes was out on the right with Chambarlhac and the cavalry in the rear.

Savary had been at the front with Boudet and reported to Desaix what had occurred. Realizing the Ninth was in grave danger from the grenadiers, Desaix formulated a plan. 'You see how matters stand,' he said to Savary, 'I can no longer put off the attack without danger of being myself attacked under disadvantageous circumstances: if I delay I shall be beaten and I have no relish for that. Go then in all haste and appraise the First Consul of the embarrassment I experience; tell him I cannot wait any longer; that I am without cavalry and he must direct a bold charge on the flank of that column whilst I charge it in front.'[24] As Savary rode off towards Bonaparte, Desaix ordered Boudet to pull the Ninth back by echelons, bringing them back into line with Guénand's brigade. Receiving this order Boudet was worried about compromising the security of his skirmishers by pulling back. He ordered Musnier to withdraw, but to take his time about it, giving the skirmishers time to rally if they could. Boudet turned his horse and headed back to appraise Desaix of the situation.

When Savary encountered Bonaparte he passed on Desaix's request for cavalry support. After reflecting for a moment the first consul said to Savary: 'Have you well examined the column?'

'Yes General,' he replied.

'Is it very numerous?'

'Extremely so, General.'

'Is Desaix uneasy about it?'

'He appeared uneasy as to the consequences that might result from hesitation. I must add his having particularly desired I should tell you that it was useless to send any other orders than that he should attack or retreat – one or the other; and that the latter movement would be at least as hazardous as the first.'

'If this be the case, let him attack: I shall go in person to give him the order.' Bonaparte pointed to a group of cavalry in the distance and continued, 'You will repair yonder and there find General Kellermann, who is in command of that cavalry you now see; tell him what you have just communicated to me and desire him to charge the enemy without hesitation as soon as Desaix shall commence his attack.'[25]

The Ninth began its retrograde movement. The 1st Battalion turned its back and marched away from the advancing grenadiers. They marched a short distance and about-faced while the next battalion retreated. It was a remarkable show of discipline to turn their backs on an advancing enemy and slowly walk away. As each battalion fell back, the adjutant-majors went out and began calling the skirmishers in. Each man would load, rush back a short distance, turn, fire, reload, and run again. All the while the grenadiers pressed forward, their spirits soaring at the sight of the Frenchmen in apparent retreat.

Boudet found Desaix and told him what had occurred in his absence. After their exchange, Desaix decided to order the attack. Boudet was to go back to the Ninth and tell them to halt. Desaix would come up shortly to lead the attack in person. Desaix then heard a final report from de Juniac, who explained his actions in clearing the enemy forward posts; Desaix promised to inform the First Consul of these deeds. De Juniac rode back to his men satisfied with the praise. Desaix next met with General Guénand and told him to prepare to advance his brigade. He told Guénand what had been said at the meeting with Bonaparte and that he was going over to the Ninth to lead the charge there.

Desaix caught up with Boudet and told him, 'Rendezvous with your second brigade, I will lead the charge here.'[26] Desaix then instructed Boudet exactly what he was to achieve. He was to split the enemy centre in two with Guénand's brigade and prevent the wings of the Austrian army from acting in concert. As Boudet rode off, Desaix went past the carabineers on the right of the line. The Ninth began marching forward towards the skirmish line. The smoke was so thick Desaix could not see anything ahead. Where were the Austrians? Wanting to judge the situation for himself, he pressed ahead and went up to the skirmish line to reconnoitre.

The smoke was dense, a wafting, sickly, sulphurous grey fog. There were momentary bursts of light as the skirmishers fired; orange and yellow flames bursting forth, with showers of tiny white-hot sparks as flints scraped strike plates and priming powder. Lead balls whizzed through the air on their murderous flight. The dark shapes of fighting men could be seen, reloading, priming, crouching over the fallen. Suddenly there was a gap in the smoke – the Austrians were just ten paces away at the edge of the vineyard. There was a thunderous volley then silence. Desaix began falling backwards from his saddle towards the floor; his body limp. The sky loomed up overhead then darkness fell. He was dead before he hit the ground.[27]

With the main line coming up behind them, the skirmishers around Desaix's body had to quickly get out of the way lest they become trapped between the two advancing lines. As they began to run left and right there was an almighty discharge. The main line of the Ninth discharged its muskets at the grenadiers from point-blank range. At the same instant three of the French guns on the road each fired a round of canister into the grenadiers from 50 paces.

After the concussion of this enormous detonation came a guttural cry of 'Vengeance!' The Ninth's bayonets came down like a wall of steel. With an insane fury they surged forward through the smoke, trampling the vines in their determination to avenge their losses. Watching on from behind, Victor described the inevitable consequence of this charge: 'The shock was terrible.'[28] Screams went up as shafts of metal entered men's bodies. For those not impaled in the first impact, there came the bayonets of a second rank, then a third. Men were pressed together and lifted from the floor in the crush. The butts of guns came raining down: skulls and necks broke, faces split. The grenadiers' ranks began to fall apart from the pressure.

General Kellermann had seen the arrival of Boudet's division along with everybody else. Earlier in the morning he had fought two major actions against the Austrian cavalry and his brigade had been considerably reduced. At 5pm there were only eight officers and 150 men of the 2nd and 20th Cavalry still in the saddle. Even when Kellermann added the 8th Dragoons to his command, he still had fewer than 400 sabres. Receiving his instructions from Savary, Kellermann was somewhat surprised by the order to charge, but nevertheless formed his troopers in a single line and advanced westward through the vines, passing several hundred metres to the right of Guénand's brigade. As he did so, Kellermann saw the discharge on his left in which Desaix was killed. Breaking out from the vines he gave the order, 'Platoons to the left, forwards.'[29] His line of troopers wheeled southwards, forming a column and then raced past Marmont's gunners. They passed an instant after the final salvo was fired into the grenadiers.

The roar of the cannon deadened the rumble of approaching hooves. Unseen in the confusion and smoke, the cavalry engulfed the left of the Austrian line. As the horses galloped by, great tears were opened in the torsos of soldiers unsure at what had just hit them. Assailed by bayonets to the front; chopped at by sabres from above, the grenadiers' resistance began to break. Only just re-formed and regaining its confidence, the Wallis Regiment was ridden down. The second wave of Kellermann's horses now hit, trampling and slicing as they went. General Zach saw Kellermann's chargers and tried to ride away. A hand grabbed him by the throat and he felt the sharp point of a sword in his back. 'Surrender,' commanded the voice. As Zach replied to the voice behind him his men began to throw down their arms in a similar gesture of submission.

The soldiers of the Ninth had not seen Desaix's fall.[30] As was his custom, Desaix had been out of uniform. Only his immediate companions saw what occurred. Riding slightly ahead of Desaix at the time he was struck was Lauriston. As he instinctively turned his face away from the grenadiers' discharge he saw Desaix falling. Another aide-de-camp, Captain Charles Lefèbvre-Desnoëttes, was out of his saddle in an instant, rushing to the prone body in the vineyard. Lauriston turned his horse and spurred it towards the body. Kneeling by the body, Lefèbvre-Desnoëttes pronounced him dead. A ball had hit the general square in the chest and exited through his right shoulder blade. There were no final words. Lefèbvre-Desnoëttes called out to a nearby sergeant and asked him to remove Desaix's body from the scene of the fighting. Adjutant-Major Pierre Barrois came over to survey the scene. The sergeant turned to Barrois and asked if he could take Desaix's overcoat. After all, the sergeant argued, Desaix had no further use for it.[31]

As this macabre scene was played out, Guénand's brigade began its advance to the north of the road. Guénand had asked General Marmont to cease firing as his infantry had to advance past his line of fire. Marmont ordered his gunners to turn their pieces round and prepare to haul them forwards on drag ropes in support of the forthcoming attack. As Guénand's men marched forwards his left-most battalion wheeled round to support the Ninth's attack on the grenadiers, while the rest pushed forwards and exited the vineyards. As the advance began Guénand felt a tremendous pain from his right hip, stunning him for a moment. Looking down and expecting to see blood, he was astonished to see the ball had struck his purse. Later examination would reveal nine coins bent over double and a large and rather nasty bruise. As Guénand sat on his horse taking in his miraculous escape, Boudet caught up with him and passed on Desaix's instruction and remained with Guénand to assist him in the next phase of the attack.

In front of them Guénand saw a terrible sight: he counted 35 guns lined up opposite his brigade. Behind the guns was the awe-inspiring sight of a line of cavalry, about 1,000 strong, in perfect order of battle heading towards him.[32] While Zach's advanced guard had battled with the Ninth, the Liechtenstein Light Dragoon Regiment had deployed north of the road. They had watched helplessly as Kellermann's cavalry suddenly appeared out from behind the vine-covered trees and onto the flank of Zach's infantry. They now trotted forwards, intent on revenging this reverse and perhaps freeing some of their comrades in arms. The light dragoons first flew into a wall of fire from Guénand's brigade. This fire was supported by the artillery, which had been pulled forwards on drag ropes. At the same time, General Kellermann saw the advance of the Austrian cavalry and ordered the remainder of his own troopers to wheel to the right to meet them. Before the Austrian horsemen could react, Kellermann was among them with just 200 men. Their small number was compensated for by the ferocity and conviction with which they fought. Kellermann's men were also mounted on horses far larger than the ponies of the Austrian cavalry.

Despite the ferocity of Kellermann's charge, he could not stem the whole tide. The remainder of the Austrian light dragoons pressed on. All over the field sergeants called out for their skirmishers to rally around them. A series of brutal and hard-fought combats took place, as sabre struck against bayonet. The cavalry tried to form up again to make a charge on the Ninth's flank, but the fire from the sharpshooters was still too strong and casualties began to mount. Several chasseurs were caught out in the open alone – those who panicked died; but for those who held their nerve, the cavalry often came off worse. There were several instances where chasseurs, attacked by one or two mounted Austrians, shot the first out of the saddle at close range then assailed the second with the bayonet. When fighting horsemen the technique was to stand on the rider's left, away from the sword arm, with the horse's head in the way of any swiping blows from the sabre. The chasseur could then aim a well-timed blow from the butt of his musket and knock the rider to the ground where he would be at the mercy of an unforgiving bayonet. It was bloody work, but the Frenchmen's tempers were now well and truly up.

In the confusion a French dragoon officer found himself charged down by a group of Austrians. Corporal Victor Mahut of the carabineers flew to his aid, running unseen by the Austrian dragoons. Mahut shot one of the dragoons dead, surprising the others so much so that they fled. Seeing his chance to escape, the French dragoon officer sped away, leaving Mahut alone with the dead Austrian and his horse. One of the Austrians looked over his shoulder and saw Mahut was acting alone. The group turned round and prepared to ride him down in revenge. The corporal had two options: load his gun or make a run for it. He calculated the odds; loading would only give him one shot; the odds were too great. However he did now have a horse, but would he be able to outride his attackers? Before he could make a choice, a shot rang out and Mahut fell to the ground wounded. Someone else had seen him and picked him off. The Austrian cavalry left him for dead and rode off. In being wounded Mahut's life had, ironically, just been saved.[33]

The shot had probably been fired from one of the Austrian infantrymen who had seen their chance to escape in the confusion following the Liechtensteins' charge. One of these – a grenadier – saw chasseur Jean Vinot alone and under pressure from two Austrian dragoons. At 1.60m, Vinot was not a tall man by any means. Seeing this, the Austrian grenadier went over to indulge himself at Vinot's expense, but the plucky Frenchman was having none of it. As the first dragoon rode at him, Vinot smacked him out of his saddle and onto the ground. He then turned on the grenadier and shoved his bayonet through the man's body. The second dragoon turned his horse and rode away as fast as he could from the enraged Frenchman.

Sharp-eyed Sergeant-Major Noël Petit noticed a group of Austrians out in the cornfield that were sniping at his men. Petit quit his position and went after them himself. Like a master huntsman he moved unobserved through the tall crops, chose his first victim and pulled the trigger. The surprised enemy skirmisher fell dead. Petit reloaded and repeated the process several times with typical cunning. Realizing they were being stalked by a master of his craft, the Austrians became unnerved. Three of them threw down their arms and allowed Petit to take them prisoner.

Of all the examples of bravery exhibited during the hand-to-hand fighting, Corporal Jean Bouvier stood out for the ferocity of his actions. At the centre of the mêlée with the grenadiers, Bouvier found a way past the grenadiers' bayonets and broke into the Austrian ranks. In a fit of rage he went about viciously bayoneting all those about him. Even amid scenes of intense slaughter and confusion all around, Bouvier stood out.

All these deeds happened in as many minutes. It was almost as if everything occurred at once. As the dragoons rode off and the last of the grenadiers threw down their weapons, Kellermann's troopers began herding prisoners together. Those of Zach's command who had escaped Desaix's onslaught now formed a mob of fugitives heading for Spinetta; as they went they spread word of the disaster which had befallen them. The Austrian artillery also saw its chance to limber up and speed away before the French infantry caught up with them. Unfortunately for the Austrian gunners their preparations did not go unnoticed for long. The soldiers of the Ninth were in the process of rallying and re-forming their formations when they first noticed the flight of the guns. Jean-Baptiste Michel exhorted his comrades in the third battalion's carabineers to follow him and courageously charged at the guns. Already shaken at the suddenness of

Zach's reversal the Austrian artillerymen began to panic at the approach of the light infantrymen. They knew full well what their fate would be if they were captured; they could not ask for any quarter. Some continued in the attempt to withdraw their pieces; some simply fled. As General Boudet later remarked, the capture of the guns was all down to the soldiers of the Ninth.[34]

After watching the successful charge, Savary went to resume his place at Desaix's side. He saw Boudet's men advancing and rode over to them, but could see no sign of Desaix. Glances were exchanged: who would tell him? In the end it was Mathieu Labassée who told Savary that the general was dead. Savary was devastated at the news and went in search of his mentor's remains. He returned to the place where he had last seen Desaix. Searching among the bodies of the infantrymen with whom he had been placed, Savary recognized Desaix's long dark hair and his tanned, scarred face. Incredibly his body and those lying nearby had already been stripped. Desaix's body was naked except for his blood-soaked undershirt. Savary tried to mop up the blood round the horrible wound with his handkerchief but there was too much. He thought about embalming Desaix's heart to send it back to his mother; but looking at the wound he realized the organ had gone. Instead he cut a lock of Desaix's hair, thinking to keep it as a memento; but he rashly put the hair into his bloodstained handkerchief and would later find it soiled by gore. Not wanting the body to be buried indiscriminately in an anonymous grave, he conspired to take Desaix's earthly remains to the rear. A horse had died a short distance away and Savary removed the blanket from under its saddle. A stray hussar assisted Savary in wrapping the body up. This stranger consented to lay the body across his saddle and to lead it by its bridle while Savary went to the first consul.

Bonaparte was watching the proceedings with a growing sense of satisfaction. Guénand's brigade had resumed its advance and the army was following in its wake, re-energized and confident of victory. As Bonaparte prepared to return to his headquarters at Torre di Garofoli, he heard the news about Desaix. The first consul was stricken with grief: 'Why am I not allowed to weep?' he asked out loud. Arriving at Bonaparte's side, Savary told him what he had done with Desaix's body. A saddened Bonaparte approved and bade

Savary to follow him to headquarters from where they would send Desaix's body to Milan to be embalmed.

It was now approaching 6pm and there was still much to be accomplished. The main force of Austrian infantry was as yet unbroken. However, having watched the remnants of Zach's advanced guard hurtle past in disarray and having heard about the arrival of French reserves, Austrian morale was brittle. Boudet's men at last appeared, screaming and cursing as they came. They smashed into Kaim's soldiers and mauled them. Boudet was everywhere, helping Guénand keep the advance moving. Braver elements of the Austrian cavalry still rushed around catching pockets of skirmishers unaware; it was chaos.

Those out on the extremities of the Austrian line were afraid of being cut off, and they began to retreat back towards Alessandria. The Austrian infantry began to become disordered in places as the crush began to get worse. On the main road the Ninth was in pursuit. Sergeant-Major Etienne Daviou decided it was time to bag a few prisoners. He rushed ahead to the nearest Austrian unit. In the confusion he grabbed hold of an Austrian officer, pulled him out of line and took him prisoner. Given the ease with which he had accomplished this, Daviou waited until he saw a second victim, then a third, then a fourth, seizing them in the same manner as the first.

The Austrian line in the centre crumbled away in front of the tide of Frenchmen. The Ninth advanced towards Spinetta where a second Austrian grenadier brigade had taken position, hoping to stem the French tide. General Victor came up in support with the remains of Gardanne's division, now resupplied with ammunition. As the Ninth faced the second grenadier brigade, a force of Austrian light cavalry came up from the south. On the Ninth's exposed flank, Kuhmann ordered his battalion to form a square.[35] Before the Austrian cavalry could fall on the Ninth they were charged by the heavy cavalry of the Consular Guard. The horse grenadiers were among the biggest men in the French army, mounted on the strongest, largest horses. They gave no quarter to the much lighter-mounted Austrian cavalry and began to push them in the direction of a deep, muddy ditch. Kellermann executed a supporting charge, clattering into the flank of the same column of Austrian cavalry.

At Marengo, where the little bridge crossed over the Fontanone stream, terrible confusion reigned. The debris of Kaim's infantry were trying to negotiate the stream at the same time as the artillery and retreating cavalry. In a panic to escape the ferocity of the French cavalry, the Austrian horsemen began to force their way through the crowd of fugitives alongside the ditch. Many of the infantry slipped in the mud or tripped over debris and were trampled, crushed and even drowned.

The last resistance was from the Austrian grenadiers who calmly fell back on Marengo covered by a screen of light troops. They took possession of the grange that had eluded them for so long in the morning battle and prepared to make a last stand. With daylight beginning to fail, Boudet asked his men to make one last effort. The Ninth raced into the gardens and buildings to evict the last Austrian defenders. They set about their task with the same extraordinary zeal they had maintained throughout the past month. At 9pm, after four hours of near continual fighting, the Ninth stopped. The village of Marengo had fallen back into the hands of the men in blue. Deafened by the incessant cannon fire, half hallucinating through fatigue and thirst, the Austrian army made its way back to Alessandria defeated. In this half-light, illuminated by the haunting flashes of musket fire, men stumbled about looking for their units and friends.

Boudet drew his men back into a line just behind Marengo. Gardanne was given the honour of reclaiming his morning position in front of the Bormida. Around 10pm the guns finally stopped and darkness consumed the field, temporarily hiding the scars of this desperate battle. The terrible cries of the wounded, fearful of the night, were unheard by the survivors, whose ears were still deaf from the gunfire and whose minds were numb except for the desire for water and sleep. Austrian and Frenchman, victims alike, crawled together to assist each other however they could, enemies no more. While the generals rode off to headquarters to stake their claims, many of the soldiers threw themselves on the ground and slept. Others sat quietly, contemplating the night sky, their senses still overwhelmed with the high of combat. While waiting calmly for their hearts to stop pounding and for the sun to rise again, they pondered what had just occurred. All was still and tranquil beneath the spectral passage of storm clouds overhead.

AN INCOMPARABLE
REPUTATION

When victory was assured, Bonaparte returned to his headquarters and awaited his generals' reports. Still deeply troubled by the death of Desaix there was little room for jubilation. A meal was cobbled together from scraps taken from a cavalry foraging party. Bonaparte's secretary saw tears welling up in his eyes at one point as he spoke of Desaix. The diligent Berthier made his first after-action report at 9pm. Reading through it, Bonaparte came to the description of the evening battle. There he saw the line: "The 9th Light Infantry, incomparable in its bravery, was in the first line; General Desaix marched at its head.'[1] It was such a glorious image. Bonaparte pictured the Ninth arriving on the battlefield as he had seen them: eager to do battle. He remembered his fallen friend Desaix. The romantic spirit in Bonaparte was aroused and inspired him to dictate a suitably heroic description of the battle for the army bulletin.

Bonaparte was a natural propagandist, an expert at captivating the imagination. He described the battle in broad sweeps, depicting his guard as a 'rock of granite'. There was a eulogy to Desaix. Although Desaix had died without uttering a word, Bonaparte imagined what his friend might have said given the chance: 'Go tell the First Consul I die with the regret of having not done enough to live in posterity.' He then inserted the line: 'The 9th Light have earned the title *Incomparable*.'[2] For evermore the names of Desaix and the *Incomparable* Ninth would be linked together.

At daybreak on 15 June, Desaix's body, wrapped in a shroud and covered by an overcoat, was loaded onto a peasant's cart and led by an escort towards the rising sun in the direction of Milan. Meanwhile, out on the field, the sunrise revealed a scene of devastation. The French line looked down on the grange at heaps of naked corpses, dead horses, broken artillery, offal and blood. The gatehouse tower loomed up like a tombstone for the two armies. Looking down on all that carnage, thoughts turned to what the new day might bring – peace or a repeat of the previous day's hell? Their fears appeared to be realized when firing was heard up ahead. General Gardanne's forward posts had opened fire on the Austrian light troops who had spent the night in front of the Bormida bridgehead. Mercifully the firing was only sporadic. Austrian riders approached with a flag of truce. They wanted time to bury their dead.

Under this flag of truce, working parties went out searching for their wounded comrades scattered over the field. The true price of victory could now be counted. Something like a third of the Ninth had gone down during the battle, about 400 of whom were either killed or seriously wounded. The remainder were lightly wounded and had moved to the rear in search of medical attention. Some had been cut off in the skirmishing, or knocked unconscious in the fighting, when they woke they went looking for their friends, anxious not to be left alone in such a ghastly place.

Almost all of the officers had picked up knocks during the battle, with 18 killed or seriously wounded.[3] It was by far the highest toll ever suffered by the Ninth in a single day. The old adventurer Sirejean had been shot from his saddle. For so long he had been denied action because of unjust suspicions levelled against him by a paranoid government. Now he lay in one of the field hospitals slowly dying – his age and the exertions and fatigue endured over the past month conspiring against him. This campaign had been his last chance before retirement to prove he was a true patriot. Near to death, among strangers, in a place of great suffering, his loyalty to France was beyond doubt. It was a cruel and sad way for him to meet his maker. Labassée directed young Pierre Barrois to take command of Sirejean's battalion. A battalion commander at the age of 25, great things awaited Barrois.

Captain Nouveau and Lieutenant Delpeuch were among those killed outright during the battle. Adjutant-Major Huguin had been shot in the left leg during the charge. He fell with captains Marthe, Delville, Rieux, Frassinet and Marc. It will be remembered how Robert Marthe had taken the place of Pierre Gros for this campaign. Poor Marthe was hit in the left leg and lost a large piece of muscle. He would never march on campaign again – and would be as lame as Gros, the man he had replaced. Among the lieutenants there had been a few dangerous wounds. Scheck was in a bad way, waiting for his right arm to be amputated. Pierre Billon had been shot through the shoulder, but would live to fight another day. Their fellow lieutenants Joindot, Errard and Thirry had also fallen to wounds, as had sub-lieutenants Berbain and Paulet. Another casualty was Drum-Major Jean Jacques Portier who took a shot in his right leg. Even the intrepid surgeon Charles Vanderbach was out of action having taken a nasty blow on the chin.

While the Ninth had fought the Austrian grenadiers, Guénand's brigade had suffered very heavy casualties. The 30th Line were particularly badly hit and Boudet was pleased how they came through such a dramatic baptism of fire so bravely. The 59th had escaped the level of casualties suffered by their sister unit.[4]

A detachment of generals and their staffs rode off towards Alessandria to begin negotiations with the Austrian commander. Boudet went with them. In the meantime the grim task of stripping the dead continued. Some spent their time collecting musket flints and cartridges out of the Austrian ammunition boxes, just in case the negotiations stalled. Others made piles of hats, coats, cartridge pouches, muskets, sabres, shoes, everything that could be recycled for the war machine.

Burying the dead was a major problem. There were no shovels. Adjutant-General Dalton wrote to headquarters complaining of this, pointing out the air had started to turn bad. Some of the Frenchmen began dousing themselves with vinegar as a precaution against disease. In some cases a dusting of earth was sprinkled over the bodies, but this would not suffice. Pragmatism called for extreme measures: the dead would have to be burned to avoid disease. All across the field pyres were made from broken muskets, carriages and vine poles. Even then, bodies kept turning up. The fighting had been scattered over such a wide area that peasants would find corpses for weeks after the battle. A ration of brandy was distributed to stiffen the division's resolve.[5]

Bonaparte eventually agreed terms with Melas; not a complete end to the war as everyone hoped, but victory enough for Bonaparte to return to Paris and cement his political power. Under the terms agreed, there would be a ceasefire and the Austrians would march out of Alessandria to a new position behind the Mincio River. Before this march began, the whole army prepared to be inspected by General-in-chief Berthier on 19 June. Weary but proud, the victorious Frenchmen wore oak leaves in their hats as a symbol of their victory.

The inspection complete, at 6pm Boudet's division was put on the march to Voghera, the men collecting a ration of bread as they left the field. Eight hours later they arrived in Voghera. They stayed there waiting for rations until 10am before setting off for Stradella, which they reached at 8pm. After just five hours in which to cook and sleep they were again put on the march, this time for Piacenza, which they reached on 21 June at 6pm. This last march was made through burning heat, summer having finally broken the veil of wet weather. They had marched for 35 hours in 48 and everyone was exhausted. Dalton wrote to army headquarters: 'The three days of marching has greatly fatigued the troops. It would be desirable if we were able to set off each day at midnight.'[6] By marching through the night they would be able to rest during the scorching afternoons.

The forced marching was necessary to shadow the Austrian army's retreat eastwards. One commentator spoke of how strange it was to see the French and Austrian armies mixed up together on the route. At Piacenza the armies camped next to one another by the city ramparts. Inside the town the adversaries were found mixed in the same inns and cafés without any apparent trouble.[7] The weary Ninth were sent back on the road, this time to Cremona. Here the heroes of Marengo made a less than positive impression on one individual. An officer from the 12th Chasseurs was billeted on a local marquis along with a score of light infantry scamps. He wrote:

> There was, in the same house, twenty chasseurs of the 9th half-brigade of light infantry, two of whom were sergeants. One of this gang (because I might term them thus) came and took from my room, which I had just left, my waistcoat in which I had three gold sovereigns and approximately eight francs in loose change. It was my entire fortune.[8]

The extreme fatigue afflicting the men of the Ninth was now recognized, and they were allowed to spend over four months recovering in billets around the villages outside Cremona. Now was the time to boil their laundry and write back to parents reassuring them they were still alive and asking for money to be sent by return. With the ceasefire in place, the depot moved from France to Milan. Along with Captain Gros came several hundred reinforcements fresh from training. Life in the Ninth must have been doubly hard for the new boys. The survivors of the arduous campaign and the fierce bombardments of Piacenza and Marengo enjoyed a tight bond. Those considered 'green' a year before now took on the air of veterans. Over the next 15 years, men in the Ninth would always be posed the question: were you at Marengo? Those who were not at the battle must have eventually cursed the very name of the place.

On the subject of reputations, a debate quickly began about Desaix's charge that would last for many years to come. On the night of the battle Brigadier General Kellermann returned to headquarters. Bonaparte said to his secretary, Bourienne: 'Little Kellerman made a lucky charge. He did it at just the right moment. We are much indebted to him. You see what trifling circumstances decide these affairs.' When Kellermann approached Bonaparte's table, the first consul said to him, 'General, you made a pretty good charge.' Kellermann was the son of a famous general, and for his conduct at the battle, he believed he deserved promotion to full general. When this was not forthcoming, the first consul's praise was misinterpreted as a snub. Bonaparte then upset Kellermann further by calling over to the commander of the horse grenadiers, 'Bessières, the Guard has covered itself with glory.' Kellermann went off and sulked. Kellermann commented his charge had placed the crown of France on Bonaparte's head. Although this was not said to Bonaparte's face, it was not long before the first consul learned about it all the same.[9]

Kellermann was piqued when Desaix's aide-de-camp, Savary, later published his memoirs and claimed the order for the cavalry charge had originated from Desaix. Kellermann published his own account and stated it was he alone who had ordered the charge that crowned the success. While it was true that the timing of the charge was entirely down to Kellermann, without Desaix's request for cavalry support, it is unlikely Kellermann would have played any role in the counter-attack.

There was a second part of Kellermann's account that Savary was unhappy with. Kellermann wrote that before his charge was executed the French troops had been broken and were fleeing from the Austrian grenadiers. Savary contested this point very strongly in a later edition of his memoirs, citing Labassée as a witness:

> General Desaix's first line was composed of the 9th Light, one of the most redoubtable regiments in the army, commanded by Colonel La Bassée [sic], who still exists. This regiment and its chief were accustomed to attach their names to every field of battle upon which they fought. They were never known to hesitate at the sight of danger; and I can attest that, as I was proceeding after Kellermann's charge, to overtake the division which was debouching, upon the left of San-Juliano [sic], I saw at the front the 9th Light regiment, which certainly did not have the air of a regiment just broken in. This accusation is rendered still more improbable by another circumstance. The First Consul was fully aware of all the occurrences of the day. The reports could not have left him in ignorance of those acts of weakness or of courage which had marked the vicissitudes of the battle. Nevertheless, he congratulated the 9th Light regiment upon its conduct, and assigned to it the title of *Incomparable*. Now, one knows that, however well disposed to distribute praises, he was never lavish of them.[10]

The evidence that Boudet's troops had played the decisive role is overwhelming. After the battle the army's chief of staff, General Pierre Dupont, introduced Boudet to an émigré serving with the Austrian army called Crossard. Dupont told Crossard it was Boudet's troops who had turned the tide of victory in Bonaparte's favour. Boudet modestly agreed, telling Crossard, 'Yes, it was my division that finished the affair.'[11] A letter dated Milan, 19 June 1800, and attributed to the aide-de-camp Lauriston, contains the following: 'You will be delighted to learn the division Boudet is considered as having saved the army; because, actually, at 2 o'clock, the battle was lost.'[12] Kellermann spoke with General Guénand in Milan soon after the battle. Guénand related: 'Kellermann agreed with it himself … without the impetuosity and sureness of my attack he would never have made the cavalry charge.'[13] Writing in 1801, the officers of the 2nd Cavalry, who spearheaded Kellermann's charge, also agreed that Kellermann only charged after the enemy had lost its appetite for fighting because of Desaix's attack. Perhaps the most significant endorsement came from Bonaparte himself, saying of the Ninth, 'It was them who decided the day.'[14]

Soon after the battle, Labassée was asked to put forward the names of men who had been outstanding in the battle and who deserved honours. Since the suppression of military decorations during the Revolution, soldiers had instead been awarded special 'arms of honour' in recompense for acts of outstanding valour. Bonaparte formalized this practice in a law of 25 December 1799. At the end of a battle the army commander would call for the names of any deserving men who might be rewarded. For infantrymen the most common reward was a musket from the prestigious Versailles workshop, with a silver name-plate fixed to the stock.

On 15 June a list was drawn up of men who had distinguished themselves and had been mentioned in after-action reports. Just two names were picked from the Ninth: Cazaux for his action at Piacenza and Chasseur Jean Vinot from Kuhmann's battalion.[15] However, Bonaparte arbitrarily awarded ten 'silver muskets' to the Ninth and asked for the names of ten deserving recipients.

In the billets and inns, over a tot of wine and cards, the men's stories began to take shape. Who had done what; who had been the bravest; who had carried Desaix's body; who had heard his last words; what had happened to his coat? All were debated with the usual embellishments and self-promotion. When it came to selecting nine more names, Labassée was genuinely stumped. In the end he simply held a lottery by company.[16] The Ministry of War was unhappy at this egalitarian approach. They wanted details of the great feats these men had performed on the field of valour. A new list was drawn up and submitted, this time with Labassée favouring some of the older soldiers. With the corps still in Italy, the final confirmation of names would not come until they returned to Paris in the following year.[17]

Summer passed into autumn and still the Ninth remained around Cremona. On 14 October a small reorganization took place when Bonaparte ordered certain half-brigades to be stripped of their third battalions. The Ninth retained their third battalion and received an influx of around 500 officers and men from three line half-brigades and the 10th Light. This made the Ninth momentarily top heavy; but after due consideration the surplus officers were pensioned off and sent back to France.[18] In the report on the reorganization there was a note that a ceremonial band had yet to be organized.[19] In the old days, the Cévennes Battalion had a band composed of Chief Musician Grimal and the three Beaumann brothers, Pierre, Antoine and Michel. The regulation of 1788 declared that the musicians would play hunting horns or trumpets and could be accompanied by the battalion's children on fifes. In the early part of the war this band was released and the Ninth had spent the war without a replacement. However, with its prestige growing after Marengo, the Ninth was going to need an impressive band to add a little pomp to parades and soirées thrown in its honour.

Officially each half-brigade was allowed eight musicians on the payroll, one of which was designated as the band leader. These would be supplemented by a number of 'hireling' musicians (*gagistes*) paid for privately by the officer corps who would each contribute one day's pay a month. Depending on the commander's whim, the band might actually have anything from 20 to 30 musicians in it. In the latter months of 1801 Labassée began establishing his band, which eventually contained 22 musicians and hirelings.

On 12 November 1800 hostilities with Austria resumed. The commander in Germany, General Jean Victor Moreau, won a decisive victory at Hohenlinden on 3 December and the Austrians were driven back to within 80km of Vienna. As an armistice was called on Christmas Eve, attention moved back to the Italian theatre. Following the Marengo campaign the Austrian army had taken position behind the Mincio River. This line encompassed the strategically important city of Mantua, which France had lost in 1799 and now wanted back. The plan was to push the Austrian forces away from Mantua, back beyond the Piave River, east of Venice. The Army of the Reserve had been re-designated as the Army of Italy and placed under command of General Guillaume Brune. When hostilities resumed, the Ninth quit Cremona and moved up to the Mincio. However it was not until Christmas Day 1800 that Brune commenced hostilities and crossed the river. The Ninth was present at the battle of Pozzolo the following day and took part in the campaign but, in the words of Labassée, 'the half-brigade did not have the opportunity to distinguish itself.'[20]

Pursuing the Austrians to Verona and over the River Adige, the Ninth at last entered Treviso where an armistice was concluded. In truth, Hohenlinden had already done for the Austrians. The treaty of Lunéville was signed on 9 February 1801, effectively bringing the War of the Second Coalition to a close. The Ninth fell back to Verona where they rested until April. As a reward for their achievements the previous year, the Ninth was recalled to Paris to form part of the city garrison. In the first days of April they marched through Turin and re-crossed the Alps into France through the Mount Cenis Pass. They arrived in Paris towards the end of May after a march of more than 1,000km.

As before in Paris, the Ninth was housed in two locations. Some returned to the barracks in the Rue de Babylone while the remainder went to the Rue d'Oursine, just south of the Luxembourg Gardens. Absent for over a year and a half, the men quickly returned to their favourite haunts. For the officers there was the chance to see their wives and children. There would have been visits to the widows too. Much had changed in the French capital since they had left. With the spectres of civil war and invasion banished, there was a sense of optimism about the place. Soldiers were at the forefront of society and those of the Ninth found themselves much in demand. The Marengo myth was now well established and at last the people of Paris could come and gawp at the 'incomparable' men Desaix had led in his final charge.

On 4 June 1801 the ten muskets of honour awarded for Marengo were finally distributed. The names of the recipients were published the following day in the state newspaper, *Le Moniteur Universel,* so their names might be read in homes across France.

On 15 Prairial [4 June], the first consul handed, in a grand parade, ten muskets of honour to the braves of the 9th Light Half-Brigade, to whom they had been granted having distinguished themselves by remarkable deeds at the battle of Marengo:

To Citizen Jean *Bouvier,* corporal, born at Pousin, canton of Privas, department of the Ardèche

To Citizen Jean *Lambert*, sergeant, born at Bouquemont, department of the Meuse

To Citizen Etienne *Daviou*, sergeant-major, born at Mecesink, department of the Meuse

To Citizen François *Camus*, carabineer, born at Reims, department of the Marne

To Citizen Joseph *Macquart*, sergeant, born at Présau, district of the Ain, department of the Meuse

To Citizen Jean-Nicolas *Petit*, sergeant-major, born at Saint-Mihel, department of the Meuse

To Citizen Victor *Mahut*, corporal, born at Lan, canton of Montagne-sur-Aisne, department of Marne

To Citizen Jean *Vinot*, chasseur

To Citizen Jacques *Julien*, sergeant, born at Champy, department of the Ariège

To Citizen Jean *Piessevaux*, chasseur, born at Bauteville, canton of Montmédy, department of the Meuse.[21]

Ten days later, on the first anniversary of Marengo, 14 June 1801, Bonaparte summoned the Ninth to a fête for the King of Etruria held in the gardens of the Ministry of War. The Tuscany region was now allied to France following the treaty of Lunéville, so Bonaparte wanted to show off his nation's martial strength. Supper was given under canvas to give the garden the appearance of a military camp. The Ninth paraded round the encampment to the delight of the spectators. It had been a beautifully clear day, and as the azure sky took on the colour of slate in the twilight, a grand spectacle began with sky rockets fired into the air. An air balloon rose up above the garden. Suspended from the basket was a fiery lancework spelling out the name 'Marengo'. By now Labassée's men must have begun to understand the importance of what they had achieved in battle.[22]

The previous August, Labassée had been asked to provide the Minister of War with the details of all the 'battles, combats, actions, sieges and expeditions' at which the Ninth had been present since September 1792. At the same time Labassée was asked to detail all the various reorganizations that had taken place. The document was completed on 21 June 1801, seven days after the fête at the Ministry of War.[23] Unfortunately the document lists only the barest essentials and, typically of Labassée, while the list of military feats is impressive, the narrative is frustratingly scant in detail, especially in the case of Marengo:

Battle of 25 Prairial [14 June], at Maringo [sic], it took, in conjunction with the other corps, more than 6,000 Hungarian grenadiers prisoner, after having put the Imperial Army into flight.

Much like his earlier claim to have been a captain of corsairs, the document if nothing else confirms Labassée was not averse to exaggeration.

The plaudits continued to follow. On 23 July 1801 Captain Cazaux was presented with his 'sabre of honour'. The ornate, gilded sabre was presented with an embroidered green scabbard and belt. The blade carried the inscription 'Combat of the Piacenza bridgehead 80 men prisoners of war 17 Prairial Year 8 [6 June, 1800]'.[24] Putting the beautiful craftsmanship and the prestige of the sword to one side for a moment, this award carried one very important benefit. Article 5 of the law of 25 December 1799 stated that recipients of such an award would enjoy double pay. There were also financial rewards for those put forward for a 'silver gun', the recipients drawing a bonus, or 'high pay' of five centimes a day.

The Ninth's stock was now fairly high in the capital. So much so that it dented the collective ego of the Consular Guard. Quarrels broke out. It takes little imagination to picture the testosterone overflowing when those dubbed 'incomparable' vied for attention in the same establishments frequented by those termed merely 'elite'. Perhaps the Guard's performance at Marengo came up in discussion? The Guard had gone home with Bonaparte soon after the battle while the Ninth remained in Italy. Out in the cafés around the Palais Royal there had been no one to challenge the predominant role the Guard claimed in the French victory. It would have only taken one wag to point out the Guard were nowhere near Desaix when he fell for the furniture to start flying. The scale of the rivalry between the two units should not be underestimated. No less a person than General Lannes had to intervene. Writing a stern order to the Guard on 10 September, Lannes reported the authors of the trouble between the two units had been hunted down, punished and driven out of the Guard. He reminded the remaining guardsmen of their duty:

> … The 9th Half-Brigade distinguished itself by its conduct in the war and in the interior, it is entitled to the respect of every corps in the army; it must find everywhere only friends, even more so in the Guard of the Consuls, formed from the elite of all the corps. Not only must all the quarrels stop, but all the feelings of friendship and mutual consideration which unite the men, must be reborn too and bring together these two corps. The general expects this from all the servicemen of the Guard, with whom he was so satisfied until now.[25]

From this order, one gets the impression blame for the unmentioned quarrel was laid firmly at the feet of the Guard. However, the problem appears to have been inspired by the choice of the Ninth's title. Three line regiments were given honourable epithets by Bonaparte: the 14th Line was *Intrepid*; the 32nd Line was *The Brave*; and the 57th Line *The Terrible*. These titles did not cause anyone to suffer a sense of injustice, but the Ninth's title did upset other units. Captain Marc Desbœufs confirms this in his memoirs:

> The 9th Light had received at Marengo the epithet of incomparable, but this epithet, poorly chosen because it seemed to imply a sort of superiority over the other corps, was never given to them by the army other than in derision.[26]

The Ninth didn't exactly enhance their reputation. In fact certain elements of the unit clearly got out of hand; something which was pointed out in *Le Moniteur* on 26 October:

> Report from the Police Prefecture, 4 Brumaire Year 10. We noticed, yesterday more than on other days, that large number of chasseurs of the 9th Light Half-Brigade were drunk on wine; that on the boulevard of the Temple, the quays and the Place de Grève, they incited several fights.[27]

Such behaviour clearly besmirched the name of the corps. A reputation was all well and good, but it had to be maintained. Labassée's men required a shake up and this came in the form of an inspection that resulted in an inventory of criticisms from the top to the bottom of the corps.

Their nemesis was General of Division Edouard Mortier, whose keen eye missed absolutely nothing. At the beginning of the inspection Mortier was clearly impressed with the senior officers he met. He described Labassée as a 'good commander, having made war with distinction.' He found Kuhmann to be 'moral' and was extremely impressed with Pierre Barrois, describing him as an 'officer recommendable by his talents and his conduct, having distinguished himself by his bravery in all the actions where the corps has found itself; of a recognized morality.' He then recommended Barrois for a promotion. Mortier was equally pleased with the composition of the corps, recording 'the carabineers and chasseurs are strong, robust and have a good air. There are several chasseurs of a height worse than mediocre but otherwise well constituted.' He also reported 'the best spirit animates them' although their 'discipline and instruction leave much to be desired.' He also commented 'it appears that subordination between ranks is not observed.'

Writing a résumé of his findings, Mortier began with the following passage:

> The inspector general congratulates the servicemen of the 9th Light Half-Brigade on the good spirit which reigns among them. He urges them to faithfully observe the duties which impose discipline on them in order to continue to merit the good reputation the half-brigade has made for itself in war.[28]

Hereafter the résumé continued in a less positive light: 'The Inspector general expected to find more instruction among the officers.' Although extremely experienced in action, none of the officer corps had any formal schooling in the theory of warfare. None had been cadets before the Revolution. The sole survivor of the pre-revolutionary officer corps was Labassée and it will be remembered that he had been at sea until the age of 20. In fact, as originally conceived, the Ninth was not intended to fight in the line of battle at all. Rigid inflexibility was not something the unit practised while rushing after the light cavalry. In fact most of the Ninth's officer corps was only formally trained to sergeant-major level. Mortier advised the officers to study theory and to form a library of military books at their own expense. A collection of good books would procure them an 'agreeable pastime', he added somewhat haughtily.

Having all but called the officers incompetent, it was only natural that Mortier would find fault with the instruction of the men. On the subject of their drill, Mortier would have been 'entirely satisfied' if several soldiers had not, in the first motion of loading, moved their feet before dropping the musket into the left hand. The sub-officers behind the ranks appeared nonchalant and did not align themselves properly. There was not enough silence in the ranks and the soldiers lacked 'immobility'. Manoeuvres were executed well by Labassée, but Mortier would have been happier if they had been carried out with 'less abandon'. When marching, the men did not steady their muskets sufficiently, which allowed them to wobble. Mortier also noticed that, in order to maintain contact with their neighbour on the right, the majority of men stuck out their elbow, bent their backs and allowed their right hand to hang freely. The regulation called for the men to keep their arms by the side, thus keeping the files close together. Mortier also focused on the guides of each company. These men were formed by the right-hand files. The rest of the company would align on them and follow their step and direction. Mortier was unhappy that they did not maintain the correct distances between the companies and did not follow exactly the path of the guides ahead of them when in column.

To remedy these faults, Mortier recommended theoretical and practical instruction. The battalion commanders were to set up a school of theory for the officers to learn the regulations on drill and internal discipline, beginning with the most basic part of the 1 August 1791 drill regulations, the 'School of the Soldier'. Lessons were to be held at least three times every ten days. The battalion commanders were to form their officers into platoons and to drill them when the sheds were not being used to train the recruits. Labassée was asked to assemble the officers at his quarters twice a month and observe their progress. At the same time, the adjutant-majors and adjutants were ordered to give daily classes to the sub-officers teaching them to execute the drill with 'great precision'. Beginning in the spring, on 1 Germinal (22 March 1802) the Ninth was to begin drilling by company and finally by battalions in order to execute the final part of the 1791 regulations, the 'Evolutions of the Line'.

Mortier next turned his attention to the uniform and equipment of the corps. The officers wore different sorts of hats. They tilted their hats over different eyebrows; they wore different types of boots and some did not appear to look after them very well. A lot of the officers wore their sword belts over the top of their waistcoats, a distinction reserved for senior officers only. Mortier then described what he called 'light infantry pantaloons'. These overalls were, Mortier conceded, 'tolerated' but they ought to have been closed on the outward seam, not fastened with buttons in the fashion adopted by hussar stable dress. These trousers, Mortier concluded, were not fit for parade uniform.[29]

The sub-officers had made a hash of sewing on their stripes. The corporals wore red stripes rather than the standard yellow, and the sleeves and collars of their shirts were too short. Some of the more fashion-conscious men positioned their epaulettes so far off the shoulder they were actually on their backs.

Their cleanliness left something to be desired also. The men's hair was not cut equally along the brow, their queues were not held by pins and some had grown curious beards under their chins. Their collars were greasy and dirty, and their coats were not beaten or brushed sufficiently. The duty officers and sub-officers were instructed to make sure the men shaved and dressed properly in future.

With regard to their armament, Mortier found the sergeant-majors and quartermaster corporals had stopped carrying muskets altogether. Another irregularity was that the sabre and cartridge belts were worn too long. While loading, Mortier noticed the soldiers had to lean backwards to reach inside their cartridge boxes. He also watched as some men were impeded or even tripped by their sabres coming between their legs on fast marches. Looking in detail, Mortier found 680 muskets had barrels shorter than that prescribed by the regulation of 9 Thermidor, Year 9 (28 July 1801). Another 60 were of Piedmontese manufacture and therefore not regulation issue. Mortier noticed some soldiers had hammered gilded nails into the wooden stocks of their muskets to identify them. Mortier was having none of this: muskets should all be plainly numbered instead.

Mortier then inspected the barracks occupied by the Ninth. The courtyards appeared tidy enough, but there was a terrible smell caused by the men urinating up the walls. Mortier preferred them to use the buckets provided. The Oursine Casern had holes in the roof and the pump did not draw sufficient water from the well. Inside Mortier found the bedchambers, stairs and corridors were unclean. The shelves were not dusted and the window-panes unwashed. The stale smell in the bedchambers implied the soldiers did not open the windows each morning. The soldiers' sacks were not made up and their personal belongings were scattered all over the place and under the mattresses. Several soldiers had obtained wooden trunks, which were not authorized. The shoes were not hung up. The soldiers' haversacks and forage caps were placed on the shelves intended for the soldiers' bread rations, while the bread was kept on the shelves with the cartridge boxes and bayonets. The beds were not labelled. The bedchambers did not have the name of the captain, the squad number and the names of the men posted on them. Nor was the penal code placed in the most prominent place.

Moving onto the administration of the corps, Mortier was concerned to find that most members of the Council of Administration were not familiar with their duties and councils were often formed of five or six persons, not the seven prescribed by law. He was fairly happy with the quartermaster treasurer, Captain Saÿvé, but pointed out several examples of 'negligence' with the deletions and surcharges in the registers.

The uniform officer, Pierre Gros, really appeared to catch Mortier on a bad day. Mortier was unimpressed with Gros' bookkeeping and found the stores were damp, thus putting the cloth in danger of mould. It appeared to Mortier that a certain Lieutenant Divers was the one doing all the work because of Gros' infirmity. Mortier instructed the Council of Administration to choose another uniform officer as the role required a great deal of 'activity and supervision'.

The inspection was also a time to fill vacant officer posts. A new vacancy had been created by the addition of a fourth battalion commander in each half-brigade. Labassée put forward Captain Baudot of the 2nd Battalion's carabineers for the position, but then a tragedy struck the Ninth. Shortly after Mortier's inspection, Battalion Commander Verger died. The cause of this untimely death is not known, but it must have been sudden as it occurred sometime in the weeks immediately after the inspection and there had been no comment by the inspector that Verger was suffering from illness. Baudot was therefore promoted to replace Verger. The vacant fourth position was offered to Robert Marthe instead, but the Ministry of War blocked the move. Marthe's reports remained positive and he had suffered an honourable wound at Marengo, but the post was offered to an outsider.

The majority of promotions within the Ninth had traditionally been in-house, passed down the line of seniority and not always to men of merit. The post was offered to a staff officer attached to the Army of the Orient named Combelle. With his attempts to promote Marthe frustrated, Labassée turned his attentions to Pierre Gros. Mortier had instructed Labassée to sack the old soldier and get someone new in. This resurrected the perennial problem of what to do with the fellow. Labassée decided to ignore Mortier and leave things as they were.

While Mortier had been conducting his inspection, Bonaparte had commissioned a new set of flags for the Ninth. No information survives regarding the flags associated with the corps before 1802. It is highly probable the Ninth was issued a flag in the national colours in 1791 along with the rest of the army, but this flag is never mentioned. In truth the flag probably went over the border with the Dumouriez traitors in 1793. In the famous painting of the battle of Marengo by Lejeune, an eyewitness to the battle, no standard is shown flying over the ranks of the Ninth. In this same painting several other half-brigades are shown with their flags unfurled. Given the Ninth's prominent role in the drama, one imagines Lejeune would have shown a flag if one had existed. The evidence clearly points to the Ninth never having been issued a flag in the republican era and, in truth, the cumbersome flags of this period were an impediment to light infantry in the field.

The new flags were designed by the engineer officer, Jean-Baptiste Challiot de Prusse. The flag was approximately five French feet square. It comprised a large sunburst with the soubriquet 'L'INCOMPARABLE' at the centre surrounded by a wreath. In each corner was a red triangle carrying the numeral '9' bordered by a green diagonal containing 11 golden hunting horns. Between each of the four triangles was a smaller blue triangle containing a flaming grenade device. The sunburst design was chosen in favour of other designs incorporating chimera heads and a Gallic cockerel. The design was particularly unusual for the predominant use of green, the traditional colour associated with chasseurs, rather than the national colours of the Revolution.

The presentation took place on Saturday 4 June 1802 and was again reported in *Le Moniteur*.[30] There was a brilliant parade in the Place du Carrousel, the grand courtyard of the Tuileries Palace. Alongside the Ninth, the 1st Foot Artillery Regiment were also receiving their flags, albeit in very different circumstances. There had been an insurrection in the regiment while it was in Turin. As punishment, Bonaparte had taken away the regiment's flags, enveloped them in black crepe and hung them in Paris' Temple of Mars.

After returning the artillerymen their standards, Bonaparte turned to the Ninth. He gathered the officers and sub-officers before him and the three new flags were carried forward by a detachment of veterans. The flags were passed to Labassée who gave them to each of the battalion commanders. Bonaparte then said:

Soldiers of the 9th Light Infantry, here are your flags. They will always serve as your rallying point. Be worthy of the inscription I have had put there. Never, not ever, can the flags of the 9th Light Infantry fall to the enemies of the state. Do you swear to sacrifice your life for their defence?[31]

The officers and sub-officers responded: 'We swear it!' The troops then defiled together while the band of the Consular Guard executed a march composed by Giovanni Paisiello. Mortier had been hard on the Ninth and they probably deserved it, but this parade had a marked effect. As Dubois' 1839 history of the corps put it: 'If something had been missing in the enthusiasm of the half-brigade, such a distinction would have been enough to electrify it.'[32]

The remainder of 1802 passed off without much action. The officers began re-learning the exercises and the sub-officers endured a dose of the same medicine. In the spring of 1803 it was time to say goodbye to an old friend when Christian Kuhmann left the corps on 24 March to take up the assistant commandant's position at the Special Military School at Fontainebleau. The venerable old soldier would live out the remainder of his days teaching the ropes to a new generation of officer cadets, while fending off their amorous intentions towards his twenty-something daughter who, one cadet wrote, had 'beautiful eyes, a lot of spirit and, as it is said, much humanity.'[33] The same correspondent described Kuhmann as an old soldier and 'truly respectable'. Another cadet, Elzéar Blaze was also struck by Kuhmann and gave a colourful description of him in his memoirs:

> ... [The commandant's] alter ego, the brave Kuhmann, seconded him most admirably. That epithet 'brave' was given to him by a man who was a consummate judge – by Napoleon himself. He was an excellent Alsatian, mangling the French language, whose hobby was discipline, and who thought of nothing but the exercise. I see him still at his door, at the moment when the battalion was getting under arms, stretching himself three inches taller, and crying: 'Heads up! Heads up! – immovable! – immobility is the finest movement of the exercise!' The antiquary exploring the Parthenon or the ruins of Baalbeck, the painter contemplating the masterpieces of Raphael or Michelangelo, the dilettante seated in the pit of the Italian Opera, the sportsman who sees his pointer make a dead set, feel less intense delight than did the brave Kuhmann in seeing a platoon manoeuvre according to principles. When a movement was well executed, when an evolution was effected in an accurate and precise manner, tears trickled from his eyes down his cheeks, blackened by gunpowder; he could not find words to express

his gratification; he contemplated his work, and admired himself. 'There is nothing finer,' he would sometimes say, 'than a soldier carrying arms. Immovable, head upright, chest forward – 'tis superb! 'tis magnificent! 'tis touching!'[34]

The successor to Kuhmann was a man from outside the corps. Jean Marie Régeau was a 44-year-old native from Calais. He had first joined the army in 1779 and remained in service until 1788. When war broke out in 1792, Régeau joined a volunteer unit called the Chasseurs of Paris and assumed the rank of captain quartermaster treasurer. After various amalgamations, Régeau found himself occupying several staff positions with the Army of the Rhine before being promoted to battalion commander by General Moreau in 1800. In time, he would be talked about as one of the finest officers in the army and would have three sons serving in the Ninth with him. Others, as we will see, were wary of his ability to spend money like there was no tomorrow, but no one could doubt the man was a character.

The sequel to General Mortier's inspection came on 30 June 1803 and was undertaken by General of Division Bonnard. The inspector commended the good spirit of the corps. The officers were now generally well instructed in theory, but some still lacked the necessary assurance when executing manoeuvres. Bonnard also identified some of the sub-officers required more training. The motions of the 1 August 1791 Regulation were carried out to Bonnard's satisfaction, except the 'abandon' with which the men executed the 'port arms' position. The inspector noted some held the musket too high and others too low. Bonnard pointed this out to Labassée and ordered him to rectify the problem promptly.

Commenting on the appearance of the corps there were still improvements to be made. Bonnard noted how the more fashion-conscious members of the Ninth still wore their cross belts too long and had difficulty reaching into their cartridge boxes as a result. Bonnard complained the men did not wash their faces and remarked their ears were full of hair powder and pomade, a comment which indirectly confirms that the men still powdered their hair white in the traditional fashion. Bonnard instructed Labassée to 'punish severely' those captains who neglected to check this in their inspections. These same captains were to forbid their men from embellishing their uniforms with 'objects of fantasy' as he termed them.

The inspector then visited the barrack rooms. He received several complaints about the poor quality of the bread, but when he tasted it himself, he found it conformed to regulations. The same applied to the 'bread of the soup'. This was a lighter type of bread that was broken up and used to thicken the soldiers' broth. While the bread itself was acceptable, the manner in which it was stored was not to his liking. The bread shelves were covered in dust. Bonnard was displeased with this and complained it would cause illness among the men. Captains who tolerated such standards must be severely punished, he advised.

Bonnard was extremely impressed with Captain Saÿvé's standard of bookkeeping; but was less enthusiastic to find Captain Gros still employed as the clothing officer. Bonnard reminded Labassée of the order to relieve Gros of his duties. Bonnard probably would have given Gros a reprieve, if he had found improvements. Alas, the registers were no better kept than the year before. Gros was still in poor health and Lieutenant Divers was still skivvying on his behalf. Bonnard felt compelled to repeat Mortier's earlier instruction.

Fortunately for Captain Gros there was a reprieve. Fifteen days after Bonnard's inspection took place, the Ninth was ordered out of Paris. There was talk of an invasion of England to settle matters once and for all between the two quarrelsome neighbours. With war renewed everyone would have their part to play, even an old salt like Gros.

6

INVASION FORCE

A decade of war had demonstrated the French army's pre-eminence on land and British mastery of the seas. From the French perspective, the surest way of bringing the conflict to a successful conclusion was to invade Britain and fight a decisive battle on the banks of the Thames. However, to get an army across the Channel, Bonaparte first needed to remove the British squadrons protecting it. The perils of relying on the French navy had been amply demonstrated to Bonaparte in 1798 when, after losing a fleet at the battle of the Nile, Bonaparte's army had been marooned in Egypt for three years. Instead of provoking a full fleet action, Bonaparte opted for a more indirect strategy. He would use his navy as a decoy to draw the British warships away from the Channel in a series of cat-and-mouse pursuits. This would give him time to land a massive army on the English coast and march on London. Within five days he was confident of parading his troops in the British capital. The war would finally be won and the paymaster of France's enemies would finally be put to rest.

Determined to launch an invasion, Bonaparte assembled an army on the northern coast of France. The Ninth was ordered to the Normandy coast on 15 July 1803 with 1st Battalion at Le Havre and 2nd Battalion at Honfleur. These two battalions were now known as the 'field' or 'war' battalions. The 3rd Battalion was henceforth designated as a garrison battalion and sent to Philippeville in the Ardennes. Before leaving Paris it was stripped of its fittest soldiers to bring the field battalions up to strength. In return, some of the older men in the field battalions were sent to 3rd Battalion where they could help train the recruits.

Throughout the summer of 1803, the Normandy coast must have appeared much like a scene from the Bayeux Tapestry. Shipwrights constructed a multitude of boats by the mouth of the Seine to transport the soldiers from Normandy to where the army was assembling at Boulogne. While the ships were prepared, Labassée presided over another reorganization. On 24 September the designation 'regiment' was restored to the French army along with the title 'colonel'. The Ninth was now properly the 9th Regiment of Light Infantry. However Labassée did not get to enjoy the title colonel as he was instead promoted to general of brigade.

On 29 September General Labassée received a complaint from Berthier, the minister of war, bemoaning the conduct of several officers. Berthier was unhappy to learn that Captain Perrin was deeply in debt, while Captain Nicolas was drinking heavily. As for Lieutenant Queleine … well, he was simply incompetent. This was not what Berthier expected of the regiment's officers – they were to buck up their ideas or face the consequences.[1]

As detachments of the regiment began travelling by boat to join the main army at Boulogne, Labassée informed the Ministry of War of several personnel changes he had made. Writing from his lodgings at Le Havre on 28 October, General Labassée explained that all the officers unable to support 'the fatigues of war' due to infirmity or wounds had been transferred into the garrison battalion.[2] Among this number was Robert Marthe, now the most senior captain in the regiment. Labassée explained how he had personally asked the first consul to make Marthe a battalion commander with a garrison command. Having seen the veteran officer on parade Bonaparte had promised this, but nothing had happened.

Other senior captains were also packed off to the depot. Despite numerous wounds and four years of 'dilapidated health', the 'brave and intrepid' Captain Delville had clung on to command of 1st Battalion's 1st Company. However he had fallen seriously ill, almost to the point of death, so Labassée sent him to the 3rd Battalion. The same applied to Captain David Fressinet who was almost completely blind. Captain Lange commanded 2nd Battalion's 1st Company. Just as he was about to leave Honfleur for Boulogne, Lange broke his leg in an accident. From his service in the navy, Labassée knew all about the perils of the sea and wanted his men to travel with a full complement of fit officers. Lange was replaced and ordered to Philippeville.

Labassée was right to be cautious about the sea voyage to Boulogne. The weather during the passage was appalling. Fearing the British navy might attack, the craft hugged the shoreline where they came under the protection of guns mounted on the major coastal promontories. This placed the ships perilously close to the rocks along the shoreline and the poor soldiers of the Ninth found themselves tossed around, soaked and seasick. In the storms a great deal of baggage and equipment was lost over the side. The regiment arrived at Boulogne in dribs and drabs; battered and bruised as if returning from a gruelling campaign. These detachments were sent 3km from the port to quarters at Ostrohove where they spent a miserable winter patching their uniforms, repairing what was left of their equipment and grumbling.

The gathering of the army in Boulogne marked the end of an era for the Ninth. In 1784 Labassée had quit the channel port to join the corps recently formed in Carcassonne. The following two decades had seen an unprecedented change in the fortunes of France. Labassée had ridden this wave of history, growing as a man, becoming a father and a leader of men. Twenty years before he had been an aspiring corsair, now he was a general of brigade in the infantry. He was the last officer from the *ancien régime*; the last in a direct line stretching back to before the Seven Years War when his father rode off and made his name in war. Labassée's private thoughts are unknown, but it must have been something like a divorce when he left the Ninth.

The obvious successor to Labassée was Battalion Commander Pierre Barrois. Mortier had recommended him for promotion the year before and he knew the Ninth like the back of his hand. He was young, ambitious and possessed a good pedigree having been in the thick of the action at Marengo. Barrois did receive a colonelcy, but tellingly it was not with the Ninth. He was directed instead to take command of the 96th Line. Labassée's successor would come from outside the corps, presumably with a verbal instruction to shake things up in a way that an insider never could.

The new colonel arrived on 22 December 1803. Aged 33, Claude-Marie Meunier was from Saint-Amour in the department of Jura on the eastern side of France.[3] He was the son of a master joiner and had pledged his life to the tricolour in 1792 as a volunteer in the 10th Jura Battalion. An impressive recruit, his peers elected him captain of grenadiers within a week. After a spell of hard service on the Rhine, Meunier was transferred to Italy where he first encountered Bonaparte. Meunier went to Egypt and was made a captain in Bonaparte's 'Foot Guides' in January 1799. Each army commander was allowed to maintain a small bodyguard to protect their person and headquarters. When Bonaparte took over command of the Army of Italy in 1796 he inherited the corps of Guides raised by General Kellermann (father of the cavalry general of Marengo fame). Initially a modest force of cavalry, Bonaparte added 400 infantrymen when he went to Egypt.

Meunier's appointment to the Guides drew him towards the inner circle around Bonaparte. It was an appointment not without its hazards. A number of Guides were assassinated during the Cairo uprising of 1798. Forty more were killed at the bloody siege of Acre in 1799. When Bonaparte quit Egypt in August 1799 he could only take 200 Horse Guides with him. The Foot Guides were left behind where they served under the indomitable General Jean Baptiste Kléber and his successor General Jacques François Menou until the army capitulated to the British after the battle of Aboukir on 2 September 1801. Returning to France after three years' absence, it was not long before Meunier found himself back in close proximity to Bonaparte. In February 1802 Meunier was incorporated into the Consular Guard with the rank of battalion commander.

The Ninth also had to find a candidate for the newly created post of Major. The prime function of the major was to command the depot and oversee the training of the recruits while the colonel led the field battalions. The post could have been filled internally, with Captain Cazaux primed for promotion; but the hero of Piacenza was sent to become major of the 2nd Light Infantry. The vacancy in the Ninth was again filled by an outsider. Forty-year-old Claude Marcel D'Eslon originated from Mirecourt in the Vosges region. He was a former horse chasseur in the King's army, who, like Kuhmann, transferred to the foot chasseurs on their creation. By 1789 D'Eslon had reached the rank of sergeant putting him in a good place to rapidly accelerate through the officer grades after the Revolution. He served in the Army of the Rhine and took several staff appointments before leading a carabineer company for a spell. He then served as an aide-de-camp to a succession of generals in the armies of the Rhine, Rhine and Moselle and in Switzerland. He finally settled in the 10th Light Infantry with the rank of battalion commander. He was brave and had personally captured a field gun and seven gunners at Rastadt in 1796, despite having his horse shot from underneath him. He had also fought bravely at Hohenlinden and seemed destined for a superior grade. He may have been slightly disappointed to play second fiddle to a younger colonel, even in such a prestigious regiment.

At Boulogne the Ninth was assigned to the corps of General Michel Ney, a popular figure with the veterans of the Rhine armies who had yet to serve under Bonaparte. The Ninth formed the 1st Brigade of the 1st Division under General Pierre Dupont, formerly Berthier's chief of staff during the Marengo campaign. The remainder of the division was made up by two line infantry regiments. Colonel Darricau's 32nd Line was a celebrated regiment in its own right, dubbed 'The Brave' by Bonaparte. They had fought in the first Italian campaign (1796–97) and went to Egypt with him in 1798. The other regiment was the 96th Line, another veteran regiment of Marengo now under the command of an 'old boy' from the Ninth, Pierre Barrois. Under Dupont, this division was destined to become one of the most celebrated in the army; although this was far from obvious at the beginning of 1804.

When the dark days of winter subsided, the work of preparing for the coming invasion began. Given the Ninth's lofty reputation, Meunier must have been somewhat disappointed at the ragged wreck he inherited. Dupont ordered an inspection of the regiment at Ostrohove and witnessed the scale of its decline for himself. On 27 February 1804 Meunier and D'Eslon co-authored a letter to Dupont setting out an action plan.[4] They agreed the regiment appeared 'destitute' and the uniforms and headgear were in a pitiful state. Dupont and D'Eslon agreed they would employ every means to 'restore all parts of the uniform, armament, equipment, linen and footwear, the discipline and bearing, the order and the work which was interrupted by the scattering of the regiment and by what it experienced from losses during its crossing from Havre to Boulogne.'

They begged Dupont to press the director of administration at the Ministry of War to send the articles of uniform they were due for the year 1803–04. Interestingly the letter implies the number of recruits exceeded the usual peacetime complement while the money allocated to the regiment remained the same. The letter finished with the following pledge: 'Be well assured General, we shall do everything possible to put the regiment back in a state which leaves nothing to be desired, at least in terms of order and discipline.' It was a polite way of informing Dupont he would have to intervene on their behalf if he wanted the men well behaved *and* smartly dressed.[5]

In March 1804 the regiment was sent south-west along the coast to Étaples, which had been designated as Ney's embarkation port. Dupont's men created a camp for themselves in the grounds of the Candal farm at Camiers, from where the English coast could be seen on clear days. The Ninth's field battalions formed three streets on which each company constructed a group of six barrack huts with a seventh for the sub-officers. Each hut was 20ft long and 16ft wide. The walls were made of cob (a mixture of earth and fine straw), whitewashed with chalk and topped with a thatched roof. Each hut had a wooden door in a green painted frame. Inside the huts a sleeping area was made by forming a bank of compacted earth two feet high covered with fresh straw. Each man slept on a woollen blanket enveloped in a distribution sack, with his haversack serving as a pillow. The sub-officers' huts also contained a writing desk for the sergeant-majors.[6]

The officers' huts were built of the same materials, but had internal divisions providing a separate living quarters and bedrooms. There were lodgings for their orderlies and log stores for fuel. Each hut had its own garden, half of which was for vegetables and the other half for flowers. The colonel's quarters were constructed in the interval between each battalion's huts. Meunier's lodgings were a grand affair with a superb garden. The parade ground was bordered with shrubs and flowers and as a finishing touch, each of the streets were named after famous soldiers and victories.

To improve sanitation, rainwater was carried away from the huts via channels which led into a canal running parallel with the road. The canal emptied into a reservoir which irrigated the soldiers' allotments where they grew their own potatoes and vegetables. Each company built a bridge over its section of the canal, connecting the sleeping quarters to the cookhouses. These were square structures containing fireplaces, benches and musket racks. The regular ration included white 'soup bread', a brown 'ration' bread, meat (usually beef), dried vegetables (rice and lentils), brandy and vinegar, which they used for purifying their drinking water. These rations were supplemented by purchased or home-grown potatoes and fresh vegetables. The lunchtime meal was a *soupe grasse* with vegetables and a small portion of beef.[7] In the evening they had a meal of potatoes flavoured with butter, onions and vinegar. The men ate with their corporals with six or seven portions served at a time in a communal mess pan, each man taking a turn to dip in with his spoon. The sergeants of each company formed their own mess, while the sergeant-majors and adjutants were permitted to eat with more refinement *en pension* at the battalion canteen.[8]

These canteens formed part of the recreational area of the camp. Just past the kitchen huts were the soldiers' clubrooms, where they learned to dance and fence. With no regulations for physical exercise, fencing and dancing were considered excellent pastimes, relieving boredom, building stamina and, in the case of fencing, developing an offensive spirit. In addition to the official regimental band, the drummers and many other soldiers must have had sufficient musical skill on fifes and fiddles to provide their own accompaniment for dancing, although it is less certain what 'ladies' may have been on hand to partner them. Beyond the clubrooms were the canteens where life's little joys could be purchased from the battalion cantineers, provided of course that the sergeant-major was not disturbed while relaxing with his evening dram and pipe. In time these canteens were joined by modest restaurants and cafés, as local entrepreneurs realized that the soldiers were something of a captive market to exploit. Some of the cafés were even equipped with billiards tables.

As this great settlement was being constructed, a major reform took place in the light infantry regiments which created a new elite company with the same high pay as the carabineers. The law of 3 March 1804 decreed that every battalion of light infantry must contain one company of voltigeurs (lit. 'vaulters'). According to the instructions, the voltigeurs were 'specially intended to be quickly transported by the cavalry to the places where their presence is necessary; they will be exercised in nimbly climbing and riding pillion behind a horseman, and nimbly descending, to form up quickly, and following on foot, marching at the trot … The voltigeurs will be particularly exercised firing with speed and great accuracy.'[9]

These companies were to be formed of 'well-constituted, strong and agile men of the smallest size'. The sub-officers and the soldiers had to measure less than 1.60m (5ft 2in.) in height; the officers, no more than 1.63m (5ft 3in.) in height. This company would be composed of a captain, lieutenant, sub-lieutenant, sergeant-major, four sergeants, a quartermaster corporal, eight corporals, 104 voltigeurs and two instrumentalists; giving a total of 123 men. Instead of drums the instrumentalists would be equipped with small hunting horns called cornets. Given their diminutive stature, the voltigeurs would be equipped with the dragoon-model musket. This was 98mm shorter than the standard infantry musket (1,417mm against 1,515mm) and 100 grams lighter (4.275kg against 4.375kg).[10] The officers and the sub-officers were armed with rifled carbines. Their uniforms would be the same as those of the rest of the light infantry but with a yellowish 'chamois' collar.

Although perhaps new in name, the voltigeurs were not entirely novel. In the King's army every infantry battalion had had its own company of light infantry for scouting and skirmishing and throughout the Wars of the Revolution, many infantry units had formed unofficial 'scout' units which performed a similar role.[11] In the 1780s the infantry chasseur battalions had been created specifically to work with light cavalry, so the concept of close cooperation was well established.[12] The real innovation was in selecting the shortest men to perform this task. Where the shortest men were often the butt of their comrades' jokes, admission to the voltigeurs at last gave them a means of achieving elite status. It also plugged the legal loophole that had left a sizeable section of the population exempt from conscription. The conscription regulation of 8 March 1800 set a minimum height of at least 1.65m (5ft 4in.) for conscripts.[13] The voltigeur law in effect meant Frenchmen previously classified unfit for military service became not only eligible, but were classed as elite troops!

By 11 May the voltigeur officers for the field battalions had been appointed. They were captains Janin and Bruyère; lieutenants Collignon and Martinet; and sub-lieutenants Lambert and Petit. The second company of each battalion was dissolved to make room for the new company and the men were exchanged with those who qualified for service with the voltigeurs. The vast majority of the men in the Ninth were above 1.65m in height so the regiment found itself 215 men short of the 360 required and so the remaining places went to short conscripts. It must have irked many to see these diminutive newcomers awarded high pay without even being blooded in action; but their time would come soon enough.

These reforms and preparations were set against a backdrop of great political events. In 1802 Bonaparte had been made first consul for life following a national plebiscite. There then came a great debate about him taking the crown of France as emperor. There had been assassination plots against Bonaparte; then a royalist conspiracy involving General Moreau, the outlaw General Charles Pichegru and the Breton Georges Cadoudal. If Bonaparte fell victim to a dagger, some feared there would be a return to the anarchy of the Revolution. The justifications can be dressed a hundred different ways, but the conclusion was something of a paradox – the French senate decided the best way to preserve the freedoms earned since 1789 was by entrusting Bonaparte and his male heirs with the imperial crown and strong executive powers.

Colonel Meunier was an enthusiastic supporter of Bonaparte and whatever his men thought privately they outwardly shared his convictions. On 4 May this conviction was expressed by Dupont in a letter to Ney:

> I enclose, my dear General, the personal addresses from the generals and colonels of the 1st division to the First Consul. They all contain the same wish, which we have already expressed at the head of the troops, that the hero of France should be invested with the Imperial Dignity. May I beg you to lay these addresses before him as the most sacred pledge of the devoted attachment felt towards him by the division he has placed under my command.[14]

On 14 May 200 cannon shots were fired in the camp of Camiers as a signal the first consul had been offered the crown. On 18 May, the first consul was proclaimed as Emperor Napolcon I and the constitution of France was changed anticipating an endorsement by plebiscite on the principle of hereditary empire. Taking Charlemagne as his model, Napoleon I began creating a new nobility from his family and closest associates. On 19 May Ney was one of 18 generals elevated to the rank of marshal of the empire. That same day Napoleon established the Legion of Honour to reward civilians and soldiers alike for services to the empire. As its name suggests, the legion was formed along Roman lines. There were four ranks in the legion: grand officer, commander, officer and legionnaire. Nomination to the legion would become a source of great pride and it came with an income. Even simple legionnaires pocketed an extra 250 francs a year.

Talk of crowns to one side, there were more pressing matters to contend with at Camiers, namely the miserly recalcitrance of the Ministry of War. Meunier wrote to Dupont on 11 June 1804 complaining about a lack of uniform provision:

I have the honour to report, General, I have just received from the depot the quantity of 1,500 shirts, 1,300 pairs of grey gaiters and 1,500 sleeping bags for both field battalions under your orders. I shall receive presently 900 pantaloons in blue linen. I must observe to you, General, that the major to whom I had written pressing for the uniforms which are due to both field battalions for the replacement of Year 12 [1803–04], warns me he has still received nothing, despite multiple reclamations which he has made, both to the Director Minister and to the Directorate of Uniforms for this object. The major tells me the regiment received this year 500 draftees from the Vosges and 215 more for the companies of voltigeurs, which makes 716 men, not including the deserters, who are daily returned to us, who have not been judged, and the minister sends him only 300 coats. There will thus be 416 men for whom the corps will get nothing; it is impossible for us to dress them. I pray you, General, to make representations to the minister, asking him to give the orders necessary for the manufacture of 800 replacement coats for the year 1804 and 716 for the recruits of this year, instead of 300.[15]

As the summer months continued Dupont trained his division hard, three times a week. When not drilling or tending their gardens, the soldiers would spend time down in the port where 400 boats had been collected for Ney's corps. The soldiers of the Ninth were trained in naval gunnery and the basic nautical arts. If the flotilla came under attack during the crossing there would be no room for bystanders. If the sailors went down to enemy fire, the infantrymen would have to know what to do.

Ney's chief of staff, General Dutaillis, wrote to Dupont on 9 July informing him that the drummers, musicians and sappers in his division were to be armed with musketoons and bayonets. Perhaps the most interesting piece of this order is the confirmation that there were then 22 musicians and six sappers serving in the Ninth. Sappers are not mentioned previously in the surviving inspection reports or documentation of the Ninth. They were strong, fierce men who were permitted to grow full beards to further display their manliness. They wore bearskin caps with a leather apron and gauntlets, sporting a badge of crossed axes on their sleeves. Although equipped with musketoons and swords, the principal armament of the sapper was a large two-handed axe, which allowed them to smash a path through obstacles, and break down doors and gates during combat.

Dutaillis also instructed each company to appoint a fifer. These might be drawn from the regimental children over the age of 14, or from weaker conscripts who demonstrated an ability to play the instrument.[16]

Having founded his Legion of Honour, Napoleon made the first distribution of the award to the troops in Paris at a lavish ceremony on 14 July 1804. He then instructed his marshals to distribute the Order to the troops on the northern coasts. Ney was not satisfied with this. His men wanted the same honour as the troops in Paris so Ney wrote to Napoleon expressing the regret his men experienced in not receiving their crosses from the emperor in person.[17] Napoleon saw an opportunity to use such a ceremony for uniting the army as never before and to help extinguish any remaining rivalries between the old armies of the Rhine and Italy. Napoleon therefore asked for all the army corps stationed at Bruges, Ostend and Montreuil to join those at Boulogne for the occasion, which would be held on his 35th birthday.

At daybreak on 15 August, an artillery salute opened the festivities. Eighty thousand troops were drawn up in a natural amphitheatre facing the sea. At the focal point was a small hill upon which a throne was raised for Napoleon and surrounded with captured flags. Behind Napoleon the coast of England could be seen. The infantry formed up in line facing the throne, spreading outwards like a fan. The cavalry formed a semi-circle behind. Amid a thunder of guns and beating drums, Napoleon arrived and a shout went up as the army greeted its emperor for the first time with an exultant shout of '*Vive l'Empereur!*'

Twenty-two soldiers from the Ninth were awarded the Legion of Honour that day.[18] The recipients stood at the head of the regiment expectant. The Legion of Honour was awarded by right to all those soldiers who had won Arms of Honour, including those who had died, such as Sergeant-Major Daviou who had died in Italy after Marengo. Of the original recipients we find the names Mahut, Bouvier, Piessevaux, Julien and Macquart present in 1804 at Boulogne. Lieutenant Pierre Donot, the commander of the swimmers on the Marengo campaign was there, along with Assistant Surgeon-Major Charles Vanderbach, who had been awarded an Épée of Honour for swimming the Ticino under fire. From Piacenza were Lieutenant Etienne and Captain Leblanc, both of whom had captured large parties of Austrians around the citadel. Sicaire Dumas from the Dordogne was a conscript who had been to Piacenza and Marengo and merited a distinction, along with Sergeant Heckenroth. One of those unlucky to miss out on an Arm of Honour after Marengo was Sergeant-Major Jacques Eudes who had been wounded in the left leg at Piacenza but had soldiered on and fought at Marengo. The same applied to Corporal Jean-Nicolas Hemard who gave distinguished service at Piacenza and Marengo. This was an opportunity to recognize their dedication along with sergeants Couade, Pérot, Metty, Toussaint, Pierron, Volsack, Lefebvre, Lanier and Andre. A few low-ranking men were rewarded, including Voltigeur Joseph Barrier, Chasseur Dumas and 40-year-old Corporal Virey.[19]

Colonel Meunier was made an officer of the Legion of Honour. His senior officers, battalion commanders Régeau and Barère also received crosses, as did Adjutant-Major Nicolas Huguin who had been shot in the leg at Marengo. Crosses were also awarded to a number of officers in the 3rd Battalion, including the Quartermaster Treasurer, Captain Saÿvé, along with captains Marthe, Pierre Gros, Reboulleau, and Nicolas Baudot of the newly formed voltigeurs. Major D'Eslon was also awarded the honour. It is unclear if any of the third battalion officers travelled to Boulogne to be at this ceremony or whether they received their crosses slightly later; one imagines they were all preoccupied with clothing and training the recruits at the time.

One name of great interest on the list is that of 30-year-old Sergeant-Major Jean Nicolas Fouquet. From the Ardennes, Fouquet was one of the Meuse Scouts who joined the Ninth during the amalgamation. He had been grievously wounded by a lance in the right leg on 1 May 1796 and had been left for dead on the battlefield. He fell prisoner and was later exchanged, returning to the Ninth when it formed the Paris garrison. He was promoted to corporal and then sergeant during the Ninth's stint in Brittany during the civil war. At Marengo he made a noticeable contribution and was badly wounded again, this time by an Austrian bayonet. He survived and was promoted to sergeant-major a month after the battle, becoming 2nd Battalion's standard bearer. His future career would be one to note.

With the awards distributed, Napoleon gave an address concluding with the words, 'You soldiers, you swear to defend, at the peril of your lives, the honour of the French name, your country, and the institutions and laws by which it is governed!'

Napoleon Bonaparte: the First Consul.

The 9th at Marengo, where they gained their fearsome reputation.

General Alexandre Berthier, the day following the battle of Marengo.

General Louis-Charles-Antoine Desaix.

The 1802 pattern flag of the 9th Light Infantry.

Top left
Jacques-Louis David's portrait of
General Claude-Marie Meunier,
colonel of the 9th.

Top right
Laure-Emilie-Felicitie David,
Baroness Meunier.

Bottom left
Self portrait of Jacques-Louis David,
showing him sketching the
coronation of Napoleon.

Above and below: The distribution of the Eagles by Napoleon, 5 December 1804.

Presentation of the Legion of Honour, August 1804.

The French infantry on the march near Jena.

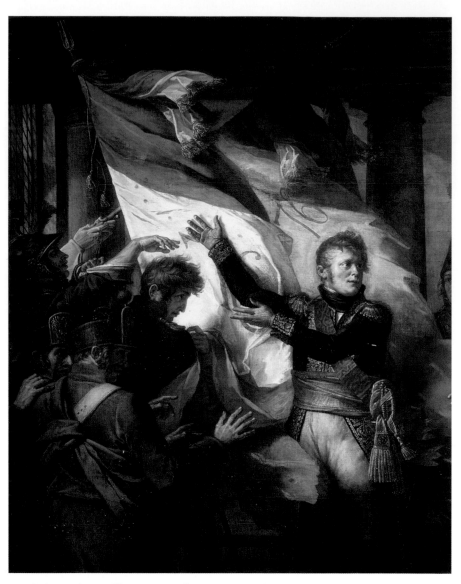

Marshal Ney, the Ninth's inspirational corps commander 1804–5.

'We swear it!' cried the assembled soldiers as one voice.[20] As they made this pledge all the corps of drummers and musicians burst into a fanfare, while the coastal artillery and the vessels in the harbour opened fire.

After this deafening acclamation, the troops filed off and the rest of the day was spent in games: dancing, running races and engaging in manly feats of strength. The men enjoyed double rations and a bottle of wine each. Dinners were thrown for the legionnaires by the likes of Prince Joseph Bonaparte, Marshal Soult and the Ministry of War. These continued until the evening when there was a firework display. To supplement the rockets and spinning wheels the infantry mounted a spectacular display. Fifteen thousand soldiers lined the cliffs facing England and commenced a rolling fire using pyrotechnic 'star cartridges'. The effect was truly spectacular and visible far out to sea.

After leaving Boulogne, Napoleon headed for Ney's corps at Montreuil. Two thirds of Ney's men had been left behind and wished to demonstrate their attachment for the new sovereign. Ney put his corps under arms and the inspection went well. Ney took them through every manoeuvre and evolution with aplomb, much to Napoleon's pleasure. The emperor then called for the oldest soldier of each regiment to be presented to him. He interrogated these ruddy-faced veterans and asked what battles they had fought in and where they had been wounded. Having listened to their stories, Napoleon granted each of them a pension.

The remainder of the summer was spent in preparation for the invasion with drills and field exercises. As autumn approached there were murmurs around the camp. What was *he* waiting for? Was the navy at fault? Some speculated Napoleon was waiting for fog to conceal his ships, or a storm to scatter the British fleet. While the speculation continued, the autumn gales began buffeting the men's huts, knocking down walls and tearing off thatch. Drill exercises were soon forgotten as the men spent most of their time engaged in repair work. Ney became concerned about his men's health. A summer of marching, serving naval guns, hauling ropes and gardening had had a tremendous effect, honing the men's strength. Ney did not want this work undone by the ravages of winter and so he resolved to rebuild the camp. The fields and riverbeds were searched for stones. When these materials ran out, pits were dug to find more. All the soldiers became carpenters or masons and very quickly a stronger camp was built.

With winter approaching Ney was also concerned boredom might set in. He therefore ordered that three large halls be built behind each regiment's huts. The first hall would be at the centre of the 1st Battalion. This would be used as a fencing room. Behind the 2nd Battalion a dancehall was constructed. The third hall was built between the two battalions and was for the officers to study in. Ney did not want his officers studying alone, fearing they might compound errors. He wanted them to assist each other and to debate. The marshal ordered each officer to give an account of the manoeuvres he had witnessed in the field. Together the officers were to learn the theory properly and clear up any areas of confusion.

While the two field battalions bedded down for a winter on the coast, the 3rd Battalion continued to train the latest conscripts and recruits. Much of what we know of the 3rd Battalion in this era comes from two inspections: the first by General of Brigade Amey, at Philippeville on 4 October 1804; the second by General of Division Mermet ten months later at Charleville.

Amey's opening impressions of the 3rd Battalion were extremely positive and demonstrate the advances Meunier and D'Eslon had made since beginning their stewardship:

> In a regiment the name of which is a eulogy, one would expect to find a love of the government, submission to the law, union and harmony between the servicemen who compose it and that is what exists in the 9th Regiment of Light Infantry.[21]

Eulogies to one side, Amey described the men's uniform as 'good', especially so in the carabineer and voltigeur companies. A lot of the men were still without coats, an order for 216 coats not having been delivered by the time of his inspection. There was also a lack of sabres and Amey authorized the order of 542 side arms, which would be provided by the arsenal at Maubeuge.

As for the type of men in the 3rd Battalion his remarks are extremely revealing:

> Independently of the old soldiers, the others can be divided into two classes: the conscripts of the department of Vosges, who are appropriate for military service,

appear to enjoy it, show willingness and do not desert. Those of the department of the Scheldt have no form, do not show either taste or willingness and desert a lot.

Investigating what might be troubling the men he wrote of the conscripts, 'One must accustom them to like their duties, rather than to dread their leaders from fear of punishment … Soldiers are all children of the same family.' Anyone maltreating a conscript would be punished severely, he warned. However, all the evidence he saw was the old sweats appeared to be treating the conscripts well. Given this he placed the blame outside the corps: 'In general the choice [of conscripts] was badly made in the departments for Year 11 and Year 12.'

The conscripts from the Low Countries were a real problem. Amey noted 141 had deserted and many more presented themselves for medical discharge during the review.[22] There appeared to be many valid medical complaints including 'accidental epilepsy' and asthma. One had a left leg two inches longer than his right, while another had a left leg three inches shorter than the right. There were even several cases of 'certified imbecility' serious enough to have men thrown out of the corps. A lot of the invalids had suffered hernias, and wounds to the right hand by sabres were not uncommon. This latter category deserves special scrutiny. Were these genuine accidents in sabre practice or deliberate mutilations to win a discharge? Elsewhere on the list of medical complaints there are several instances of the amputation or paralysing of the right index finger – the trigger finger. A soldier unable to pull a trigger was of no use to anyone. Amey was no fool. The names of 11 conscripts suspected of deliberately mutilating their fingers were sent to the Ministry of War for further investigation.[23]

Of the remainder, General Amey noted how the instructors were zealous and the soldiers were willing, and considered progress would be guaranteed. Already he noted 'proof of instruction' in the way they performed a firing exercise, marching and arms drill. The men had already been schooled for six to eight months and the inspector asked for the rate of instruction to be accelerated but cautioned against graduating the soldiers beyond the 'school of the platoon' into the 'school of the battalion' until they were satisfactory in the former. Interestingly he remarked there were limits to what could be taught by drills. He wrote, 'It is not through multiplied exercises which one acquires an imposing presence in the movements; it is not by frequent marches that one obtains the necessary accuracy and self-assurance in the step. It is thus essential to make, when the weather allows it, frequent military promenades, with packs on the back.' Amey also found some of the officers too slow in the delivery of commands. The inspector gave them some advice, writing, 'an important point that Messrs the officers and sub-officers should not lose sight of, it is the firmness and the uniformity of commands, without which you should not expect any regularity in the execution.' What Amey was referring to here was the importance of instructors developing a rhythm, or cadence, in the delivery of command. When the winter came and made outdoor activities difficult, Amey asked for the conscripts to be taught lessons in theory. This would perfect their education before being sent to the field battalions preparing to invade England.

Many of the soldiers in the 3rd Battalion were now long in the tooth. Napoleon awarded a 'high pay' to those with over ten years' service. At the time of Amey's inspection there were 53 men in the 3rd Battalion eligible for this benefit. By now the armourer Antoine Regnier could claim 35 years' service; Master Kastner the cobbler claimed 13 years and Marc Thionville the tailor, 11 years. Some of the veterans had as much as 25 years' service in 1804. Given the meteoric promotion achieved by some in the revolutionary era, it is sobering to find men who had been with the corps for 20 years still ranking as chasseurs. Literacy was a factor, but as with any organization some men did not feel it necessary to push themselves to the fore.

Although breaking the chronology of this account somewhat, it is interesting to compare Amey's findings with General Mermet's inspection of the same battalion on 18 August 1805. It was less congratulatory in tone. While the men's spirit was 'excellent', Mermet complained there was 'little immobility in the ranks.' The inspector was concerned about the physical qualities of the men he saw: 'Many men are malformed, weak and inappropriate for service in the light infantry.' The battalion was also overspending on shoes, the price they were paying was 'exorbitant' and there were irregularities with the uniform. The officers' coats were tailored individually with non-regulation numbers of buttons.[24] The soldiers' waistcoats were without sleeves, which was against the regulations, although it cut costs and perhaps made for a more comfortable fit. The visors on the shakos were poorly placed, the soldiers' plumes were poorly fastened and got in the way during arms drill. In many cases the packs were being worn too low and were also hindering the men as they opened their cartridge pouches.

Since Amey's inspection the previous October, the 3rd Battalion had received just 65 new conscripts. Why then the change of opinion? Partly, no doubt, down to the inspector. Perhaps Major D'Eslon and Amey had shared a good table together? One strong possibility is that the best of the conscripts had been sent to the two field battalions at Camiers in exchange for those no longer fit for service. This is borne out by some of those proposed for retirement by the inspector: Chasseur Pelet (30) was injured in the left foot by an accident while building the huts at Camiers; Chasseur Deschamps (27) injured his right hand in an accident on board a gunboat. There were a number of others suffering from rheumatism. In each case it was said they could no longer support the fatigues of war.

Of course, ex-soldiers still had a part to play in Napoleon's France. He ordered all soldiers being granted a discharge either through length of service, wounds or infirmity, would go home in a uniform coat in good condition. If the soldier was a sub-officer, carabineer or elite soldier, he would also be allowed to take his sabre home with him. This perk was not an act of charity. Seeing the old soldiers coming home like vagrants would have shaken people's faith in Napoleon.

Some of our old friends in the officer corps were also recommended for a pension by Mermet. Captain Marthe was put forward for retirement at the age of 53. Mermet graciously complimented him on the presentation of his company's accounts and the state of propriety in the barrack rooms he commanded. There was no mention of a note left by General Amey, the previous inspector. Giving his opinion of the officers Amey had said of Marthe: 'Is a little inclined to drink.' Perhaps this is why pleas for promotion were ignored repeatedly? It was time for Marthe to bow out, leaving two young sons enrolled in the regiment.[25]

Another departure was Captain Edme Reboulleau, who heralded from Labassée's home village and was possibly his brother-in-law. Reboulleau had been seriously wounded at Piacenza with a shot through the body and many had feared the wound was mortal. The wound was causing him so much trouble that he asked for retirement at the age of just 31. One character not yet departing was the indomitable Captain Pierre Gros, temporarily given command of the 3rd Company, proudly displaying his legion of honour to the recruits. Relieved of all administrative duties a role had been found for Gros as recruiting officer.

While some careers were ending, others were making steady progress. Mermet recorded two chasseurs being transferred into the Imperial Guard. Despite the trouble which had existed between the Ninth and the Guard, it must be recognized that all good soldiers aspired to join Napoleon's elite corps where service conditions were much better. Chasseur François Vildier, 26 years of age and 1.775m in height, had served in the campaigns since 1800; Chasseur Pierre Antoine Lanthonne, 28 years of age and 1.705m in height, had only served with the army on coast, but had worked previously in the Versailles armaments. The inspector recorded: 'these two servicemen are very young in service to join the Imperial Guard, but they have been asked for by the Colonel of Chasseurs.' The normal requirement for entry in the Guard was *five years of service and two campaigns, with a minimum height of 1.76 metres.* This example demonstrates how, as always, rules were ignored when they proved inconvenient.

———————

Napoleon's coronation took place at Notre Dame Cathedral in Paris on 2 December 1804. Three days later the Emperor awarded new flags to the army. The Ninth sent a deputation down from the coast to assist at the coronation and receive the new standards. Since the Revolution, the Phrygian cap (or liberty bonnet) and Gallic cockerel had been popular French symbols. Napoleon broke with these and chose the Roman eagle as the new national emblem. The eagle standard was made from gilded bronze cast in six parts, and weighed 1.85kg. The eagle's head was inclined to the left and its wings slightly spread. It perched on a plinth with its right talon on a 'spindle of Jupiter' without lightning bolts. The regimental number was displayed on the front and back of the plinth, which was 40mm high and 120mm wide. With plinth, the eagle measured 310mm in height and 255mm from wing tip to wing tip. At the bottom of the plinth was a 60mm socket, into which was affixed a blue staff.

Given the weight of the eagle compared to the traditional pike-head finials, the accompanying flag was considerably reduced in size to 810mm square, approximately half the size of the 1802 model. Napoleon is said to have attached no special significance to this flag, it was the eagle he prized. Even so, its colours were an important reminder of the national colours of the Revolution. The tricolour flag was made of oiled silk and consisted of a central white lozenge with the corner triangles alternately red and blue. The lozenge was charged with golden lettering, which in the Ninth's case displayed the message 'L'EMPEREUR DES FRANÇAIS AU 9e REGIMENT D'INFANTERIE LÉGÈRE' on one side and 'VALEUR ET DISCIPLINE' with the number of the battalion on the other.[26] In the coloured triangles were golden wreaths containing the regimental number. The Ninth received two eagles, one for each of its field battalions.

The ceremony was held on the Champ de Mars in Paris. Huge porticos had been set up on the façade of the École Militaire and in front of these a platform at first-floor level on which Napoleon would sit surrounded by princes and princesses, politicians, the marshals of the empire and other dignitaries and ladies. The balcony was decorated with banners and crowned with eagles. Descending down from the balcony onto the Champ de Mars was a huge staircase on which Colonel Meunier sat with the other colonels of the army and the presidents of the departmental electoral colleges. Meunier held one of the regiment's new eagles. Meunier and his deputation sat there from 6am. The weather was awful. It had been snowing and the rain had brought about a thaw. The Champ de Mars was a sea of slushy mud.

Napoleon set out from the Tuileries at noon. In due course the imperial cortège came into view led by the horse chasseurs of the Imperial Guard and a squadron of Mamelukes, who had remained in French service after the evacuation of Egypt. The emperor and empress went inside the École Militaire and donned their imperial insignia. They climbed out onto the platform and took their thrones. As they came into view there was an artillery salute and a fanfare of trumpets. The remainder of the military delegation formed a large column and marched forward to the steps where their colonels were now stood.

The crowds of onlookers fell silent as Napoleon rose to address the throng. In a loud clear voice he spoke. 'Soldiers, behold your standards! These eagles will always serve you as a rallying point. They will go wherever your emperor may judge their presence necessary for the defence of his throne and of his people. Will you swear to sacrifice your lives in their defence, and to keep them always by your courage on the path to victory? Do you swear it?'

Meunier and the other colonels held their eagles aloft, pointing them towards Napoleon as if taking his blessing. 'We swear it!' the colonels replied. This pledge was repeated in turn by the column of soldiers behind the colonels. Sergeant-Major

Fouquet was one of the deputation standing in the slush. Bursting with pride and his new cross of the Legion of Honour on his chest, it would take more than bad weather to ruin his memory of this day.[27]

But what of the Ninth's precious 1802 colours, the ones Bonaparte had given them at the Tuileries? It is well known that there was an oversight – no plans were formulated for the republican colours each regiment handed in; there was no one to receive them and they ended up discarded to the side of the platform in the pouring rain. The official story is that these colours were retired to the Invalides and were later destroyed in 1814 to prevent them falling into enemy hands. However, at least one of the Ninth's 1802 flags was retained by the regiment, perhaps at the depot as a souvenir. Its story will be told later.

Colonel Meunier, officer of the Legion of Honour was kept busy over the remainder of the winter making plans for his marriage. His fiancée was Laure-Émilie-Félicité David, one of the twin daughters of Jacques-Louis David, an artist and a prominent figure in Napoleon's new court. From the *Tennis Court Oath* of 1789, the pencil sketch of Marie Antoinette on her way to execution and *The Death of Marat*, David's paintings were, and remain, an iconic visual record of the Revolution. He would immortalize the first consul in the same way, with the portrait *Napoleon Crossing the Alps*, showing him mounted on Alexander the Great's horse, Bucephalus. From David's perspective, the up-and-coming, energetic Meunier was an excellent match for his daughter. Napoleon thought so too and gave his blessing to the match. The wedding took place on 28 March 1805 with Napoleon and the Empress Josephine signing the wedding contract.[28]

By marrying David's daughter, Meunier consolidated his position among the social elite. In the process of immortalizing Napoleon, David would also promote his own family in the process. In his painting *The Coronation of Napoleon*, David put himself and family in the viewing gallery immediately above Napoleon's mother looking down over the coronation.[29] More subtly, when painting his *Distribution of the Eagles*, he ensured that the eagle held highest above all others at the centre belongs to the Ninth, his son-in-law's regiment.

Alas, the honeymoon must have been very short-lived. On 20 March the minister of war, Marshal Berthier, sent Ney his embarkation instructions. Dupont's division was to embark on the 'fifth and eighth divisions of gun-sloops, and the ninth and tenth divisions of gun-barges, forming part of the first squadron'.[30] The craft built for the invasion were designed to have a shallow draft to approach close into the shore and be hauled up onto the beach if necessary. The gun-sloops were 20–25m long and had an armament of four 24-pounders and a howitzer; some were large enough to carry 36-pounders. Each had a crew of 22 sailors and could carry a full company of infantry, the larger ones taking up to 200 men. The gunboats resembled small fishing craft and were designed to transport the horses, ammunition and artillery. One gunboat was assigned for the Ninth's baggage.

Ney's troops began practising embarkation drills, one division at a time. Once this process had been perfected, Ney organized a full-scale exercise with his entire corps. Assembled on the beach, each column was placed opposite the boats assigned to it. At this point the men had no idea whether it was an exercise or the real thing. The companies were formed in sections. A signal gun fired. The generals and their staff dismounted and put themselves at the head of the troops they were to lead. There was a drum roll and the men sheathed their bayonets. When the drum roll ceased, a second signal gun fired. The generals gave the order to embark. A third gun fired. The command to march in column was given and the men surged forward onto their respective boats. Within ten and a half minutes the process was complete and 20,000 men were embarked, wondering what awaited them on the English shore. Another signal gun was fired and the drummers beat 'to arms'. The soldiers quickly formed up on the decks of their gunboats and barges. Another signal gun was fired. Believing this was the signal to raise anchor, thousands of voices spontaneously cried out '*Vive l'Empereur!*' They were bitterly disappointed when told it was the order to disembark. Thirteen minutes later the grumbling soldiers were back on the beach formed in line.

They practised assault landings in a novel way. The soldiers of the division would form up on land in groups, each representing a boatload of soldiers. They would pretend they were just reaching the shore and as their imaginary boats struck the invisible sands, the drummers would beat the charge. The voltigeurs would 'leap' from the craft and rush to engage the enemy forming a protective cordon behind which their comrades would disembark and form up.[31] Ney was extremely satisfied with these preparations. All they needed was for the French navy to lure the British fleet out of the Channel and the invasion could begin.

On 26 June Ney wrote to Dupont informing him he was expecting the emperor to review the camps. He ordered Dupont to have the regiments under his orders dressed as smartly as possible and to ensure that each soldier had all the regulation equipment. Indulging in a little fantasy, Ney said he wanted everyone from the rank of captain down to be dressed with white breeches, gaiters and collars; with the colonels and their staff dressed in white breeches, riding boots and silver spurs.[32] 'My intention,' he added, 'is also that the sub-officers and the soldiers of light infantry have a pair of white gaiters, if the Council of Administration can meet this expense without being too much embarrassed.'

On 8 July more detailed orders arrived, this time from General Dutaillis, Ney's chief of staff. The minister of war had made a preliminary inspection of the troops and found little uniformity between the different divisions of the army. To clarify what was expected in future, detailed guidance was provided. The instruction stated that all the troops in each company should be lined up by length of service, with the officers placed on the extreme right. Before the inspection began the company was to be inspected by the sergeant-major, then successively by the captain, the battalion commander, the colonel, the general of brigade and, finally, the general of division.

When the dignitary arrived, all the officers were to salute by raising their épées to the shoulder. The captain should present the company register with his left hand. If a roll-call was asked for, the soldiers called should reply in a loud voice 'Present'. The captain would explain the case for any absentees. As the review took place, the captain and sergeant-major were to follow level with the dignitary making the inspection, on the reverse side of the company. The colonel and the surgeon-major were to follow directly behind the dignitary with the respective battalion commander, adjutant-major and adjutant sub-officer.

The musicians, drummers, voltigeur cornetists, fifers and sappers were instructed to sling their musketoons over their backs with bayonets fixed. The musicians were to hold their instrument in hand; the drummers to have their drums ready to be beaten; the cornetists with their instrument over the left arm; fifers holding their fifes in the right hand; and sappers their axe on their right shoulder, the blade facing outwards. If the dignitary asked to see inside the men's haversacks, the captain was to come to the front and centre of the company and give the following orders: 'Attention – Platoon! About face! Order arms! Ground arms! Face front! About face! Ground packs!' He would then say in a loud voice: 'Place your effects by the regulation and have your pay books to hand!'

The soldiers' linens and footwear was to be placed on the ground in front of each man in the following manner:

i.   The linen distribution bag
ii. The second pair of shoes with the soles turned upwards and the spare gaiters (grey, black or white)
iii. The stockings of thread and wool
iv. The shirts and on either side the pocket handkerchiefs and the black and white collars
v.   The hide haversack
vi. The man's petty equipment (shoe buckles, turn-screw, worm, two spare flints wrapped in their leads, a bag of hair powder, brushes, etc.)

The men's vent picks were to be attached to the third button on the lapel and passed under the cross-belt during the inspection. Water canteens were to be suspended by a hide belt over the left shoulder and on the right-hand side, placed over the cross-belts. Each man was to have a small phial of glass or white metal placed in his cartridge box filled with oil for keeping his musket in working order. All the men's weapons, equipment and uniform were to be labelled with the initial letter of the company and the man's number. If, God forbid, a soldier wanted to present a complaint during the review, he was to present arms and offer the dignitary a written petition with his right hand, at the same time explaining verbally the cause of his complaint. Drummers were to present complaints by giving a single beat of the drum.

As the date of the inspection approached, the main concern became Ney's order to have the men in white gaiters. Colonel Darricau of the 32nd Line wrote to Dupont on 7 August in something of a panic. The inspection was to be held the following day. He informed Dupont that the regiment had experienced great difficulty obtaining white linen for the gaiters. He had 30 tailors working on the gaiters and indicated each worker could make one pair of gaiters per day. At this rate it would take two months to manufacture the required amount and he had been given less than a month's warning. Worse, there were other items the tailors had to work on. He was therefore faced with a dilemma. The officers had all been issued with white gaiters, but the men behind them would have to be in black. Darricau therefore ordered his officers to wear boots for the review.[33] Meunier must have been in a similar predicament, judging from the irate post-review letter Ney sent Dupont on 8 August 1805:

> The colonels of 9th and 32nd regiments are, my dear General, the only ones in the army who found it impossible to execute the orders which I gave so the corps could be presented to His Majesty uniformly dressed. They could at least have had you warn me earlier of this.[34]

Ney asked Dupont to instruct the two colonels to make up any shortfall in white gaiters as soon as possible by coating their existing grey gaiters with a mixture of white dye and glue. They could get the recipe for this concoction from the colonel of the 59th Line.

Given they were about to mount the largest seaborne invasion ever attempted, Ney's concern about white gaiters may have seemed somewhat frivolous. In the previous war they had fought and been victorious in bare feet and rags. Fortunately for Meunier, all talk of white gaiters was soon forgotten and it is unlikely they ever complied with the request. Napoleon was at Boulogne waiting for his fleet to arrive. If the French navy could just keep the Channel clear for five days he would have an army of 150,000 men in south-east England. The waiting was beginning to irritate him and his impatience grew when British sails were observed off the coast.

Napoleon ordered his troops to go out to fight them. Therefore, on 12 August, Ney earmarked 3,000 men for the task, including the two divisions of gun-sloops manned by the Ninth. Quite how our intrepid chasseurs would fare against British warships we will never know, for the weather was atrocious. A fresh westerly wind whipped up the Channel making it impossible to commit the flat-bottomed boats to the open sea. Instead they bobbed around in the harbour until 5.30am when they were ordered to come back ashore. Ney saw his men had spent a 'rough night' out in the harbour, but informed Napoleon that they were more concerned at not having had the opportunity to engage the enemy.[35]

Still they waited 'minute by minute' for news of the navy and the order to set sail. On 21 August an embarkation was ordered at 1.30pm. Again Ney's troops clambered onto their boats only to be informed that it was a drill. The army was like a coiled spring, a dart aimed at the heart of the perfidious British beast. Everything was prepared for the invasion. All the artillery was loaded, the rations were stowed and the hospital equipment placed on board. The army could not be kept at this level of readiness forever without boredom and malcontent setting in. At last, a week later at 5pm on 27 August 1805, a courier arrived with urgent orders for the division. Dupont broke open the seal to the message and scanned the handwritten message. Around him his staff waited impatiently for news. Should they have the men prepare to embark? No. There had been a change of plan. In the morning the division was to make all speed for the Rhine frontier.[36] The Austrians were advancing through Germany supported by the Russians. There was not a moment to lose.

WAR ON THE
DANUBE

On 19 August 1805, nine days before setting off for the Rhine, a new officer was posted to the Ninth. Aged 32, Adjutant-Major Maurice Godet arrived under something of a cloud. A soldier since August 1792, Godet had fought a myriad of combats and had been seriously wounded when an enemy cavalry regiment rode over him. Godet considered himself lucky to have received just five sabre wounds in the affair, one of which had nearly removed his nose. He had been to Malta and Egypt in 1798, serving in Desaix's division, but was struck with ophthalmia and ordered back to Europe. His eyesight recovered in time for the Marengo campaign serving under General Chabran, and Godet was praised for leading a column against Fort Bard.

Godet's problems began in the spring of 1802. When voting in the plebiscite on the life consulate, Godet voted against the idea, signing his name in the 'no' column (there was no such thing as a secret ballot). In total 8,271 Frenchmen shared Godet's opinion; but over three and a half million voters did not. Returning from Italy, Godet went to Ostend where the 21st Light formed part of Marshal Davout's corps. He was rather expecting high things of his career, but when the colonelcy of the 21st Light came up, the position went to another man, Jean Joseph Tarayre. The new colonel took an instant dislike to Godet in whom he saw a jealous rival. Tarayre recommended Godet for a transfer, describing him as 'dangerous' and accusing him of turning the officers against their commander.

When the question of Napoleon's coronation came up in 1804, Godet adopted a more prudent stance. The officers of his regiment were gathered together by the colonel and told the vote would be held the following day. To avoid a crisis of conscience Godet decided to abstain, keeping a long-standing dinner engagement with the officers of the 51st Line. Over lunch the discussion was about the vote. Godet was convinced that all the captains he dined with would have come out against the idea of a hereditary empire if there had been no influence on the vote. The elder officers had won their positions under the banners of the republic, fighting against monarchs and tyranny. At a separate meeting with Godet, Colonel Magnier of the 13th Light put it succinctly: 'For the first consul, they'd pass through fire – for an emperor, no!'[1] However, when the captains of the 51st Line were called in by their colonel to vote, each returned with their heads bowed admitting they had voted *yes*. What other choice did they have? Godet became anxious. What would it mean for his own career if he was the only officer in the 21st Light not to endorse the plebiscite? He returned to his own camp and signed the document with the other officers without saying a word.

Unfortunately the damage had already been done. At dinner, Colonel Tarayre had told Marshal Davout one of his officers was refusing to vote and was causing trouble in the regiment. The following day Davout inspected the 21st Light and led Godet for a little walk. Godet was on one side of the marshal, the colonel on the other. Davout came straight to the point and accused Godet of not signing and seeking to cause an uprising. Godet denied it. Davout then asked what Godet had been doing in the *Café de Commerce*, the supposed base of his seditious operations. Godet answered he had never heard of such a place let alone set foot in it. The marshal looked at the colonel and asked if he had singled out the wrong man? Somewhat humiliated by the affair the colonel lowered his head and confirmed Godet had indeed given his signature. Davout gave Godet a brief discourse on the dangers of political clubs, tapped him on the shoulder to emphasize his point and went on his way.

This incident clearly indicated the colonel was out to get Godet. The tension increased when Godet learned the colonel was trying to promote the most junior captain over his head to a vacant battalion commander's post. Captain Brémond had only been a sergeant-major when they went to Egypt and Godet snottily dismissed him a 'courtesan'. In order to curry favour with the colonel, Brémond challenged Godet to a duel. Godet readily accepted. At the appointed time and place the two parties met outside the camp. Godet had been in action many times and had been called out to a duel once before. On that occasion sabres had been demanded as the weapon of choice. It was early in his career and Godet had only ever held a sword while on parade. He had certainly never frequented a master-at-arms' fencing school. Nevertheless, Godet swished and parried the sword around as if an expert, so much so his adversary got cold feet and offered conciliation. Perhaps this trick would work again? Through his seconds, Godet asked for sabres. However Brémond refused saying he had damaged his wrist in Egypt and would be at a disadvantage. Duelling etiquette would not permit such a disadvantage, so pistols were chosen.

As the two men prepared, a third party asked for conciliation. Godet rebuked him fiercely. While the seconds loaded the pistols, Godet asked what rules would be followed? Brémond's seconds asked for a distance of 40 paces between the two adversaries. Godet was furious. At that range there would be so many attempts to hit one another the garrison would be alerted and would put a stop to it. Perhaps this was Brémond's plan? Godet angrily recommended 'three paces, blindfolded' instead. This would have been suicidally close, so the seconds eventually agreed for the two men to advance towards two hats placed on the ground, ten paces apart. When they reached the hats, they could fire at will. With mounting tension, both men advanced and arrived at the hats simultaneously. Both men raised their pistols to eye level and took aim. Brémond was fastest to the trigger, with Godet firing a fraction later. Godet heard his adversary's pistol ball whistle past his head and in turn watched as Brémond crumpled to the ground mortally wounded.

In the fallout from the duel it was clear Godet could not remain in the regiment. A solution was found and he was sent to the camp at Camiers to join the Ninth. In so doing he replaced an adjutant-major described to Godet as 'quarrelsome, brutal and poorly looked on by the officer corps'. This officer had fought a duel with a brother officer whom he had seriously wounded. The latter had been considered the wronged party and so justice was not seen to have been done. The adjutant-major was forced into making the transfer, conveniently creating a vacancy for Godet.[2]

Arriving at Camiers, Godet presented himself to Meunier. He was frank with Meunier and told him this was not an ideal situation for him, at his rank, to be moved sideways rather than to be promoted. In reference to his duelling episode and the sour end to his time with the 21st Light, Godet asked Meunier not to judge him on prejudices, but on his manner of service: 'Be at ease,' Meunier reassured him. 'Serve well and, as you do, shall be done unto you.'

Godet was pleasantly surprised to find a friendly face in the Ninth. The commander of 1st Battalion was 44-year-old Jean Marie Régeau, who had replaced Kuhmann. Régeau had been quartermaster treasurer of the 21st Light and was well known to Godet. His old comrade overwhelmed Godet with congratulations and expressed great happiness at their serving together again. When Godet used the formal address of '*vous*', Régeau was indignant and insisted he should use the familiar '*tu*' except when in front of the men.[3]

Godet learned a great deal about his new comrades on the march to the Rhine. Nine days after Godet was posted to the corps, on 28 August 1805, the Ninth marched off to do battle with Austria, with 1,850 men under arms, approximately 800 of which were veterans of previous campaigns. During the first stage of the march, to Arras, Godet witnessed Adjutant-Major Huguin drunk, lying on his back on the side of the road 'snoring like a clergyman after dinner' as the regiment marched past.[4] Then as the regiment marched through the Champagne region, the men drank themselves silly on the regional produce. Reflecting on the regiment later in life, Godet penned the following passage:

> It was such a brave regiment the 9th Light Infantry; the officers were brave; the soldiers were brave. But, these qualities were tarnished by a great number of officers, and some of the most influential captains, by their tendency to abuse drink, especially brandy. I can still see Captain Gabriel leaving his bivouac, looking through haggard eyes and stupefied, mounting his horse only then to fall from the opposite side, with the soldiers shouting: 'he's up, he's not up, etc …' and, on another occasion, Captain Aubry of the 2nd Battalion's carabineers whom we were obliged to leave stretched out on the side of the road while the corps marched on the enemy. Indeed! This capital fault, which could have had the most damaging consequences and could have led to a serious suffering of discipline, never had that result or influenced the spirit of the soldiers. That corps had an admirable spirit![5]

As the march through France continued, there was another example of the Ninth's admirable esprit de corps. By 1805 the field battalions were composed of a great many men from the Vosges region in eastern France. The regiment was going to pass very close to their homes and, as Godet put it, there was not one of them who did not want to see 'his parents, his cows, his oak trees and his valleys' one last time before going into action. For several days Meunier and his senior officers debated what to do. If they granted leave to everyone, the regiment would be considerably reduced. If no leave was granted, there was the risk that men would go home anyway and, having deserted, would be extremely unlikely to return. When it was Godet's turn to express his opinion, he advised Meunier to grant leave to everyone and to appeal to the men's honour and loyalty. When the moment arrived Meunier authorized the company captains to grant leave to everyone who asked for it, with the condition they returned in time for a review at Nancy, the day after the regiment was scheduled to arrive.

With the regiment reduced to fewer than 200 men, Meunier was extremely concerned. This was his first command and his reputation would be destroyed if his men did not return. His anxiety grew worse at Nancy when hardly any came back. More returned by Lunéville and at Saverne the regiment was 'respectable' again. By the time it reached the Rhine, only three men were missing, all of whom would catch up before the first action. Meunier was jubilant and mightily relieved. Spirit in the regiment was very high.[6]

While the men were scattered across the country lanes of eastern France, the officers had taken a liberty of their own. After the regulation of 24 June 1792, soldiers of all rank were required to wear their hair long in a 'queue', rolled up in a black ribbon and held in place with a pin.[7] This regulation fixed the maximum length of the queue at eight French inches, but Godet's reached down to the small of his back in a style known as a 'queue à la Frédéric', in reference to Prussia's Frederick the Great. It was, Godet admitted, a useless appendage. Since Egypt, Napoleon had worn his hair cropped short in the Roman style, or *à la Titus*. This fashion was spreading and for several days, as the officers supped together at inns along the route, the subject of their hairstyles came up. Although Meunier was present at these discussions, he would not give an opinion one way or the other. Although all the officers agreed the queues should go, without Meunier's approval no one would take the plunge. At last, when the regiment stopped at Toul and the men were dismissed, Godet said, 'My faith, I'll take the risk, whatever comes my way. Adieu, long queue!'[8] As he said this, Godet had his eyes on the colonel, who remained impassive. Godet took this for a tacit approval and, by the time they marched off, his queue was a souvenir in his pocket. When the regiment arrived at Nancy, all the officers followed suit and had their queues cut off, Meunier included.

On 25 September the regiment arrived at Lauterbourg where Dupont's field artillery was waiting for him. There were 200 gunners manning two 12-pounders, four eight-pounders, two four-pounders and four howitzers, plus associated limbers, horse teams and ammunition caissons. The division had also been joined at Hagenau by 400 blades from the 1st Hussars, old friends from Marengo. The Ninth had a field strength of 1,850 men (less the three still scurrying along to catch up); the 32nd and 96th a field strength of 1,700 men each. In total Dupont commanded 5,850 men of the 1st Division of Ney's VI Corps.

Ney's engineers had thrown a boat bridge over the Rhine below Lauterbourg opposite the village of Durlach. The passage into German lands was marked with great ceremony. The entire corps was in full dress uniform with oak-leaf garlands on their hats symbolizing their previous victories over the Austrians. Dupont's division led the way with repeated cries of 'Vive l'Empereur!' The division's vanguard was composed of 1st Squadron, 1st Hussars, with the first company of voltigeurs behind. They were followed by a four-pounder gun and a howitzer. This vanguard was followed by the remainder of the Ninth's 1st Battalion and then the 2nd, with the second voltigeurs at the rear. A detachment of ten gendarmes followed, watching out for stragglers. The 32nd Line came next followed by the remainder of the artillery. Behind these came the 96th Line led by Colonel Barrois. Behind Dupont came the infantry divisions of General Loison and Malher, the second brigade of which was commanded by General Mathieu Labassée. General Tilly followed with a brigade of cavalry.

At the tail of the column, the corps' park clanked and trundled forwards. This consisted of the wagons containing the headquarters equipment, the canteens, medical supplies, engineers' tools and caisson after caisson of ammunition. With the park came the baggage of the corps. In this convoy was a sergeant 'baggage master' and 12 chasseurs from the Ninth guarding their regimental wagons containing the officers' portmantles. Finally at the very tail of VI Corps was a rearguard of four companies from the 59th Line. Let it never be said Napoleon's armies went to war unimpeded by baggage.[9]

The Ninth was directed eastwards through the Black Forest, passing Ettlingen and Pforzheim, then turning south-east towards Stuttgart where they arrived on 1 October. The marches began to feel tiring and long. Rations were scarce, but potatoes were in season and so the French soldiers were like blight. At Stuttgart the governor refused to open the city gates. Drums were heard inside the town and the garrison was seen to take up arms. Ney brought up artillery for a show of force. At the same time Dupont ordered the 32nd Line to prepare for an assault and a detachment went forward led by the regiment's sappers, axes at the ready. With the remainder of Dupont's division arriving and a few cannon balls fired at the town, the governor finally opened the gates lest the city be taken by force. Once inside, the Frenchmen were welcomed warmly and two days of rest were permitted. Some believed the resistance had only been a token gesture and the elector of Württemberg was really a supporter of Napoleon.

On 3 October Dupont quit Stuttgart and marched in the direction of Oberesslingen following the River Neckar eastward through Göppingen to Heidenheim on the River Brenz. Reaching the river on 5 October the division bivouacked on the heights overlooking the Brenz and had a day of rest. Here they turned left and headed north-east to Neresheim before turning southward and falling down on the Danube valley, arriving at Höchstädt on 7 October. Here the Ninth bivouacked behind the town on the battlefield of Blenheim where the French had lost to Marlborough in 1704. The purpose of these long and complicated manoeuvres was that Napoleon was repeating his strategy of 1800. The Austrians were drawn forwards into the Black Forest by various French feints. While the Austrian General Mack advanced westwards, Napoleon's army swept in a clockwise arc north of the Black Forest and down to the Danube behind him. As at Marengo five years before, the Austrians were cut off from Vienna. Ney's VI Corps now formed the right flank of the Grand Army, followed by the corps of Lannes, Soult, Davout, Marmont and Bernadotte. Napoleon hoped the Austrians would now turn eastwards in a bid to recover their communications with Vienna and in so doing, run into the Grand Army. Napoleon set up his base of operations at Augsburg; Soult was ordered south to Landsberg while Bernadotte and Davout were ordered east towards Munich to guard against an approaching Russian army under Kutuzov. Ney, Lannes and Murat were sent westward towards Ulm to make contact with the Austrians and bring about a decisive battle. The snare now appeared to be sprung. It was all so much like Marengo five years before; and just like Marengo, the Austrians reacted by doing something Napoleon did not expect.

On 8 October Murat and Lannes were on the south bank of the Danube while Ney's corps remained on the north bank. Dupont set out in the early afternoon heading for Bissingen-Ob-Lontal, which he reached at 3am. It was a dreadful day to be on the road. The weather broke and the French were drenched by icy rain. Stragglers began falling behind and at Stotzingen around a hundred of them took the wrong fork and ran into an Austrian forward post on the Languenau road. Despite being without officers, the stragglers united and opened fire on the Austrians, retiring northwards in good order on the village of Stetten where they rallied with some other soldiers who had dropped out of the march from fatigue. The Austrians tried to force their way into the village but the French defence held. As the Austrians retreated the stragglers forgot their exhaustion and hurried to catch up with the rest of the division.

At daybreak on 9 October, Dupont sent a battalion of the Ninth south-west with 30 hussars and a four-pounder gun under the command of Squadron Commander Jean Louis de Crabbé, one of Ney's aides-de-camp. They encountered the Austrians on the plain between Languenau and Albeck. After reporting their find to Dupont, Crabbé attacked without waiting for support. At first they did well, pushing the Austrians back to the outskirts of Albeck. Crabbé then paused, waiting for the rest of the division before capturing the village. The Austrians mounted a counter-attack, knocking out the French four-pounder and pushing the Frenchmen back to a wood to the north of the village. A hussar was killed, along with two men from the Ninth. Three more chasseurs were wounded in the action, the first victims of the campaign.

Dupont arrived before Albeck at 6pm and formed the Ninth in column on the road. The general dispersed the two voltigeur companies either side of the road, supported by two squadrons of hussars. The voltigeurs set out on the flanks, with the column marching swiftly in the centre. Watching this dense mass of troops heading towards them, the Austrians in Albeck quickly cleared out under the cover of darkness. In the darkness the two voltigeur companies entered the village from opposite sides and opened fire on one another. Fortunately no one was wounded.

Throughout the day Dupont's men had heard heavy firing on their left. Malher's division had been ordered to seize the bridge over the Danube at Günzburg. After a sharp action, Malher passed over to the right bank. The following morning Dupont sent out patrols to probe the Austrian positions. Although there were several sightings, no action developed so the division spent 10 October resting as much as the ugly weather would allow.

Meanwhile Napoleon was weighing up his options. He believed the Austrians were planning to escape from Ulm by marching along the River Iller to the south of the city. Napoleon ordered Ney to press forward and surround Ulm. On the evening of 10 October Ney ordered Dupont to close in on Ulm from the north and summon the commander there to surrender.

Support for this advance would come from a division of foot dragoons under Baraguey d'Hilliers located at Stotzingen. These foot dragoons were an unhappy lot. When planning the invasion of England, Napoleon had decided some cavalry units would have to find their mounts on the other side of the Channel. There had then been neither time nor resources to provide them with horses before marching against the Austrians. In response the dragoons grumbled everywhere they went. They inspired little confidence.

At 8am on 11 October Dupont received another instruction from Ney. The marshal recommended Dupont obtain ladders to scale the walls of Ulm. He optimistically described the Austrians as being struck with terror and reported they were retiring on Biberach and the Upper Tyrol. His instructions concluded: '... It is therefore likely that Archduke Ferdinand will have left only a weak garrison at Ulm, with orders to hold on until the last extremity; but our preparations and our threats will doubtless decide the commandant to surrender without running a risk of a fight.'[10] Dupont's division marched off at 11am. The Ninth had 1,763 men under arms. The remainder of the force consisted of the 32nd Line (1,662 men), 96th Line (1,721 men), the 15th and 17th dragoons (673 horses) and the 1st Hussars (375 horses), although half of the hussars were away on reconnaissance. The artillery and train counted for another 250 men, with 11 guns (two 12-pounders, six eight-pounders, two four-pounders and one howitzer). One of the four-pounders was still out of action from the skirmish at Albeck, but it was compensated for by the addition of three howitzers attached to the light cavalry.[11] The reserve force under Baraguey d'Hilliers consisted of another 4,500 men and ten guns. However these forces were spread out over a considerable distance and would take far longer to come to Dupont's aid than Ney had anticipated.

There were clues that something was amiss when intelligence reports arrived from Dupont's cavalry patrols. Dupont learned that the Austrians occupied Elchingen and Thalfingen, and were on his left and sending patrols out on his right towards Dornstadt. Some captured Austrian officers assured Dupont that their entire army had bivouacked the night before to the north of Ulm and were already formed in order of battle in that direction. Dupont had been told the Austrians were retreating southwards and to expect light resistance. The intelligence suggested the opposite might be true.

Unknown to the French, the Austrians had decided to escape to Bohemia using the routes to the north of Ulm. Their audacious plan would see them escape the French noose, cut Napoleon's own lines of communication to the north of the Danube and effect a junction with the Russians. In their plan, the Austrian advanced guard under Prince Ferdinand would quit Ulm and head towards Dornstadt. Once the advanced guard had cleared the route, the remainder of the Austrian army was ready to follow that same evening. If successful this plan would severely embarrass Napoleon, if not cost him the campaign.

Passing through the woods beyond Albeck at around 1pm, the Ninth arrived at the hamlet of Haslach a league and a half (6km) from Ulm. Dupont looked out across the fields and realized the sum of his fears. The Austrians were present in great strength and on the march. Looking down a gentle valley to the right of the road, the French could see the enemy advanced guard, composed of 400–500 men, with their right supported by a wood. Behind this line, rising up towards the village of Jungingen was a square formed by a similar number of men with a considerable reserve crowning the heights in front of the village.

The Ninth's voltigeur companies were engaged and quickly forced back. The Austrians began deploying artillery to bombard Dupont's column. There was little time to prepare for action. The Ninth was ordered to execute a turn to the right, changing their front and deploying in line formation along the Ulm road facing the Austrians. The artillery was deployed to the right of the Ninth and began returning fire on the Austrian guns. The 32nd executed a similar change of front and took position behind the artillery. The 1st Hussars were deployed to cover the Ninth's open flank on the left while the 96th Line remained in the rear as a reserve.

The Austrian artillery fire was directed principally on the French battery, but the majority of the victims were in the 32nd Line standing behind in support.[12] While this artillery duel was engaged, the Austrians directed several columns of infantry on the French right flank preceded by a strong force of cavalry. Dupont committed the 96th Line to the right of the 32nd. On the extreme right a company of chasseurs under Captain Balson was posted with a detachment of 17th Dragoons to cover a small wood the Austrians appeared to be attempting to turn.

As the Austrian deployment progressed Dupont had to make a quick decision. If he remained on the defensive he would be overwhelmed by superior Austrian firepower. If he tried to retreat he would find himself harried by hordes of enemy cavalry. Dupont therefore decided on a third option – a ridiculously dangerous option – but perhaps his only chance of avoiding disaster. With the Albeck wood behind his back, the Austrians could not be sure whether Dupont was alone or if his division was screening the advance of a much larger force coming up behind. If Dupont acted boldly; acted as if he were expecting reinforcements to arrive in the near future, the Austrians might not press their advantage and Dupont could gain time to disengage under the cover of night. To sustain the morale of their troops, the French officers went along the line telling the men they would soon be supported by Ney and Lannes who would arrive by the bridge at Elchingen.[13] Of course this statement was untrue. The only hope they had of support was the foot dragoons at Stotzingen over 20km away. Dupont dispatched a message to General Baraguey d'Hilliers urging him to press his march and come up in support.

These dispositions made, Dupont rode over to Colonel Meunier and informed him it was his intention to charge the Austrian line. It was an exhilarating moment. The drummers beat the charge and both battalions of the Ninth swept forward in line, musicians and all, descending into the valley like a torrent. The men stomped their way through hedgerows and bushes, down to the bottom of the valley and up the other side, heading straight for the nearest Austrian corps.

Without firing a shot the Ninth presented its bayonets to the Austrian line, which was overthrown onto the square behind. A few shots were fired from this formation before the Ninth descended on it. Soon the Frenchmen were pell-mell with their Austrian adversaries. The square broke up and turned on its reserve. This third line at least attempted some defence, but was still swept away in the charge.

The Ninth entered the village of Jungingen on the other side of the valley. There were Austrians everywhere: in the houses, alleyways and the orchards outside the village. Godet watched as his battalion broke up around him and became scattered into groups. If a soldier saw a group of Austrians he would shout 'this way, charge!'[14] The nearest group of drummers would beat the charge and race off after him, followed by a mob of chasseurs. House by house the Austrians were evicted or captured and the village slowly cleared. Dupont ordered the 96th Line forward to support the Ninth and soon Barrois' men were helping round up some 2,000 prisoners captured by the light infantrymen. These were disarmed and escorted back to the 32nd Line, which had remained in reserve supporting the artillery. The Austrian prisoners were then formed into platoons and incorporated into the French line, so as – from a distance – to give the impression of a formidable reserve.[15]

On the left of the line Colonel Darricau took a battalion of the 32nd to defend the road from a force of Austrian cavalry advancing in that direction. Dupont ordered General Sahuc to attack the enemy cavalry with his brigade of dragoons. The 15th Dragoons formed the first line with the 17th directly behind. The 15th charged and pushed back a force of Austrian horsemen. In turn the 15th were charged by twice their number of Austrians and retreated. The 17th came up in support and drove their assailants away. Seeing Jungingen in French hands behind them, the Austrian cavalry retreated lest they become cut off.

Meanwhile, Meunier put himself at the head of his 2nd Battalion and pushed out beyond Jungingen to see what lay beyond. He found himself facing a mass of enemy troops that he estimated to be 25,000 strong. There was nothing he could do in the face of such numbers and immediately fell back on the village, preparing for its defence. Before long the Austrians arrived in force, fusillading the village. The light infantrymen returned fire from the cover of the buildings and from behind walls, but eventually the Austrians charged and drove the light infantrymen out and took some prisoners. The Ninth rallied and recaptured the village, supported by the 96th Line. As more Austrians arrived a fire-fight raged around the village, and it changed hands again through the course of the afternoon.[16] At one point in the action, Sergeant-Major Fouquet stood clinging onto the eagle for dear life as the flag's silk was torn to shreds by a hail of shot. The pole was struck and before long 2nd Battalion's standard was cut into three pieces. Miraculously Fouquet survived and somehow kept the standard aloft for his comrades to rally round. He was later made an officer for his gallantry under fire.[17]

While the struggle for Jungingen ensued, attention focused on the French right. Fourteen squadrons of Austrian cuirassiers commanded by General Schwartzenberg threw themselves against a detachment of the 17th Dragoons. Captain Balson of the Ninth formed his company of chasseurs into a square and was surrounded by two squadrons of Austrian cavalry. As the Austrians stood off, Balson had his men drag a dozen wounded French dragoons into the middle of his little square. For three hours he was cut off from any support. Meanwhile, four companies of the 2nd Battalion of the 32nd were directed to the wood on the right to prevent the Austrians from turning Dupont's position. Here the Frenchmen found the remains of a redoubt dating from the time of Moreau's campaigns in Germany. They quickly occupied it and used its ditches to their advantage. The remainder of the two French dragoon regiments also made a charge on this side. This time they entered into a general pell-mell combat which spilled into the woods.

As the Austrians began to realize Dupont's men were unsupported they became emboldened. Fighting around the redoubt, the 32nd Line lost contact with the rest of the division. Meunier abandoned Jungingen in the face of a determined Austrian push. Over 150 soldiers were taken prisoner. Some of the wounded were abandoned in the rush; others were cut off inside the buildings and captured.[18] As the Austrians secured the village, Meunier retreated back across the valley, surrounding his wounded with the regiment formed in a square to better resist the enemy cavalry. Everywhere the French were hard-pressed, but the Austrians seemed unable to deal a killer blow. They too had been surprised by the ferocity of the action.

By 5pm the sun had set and both sets of opponents began thinking about the approaching night. An hour later the fighting was over and both sides regrouped on their respective sides of the battlefield. Dupont's thoughts turned to securing his wounded and withdrawing to Albeck. Out in the field a number of guns had been dismounted by Austrian cannon balls and had to be abandoned. Horse teams had been killed and everywhere the slush of snow and rain made it difficult to recover the surviving pieces. In the darkness and haste to escape, a 12-pounder turned over in a ditch. The same thing happened to an eight-pounder. Pushing back on Albeck the other 12-pounder also turned over into a ditch. Dupont's artillery was therefore reduced to four six-inch howitzers and a damaged four-pounder.

More bad news awaited the division at Albeck. During the fighting the Austrian cavalry had carried on into the French rear, seized the baggage and pillaged the park. The officer in charge of the park panicked and rather than forming the wagons into a barricade, had abandoned them in a dash for safety. Twenty-one artillery caissons had been lost; along with six infantry caissons and four peasant carts loaded with infantry cartridges. With the wagons, the officers lost the portmantles containing their private possessions and Dupont lost all his charts. More crucially the division lost its medical supplies, which must have made caring for the wounded extremely challenging.[19]

Dupont's men could rightly feel aggrieved at having been left to face the Austrian army alone without support. The finger of suspicion was quickly pointed at Baraguey d'Hilliers' foot dragoons. Ney had ordered them to Albeck to support Dupont, but they had missed the entire battle as, due to the lack of provisions and awful weather, the division had spread out their bivouacs and consequently had taken longer to assemble before setting out to support Dupont, only reaching Albeck at 4pm. Approaching Albeck, Baraguey d'Hilliers' division ran into a chaotic mixture of wagons, soldiers and 'dismayed women' who had been chased out of Albeck by the Austrian cavalry. Everyone spoke of defeat, of Dupont being surrounded, of his artillery being taken, of his cavalry being overwhelmed. By the time the foot dragoons passed through Albeck it was 7pm. As they did so they encountered 'the debris' of Dupont's division on the plateau outside the village, withdrawing from the battlefield.

After the battle Dupont sent Ney a report on the battle: 'I can express to you, all the admiration which the valour of our troops inspired in me. The result of the battle attests none are more daring and devoted. 5,100 men fought for four hours an army of 25,000 and beat it completely.'[20] Dupont admitted 600 Frenchmen had been killed or wounded. The Ninth had lost eight officers wounded, including both voltigeur captains, Jean Janin (1st Voltigeurs) and Simon Paul Bruyère (2nd Voltigeurs). In addition captains Bernard and Mittour; lieutenants Bonneau, Donot, Paulet, Vadel and Garouste; and Sub-Lieutenant Lambert were also wounded.[21] Of the men, ten had been killed outright in action; 125 wounded had been recovered from the battlefield and 171 were taken prisoner (including 34 wounded).[22] Among the wounded being carried away that dark and miserable night was Vosgian Thomas Matouillot from Sandaucourt in the Vosges department. Just two days shy of his 23rd birthday Matouillot had captured an Austrian flag during the battle before receiving a gunshot wound. He would later receive the Legion of Honour for this feat. In the same action, a hero of old, Jean Piessevaux, was shot in the right thigh during the battle. Three of the regiment's musicians were taken prisoner in the action along with little Hervé Cannue, a 21-year-old drummer in the 2nd Battalion, just 1.45m tall (4ft 9in.). These losses left the Ninth with a potential strength of 1,442 men that evening, although many would have been away from the ranks assisting their wounded comrades.

Dupont claimed to have taken 4,000 prisoners, four guns and two flags. In truth any claim of victory was optimistic, but Dupont had achieved his principal goal – survival. He had been badly misinformed by his superiors about what to expect and had been lucky to hold out until nightfall. Just how out of touch his commanders were was made abundantly clear after the battle when Dupont received a new order from Marshal Ney. It instructed him that all the operations around Ulm had been placed under the command of Prince Murat by order of the emperor. In his wisdom Murat had ordered the concentration of all the French forces on the right bank of the Danube to deliver the final blow to the enemy. Dupont was therefore ordered to find a crossing at either Günzburg or Gundelfingen and leave behind a reconnaissance force of one battalion of the Ninth and two squadrons of the 1st Hussars. Baraguey d'Hilliers was also ordered to conform to these orders and evacuate the left bank. There was no time to reason with these orders as it was clear no assistance would be coming from Ney in the morning and there was every chance the Austrians would be back in force. Dupont had very little artillery left and he had lost his ammunition reserves. There was nothing for it but to make for safety, even if it meant uncovering the French lines of communication.

The following morning the division set off for the Danube, leaving a squadron of hussars on the heights of Albeck to screen the movement from the Austrians and protect the evacuation of the wounded. Although Dupont claimed a victory the previous day, his men were jumpy. No one had come to help the day before and they had all seen how numerous the Austrian army was.

Passing through Languenau their fears gave way to the most remarkable scene of disorder. As the division was pushing through the village a horde of dragoons from the rearguard came charging through the village shouting 'Form a line! The Austrian cavalry is coming!' A desperate panic gripped everyone. Equipment and weapons were thrown to the floor. Overcoats were torn off and discarded as everyone bundled their way out of Languenau into the fields beyond. Once outside, the infantry formed columns and prepared to renew the previous day's action; but no one came. The whole sorry incident turned out to be something of a practical joke. The hussars forming the rearguard at Albeck were retiring and, not getting on with their cousin dragoons, they played a prank on them. Acting as a hostile force the hussars assumed an attack formation against the dragoons and sent them reeling.[23]

Order resumed, the retreat continued eastwards towards the River Brenz. During this retreat, Surgeon-Major Charles Vanderbach again had an opportunity to distinguish himself. A messenger with dispatches for the emperor needed to cross the Danube but the bridges all appeared to be in Austrian hands. Having swum the Ticino under fire in 1800, Vanderbach this time crossed the Danube on his horse, despite the river being swollen by the heavy rains, taking the messenger with him.

That evening Dupont wrote to Ney informing him that he occupied the line of the Brenz with an observation post covering Albeck. He clearly stated the need for his men to rest: 'The excessive fatigue and the heat of yesterday's combat make it necessary for my division to rest. It will nevertheless be ready to march and to fight with [the] same audacity as soon as it receives munitions and a few artillery pieces ... infantry cartridges are equally necessary for us.'[24]

On 13 October the Ninth found themselves at Sontheim encircled by a swarm of Austrians not quarter of an hour's march away. The roads were impassable and although some of the officers found a comfortable billet, the majority of the men were desperately cold, tired and hungry. In the early hours of the morning came disturbing news. The rest of the army had finally accepted the Austrians were attempting to escape on the north bank of the Danube, not the south as Napoleon had anticipated. Dupont's order to cross the Danube was rescinded. The division was ordered to turn round and advance back towards Albeck and an inevitable encounter with the Austrians. The order from Ney had been written at 1am that morning and included the line, 'despite your troops' fatigues, it is of the final importance your division retakes this position [Albeck].'[25] Godet saw the troops were greatly concerned at the prospect of going up against an entire army alone for a second time. Matters were made worse by the rumour of a flood having carried away the bridges on the Danube. Morale could not have been improved by the absence of Colonel Meunier. The strain of the previous few days had exhausted him and he was bedridden with a fever. When the regiment marched out at 7am he was left behind in the care of the local inhabitants.

The division advanced until it came across a large Austrian corps at Languenau commanded by General Werneck. There was a fruitless exchange between the two advanced guards in which two chasseurs from 1st Battalion were killed. Chasseur Simon Rateau had his nose nearly cut off by a sabre while fighting two Austrian hussars. Despite this painful wound the intrepid chasseur dismounted and killed one of his assailants and took the other prisoner. This act of heroism aside, the clash appeared to achieve nothing but draw more Austrians towards the fray. Dupont took the cautious option and decided to retreat back onto the Brenz to cover the communications of the army. This time he went as far back as Gundelfingen.

This time Dupont was proven to be overcautious. During the night he learned that Ney and Murat had crossed the Danube at Elchingen and the Austrians had fallen back towards Ulm. On the morning of 15 October, Dupont was ordered back to Albeck. By now his men were sick and tired of plodding up and down the same muddy route in the icy, pouring rain. Rations were non-existent. Dupont was obliged to send a commissariat officer down-river to Lauingen with a detachment of hussars looking for food.

Meanwhile the Ninth was ordered to form the head of the column, with their route scouted by a squadron of 1st Hussars. The 32nd Line followed immediately behind, then the artillery and finally the 96th Line with the remainder of the hussars closing the march. This order of march took some time to organize. The 32nd had to halt to allow the Ninth to pass them and the two regiments became mixed and disordered. While the officers were trying to sort out their men, two cannon shots were heard from a nearby wood. An ambush had been set which the 1st Hussars had missed. Six thousand Austrian cavalry deployed on the division's flank. If they had immediately charged the French infantry there would have been a bloodbath. Instead they hesitated and brought up a battery of guns. While the 32nd began forming a line, they came under heavy artillery fire. There was nothing they could do in reply as their musket barrels were filled with rainwater and could not be made to fire. Realizing his men's predicament, Colonel Darricau of the 32nd ordered his men to form a square. The artillery was bogged down further along the road and was equally useless. Nonetheless, the officers disguised their unease and encouraged their men to dry off their muskets as best they could and prepare for combat. A battalion of the Ninth tried to attack the Austrian artillery, moving up to within musket range of the guns and commencing a sporadic, ineffective fire. After a few dozen musket shots, they were forced back by a volley of canister.[26]

Still the Austrians waited. Although their artillery was playing havoc with the motionless infantry, it was not enough to decide the issue in their favour. The Austrian cavalry appeared to be waiting for infantry support to come up before becoming engaged. This allowed the French all the time they needed to regain the initiative. The artillery was dragged into place and began returning fire. The 96th came up and formed up on the right flank. On the left flank the Ninth executed a change of front to the right, prolonging its left towards a ravine. The regiment then executed a march onto the right flank of the Austrian line. Watching the Ninth moving on their flank, the Austrians withdrew their artillery and melted back into the woods.

Just as it appeared the day had been won, there was a considerable scare. A regiment of cavalry in white capes rode into view. They were at first taken for the Austrian de la Tour regiment but an officer from the 32nd recognized them as being French. The regiment was indeed the 1st Dragoons and they were unceremoniously informed that if they did not remove their white capes Dupont's jittery troops would certainly open fire on them if they came any closer.

The division carried on to Albeck. By now the village was ruined and offered neither shelter nor sustenance. Dupont recorded the hardships in his journal: 'During this day the troops had to support all the miseries and fatigues of war combined; they were without rations, the enemy having cut the road to

Gundelfingen and taken the convoys which the war commissary directed towards them and the rain, the hail and the snow not having stopped falling abundantly for a moment, especially at the moment of combat at which point no musket could fire.'[27] Despite these hardships, Dupont was blessed with hardy men. They gathered what firewood they could, ignored their hunger and began cleaning their muskets ready for a new day of fighting ahead.

During the night reinforcements arrived in the guise of Murat's cavalry corps. The village of Albeck was filled with horses stomping through the slush, neighing and snorting in the night air. At last Dupont's men could learn news of what had occurred elsewhere while they had been marching up and down the Albeck road. And it was good news. When Napoleon heard of Dupont's narrow escape at Haslach, he ordered Ney and Murat to cross the Danube and reinforce Dupont. There had been fierce fighting at Elchingen where 9,000 Austrians tried to prevent Ney repairing and crossing the bridge. Ney had shown extraordinary leadership and the battle had been won. Ney was now closing in on Ulm from the north. Soult and Lannes were south of the Danube and Marmont's corps and the Imperial Guard were closing in fast too. A considerable body of Austrians were still shut inside Ulm largely thanks to Dupont's efforts on 11 October, which had prevented the Austrians from escaping.

Buoyed by this news, Dupont went on the offensive and attacked the rearguard of an Austrian force, led by Archduke Ferdinand, which was trying to escape Ulm. A battalion of Austrian infantry were guarding the bridge at Anhausen, but laid down arms at the sight of the French cavalry reserve coming up the road. Everywhere along the road was the sign of pursuit. The ground was littered with the bodies of horses and men, helmets and cuirasses, weapons of every kind, wagons, and baggage. The Ninth rounded up the prisoners taken by the cavalry and a very interesting opportunity presented itself. The soldiers of the Ninth had been suffering from the continual rain and also from the cold while sleeping exposed in the bivouac every night. At this time French troops were not issued with greatcoats, so the Ninth forced the Austrians to hand theirs over. That night they arrived in Herbrechtingen, a small town on the Brenz where the Ninth took 600 prisoners along with 40 caissons containing various munitions. The Austrians had lit their campfires prior to the French arriving and these were put to good use by the Frenchmen, who were also enjoying the warmth of their new greatcoats. The sensation of warmth must have been some compensation for the hardships they had suffered.

On 17 October the division set out again on Murat's heels, heading for Nordlingen. By then all the captains in the Ninth had obtained horses to ride on the march. Godet bought himself an enemy soldier's horse for three sovereigns from one of Murat's troopers. They were rejoined by Colonel Meunier who had been left at Sontheim with a fever. Although cured, he had not had much opportunity to rest. The day after the regiment set out for Albeck he was warned a column of Austrian cavalry was heading into town. Throwing himself onto his horse he had raced out of the town with the Austrians in close pursuit. Meunier owed his survival to the speed of his horse. One by one the Austrian riders following him dropped out of the pursuit until only a single determined foe remained. After a race of two leagues (8km) the Austrian finally relented and allowed Meunier to escape. When his heart stopped pounding Meunier noticed his fever had disappeared.[28]

Returning to the pursuit, the Ninth caught up with the Austrians at Nordlingen. The town was fortified and contained the main Austrian artillery park, consisting of more than 1,000 vehicles. Realizing they were unlikely to shake off their dogged pursuers, generals Hohenzollern and Werneck proposed a capitulation. On 19 October Dupont's 4,000 men took the surrender of 6,086 Austrians and 25 heavy-calibre guns. Many in Dupont's division were amazed to see the Austrians give up without a fight, but they were thankful nonetheless.

During the pursuit Godet was feeling flush with cash so decided to buy his orderly a horse. Arriving at Nordlingen the Ninth spent the night there and took lodgings. Godet was billeted with some dragoons whose horses were stabled with his. In the morning Godet found the dragoons had gone and his orderly's horse was missing. He enquired after his host who told him the dragoons had indeed taken the horse. Godet felt aggrieved that his host had not thought to warn him. He put the civilian under the charge of one of his corporals, and marched him off at bayonet point to the local magistrate. Arriving at the town hall Godet found the local magistrates in session. He outlined his case against the host and claimed as the host had taken the horse from him to put in his stable, he was responsible for its security. By not informing Godet of the theft, the host was liable. The magistrates debated the matter for a short time and found Godet's claim appeared just and reasonable. The host was condemned to pay the price of the horse, which Godet estimated at ten sovereigns, which was credited to him on the spot. The purchase of the horse proved to be a tidy speculation after all.

The pursuit of Prince Ferdinand continued. It felt like their relentless march was intended to wear out the legs of the Austrian horses. Everywhere there were piles of muskets on the road, dropped by the Austrians when Murat's horsemen had caught up with them. The most pressing concern on the march was food. Each man had been issued with 60 rounds of ball and cartridge but no rations. Godet admitted they had to steal bread and wine where they could find it.

That night they reached Gunzenhausen, a town in Prussian territory. The Austrians had violated Prussian neutrality to escape the French, so the French felt a precedent had been set and did the same. Following their own interests, the Prussians had remained neutral in the war and the French wished them to remain so. Ransacking Prussian towns was therefore out of the question. The Ninth was marched through the town and were not allowed to break ranks within its walls lest they committed pillage. They were absolutely famished, but were assured rations would be delivered to their bivouac on the other side of town. To make absolutely sure there was no trouble a company of carabineers was posted at the town gate to make sure no one was tempted to return. At 10pm the regiment halted in a very wet meadow, without any issue of fresh straw and only enough wood for a few fires. Typically enough, no rations arrived and orders were issued for the march to recommence one hour before first light. Hearing this, several chasseurs defied their fatigue and went off into the night to procure food, having more faith in their own resources than the military supply system.

On 20 October Murat's troops assembled at 8am in front of Erlbach. The order of march was formed, led by the 1st Hussars, the Ninth's 1st Battalion, followed by the horse chasseurs of the Imperial Guard, the 1st and 2nd carabineer regiments, and the 1st division of dragoons, followed by the remainder of Dupont's division. The Austrians were said to be a few hours ahead and preparing to destroy the bridge at Rednitz once their troops had passed. Naturally enough Murat did not want to allow time for this to happen and so the race was on. All along the route Austrian fugitives indicated that the French were not too far behind their prey. After such a wretched night the men of the 1st Battalion were absolutely shattered and were asked to stand aside to let the cavalry get past.

By Schwabach the men were dropping on their feet, and a hasty distribution was made of a little bread and a bottle of wine to each man. This revived the Frenchmen and Dupont was happy to watch his men resume their march, singing all the way to Nuremberg.[29]

By the time Dupont's men arrived, the remnants of the Austrian infantry had already surrendered to Murat's cavalry on a plain outside Nuremberg. In total the French took 2,000 prisoners, two flags, 600 horses, 32 guns and their caissons and 50 baggage carts. Prince Ferdinand escaped, but this was inconsequential compared to the men and equipment he had lost. The Ninth bivouacked outside of the town and woke to the joyous news that the pursuit had been called off. The distance from Albeck to Nuremberg is 40 leagues (160km): they had marched this distance in four days in bad weather without much food. It was a Herculean effort.

While this pursuit had been in progress, on 17 October General Mack and Marshal Berthier signed a convention in which the Austrian garrison surrendered. In total the Austrians had lost around 50,000 men as prisoners around Ulm. It was a startling success, but the outcome could have been very different had Dupont's division not disputed the day at Haslach. How different would the 1805 campaign have been if Dupont had remained passive and left the road from Ulm open to the Austrians? What would have occurred if the Austrians had regained their lines of communication with Vienna and joined with Kutuzov? Once again the Ninth had played a decisive part in defeating an Austrian army. However the campaign was far from won. Somewhere out beyond the forests and hills was a Russian army marching westward towards them.

On 22 October Dupont quit Nuremberg to rejoin the Grand Army, arriving at Landshut on 27 October after a journey of more than 200km. After two days' rest the division turned south-east and marched to Vilsbiburg. A division of Batavian troops was also destined to spend the night there so Dupont pushed on four leagues (16km) further to Gangkofen. This march was extremely fatiguing for the troops, trudging through the rain and snow over detestable roads. The next day they arrived at Eggenfelden. The town had suffered greatly from the passage of soldiers. Many of the houses had been abandoned and in the night there was a fire in the town that blocked the main road. On 1 November they went to Griesbach, arriving at Passau on the Danube the next day for a four-day halt. Dupont ordered the citadel there to be garrisoned and for the bridges over the Inn and Danube to be repaired. Six hundred of his men were sick, suffering from fever or extreme exhaustion, so Dupont ordered a hospital to be formed. Meanwhile the officers tried their best to make up for the losses of Haslach. Since their portmantles had been pillaged they had nothing but the clothes they stood in. Now was a chance to wash and buy new linens.

On the evening of 5 November, Dupont took command of a division of Batavian troops. Preparing to march out the following morning, Dupont appointed the commander of 2nd Battalion, Jean Barère, as garrison commander and gave him 500 French soldiers and a few hundred Batavians to guard the army's lines of communication. On 6 November Dupont left Passau and marched towards Linz on the eastern side of the Danube. They were now in Austrian territory and arrived at Hofkirchen after a march of 13 leagues (52km). Then it was on to Lembach and Neufelden, before arriving at Ottensheim on 7 November at 8pm. On the road from Passau to Linz Godet found himself billeted with Battalion Commander Régeau. Despite his many excellent qualities, Régeau was something of a spendthrift. Even before the regiment crossed the Rhine, Régeau had made 'several attacks' on Godet's purse. Expecting hardships ahead, Godet always held back a few coins for times of dire necessity. Now the two were room-mates, Godet's purse was back in the line of fire. When Godet refused to share Régeau's profligacy, the battalion commander's ill humour increased accordingly.

At Ottensheim Dupont was informed that he was now under the command of Marshal Mortier and he was to press forwards and join Gazan's division further along the Danube in the direction of Vienna. They quit the town early on 8 November and arrived at Linz at 9pm. The roads along the river proved impractical for artillery, so the guns were embarked at Linz before the division resumed its march. That night they arrived at Mauthausen where they at last found considerable stores of rations. On 9 November they marched to Grein. The road along the Danube was awful and proved dangerous for cavalry. On the way Dupont recorded an incident when the division came across a stray Russian soldier who blundered into the middle of the column. Dupont described how the encounter gave great pleasure to his soldiers, who were quite amazed to see the Russian was a young conscript just like many of them, not some hideous, indefatigable beast. As they marched along they passed the Russian hand-to-hand down to the tail of the column, the sound of laughter following his passage through the ranks. Arriving at Grein the division was billeted while Dupont took up residence in the impressive Schloss Greinburg. The following day they arrived at Marbach.

After his success at Ulm, Napoleon had pushed on towards Vienna passing along the right bank of the Danube. Having encountered the Russians at Amstetten, Napoleon saw the need to protect his flank from threats on the other side of the Danube. So, while the bulk of the Grand Army remained on the right bank, Marshal Mortier passed to the left bank at Linz with Gazan's division. In order to support Mortier, a flotilla of riverboats was assembled in order to maintain contact between the French forces either side of the river. Unknown to Napoleon, Field Marshal Mikhail Kutuzov had crossed the Danube at Krems, burning the bridge behind him. The wily Russian had recently learned of Mack's defeat and decided not to risk his army defending Vienna. Instead the whole Russian army moved onto the northerly bank of the Danube. When Mortier's scouts blundered into the Russians at Krems, Kutuzov grasped the opportunity to crush Mortier's isolated force. Mortier had not helped matters either; the lanky marshal had been so eager to press ahead he had embarked Gazan's division on boats at Grein. Even by forced marches it proved impossible for Dupont to catch up and the latter remained a day's march behind.

At dawn on 11 November, Dupont quit Marbach heading for Spitz. During the march they heard the unmistakable sounds of battle echoing down the Danube valley ahead. Dupont ordered his division to double its pace, and by the time they reached Spitz the men were literally dropping from fatigue. By then the firing had ceased and Dupont supposed Gazan had only been engaged in a rearguard action.[30] Dupont had received an order to position himself in this village and to throw a few advanced posts ahead. However, he was very concerned about the interval between himself and Gazan. Therefore he ordered the 1st Hussars and the Ninth to overcome their fatigue and push on another two leagues to Weissenkirchen. The 96th were kept in reserve at Spitz while the 32nd were sent to a midway point on the road. This was to prove a most useful precaution.

Riding ahead of the Ninth, Godet had been sent to arrange the regiment's billets at Weissenkirchen. The sound of gunfire through the day had not troubled him unduly, but he was concerned by the terrain around him. After Linz the left bank of the Danube was closed in by mountains, some of which came very close to the river and formed narrow defiles. In places there were paths leading up into the mountains, or depressions cut by brooks during the spring thaws. In effect this mountain provided a screen behind which an enemy could manoeuvre unseen. Godet made these remarks to a staff officer who had earlier been sent by Mortier to Dupont. As they rode along, the captain told Godet about the Russians crossing the Danube at Krems. This news increased Godet's sense of unease.

The two men went their separate ways at Weissenkirchen; the captain to return to Mortier and Godet to the municipal house to make the billeting arrangements. Once this task was done, Godet went to greet the regiment as it arrived and to distribute the billet notes, assigning men to particular houses. It was about 4pm and getting dark. The regiment arrived and to Godet's surprise, it showed no sign of halting. Godet went to Meunier and informed him that they had reached their destination. 'Ah! It would have been a good billet,' Meunier replied ruefully, before adding, 'We are marching on the Russians.'[31]

As the regiment exited Weissenkirchen they saw half a dozen hussars firing their carbines at a large column of Russians coming down a ravine. Godet's soldierly sixth sense had proved correct. When Kutuzov realized Gazan's division was isolated in front of him, the Russian ordered his frontal attack be supported by a flanking march to the right. A force of 6,000 Russians led by the Austrian General Schmidt were directed in an anti-clockwise arc around Gazan's position, and down through the mountains behind him to cut his line of retreat at the village of Dürnstein. Six hundred Russians had already reached the bottom of the ravine and were deploying in a gorge, ignoring the shots from the hussars.

While riders were sent to bring the rest of the division up, Meunier's first act was to assume a defensive position, anchoring his right on the Danube and throwing a few companies to protect his left flank. However, as they watched, they realized the Russians were not interested in them, but were turning left at the bottom of the ravine and marching towards Dürnstein, with their backs to the Ninth. Advancing to attack the Russians, the Ninth came to an area where the gap between the mountains and the river broadened into a small flat plain. Meunier deployed his men in this plain and ordered them to open fire. While the main body of Russians continued to march towards Dürnstein, Godet noticed a small party gathering by the river, to the right of the Ninth. Godet pointed this group out to Meunier and asked what should be done about them? 'All our men are deeply and seriously engaged,' the colonel replied.[32] This was not quite the case. A large number of chasseurs had been unable to deploy in the narrow space and found themselves in the rear unable to fire. Godet told Meunier he was going to gather them together and drive the Russians away from the flank. Godet rode over to the men and pointed out the Russians advancing on the flank. He led the chasseurs over to the right and barred the Russians' progress. Seeing their passage blocked, the Russians fell back without firing a shot.

While Godet had been dealing with the Russians on the right, Meunier ordered Régeau to take a few companies to try and block the ravine. Gunshots echoed throughout the mountains and men were struck by falling rocks and trees.[33] In time Régeau's men managed to cut the path, preventing any more Russians coming down to the aid of their fellows below.

Below them the firing was now engaged all across the line as the Russians were forced to turn about and engage the main body of the Ninth. By the time Dupont arrived at the head of the 32nd Line, the Ninth had nearly spent all its cartridges and urgently needed relief. Dupont ordered the 32nd to replace the Ninth. The line infantry marched forward in a column of platoons and, arriving to the left of the Ninth, the 1st Battalion turned its head to the right. Marching along the front of the Ninth, the platoons wheeled to the left and formed a line between the Ninth and the Russians. Seeing the Russians were pressed into a fairly enclosed space, Colonel Darricau ordered a bayonet charge. The drums rattled and the battalion rushed forward in line, the 2nd Battalion formed in a column behind in support.

The Russians stood to meet the charge bravely and in the darkness a confused mêlée ensued. The men fought hand-to-hand for some time without result. As the impetus of the fight began to subside there was great confusion. The Russian officers appeared to want to surrender, but their men did not. There was so much shouting that the French officers' offers of surrender could not be heard. In the confusion some of the Russian soldiers began laying down their weapons, indicating to the French soldiers that this is what they wished them to do.

The French misunderstood and went forward to round them up. Of course the Russians then retrieved their weapons and began fighting again. The whole business was descending into a bloody farce. The French officers were forced to go from man to man prising their men away from the Russians because they were sustaining casualties for no tangible gain. As the two sides faced one another in the darkness something of a stand-off developed.

Meanwhile, the hussars had been performing a useful service. The artillery train was too far off to be of use, but the hussars spontaneously rode back to the train and loaded themselves up with musket cartridges. They distributed these to the soldiers of the Ninth who were taking a rest following the arrival of the 32nd. Resupplied with ammunition, many of these men went forward and stood in the line with the 32nd.

Dupont was becoming impatient. He ordered Colonel Darricau to gun down the Russians. As this decision was made the Russians set fire to some nearby houses behind their line. They did this knowing the French would be dazzled by the light, and while the Russians remained in the shadows, the French would be illuminated before them. They were not allowed to profit from this arrangement. Colonel Darricau ordered his drummers to make a short roll. He then ordered the men to commence two-rank firing. This rolling fire, delivered from a range of less than ten paces and bolstered by the additional firepower of the Ninth, was absolutely murderous. The Russians hardly had time to respond as the French balls thudded into the densely packed mass. At such a close range each ball could pass through several men. The Russians also fell to ricochets as they fled, trying to reach the mountains or throw themselves into the Danube to escape. About 300 prisoners were taken and 600 Russians killed or wounded, General Schmidt lying among the dead.

An eerie silence fell across the field of battle and the French looked to bivouac among the dead. A company of grenadiers was sent to bar the narrow pass into Dürnstein. Around midnight a group of horses was heard approaching. The French sentinels called out the challenge 'Qui vive?' and were somewhat surprised to hear the reply, 'His Excellency Marshal Mortier!'

Mortier was at the head of the survivors of Gazan's division. As the Frenchmen snaked their way forward, following a lantern at the front of the column, Dupont's men began to learn what had occurred that day. Mortier had left Dürnstein in the morning and arriving at Stein they had seen the smoke from the burning bridge at Krems. Initially believing he was only facing a rearguard, Mortier soon realized the Russians had set a trap for him and he was lucky to have made his escape. Arriving at Dürnstein it was only when he saw the piles of Russian corpses by lamplight, Mortier realized there had been a second action. None of them had heard the fighting, but with a chill they quickly grasped how close the Russian plan to encircle Gazan's division had come to success. The pass at Dürnstein was so narrow that a handful of Russians could have blocked the Frenchmen's escape route. Had Dupont not pushed his forces further than ordered, Mortier and Gazan would not have escaped.[34]

In the morning the cost of the battle could be properly assessed. Dupont was particularly pleased with his division's performance, given the Russians' martial reputation. He described the foe as a 'robust enemy, semi-barbarous and redoubtable with cold steel.'[35] The Ninth had taken two flags in the battle. The first was seized by Captain Pierre Leblanc who killed the standard-bearer; the other by a carabineer drummer named Drapier. In return the Ninth had lost 19 men killed and 58 wounded. Sub-Lieutenant Camille Reboulleau was killed, while wounds were suffered by captains Pierre Grandidier and Nicolas Gabriel, the notorious tippler.[36]

The nature of the fighting at Dürnstein can be gauged by information found in the regimental rolls. Elements of the 1st Battalion carabineers appear to have charged into the Russian ranks, presumably joining the mêlée started by the 32nd Line. Carabineer Sebastian Robin was noted for the way he penetrated the enemy ranks before falling to a gunshot wound. Two of his comrades were killed outright, Carabineer Louis Jarry was twice bayoneted in the mêlée but survived, while 14 others fell to gunshot wounds. It was a similar story with the 2nd Battalion carabineers. Six more carabineers were killed in the action. Pierre Guettard received two bayonet cuts to the head leading a charge towards the Russian ranks. Carabineer Jacques Bertrand was also wounded in the charge while fighting several Russians. In reward for a wound to the arm he later received the Legion of Honour. Two more carabineers were wounded by bayonets, while four others received gunshot wounds.[37]

The 1st Battalion's 1st Company also appears to have got close enough for one corporal to suffer a bayonet wound in the neck, although this may have been from fighting in the ravine. Chasseur Jean-Baptiste Hytier in 7th Company was shot and bayoneted twice in the fray. Of the chasseur companies, in total five men were killed and 17 were wounded, one of whom later succumbed to his wounds. The 1st Battalion voltigeurs did not receive a single casualty while the 2nd Voltigeurs had four men wounded, including one of the cornetists. Two of the voltigeurs were wounded by sabre cuts to the head, perhaps by Russian officers. In the 2nd Battalion six chasseurs were killed, while 15 more were wounded (four by bayonet, the remainder by gunshot).

Having taken such a mauling the previous day, Marshal Mortier assembled his forces at Spitz and crossed the Danube, embarking his men on the riverboats used for transporting the artillery. There wasn't time or resources to care for the Russian wounded. The Frenchmen lit fires around which the unfortunate Russians gathered for warmth and consolation in the extreme cold. Mortier's troops began crossing the Danube at Spitz around 4am and did not finish until midnight. Hardly had the crossing finished when the men were ordered back to the left bank. According to Dupont's journal an officer of the 1st Hussars was sent to the Russian commander Kutuzov to deliver a letter from Colonel Bibikov, a relative taken prisoner during the fighting. While in the Russian camp Kutuzov told the officer he was leaving 1,300 wounded in the hospital at Krems to the generosity of the French. This indicated Kutuzov was abandoning his wounded and retiring. Therefore, on 13 November Mortier ordered his troops back across the Danube to resume their original mission.

Once back on the left bank, Godet noted how some of the Russian wounded had burned to death in the fires the French had left for them. He supposed the cold had been so great the Russians had pressed towards the flames and had fallen into them as their strength gave out. Other Russian soldiers had died from the cold while sitting in front of fires that they had been too weak to keep alight. It was a sorry sight. As they passed beyond Dürnstein, the ground over which Gazan's division had fought was all too apparent by the number of corpses littering the ground. Dupont reckoned the ratio of corpses was 20 Russians for every Frenchman. As usual the dead had been plundered, either by the survivors or the local inhabitants.

On the night of 14 November they bivouacked in front of Krems on the ground occupied by the Russians at the beginning of the battle. The following day they pushed on to Hadersdorf. The Ninth formed Mortier's advanced guard and there was a brief skirmish with a Russian rearguard near Haindorf, but no casualties were reported. They remained at Hadersdorf while Marshal Bernadotte's corps passed them. On 17 November the division quit the Danube as the river turned southwards and instead headed north-eastward towards Moravia. They bivouacked at Hagenbrunn and were at last reunited with the Grand Army.

In their absence, tales of the bloody combat of Dürnstein appeared to have captured the army's imagination. The action was mentioned in two bulletins, the first on 13 November recorded: 'This day was a day of massacre; piles of corpses covered a narrow battlefield. More than 4,000 Russians were killed or wounded; 1,300 were taken prisoner. Among the latter are two colonels. On our part, the loss was considerable. The 4th and the 9th of light infantry suffered the most.' The bulletin of 14 November confirmed 'the 4th and 9th regiments of light infantry and 100th and 32nd regiments of heavy infantry covered themselves in glory.' To reinforce the bravery of Mortier's troops, an order of the day on 14 November confirmed: 'The Emperor shows his satisfaction in the 4th Regiment of Light Infantry, in the 100th of Line, in the 9th Light Infantry, in the 32nd of Line, for the fearlessness which they showed in the fight of Dürnstein where their firmness to hold the position which they occupied forced the enemy to leave the one it had on the Danube.'[38] The details may have been slightly exaggerated but the effect was to demonstrate to other French regiments that the Russians were by no means invincible. With Kutuzov's army still out there, Dürnstein became an invaluable propaganda victory for Napoleon.

Despite the plaudits, the truth was Dupont's division was largely spent as a fighting force. Haslach, the pursuit of the Austrians to Nuremberg, Dürnstein and weeks of exposure to foul weather had taken its toll. As the Grand Army made its final manoeuvres in the Moravian countryside before the concluding battle of the war, Dupont was ordered to form part of the Vienna garrison. To ensure no slight was felt at not being with the Grand Army, when issuing this order on 18 November, Napoleon said: 'It is time that this brave division rests.'[39]

THE NINTH'S
CAMPAIGN IN PRUSSIA

upont's battered division entered Vienna on 19 November by the Moravia Gate. The Ninth was assigned the Kempandorf barracks, a verminous pesthole they found in an appalling state.[1] The straw was stained and there were few blankets; but at least it had a roof and was some respite from the slush and mud they had traipsed through to reach the Austrian capital. Things were much better for the officers who could lodge with the townsfolk. Adjutant-Major Godet's landlord was a silk manufacturer from the Island of Frioul near Marseille. Godet had the distinct feeling this benevolent host was eager to marry him off to his only daughter; but Godet had no intentions of being hitched and nobly left the daughter to others less circumspect.

In addition to Dupont's troops, Gazan's division had also been sent to guard Vienna, along with the corps of Marshal Davout. It was a strange sort of occupation. The Viennese appeared to hold no grudge against the French who were, it seems, more preferable guests than the Russians before them.[2] The soldiers went sightseeing and the civic guards patrolled the streets jointly with their Gallic counterparts. However, the sense of harmony was shattered on 29 November when an order arrived from the Grand Army, which was assembled near the Moravian capital, Brno. Davout was ordered to make haste and rejoin the army by forced marches as Berthier was expecting a 'bloody battle' at any moment. The scare continued when the Ninth's 1st Battalion was ordered out of Vienna the following day to the village of Jedlersdorf to guard the bridges over the Danube. They were ordered to send patrols westward towards Russbach looking for signs of the enemy. Had Napoleon been trumped? Were the Austrians operating at his rear?

The uncertainty proved short-lived. On 2 December the battle of Austerlitz was fought and Napoleon won a famous victory against the combined forces of Austria and Russia. The soldiers of the Ninth learned about the battle the following day. Missing Austerlitz must have been something of a double-edged sword. On the one hand many of them would surely have fallen in action if they had been present at the battle. At the same time there must have been some rancour that they had missed the deciding battle of the war. The brilliant battle of Austerlitz far eclipsed their efforts around Albeck and at Dürnstein, reducing Dupont's efforts to something of a footnote in what was arguably Napoleon's greatest victory. They did not share the first anniversary of the coronation with their Emperor in the bivouac; nor did they bear witness to the famous 'sun of Austerlitz'. They would never be able to say 'I was at Austerlitz'. Marengo would remain the Ninth's special day.

There is evidence of some sense of frustration in the regiment from Battalion Commander Barère who had been left as a safeguard at Passau with 500 men and some Batavians. He wrote to Dupont on 13 December 1805, describing an earlier letter which went astray:

> ... [I] depicted the regrets which I felt at the fact I was not admitted in the glory of sharing your perils and dangers. Occupied with shutting myself in with palisades and covering myself with the ditches which surround the citadel of Passau, I pointlessly hoped to encounter again the enemy whom you beat completely in the affair of [Dürnstein] and whom His Majesty the Emperor completely annihilated at the battle of Austerlitz. So thus vanished the only means I had to get myself promoted from the rank in which I have stagnated for more than thirteen years ...[3]

Dupont did not ignore this. Although he could do little about Barère's promotional prospects, when Dupont drew up a list of men recommended for entry to the Legion of Honour on 30 December, he placed Barère's name at the top of the list. Such a compassionate gesture demonstrated Dupont's fine qualities as a leader.

Although they had missed Austerlitz, the Ninth had received honourable mentions in the army bulletins during the campaign. Colonel Meunier profited from a substantial windfall of cash from the Vienna bank, his bounty for a successful campaign, and was promoted to the rank of commander of the Legion of Honour. While in Vienna he splashed out on an attractive carriage that became his pride and joy. The only grumbles Godet heard in Vienna were those of his old colleague Régeau. These had nothing to do with glory and recognition, but everything to do with money. The spendthrift had been too free with his purse again and expected Godet to bail him out. One evening Godet met some officers from the 30th Line he remembered from the camp at Ostend. They stayed up late drinking at a café. Régeau joined Godet and sat impatiently smacking his sabre scabbard on the Viennese cobbles, grumbling quietly below his breath and grinding his teeth. Godet suspected he was spoiling for an argument and ignored him, keeping his money and company to himself.

The Ninth's mission in Vienna was one of maintaining order; however, as had been the case in Paris, some elements of the regiment were unruly. A record survives of the trial in Vienna of two soldiers from the Ninth who were accused of 'rape and devastation by force of arms'. The two defendants were sappers Jean Devigny, aged 28 and in service since 11 September 1795, and Charles-Joseph Delorme, also 28 and in service since 19 June 1800. Although described as a sapper, Devigny was listed a corporal in 3rd Company, 1st Battalion; likewise Delorme was a corporal in the 5th Company of the same battalion. Both had skills from their pre-army careers that were useful for sappers. Devigny was a nail-smith while Delorme was a butcher.

The military justice system under Napoleon had been devised in 1796 and remained in use for more than half a century. Judgements were made by a council of war composed of seven judges: a colonel (Darricau of the 32nd Line) who chaired the sessions; a battalion commander (Bouge of the 32nd); two captains (Segond of the Ninth and Vallat of the 32nd); a lieutenant (Renellon of the 96th); a sub-lieutenant (Julien Leprest, 9th Light) and a sub-officer (Sergeant-Major Lalande of the 32nd Line). By custom, each of the seven judges was over 25 years old and none could be related to or in any way allied with the accused.[4]

Another captain would perform the duties of 'reporter', in this case Captain Renouvier of the 32nd Line. The reporter would conduct the investigation against the accused, collecting evidence and witness statements. Before the trial, the reporter would build a case against the accused then visit them and read out the accusations. The reporter would then take a signed statement from the accused outlining their defence. With the evidence collected, the reporter would notify the council of war and a date for the judgement would be set; in this case 20 December 1805. The trial was held at Darricau's residence, the townhouse of the Prince of Liechtenstein in the Alstergasse, number 107. Councils of war were open to the public, but to deter unruly behaviour the number of spectators was limited to three times the size of the council and its attendants.

The trial began with Darricau ordering the clerk of the court (a sergeant-major appointed by the reporter) to place a copy of the law of 13 Brumaire Year 5 (3 November 1796) on the bench before him. This was an important protocol as this law set the procedure of the court. The Reporter then began by reading out the statements for and against the accused. In this case there were nine witness statements against the two accused men. Although the specific details are not given, it was alleged Devigny had committed rape and Delorme was an accomplice in the act, presumably restraining the victim. The same two then caused criminal damage, 'devastating' the establishment of the innkeeper Millegg.

Having heard the case, Colonel Darricau summoned the two accused men into the chamber. As required by law, both were escorted into court unchained and as free men. Each of the accused was allowed an advocate to help in their defence. In theory the advocate could be a civilian, but was most commonly a fellow soldier either asked for, or appointed by, the reporter. The two men were asked to confirm their names, age, profession and place of birth. With their identities established, the Reporter gave a summing up of the prosecution's case against them. In turn the accused and their advocates were asked if they had anything to add to their earlier statements. The evidence must have been fairly damning because neither man spoke out. Finally Darricau invited his fellow judges to ask questions of their own. No comments were made.

It was now time for deliberation. Colonel Darricau asked for the two accused to be returned to prison by their escort and for the public to be cleared from the chamber. The reporter and clerk of the court were also required to withdraw. Other than the seven judges only one man was permitted to remain behind. This was the imperial commissar, another captain (Theurel of the 96th) who was appointed by General Dupont to independently ensure the judges acted legally and applied the correct sentencing.

Having heard the evidence, Darricau as chairman put a simple question to the other six judges. 'Are Jean Devigny and Charles-Joseph Delorme guilty of the crime of rape and devastation by force of arms?' Votes were cast in reverse order of rank, commencing with the sergeant-major and ending with the colonel. This practice prevented subordinates being influenced by the opinions of their superiors. In order to find the man guilty a simple majority of four votes was required. Jean Devigny was unanimously declared guilty of rape with the help of an accomplice. Delorme was found not guilty after having three votes cast in his favour before Darricau made the casting vote.

After establishing Devigny's guilt, the imperial commissioner read out the punishment required by law: 'A rape committed by a serviceman or any other individual attached to the army or a supernumerary, will be punished with eight years in chains; if the culprit was aided by violence or the efforts of one or several accomplices, or if the rape was committed on a girl of less than 14 years old, the punishment will be of 12 years of chains. If the girl or the violated woman died from excesses committed on her person, the culprit will be punished by death.' Given the verdict, the imperial commissar concluded Devigny ought to be sentenced to twelve years in chains. A second vote now took place to ensure the judges endorsed this sentence with a majority of five out of seven votes required to pass it. The vote was unanimous. Darricau dismissed the other charge of devastation against both men, but ordered Devigny and Delorme to collectively pay the sum of 11 florins, 41 kreutzers to the innkeeper.

With the judgement passed the doors were reopened and the reporter and clerk of the court returned to hear the verdict. Darricau announced the decision and ordered 200 posters be printed with the decision recorded in French and German. The reporter was then instructed to go to the prison and read the judgement to the accused in the presence of a guard under arms. Cleared of both charges, Delorme was allowed to return to the regiment immediately. Devigny had no right of appeal. There was merely a 24-hour delay before the sentence was enacted to allow for last-minute evidence to emerge. If he remained free of sickness and disease his next Christmas as a free man would have been in 1817.[5]

The day before the trial, on 19 December, Napoleon ordered a grand parade for Mortier's corps at 12.30pm. It appears the soldiers had scrubbed up well since arriving in Vienna and the emperor expressed his satisfaction to the heroes of Dürnstein in an order of the day, dated 21 December. It read 'the emperor has seen with pleasure, in the review which he has passed, the fine bearing of Dupont's division and that of General Gazan.'[6] After the inspection, the Ninth lined the streets of Vienna and watched the passage of the Russian prisoners defiling before the emperor of the French. This proved the final act of a glorious, but costly campaign.

Most of the wounded officers had recovered sufficiently well to resume duty. Meunier wrote to Marshal Berthier, the army's major-general and minister of war, explaining two of those wounded at Haslach now required replacement. Voltigeur Captain Jean Janin had been evacuated to Landau where the 3rd Battalion had been in garrison since the opening of the campaign. The other officer unable to make active service was Captain Paulet. Meunier requested the two officers be replaced with officers from the depot.[7] Also from the depot came a detachment of 200 reinforcements and a consignment of greatcoats which had been manufactured in France.[8]

The two field battalions of the regiment had crossed the Rhine with 1,850 men. On reaching Vienna there were 43 officers and 1,164 present under arms, including a modest detachment at Passau under Barère; another 82 were detached with some pontooneers at Lauterbourg. In other words, they had lost 561 men. Accounting for these, there were believed to be 344 sick and injured at various hospitals scattered along the route they had marched, and 253 had been taken prisoner over the course of the campaign. Given the slowness of communication, returns are open to inaccuracies. According to the regimental rolls, the regiment had lost 33 men killed in action; 23 more would die of wounds after the campaign. Between September and December 1805 (and including those in the depot), 19 men would die of sickness or unattributed 'natural' causes (often recorded as 'died suddenly').

The process of informing the relatives of the dead appears to have been somewhat sporadic. There was a postal system, with letters handled by the regiment's baggage master, in the Ninth's case Sergeant Pierre Renaux. Relatives could read or hear of the army bulletins and would know their son's regiment had been engaged. Relatives would also gain news from their neighbours. When all the young men aged 20 in a district were conscripted into the same regiment, a letter from one would be shared round. Most families would have learned of the death or wounding of their sons in this way. If no news came the families could write to the regiment, or to hospitals asking for news. A letter of this sort does survive, which although dated from before the 1805 campaign, illustrates the problems parents faced very well.[9] It was written on 11 May 1805 by Marie Valance to the director of the military hospital at Amiens:

> I have a son, a chasseur in the first battalion, fifth company in the Ninth Regiment of Light Infantry who since 17 January last has not sent any news. He mentioned to me that for four months he was sick and at the hospital of Amiens. Since then his companions have written they have not seen him anymore. One of them mentioned he had died and it must have been in Amiens. He is called Dominique Aubert, son of Dominique Aubert and Marie Valance, native of Corcieux, twenty-one years old having fallen to the fate of conscription in 1804 for the commune of Corcieux. Please Sir, search the registers of deaths at the hospital entrusted to your direction and in case he has died, send me his death certificate. Receive in advance my thanks and believe me your devoted servant.[10]

Aubert had in fact died on 27 February 1805 in Amiens hospital with the cause of death given as a 'mesenteric obstruction'. In this case it appears the mother was not kept waiting long for a reply. A mark on the letter indicates a reply was sent on 24 May 1805. However, when the hospitals were in Germany, or later East Prussia and Spain, the wait for confirmation must have been far longer.

On 26 December Napoleon signed the peace of Pressburg, a condition of which was that the French had to evacuate the Austrian capital immediately. On 29 December the regiment was sent to Munich to participate in the marriage ceremony of Napoleon's step-son, Eugène de Beauharnais, with Princess Augusta, the daughter of the King of Bavaria. The men appear to have behaved themselves at the wedding celebrations and after this was completed, the regiment was sent to Frankfurt, which it reached on 8 February.

At Frankfurt Godet procured himself a billet at the home of Mr Villemer, banker to the King of Prussia. With his host he enjoyed good food, entertainment, promenades in the city and walks through the countryside. It was the perfect panacea to a hard campaign. The banker also arranged for Godet to take an hour of German lessons daily with his children's tutor. Godet threw himself into this and rued they did not remain in Frankfurt long enough for him to become truly fluent.

After the peace of Pressburg, the old Holy Roman Empire was broken up and in the vacuum created by Austria's defeat, France was able to extend its hegemony over the German-speaking states. Napoleon cajoled the Prussians into a treaty, in which they gave up several pieces of territory for Napoleon to distribute as he saw fit. On 15 March 1806 Napoleon appointed his brother-in-law, Marshal Murat, as grand duke of Berg and Cleves, the region along the east bank of the Rhine from Wesel to Bonn. To help cement Murat's control over his duchy, the Ninth was sent to Wesel. Command of the city was ceremoniously handed over to Colonel Meunier by the outgoing Prussian military authorities.

As garrison commander, Meunier enjoyed a very lucrative perk. In peacetime the ditches of a fortification were used for grazing livestock and the local population paid the garrison commander for the right to forage there. Despite it being only March of 1806, the outgoing Prussian commander had sold the forage rights for the whole year. Godet interceded on Meunier's behalf, believing the Prussian had overstepped his authority. Godet rightly claimed the French ought to receive the income from the time after they commanded the garrison. Meunier was wary of pushing the matter as he did not want to be seen to be provoking an international dispute with the Prussians. Instead he authorized Godet to deal with the matter unofficially. After some complex negotiation, in which Godet warned the Prussian commander he would send the citizens of Wesel directly to his door seeking compensation, the Prussians relented and made a deal. Meunier personally netted over 3,000 francs from the Prussians in compensation. The colonel sent Godet a bag containing 15 sovereigns as his share of the spoils. Godet was not sure if he should be insulted or pleased by the gesture.

While in Wesel Meunier announced to Godet that he wanted him to transfer away from the field battalions to the depot at Landau. Godet protested, claiming he was too young to go to the depot, but Meunier explained that the government would not allow him to retain three 'first-class captains' with the field battalions.[11] The 3rd Battalion's senior captain had been Pierre Gros, who finally took retirement in 1806. Having been promoted to the rank of captain very quickly in the Revolution, Godet was the next longest-serving captain in the regiment. It was therefore necessary for him to join the depot battalion as Gros' replacement.

Meunier told Godet he wanted him to take over the regiment's recruitment details in the Vosges department. Godet was equally surprised to hear this. Fifteen days before, Godet had heard Meunier promise this plum posting to Captain Paulet, who had been badly wounded at Haslach. When he questioned Meunier's change of heart, the colonel asked him to go as a favour saying, 'Go there, oblige me; when you are there I can be sure what is going on. We are at peace with the whole world and there is no sign this state will soon change. But if, against all appearances, [war] comes, I will recall you right away.'

At this Godet knew he had to accept before the request became an order and soured his relationship with the colonel. However, by accepting the post Godet caused friction with the other officers. Paulet was in his mid-40s, had been in the army since 1780 and now had a family. The chance to take old Gros' job based at Épinal in the Vosges would have been extremely desirable and he was clearly disappointed to learn the post was going to a much younger man. Battalion Commander Régeau appears to have stirred things up, saying Godet had deliberately intrigued for the job. However Godet made his peace with Paulet and assured him his conduct was honourable.[12]

On the day of Godet's departure the men had a surprise for him. Called to the front of his quarters, Godet was met by the whole corps of sub-officers, with Drum-Major Gilles Marneuf at their head.[13] Godet had only been with the regiment for seven months, but always had a soft spot for sub-officers. They expressed their regret that Godet was leaving the field battalions and thanked him for his conduct on campaign. On the way to the depot Godet had one last unexpected farewell. At Düsseldorf he came across the 96th Line conducting manoeuvres. Taking a few moments to watch his companions from Dupont's division, Godet was joined by Colonel Pierre Barrois. Seeing a man in the blue of his old regiment, Barrois lavished praise on Godet. Such recognition swelled his heart with pride.

Returning to matters of state, by the spring of 1806 Napoleon had extended French influence far beyond the Rhine frontier. He had tied himself to Bavaria through the marriage of his step-son Eugène; the Duchy of Cleves and Berg had been awarded to his brother-in-law Murat; Neuchâtel was given to the faithful Berthier; while his brother Louis Bonaparte became King of Holland. Watching French influence spread, a war faction began to grow in Prussia intent on revenging itself for what it considered an insulting treaty with the French.

Before this conflict erupts we must introduce a newcomer to the field battalions of the Ninth in Germany. Although the majority of recruits came to the Ninth from conscription, there were still occasional batches of volunteers eager to enlist with a renowned regiment. Our representative of these men is Jean Baptiste Cardron. Enrolled on 25 April 1805 as Number 2,350, Cardron was born on 8 May 1786 at Philippeville in the department of the Ardennes.[14] Although perhaps modest by today's standards, Cardron was one of the tallest men in the regiment at 1.80m when he was enrolled just two weeks shy of his 19th birthday. He was described in the rolls as having a long face, a high forehead, grey eyes, a large nose, medium-sized mouth and a long chin. Before joining the army he had diligently studied a number of military books. As recruits went, he was the perfect specimen. Having lost his father Etienne, a master baker, in 1787 while still an infant, Cardron was understandably very attached to his mother Victoire and his sister Marie-Josèphe. He diligently wrote to them throughout his military career and, with equal diligence, they preserved his letters.

Promotion came very rapidly to Cardron, being made sergeant on 7 October 1805 in the 3rd Battalion. This promotion was no doubt down to his many excellent qualities, but was perhaps also a result of some patronage by Battalion Commander Régeau, who appears to have been something of a family friend. Towards the end of 1805 he made up part of a force of 200 reinforcements sent by the 3rd Battalion from Landau to Vienna. One imagines Cardron being disappointed to learn peace had been made while he was on the march.

We pick up Cardron's trail in Bonn and with it the inkling of new hostilities. The Ninth arrived there on 16 September 1806. That same day Cardron wrote to his mother: 'I can hardly believe, like everyone else, that the King of Prussia would ever dare to confront France.'[15] Six days later he returned to the subject in a tender letter to his sister:

This time there is no longer any doubt; war with Prussia is a certain thing. For four days, several regiments, which like us were on this bank of the Rhine, have re-crossed and directed themselves on Frankfurt. Today our whole division puts itself on the march and our initial destination is also Frankfurt. Thus your brother is going to learn what it is to make war. Our poor mama is going to be very sad when she learns that hostilities have resumed. Try to console her … and if the hazards of war do not allow me to see you both again, you have enough character, make yourself right in thinking that, on your own, you can give our good mama the care she might expect from both her children.

That evening, the regiment was ordered to march at 5pm. Dupont reassembled his renowned division and the Ninth was designated as 1st Brigade, 3rd Division in Marshal Bernadotte's I Corps of the Grand Army. Cardron was just able to scribble a few last-minute notes. Among them he said he had seen 'Mr Régeau' ten days previously and the officer had assured him he would win his officer epaulettes in the coming campaign.

While Cardron was contemplating his first campaign, Surgeon-Major Charles Vanderbach was preparing for the inevitable casualties to come. As his division was re-formed, Dupont put Vanderbach in charge of the division's medical services. On 27 September Vanderbach took possession of all the supplies at Mainz, which included 54kg of linen bandages (banded and compressed), 12.5kg of lint, a mattress and an amputation chest. For use with the Ninth, Vanderbach retained a double amputation chest and a complete set of trepanning instruments. The medical equipment was supposed to be carried in four-wheeled ambulance caissons, but Vanderbach's experience from the previous campaign had taught him to think differently. Dupont's division had lost its ambulance caissons at Haslach with the rest of the baggage and Vanderbach did not want a repeat of this. In order to keep the equipment close at hand, Vanderbach asked for each regiment to be given a horse to carry the medical equipment.[16]

Also on the subject of equipment, in a letter from the 32nd Line's Colonel Darricau to Dupont on 5 October, he reported the Ninth had no cooking pots, pans or camping tools.[17] These unpopular items were perhaps considered unnecessarily cumbersome for light infantrymen when comfortably billeted on German homes.[18] The regiment also appears to have returned its greatcoats to stores in July and did not think to ask for them back in time for the coming campaign. It is unlikely much could have been done before the King of Prussia gave Napoleon an ultimatum on 7 October, asking him to evacuate Germany at once. Hostilities began almost immediately and culminated in the French double victory at the battle of Jena-Auerstadt a week later on 14 October. The formidable reputation of the Prussian army was shattered and, as Napoleon remarked, France's defeat at Rossbach in the Seven Years War was finally avenged. However, it was not a victory in which the Ninth had a share.

On the eve of the great battle, Napoleon misjudged the enemy's dispositions, thinking he had the bulk of the Prussian forces in front of him at Jena (96,000 to 55,000 in the French favour), while Davout's III Corps (some 26,000 men) found itself facing the strongest part of the Prussian army, some 60,000 strong at Auerstadt. Bernadotte found himself between these two camps with a further 20,000 men. Bernadotte had received an initial order to march from Naumburg to Dornburg. Berthier then sent a revision, which stated if Bernadotte was still at Naumburg he should march to support Davout. This message came to Bernadotte via Davout and most commentators seem to agree, Bernadotte was 'piqued' at what seemed like receiving an order from a fellow marshal rather than the emperor directly. Despite still being at Naumburg, Bernadotte pigheadedly ignored the second order and marched for Dornburg as earlier instructed. By the time they arrived at 11am, the cannonade of two separate battles was clearly audible to the north and south of them. Bernadotte seemed unperturbed and left Dupont at Cramburg to guard the bridge over the Saale while he halted with the rest of his corps. Finally he marched towards the battle to the south and joined it at Apolda. Had he arrived several hours earlier he might have cut off the Prussian army's line of retreat.[19] Napoleon was understandably furious at Bernadotte's conduct. This was the first real sign of rivalry among his marshals, which would surface more openly in the years ahead. Many expected Bernadotte to face a court martial for failing to obey orders and be shot as an example, but this time the emperor allowed the matter to pass.

The Ninth's reaction at missing Jena is not recorded. There was no dishonour in them missing Austerlitz, but this was an entirely different matter. Bernadotte had disgraced them by association. Still there was time to make amends. As the remnants of the Prussian army fled northwards, Bernadotte's fresh army corps was sent in pursuit. Here at last the soldiers of the Ninth would have the opportunity to shine in a blistering march up to the Baltic Sea.

Marching at the head of Bernadotte's corps, Dupont's division arrived before Halle at 10am on 17 October. The town was on the far bank of the River Saale. The approach to the town was by a series of three bridges which crossed various branches of the river. The Prussian rearguard under Prince Württemberg had decided to make a stand at this excellent defensive position, placing 4,000 men and a number of guns guarding the bridges and the town gates. The remainder of Württemberg's corps (approximately 8,000 men) had taken up position behind Halle.

The Prussians had a detachment protecting a ford on the French right. The Ninth's 1st Battalion and a squadron of 4th Hussars were sent to check this detachment and after driving them off, remained in that part of the field in observation. Making up for his poor start to the campaign, Bernadotte was very much back on form. With Rivaud's division arriving to support Dupont, the Marshal rode up to the 32nd Line and harangued them: 'Soldiers! Go into Halle like it was butter.' [20] It was not the most eloquent harangue, but it proved perfectly adequate in the circumstances. The 32nd boldly advanced to within artillery range. At this point 1st Battalion deployed into line to the right, with its left on the road. The 2nd Battalion remained behind the left in column, directly opposite the bridge. Marching through a hail of shot and musketry, Darricau ordered a bayonet charge. His men rushed forward to close the gap between themselves and the Prussians and a series of mêlées soon developed. As the Prussians manfully fought for possession of the bridge, they noticed their own gunners were lining up artillery to protect the city gates. Heavily engaged in front, the Prussian soldiers feared they were about to be fired on from the rear by their own artillery. Resistance began to crack. The 32nd's 2nd Battalion came up at the charge and thudded into the Prussian defenders. Everywhere the Prussians began surrendering.

Colonel Meunier had been following the 32nd with his 2nd Battalion. As the impetus of the 32nd was slowed by taking prisoners, Meunier saw what had to be done. He ordered Captain Balson to take two companies and bayonet charge the Prussian barricade across the final bridge. It was a bloody business. Balson launched his men against the Prussian artillery. Three guns were seized and

300 Prussian grenadiers threw down their arms, but not before Balson fell severely wounded at the head of his troops.

The French soldiers entered the town mixed up with fleeing Prussians; Prussian reserves began entering the town from opposing gates and a fierce fire-fight commenced. Confusion reigned when French cavalry came clattering through the town, causing their compatriots to take shelter on the sides of the streets, which were soon covered with dead horses, broken carriages and the barrels of abandoned Prussian cannons.

Fresh reserves were needed, so Colonel Barrois arrived at the head of his 96th regiment and charged through the town securing the Magdeburg Gate on the left. The 32nd and Ninth charged towards the Leipzig Gate on the right. There before them, drawn up in two lines, was the Prussian reserve, some 20,000 strong. The artillery had already been trained on the gates and it was not long before the French found themselves under intense fire. The Ninth and 32nd rallied inside the town and began barricading the gates, buying time for Bernadotte to bring up reinforcements. Rivaud arrived with his division, then Drouet, and openings were made to allow the troops to pass out onto the flanks of the Prussian force. Seeing his troops pushed back on all sides, the Prince of Württemberg abandoned any hope of recapturing the town and began to withdraw his forces towards Landsberg, protected by the cavalry. The French followed the Prussian rearguard for three leagues (12km), before retiring back towards Halle with the evening drawing in.

Given the difficulty of the position, French losses were fairly modest with reports of 40 killed and 300 wounded for the whole of Bernadotte's corps. The Ninth had nine men killed, including Carabineer Laurent Marchand who had been made a member of the Legion of Honour on 14 March 1806 after being distinguished in the campaign of the year before. Five officers were wounded, including Meunier (grazed by a canister round in the chest), captains Malgontier and Rivet, along with Lieutenant Berbain. Captain Balson had also been badly wounded in the capture of the second bridge. When they carried him off to the surgeon he was found to have been shot through the belly and head with seven bayonet wounds to match. Miraculously he would fight again.

Dupont was typically upbeat. 'The winning of a bridge,' wrote General Dupont to Marshal Bernadotte in his report, 'is the most difficult operation in war.

That of the Saale was loaded with infantry and protected by canon; but I had such confidence in my brave battalions that the occasion was gloriously justified. The order to charge was given; they advanced with the most amazing intrepidity and braving a shower of canister and ball; this extraordinary audacity terrified the enemy, despite the almost impregnable position they occupied.'[21]

On the evening of 17 October, Dupont's division bivouacked on the battlefield near Diemitz. It remained in this position resting during the following day. With autumn closing in Bernadotte made a requisition of cloth at Halle to make greatcoats for Dupont's troops. The troops were also resupplied with ammunition. Having rested throughout 18 October, Bernadotte put his corps back on the march the following day in the direction of Brandenburg. Arriving at Alsleben in the evening, Dupont was ordered to detach three companies to escort the large numbers of prisoners rounded up during the pursuit. The Ninth's 1st Company 1st Battalion, was chosen for this duty, with one each from the 32nd and 96th.

The long march through Germany continued. While much of the Prussian army had collapsed, a body of 22,000 men rallied around the Prussian general Blücher. Seeking a passage to the city of Magdeburg, Blücher crashed into Dupont's division at Waren on 1 November. After a brief clash between the French cavalry and the Prussian rearguard, the French infantry passed through Waren and began deploying into line on the plain beyond it. Ahead of them the Prussians had crossed a marshy stream and burned the only bridge. On the far bank was a dense fir forest swarming with Prussian jaeger. Bernadotte ordered the 32nd's voltigeur companies to wade over the stream and engage the Prussians in the trees.[22] They went across, up to their chests in water and clambered up the far bank before opening fire. The thicket was so dense the French voltigeurs had trouble penetrating the woods and took their time to get onto the flank of the Prussian skirmishers, forcing them to begin retiring or risk becoming ensnared. In the meantime some infantry sappers began dismantling a shepherd's cabin to gain wood for making a bridge. As this work continued a few other detachments waded across to aid the voltigeurs.

By 5pm the division was on the move again and the woods cleared of Prussian sharpshooters. As the head of the column came into the clearing, they found the Prussians lined up on a ridge before them. The Prussian right was at the village of Nossentin with the cavalry on the left wing. The artillery was trained on the main road as it exited the wood. Marching at the head of the column, the Ninth was met with a violent fire. Remaining in column the regiment pressed forward allowing space for the 32nd to partly deploy to its right and the 96th to the left, against Nossentin. An officer of the 32nd witnessed the Ninth fall into difficulty. '... I saw the battalion of the 9th which was on our left, make a retrograde movement. It threw itself behind a large farm where it re-formed. I quickly went to see what had happened. I recognized this battalion had been engaged in column in a sunken lane with steep edges surmounted by hedges. It could not deploy and had received in this situation an intense fire of musketry and artillery to which it could not reply.'[23]

Something of a stalemate ensued and the Prussians were able to retire under the cover of night. Where the French may have begun to feel themselves invincible at Halle, Waren proved a timely caution. Meunier had used his regiment as a battering ram and had not tried to deploy his men or manoeuvre them at all. The regiment suffered accordingly with seven men and Captain Guittard of the 1st Carabineers killed. Serving in Guittard's company was young Sergeant Cardron, who was struck by a musket ball in the right shoulder in the action. In a letter home dated 11 November 1806 he spoke of his wound and the fighting:

... I was wounded in the shoulder. It was a blow from a ball that fortunately only entered the flesh and stopped on the bone; I suffered a lot in the first moments but now, thank God, I almost do not feel any pain and I hope to be soon restored. You would never have known about this accident if I had not been afraid some imprudent person might make it worse by announcing this piece of news to you. I believe it is useless to ask you not to be alarmed, but this letter in my handwriting should calm you, because the wound I received was in the right shoulder and it does not hamper the movements of the hand.

In this accursed affair, which lasted near two hours, our regiment and especially our unfortunate company suffered a lot. We have had five killed, among whom is Georges the wigmaker; 17 wounded including three sergeants, Sub-Lieutenant Gros and two corporals; but our greatest loss was our unfortunate captain who was hit by a canister round in the throat and was killed leaving a wife with four children. This company, detested by the colonel, we don't know why, was sent to seize five cannon which played on us with canister since the beginning of the action and inconvenienced us a lot. We overcame them and we took them, but we paid well for it.[24]

This letter is interesting for a number of reasons. As mentioned in the previous chapter, it confirms the way soldiers would write home with news about one another. Cardron's motivation here was to write home before his mother learned about his wound from someone else. Perhaps more interesting is the accusation that Colonel Meunier detested the first carabineers. Was this youthful overreaction? When a hard job needed doing, the colonel relied on his carabineers; it was the price of wearing the badge of the flaming grenade. Real warfare was not a pageant.

Under the cover of night Blücher resumed his retreat. Running out of options the Prussian general directed his men towards the neutral Hanseatic city of Lübeck, hoping to find a means of shipping his men to East Prussia. Hot on his heels came Bernadotte's soldiers. They reached Passau, then Schwerin. On 5 November they marched until midnight over roads where the mud reached halfway up their legs. After three hours' rest they were back on their feet and in pursuit. As the sun came up they could see the Baltic and Lübeck in the distance. By now the road was littered with French stragglers unable to maintain the pace so Bernadotte called a halt.

Several thousand Swedish troops had come ashore at Lübeck, but were now hurriedly trying to reach their ships at the approach of the French. Marshal Bernadotte directed General Rouyer with the Ninth to the nearby port of Schlutup where a party of Swedish troops were attempting to embark. A few shots were fired at the Ninth so Rouyer brought up some artillery. Fearing the worst, 600 Swedish troops laid down their arms. Meanwhile Bernadotte made a junction with Murat and Soult. The following morning Lübeck was taken by storm. Dupont's troops played no part in this attack, but they moved into the city that evening. Blücher had escaped them again, but finally asked to surrender the following day with full honours granted.

Having missed Jena at the outset of the campaign Bernadotte's troops had gone a long way to regain a sense of honour and achievement. From 8 October until 6 November, the Ninth had made 27 marches, some more than 12 leagues (50km) in length, covering more than 175 leagues (700km) with only two days of rest. They had fought two very hard actions at Halle and Waren and were, Bernadotte admitted, absolutely exhausted. In addition there had been something of a breakdown in discipline. After leaving Brandenburg there had not been a single distribution of bread. With the length of the daily marches there had been no time to punish the looters. There was also a tail to the corps composed of stragglers, who were only capable of making half marches. Bernadotte wanted 12 days' rest to allow these things to be put in order.

Sure enough the Ninth was given 12 days by the coast on the River Trave until 19 November. Once everyone had a chance to catch up, the returns showed the regiment was still strong. The 1st Battalion had 31 officers and 837 men present under arms, with two officers and 86 men in hospitals; the 2nd Battalion had 25 officers and 998 present men, with three officers and 183 men in hospitals. In addition there was a company of 1st Battalion (three officers, 107 men) on prisoner escort duty. On 19 November, I Corps was ordered to Berlin. It left the Lübeck area the following morning and reached the Prussian capital on the 28th.

Final word on the campaign should perhaps go to Cardron. What was his verdict on his first taste of action?

Lübeck, 11 November 1806

Finally, my good mama, after many hardships and fatigues, I can give you my news and draw you from the cruel anxiety into which a silence of nearly two months has plunged you. But if you had known of the marches we have made until this moment now, you would admit to the impossibility of writing to you. Other than that, the army's post is so badly served that I strongly fear this letter will not reach you.

Since our departure from Bonn, we have not had a day of rest, counting from our passage of the Rhine we have always marched the whole day long, always chasing the Prussian forward posts before us. But since a month ago when we had a hard affair and where thank God, I got out with my trousers clean, we have marched day and night in pursuit of a corps of the Prussian Army. Having fought it, finally, on the 6th, our Army Corps having met them once again, attacked it in the city of Lübeck, taking that town by assault and that same day and the next day, aided by Prince Murat, we took prisoner 35 thousand men all that remained of the Prussian's invincible army. After this incident they put us into billets, which makes us hope that soon we will have peace …

I am in the division's field hospital established in this city. Every care is taken of us and we are well, so stop worrying.[25]

There were no signs of officer's epaulettes yet, just the distinctive mark of his first scar. There would be many more to come.

9

THE BROKEN EAGLE

On 14 December 1806 two young sub-lieutenants were posted to the Ninth from the Special Military School at Fontainebleau. This was the academy where our old friend Christian Kuhmann had been put out to grass. One of these keen and eager graduates was Amédée Merle, a compatriot of Colonel Meunier from Saint-Amour in the Jura and the son of one of his best friends. The other was Félix Girod, son of Jean-Louis Girod de l'Ain, a noted politician and former president of the French Legislative Corps. Like Cardron, Girod was a volunteer, but whereas Cardron, the son of a baker, had enrolled as a soldier and hoped to work his way through the ranks, Girod had used his father's wealth and influence to fast-track himself into the officer corps. This was the imperial interpretation of equality.

Girod had enrolled at Fontainebleau a year before, at the age of 16.[1] He had been born two months after the storming of the Bastille, on 6 September 1789, and had grown up entirely within the great vortex of events which followed. Except for the brief window of peace after Marengo, his life had been surrounded by social, political and military conflict. Given this, his desire to join the army is unsurprising. However, being below average height, having what he admitted was a 'weak constitution',[2] and after receiving a 'pious' education, many were surprised by his choice of career. While his eldest brother Amédée was earmarked for a career in law, Félix emulated the next eldest brother,

Marc, who enrolled in Fontainebleau and constantly wrote letters telling Félix of the hardships at the school and warning him not to go. These letters only acted as a lure to the little fellow.

Life at Fontainebleau is well described in the popular memoir of Elzéar Blaze, whose pen so wittily caricatured Kuhmann. Girod's own memoirs describe the life of young cadets equally vividly. His first concern was the size and weight of the infantry musket. It was almost as tall as Girod and he found the weight extremely challenging. Recognizing his slender build, the masters at Fontainebleau assigned him to one of the bigger cadets for extra tuition. Boys being boys, the larger tormented the smaller with two or three hours' arms drill every day.

Girod spent the winter of 1805/6 without a greatcoat or a brazier to warm himself. He rose at 5am and worked until 9pm, the day punctuated with meagre meals. Everything about their day was formulated by old hands such as Kuhmann to replicate garrison service as experienced by common soldiers. The only concession to their anticipated higher station was in not having to cook their own meals.

Of course, the Spartan regime was there to teach the cadets useful lessons, not to starve, maim or scar them for life. The regime taught them to be resourceful. Girod had Turin chocolates smuggled in, a gift from his father. He did not eat them, but swapped the chocolates with his comrades in return for wine, confessing his ration of half a bottle per meal was not enough for him. Great lengths had to be taken to supply such contraband. Kuhmann's chief, General Jacques Nicolas Bellavène, ordered a crackdown, informing the school porter he could keep any confiscated foodstuffs for his family's table. Again, the crackdown only served to teach advanced resourcefulness. The school jailer was found to be less zealous than the porter and it was known he would look after the cadets from rich families. When one wanted to enjoy one's treats, it was a simple matter to be thrown into the guardhouse on some silly charge and then make the necessary arrangements.

Girod remained at the school until 1 November 1806. His memoirs record the feeling of relief to get away from the bullying of older, bigger cadets, from the jealous rivalries and the monotonous daily routines. In fact, the hard knocks endured would prove far more useful to him than the treatise he wrote on the campaigns of Hannibal. When Girod's commission came through, he was posted to the 72nd Line, then stationed in Holland. *Holland*? Girod hadn't spent a year at Fontainebleau to be posted to a military backwater. He wanted a posting with the Grand Army, by preference with the light infantry where there was perhaps the best chance for independent command and rapid promotion. He had the necessary strings pulled and was rewarded with the provisional posting to the 9th Light. He was ordered to get his uniform and equipment in order and be ready to leave Paris with a detachment of officer cadets bound for the Grand Army in eight days.

When the fateful hour came, the officer cadets left Paris in style – 50 teenagers riding in hackney carriages believing themselves the epitome of soldiering. They supposed they would travel in this manner all the way to the enemy picket lines; but at the first relay the realities of the Napoleonic system of warfare were made abundantly clear. Safely out of sight of cheering relatives and weeping sweethearts, they were unceremoniously turfed out of their comfortable carriages and transferred into straw-filled peasant carts, a dozen at a time. Without any type of suspension, these carts laboured their way eastwards, over hills and broken roads with the cadets balanced precariously on their portmantles, praying for the journey to come to an end.

Travelling 25 leagues every day (100km), they would climb down from the carts each evening and collapse from fatigue. Their route took them through Mainz, Hanau and Eisenach, but after such an appalling journey there was no appetite for sightseeing. After Erfurt they first noticed the tell-tale signs of a land scarred by war. The long lines of bivouacs were marked by countless cook fires, and uncultivated fields. All the nearby houses were abandoned and were half-burned or demolished. Every now and then was the unmistakable sight of a raised mound of freshly dug earth – mass graves.

Their journey continued towards Berlin, crossing the Elbe at Wittenberg and then arriving outside Potsdam where the transport would go no further. Still, it was only 12 leagues (48km) to army headquarters so the detachment set out on their first meaningful route march. Girod placed himself at the head of the detachment trying to prove his courage. By the evening he noticed his legs begin to falter. One by one his comrades passed him until he became the last man. Fatigue tightened its grip on Girod and he faltered, falling further and further back until his comrades were out of view. Night fell. Girod found himself on a road edged by a German forest, hungry and feeling very vulnerable and alone. In fairness to him, like a good soldier, he controlled his fear and used it to spur himself on. Luckily he had become friends with one of the detachment, who went back to find him. Girod was helped into his billet, where he collapsed in a heap on the floor and had to be spoon-fed, not having the strength to sit at the table.

The next day the resourceful officers procured transportation to Berlin and arrived that same day in the Prussian capital. Like a small cog in some enormous clockwork device, Girod arrived in Berlin on exactly the same day the Ninth arrived from Lübeck (28 November 1806). The following morning Girod nervously presented himself at Colonel Meunier's quarters. He arrived just as Meunier was giving the daily orders to a gathering of sergeant-majors. On one side of the room was Meunier, the old warhorse who had been browned by the suns of Italy and Egypt, and a room full of sergeant-majors, wizened beyond their years and come to take orders from *their* colonel. On the other side of the room was a puny youth with no bristles on his chin, fresh from school, come to claim a coveted sub-lieutenancy from one of these very same sergeant-majors. What right did Girod have to stand in the way of these veterans? Was he better than them because his father was a wealthy politician, not a wood-turner, or baker? The resentment towards Girod and the new imperial class system was etched on the face of each man.

Meunier played the scene to his own advantage, using it to curry favour with his sub-officers. He told Girod he had no notification from the minister of war about his arrival. Girod meekly asked permission to follow the regiment while waiting for the nomination to arrive. Meunier tersely replied *his regiment* was setting off the next day at 8am and Girod was free to follow, *if it pleased him*. The conversation concluded, Meunier turned his back on Girod and dismissed the sergeant-majors, all of whom were beaming in delight at the way Meunier had squashed the unwelcome newcomer.

Girod was understandably upset. Having made such a poor first impression he resolved to secure a second interview with Meunier in the hope of winning the colonel round. While plotting this he was somewhat surprised to see Meunier bounding towards him, all smiles and handshakes. Meunier said he would be charmed to have Girod as one of his officers; but he should remain with the cadet detachment until they reached army headquarters and the posting was made official. He could join the regiment then. Girod was flabbergasted at the change in Meunier's attitude. He later attributed this to the officer leading the detachment of subalterns putting in a good word on his behalf. It was more likely the ambitious Meunier realized who Girod's father was.

Although the Prussian Army had been quickly vanquished and Berlin had fallen to the French, the Prussian king, William III, was in no mood to talk peace terms. He retreated into East Prussia with his court and set himself up at Königsberg (Kaliningrad). Fearing a sudden expansion of French hegemony into central Europe, Russia again stepped forward to challenge Napoleon. In November 1806 a 62,000-strong Russian army under General Bennigsen marched westwards to protect Warsaw. Despite the onset of winter, Napoleon saw the need to advance into Poland and establish himself on the Vistula. Failing to do so would find him at a disadvantage in the spring.

On 29 November the Ninth quit Berlin and marched towards Thorn (Toruń) via Frankfurt an der Oder. At the same time Girod rejoined his detachment and marched eastward on the road to Custrin. They arrived two days later after a horrific march. The villages were ravaged and deserted. At the approach of French troops the church bells would ring and the inhabitants would flee with their possessions deep into the woods. The roads over marshy ground were near impossible to walk on; heavy rain, the passage of horses and vehicles turned them into quagmires. The men advanced at a snail's pace, struggling to hold onto their shoes in the mud. Girod came across the bodies of several men from the Imperial Guard. They had reached the end of their strength and had taken their own lives rather than face more suffering.

The wind blew up into a gale one night. Hailstones thrashed Girod's face and visibility was so bad that even the local guide leading the detachment became unsure of the way. The guide took the bridle of the captain's horse and slowly edged his way forward. The first man behind the horse took hold of its tail and the men behind each took hold of the coattails of the man in front lest they become lost. Every now and then one would fall into a water-filled ditch and drag his comrades over with him. Each time they would rise up and start off again, each holding on, guided by lights in the distance which promised a return to civilization and warmth. Arriving at Custrin, Girod fell into a tavern overflowing with grenadiers from the Imperial Guard. Totally exhausted, Girod demanded wine. He was given a bottle and drained it like it was water. Brandy was thrust in his direction, but the room was growing too hot and his legs were unsure of themselves. Drunk, he staggered to his billet, tore off his waterlogged uniform and fell asleep naked on a bale of straw.

In the morning he was woken by a feeling of extreme hunger, so he devoured the remnants of the previous night's supper. Girod's clothes were still soaked through but he had no choice but to put them on wet. His portmantle had been put onto a wagon the day before, but the wagon had vanished in the night. One of his comrades had been placed in charge of the wagon, but soaked to the bone and frozen by the cold, his strength had given up and he fell out of the wagon into a ditch where he spent the night unconscious. He was lucky to be saved by an officer travelling post on the same route.

After Custrin the march took the Frenchmen into Poland. It was a very poor country, populated by oppressed serfs and Jews who hawked their goods to the French soldiers wherever they found them. There appeared to be few major roads and so the conditions underfoot remained treacherous. At last they arrived in Posen (Poznań) and were shown to Imperial General headquarters. They were presented to Napoleon who listened to their tales of woe about following the army in a country exhausted of every resource. Napoleon granted each of them a gratuity of 300 francs and offered to make good any losses of equipment they suffered on the way. Girod also received his commission for the Ninth and did not delay putting himself en route to join them along with Sub-Lieutenant Merle, the son of Meunier's friend.

The Ninth had already crossed the Vistula at Thorn and were some way beyond. Girod and Merle reached the city without incident, sharing the road with various regiments they found heading in the same direction. Resting at Thorn for two days to rebuild their strength, they learned Bernadotte's corps was cantoned around Mlawa. The two subalterns finally reached Dupont's headquarters on 31 December. They were told the Ninth was posted a further four leagues (16km) down the road. The two officers doffed their hats and scurried off hoping to reach the regiment before nightfall. However, they miscalculated the length of daylight remaining and found themselves marooned in the darkness at a small hamlet composed of three or four abandoned and devastated houses.

Sharing their plight were two sub-officers from the regiment on their way back to the corps. Lacking any food the four men agreed to share whatever morsels they could find in this desolate neighbourhood. French soldiers were famously resourceful and before long Girod heard the unmistakable squeal of a little pig being held from the ear by a ravenous Frenchman. It was a miracle. Without cooking pots and pans they built a large fire and butchered the unfortunate animal, grilling small pieces of meat over the charcoals. After this delightful meal, the four men sprinkled some straw around the fire and went to sleep.

In the morning the four damp wretches rose to greet the new year, it being 1 January 1807. It was freezing cold and their thoughts were of home, where friends and family were at that very moment lavishing gifts on one another and eating bonbons. Their only consolation was that the regiment was not too far away. Before long Girod and Merle presented themselves to Meunier who was lodged in the castle of the local overlord. They were rewarded with an excellent lunch.

Meunier assigned Girod as sub-lieutenant in the 1st Voltigeurs. Given his modest stature this was an excellent posting and one in which he would have ample opportunity to build a reputation *if* he had the stamina and luck to survive. This company was found in the little town of Vittemburg, halfway along the road between Warsaw and Königsberg. On his arrival Girod found the voltigeur officers playing the carabineer officers at a card game called *la drogue*.[3] It was a game played by those who had neither 'money nor credit', or those who were not prepared to risk their fortune on cards. The game was played by two pairs of players. The object was to go through the deck of cards making pairs. One card was omitted from the deck at random (*la drogue*) and whoever was unable to play at the end of the game was made to wear a long piece of slit wood over the nose. It was a painful forfeit and produced 'an amusing grimace'. If you were caught cheating, a second pincher might be applied.

Meanwhile Bennigsen's Russians were getting closer. The regiment was ordered northwards to the banks of the Vistula Lagoon (Frisches Haff). Here they were in East Prussia and the local language reverted back to German, with which they were more familiar, although the majority only spoke three words: '*Ich logieren hier*' (I'm staying here).[4] The 2nd Voltigeurs were engaged in a minor skirmish in which Sub-Lieutenant Dunoyer was captured with 12 men. In this skirmish he had been asked to scout ahead and recklessly gone too far. Dunoyer was another graduate from Fontainebleau and although he had been with the regiment longer than Girod, and had been wounded at Halle, he was still considered inexperienced and was blamed for the error. Girod took note: it could very easily have been him.

On 24 January Girod found himself at Braunsberg. The cold weather, forced marches and poor diet had taken their toll on him. He had badly blistered feet, was suffering from dysentery and had a fever. Meunier was not a heartless colonel. He took pity on Girod, sitting next to him at dinner. Only three days before, Meunier had written to Dupont complaining that many of his men were barefoot.[5] Girod was praying for a quiet night and some rest, but as soon as the officers finished their supper, there were alerts caused by nearby enemy outposts. Between 11pm and midnight, they received the order to prepare to march out. Hearing about Girod's blistered feet, another officer advised him to throw an entire egg, including its shell into each of his boots, assuring him he would not suffer as much on the march. Meunier had a more practical remedy. He had his private caleche following him and offered Girod to ride in it.[6] Girod obtained his captain's permission and took advantage of this offer. The only trouble was that as he was not walking he felt the cold more and with his feet covered with the broken eggs, he thought they would surely freeze. It was two or three degrees below zero.[7]

Later in the morning of 25 January, the wagon train Girod was travelling with stopped to allow a party of soldiers to scurry by. There was a rumour the Russians had been encountered in strength and this was soon confirmed by the sound of artillery booming in the distance. Ignoring his painful feet, Girod jumped down from the caleche and hurried forward to rejoin his battalion. The 8th Line from Rivaud's division had encountered the Russian advanced guard led by Bennigsen near Mohrungen (Morąg). While the 8th clung on to a position in front of Georgenthal, Marshal Bernadotte hurried to the scene from the direction of Osterode, arriving around 11am with a brigade of Drouet's division (27th Light, 94th Line) and both battalions of the Ninth. At this point the rest of Dupont's division was still several hours' march away from the field.

By the time Girod arrived, the Ninth's 2nd Battalion had been sent forward to seize the village of Pfarrersfeldchen, which was occupied by Russian sharpshooters. This battalion advanced over a frozen lake to attack the village from the flank with its voltigeurs deployed. The battalion quickly drove the Russian skirmishers away and took up defensive positions around the farm buildings and gardens. The Russian 25th Jaeger were ordered to counter-attack the Ninth, but the Russian regiment was recently formed and inexperienced. When the regiment came within range of the Ninth's muskets, it was met by a furious fusillade and fell back in disorder. The Russians responded by launching a counter-attack, this time with two companies of the 5th Jaeger and six companies of the Escatherinoslav Grenadiers. The Russians were in no mood to trade volleys with the Ninth, but pressed forward in a manner that showed they wanted to fight hand-to-hand. The bayonets of the Russian troops came down with a tremendous 'hurrah!'

At some point in the fighting the 2nd Battalion's commander, Rameaux, was wounded along with Surgeon-Major Ballesdent and several other officers. The Russians also killed Lieutenant Donot, the commander of the swimmers on the Marengo campaign, and the battalion's eagle bearer, Sergeant-Major Hautecoeur.[8] With their battalion commander out of action, the French officers looked at one another for inspiration. The battalion was dispersed around the farm buildings and had already fired off a great deal of ammunition. The battalion was unsupported and it was extremely unlikely any assistance would arrive before the Russians. A shout went up to rally the battalion on the far side of the village. The drummers beat the recall and with Russians getting closer, the light infantrymen raced off through the snow.

As the Russians entered the farm they encountered small pockets of resistance where groups of chasseurs had holed themselves up in buildings and had not realized their comrades had already retreated. A group of 14 chasseurs from 5th Company found themselves cut off and surrendered, only to be rescued by their sergeant, Joseph Nicolas Cuinat, who ran back into the farm with a corporal and chased off their Russian captors. Some were not so lucky and found their demise on a Russian bayonet.[9]

While these private contests were being fought, the battalion's eagle guard came into desperate trouble. After Hautecoeur's demise, the eagle had been picked up and guarded by a group of carabineers. In the hasty retreat this group was singled out by the Russian sharpshooters. Trudging through the knee-deep snow, two more eagle bearers were shot down in quick succession. A carabineer seized the flag up from the snow and ran with all his might, but he could not escape. Turning to face the Russians, the carabineer saw a group of jaeger bearing down on him. One of them was an officer on horseback. Unable to outrun them, in desperation the carabineer threw the eagle like a javelin over a wall in the direction of his retreating comrades hoping it would be saved. He then turned to face his assailants, wounding Captain Reitzenstein of the 5th Jaeger before falling himself. As the carabineer winced from his wounds, he watched a party of Russian troops run by and retrieve the flag. He must have been distraught as he watched the blue staff held aloft victoriously by Adjutant Basile Borodkine.[10]

Witnessing the flight of the battalion, Marshal Bernadotte ordered Meunier to advance in support with 1st Battalion while he rode among the retreating light infantrymen to rally them. The 1st Battalion advanced and took position alongside the rest of the French line on the frozen lake. Girod was concerned at the ominous cracking sounds from the ice beneath his feet. The Russians brought up several guns and began firing ricochet shots across the lake to try and break the ice and drown the Frenchmen. Fortunately it held firm.

It was now 2pm. A fierce fire-fight raged along the French line without either side gaining the upper hand. On the far side of the field, Dupont approached with the 32nd and 96th. Seeing the French line heavily engaged to its front, he quit the road and marched cross-country at the Russian flank. As Dupont's men advanced across the frozen lake they also noticed the elasticity of the ice underfoot. There were several cracks. The Russians began lobbing shells but were again unsuccessful in breaking the ice. Ignoring the peril, Colonel Barrois had his regiment help pull the artillery into position across the frozen lake. Dupont's gunners managed to find a position where they could enfilade the whole Russian line. Every shot fired from the French guns bounded its way through the Russian line causing carnage and confusion. Colonel Darricau now made the decisive move. As the Russians began to retreat, he ordered 500 fusiliers to advance in skirmish formation against the village of Georgenthal behind the Russian lines. His men raced through the snow and occupied the houses. As the Russians began to retreat they had to pass through Georgenthal and were exposed to point-blank fire. The battle was declared in the French favour.

As the fighting raged around Pfarrersfeldchen, a large party of Cossack horsemen made a long detour around the two armies. The French baggage train had taken refuge behind Mohrungen. The Cossacks swept down on the train and seized everything they could get their hands on. Bernadotte's personal baggage was lost, along with all the contributions they had exacted from the population of East Prussia. Of this sum, 12,000 francs had been promised to Colonel Meunier as his share of the spoils. He was understandably upset at losing out on such a sum. In truth he had far bigger problems to deal with. Once the 2nd Battalion rallied they realized with horror that the eagle escort had not made it out. After a search of the field after the battle, they would have found the bodies of the men last seen defending it. On the evening after the battle, as the soldiers prepared to bivouac in two feet of snow, rumours began to spread among Dupont's other regiments that the Ninth had lost an eagle. Meunier had sworn a personal oath to Napoleon to defend the eagle. When the newly crowned emperor had asked, 'Will you swear to sacrifice your lives in their defence' it had not been empty rhetoric. This would be the end of Meunier's promising career. In fact, the disgrace was such it might even oblige him to take his own life. However, just when it seemed inevitable that the loss of the eagle would be exposed, he experienced an enormous stroke of luck.

According to Girod there had been an accident before the battle in which 2nd Battalion's eagle had been damaged. The eagles were not cast as a single piece, but in sections. In this accident the eagle section broke away from the plinth on which it stood. The 'bird' section was wrapped up and put in a caisson until a smithy could be found to make the repairs. The 2nd Battalion therefore marched under the flag, the staff and the gilded plinth, which bore the numeral '9'. This is what was captured, the fact the eagle was missing from this assembly can only be considered a technicality. There was a mad dash back to the baggage train to recover the eagle, but of course, the Cossacks had made off with all the regiment's caissons during the battle. Meunier must have experienced a second moment of despair, but luck was still on his side. It turned out that the caisson containing the broken eagle had been missing for three days – it was not with the other caissons when the Cossacks attacked and arrived later in the day. The officers hurriedly pulled the 'bird' from its wrappings and mounted it on a long hop pole. After conspicuously parading it in view of the other regiments the rumours of losing an eagle ceased. To cover himself, Meunier put out a story that the eagle had indeed fallen to the enemy while the regiment had been dispersed in skirmish formation, but his men had heroically re-conquered it. What reason did anyone have to doubt him? It was a glorious story. When Napoleon heard the tale he included it in the 55th bulletin of the Grand Army, dated Warsaw, 29 January 1807. The language used in this bulletin leaves no doubt of the dishonour of losing an eagle:

> … The mêlée was very lively; the eagle of the 9th Regiment of Light Infantry was seized
> by the enemy; but, at the sight of this insult with which this brave regiment was going
> to be tarnished forever, and which neither victory nor the glory acquired in hundred
> fights would have washed away, the soldiers, animated by an inconceivable ardour,
> rushed on the enemy, routed them and retook their eagle.[11]

Although Napoleon's bulletins were famous for their economies of truth, in this case, no fault can be laid at the emperor's feet. Meunier had deceived Napoleon over what really occurred and in their lifetime, all but one of the officers promulgated this falsehood. It is uncertain when the emperor finally learned the truth from the Russian gazettes, but he did. By then it was too late to amend the heroic story as it had been told to the French public. There was little to gain from exposing the son-in-law of Jacques-Louis David as a liar. However, as a precaution against a repeat of the unfortunate incident, Napoleon ordered all his light infantry regiments to send their eagles back to the depot, lest they suffer a similar experience while skirmishing.[12]

There is one last twist to this story. The Russians were naturally jubilant to seize the flag as a trophy and all their accounts agree that the standard had been damaged with the eagle itself absent, confirming Girod's story. This did not diminish the triumph of seizing the standard in any way. The flag was taken to St Petersburg and deposited in the Cathedral Notre Dame de Kazan on

31 March 1807. In 1969 General Serge Andolenko, a Russian émigré in French military service, produced an excellent work entitled *Aigles de Napoléon contre drapeaux du Tsar*. In this work Andolenko raised an interesting question about the Ninth's broken eagle. He quoted General Ermolov, who described the capture of the flag and included the words, 'This flag had been given under the Republic to the half-brigade, which received the name *Incomparable*.' The history of the Russian 95th Regiment also commented: 'This flag had been given, under the Republic, in recompense of the bravery, to the half-brigade which carried the name of *Incomparable*.'[13]

The silks attached to the eagles in 1804 were uniform in presentation. None bore regimental mottos. This made Andolenko wonder if the Russians had actually seized the 1802 pattern flag, the flag with the motto 'Incomparable' emblazoned on it. Why else would General Ermolov describe it as a flag given under the Republic? Did the Ninth really attach their 1802 colours to the eagle staff? Apparently there was a precedent for this. Andolenko cites the example of the 57th Line, which Napoleon dubbed 'The Terrible'. Before the eagles were distributed Napoleon ordered the colonel of the 57th to return a set of flags that bore the title 'The Terrible.' When the eagles were distributed, the 57th's eagle had been fitted with the old flags. Had Napoleon done this same service for the Ninth? When Fouquet was questioned about the ceremony in 1839, he reported handing over two of the 1802 flags in return for the two new eagles. We know at least one of the 1802 flags was retained; but were all three? The romantic in us may prefer to picture the Ninth marching into battle under its special green and sunburst flags affixed below a gilded eagle; but the sceptic in us must admit the tattered cloth which the Russians took away at Mohrungen was probably the 1804 tricolour.

The day after Mohrungen the French retreated south to Osterode and then turned westwards through the snow in the direction of Thorn. Although they had been victorious against the Russians, Napoleon wanted to lure the Russians into a trap. As the Russian commander General Bennigsen pursued Bernadotte's corps towards the Vistula, Napoleon would manoeuvre the remainder of the Grand Army onto Bennigsen's left flank and rear. It was a brilliant piece of strategy, but if Bernadotte's men were caught by the Russians they would be dreadfully exposed. Given the weather, the poor condition of the roads and the swarms of Cossack light horsemen all around them, there was every chance of the Russians catching up with them.

On the evening of 26 January, the Ninth's 1st Voltigeur Company found itself ahead of the regiment scouting the march. They came across a village and discovered a cache of wheat flour. One of the voltigeurs had been a baker in Paris before joining the army and was able to bake bread for the whole company. It was a luxury they had not enjoyed for many days. As soon as the company settled down for the night, the remainder of Dupont's division arrived and turfed them out. The voltigeurs were again ordered forwards ahead of the regiment and spent a wretched night under arms in a blizzard watching the edge of a forest. In the morning one of the sentinels killed a Cossack. It was the first one they had seen up close and many of the little Frenchmen came to gawp at the unfortunate wretch. Later in the day the voltigeurs came under attack by a body of cavalry that had used the woods for cover. There was a mad scramble to avoid being surrounded and they reached the safety of the regiment only after losing a corporal and five men captured in one of the advanced posts. That evening there was another scare when two chasseur companies given up for lost strayed into the picket line and caused a brief fire-fight. It was bitterly cold. That night Sub-Lieutenant Girod fell asleep in the open and woke to find himself under a mantle of snow. He was surprised how warm the snow had kept him through the night.

The regiment marched off and arrived at Liebemuhl (Miłomłyn). All the houses in the village were engulfed in flames for no apparent reason, another senseless calamity of war. On that particular day the 1st Voltigeurs rotated with the 2nd and went to form the regiment's rearguard. They could hear Cossacks hurrahing in the distance but suffered no serious trouble from them. It was a reminder that the Russians were still perilously close. In the afternoon they came across a farm that had thus far escaped the ravages of war. The soldiers of the Ninth swooped down upon a flock of sheep, which they served for dinner. Marauders were sent out to scour the neighbourhood and on this occasion they returned loaded with poultry and other welcome supplies. In their absence the mundane chores were carried out by the rest of the men. Fresh straw was gathered, and barn doors, carts, ploughs and other wooden equipment were broken up for firewood. This operation was carried out with no thought for the farmer whose livelihood they ruined.

On 29 January the march continued without any sign of the Russians. Bernadotte's corps took up position around the town of Löbau (Lubawa), with Dupont's division to the north-east at the village of Rozenthal. Towards midday both voltigeur companies of the Ninth were sent to the village of Grabaü (Grabowo) two miles distant. This village was already occupied by 50 troopers from 4th Hussars under Squadron Commander Eugène Merlin and a brigadier-general whom Girod did not name in his memoirs for reasons which will soon become apparent.[14]

The general in question had asked for a battalion and artillery support to be sent to Grabaü so he was somewhat stunned to see two weak companies arrive, totalling no more than 120 men. The voltigeurs sent out some forward posts and as it had been a quiet day, the commanders of the voltigeur companies (Captain Dongée of the 1st and Lieutenant Grandjean of the 2nd) decided to billet their men in the houses. The village was Polish and the reception given to the Frenchmen was more favourable than in the Prussian villages they had encountered. Girod took the opportunity to make running repairs. He had not removed his boots for days and the sores on his feet needed to be dressed. He therefore stripped off and took the opportunity to wash his shirt. While he was doing this, the local villagers kept coming in and speaking excitedly in their local dialect. In no mood to converse, the French officers rudely shooed the Poles away. However, as they pushed the villagers in the direction of the door they heard a blood-curling shout of *'to arms!'* outside.

Of course, the Poles had been trying to warn Girod and his colleagues. They realized this when the group of officers saw the main guard of hussars gallop past, having not even had time to bridle their horses. Girod's comrades were still fully dressed and they looked at their young colleague with commiseration as they hastily ran out to join their companies, each bidding Girod *adieu*, believing he would be captured. The peasants to whom Girod had been rude now came to his salvation by helping him dress. One fetched his boots, another held his breeches; one offered him his épée, another his hat. The linen was still damp so Girod abandoned it. He ran out into the street still buttoning his clothes up as the enemy cavalry came galloping into the village from one end. The voltigeurs were at the other end and had taken up position in a cemetery surrounded by a high wall. With his heart in his mouth Girod reached the safety of his comrades in the nick of time.

While perfect for infantry, the position was not large enough to take the French hussars and their horses as well. The general decided they should make a run for it, which was all well and good for him on his swift horse, but the voltigeurs would have been very exposed on the open plain. Captain Dongée accepted the order, believing he did not have the authority to do otherwise; however Lieutenant Grandjean was having none of it. Grandjean was a close relative of General of Division Charles Grandjean, a distinguished general in the Grand Army. Possibly the lieutenant felt this connection might count in his favour should he later be tried for insubordination. In any case Grandjean told the general he could do what he liked, but *his* company of voltigeurs was staying put in the cemetery. The general decided to remain after all.

Rather than remain in the cemetery, the voltigeurs formed up outside with their backs against a sort of palisade formed by drifting snow. This allowed the hussars to form up alongside them to the left. Commander Merlin harangued the infantrymen with stirring words: 'Brave chasseurs of the Ninth, remember Marengo where your regiment acquired the glorious surname Incomparable. Remember Krems (Dürnstein), Halle and all the other places where you have maintained your reputation.'[15] Each time Merlin said something, the general would half-heartedly say 'yes chasseurs, yes' and repeat whatever had just been said. He did not inspire much confidence.

In the meantime a mass of enemy cavalry about 800 strong formed up in front of them and prepared to charge. The majority were Prussian 'Death Hussars', so-called because of the death's head badge they wore on their shakos. They were intermingled with a large number of Cossacks who had joined with them, lances at the ready. The Frenchmen waited coolly to receive the charge and as the mass approached a Prussian colonel called out, 'Frenchmen, surrender. No harm will come to you.' No sooner had he finished uttering these words when the voltigeurs let fly a volley from 30 paces. The colonel fell dead, pierced by two balls, his body landing among those of his comrades. Twice more the cavalry charged and each time they were met with a vicious fusillade. The horsemen retreated and regrouped in the distance to consider their next move. Meanwhile the French hussars began passing their cartridges to the voltigeurs who were already running perilously low.

At the beginning of the action a hussar trumpeter had been sent back to Rozenthal to alert Dupont to what was occurring at Grabaü. The trumpeter galloped as fast as his horse would take him and presented himself at Dupont's headquarters, recklessly informing him that the men at Grabaü were so badly outnumbered they were now almost certainly either dead or captured. Unaware of the composition of the forces ranged against him, Dupont adopted a prudent stance and ordered his division to stand under arms waiting for the enemy. Colonel Meunier was reluctant to write off both his voltigeur companies on the word of an overexcited trumpeter, so galloped off over the snowy fields in the direction of Grabaü himself. It wasn't long before he heard the tell-tale music of his voltigeurs at work. Convinced his men could be saved, Meunier rode back to the division, borrowed several voltigeur companies and a little light artillery, and led them the two miles down the road to Grabaü. Arriving in range, Meunier had a howitzer prepared for action. Typically enough the first shell flew straight at the Frenchmen it was destined to protect and it was lucky no one was injured by the blast. Seeing the relief force coming, the Prussians and Cossacks made off, cursing under their breaths. They left a heap of horses and over 60 of their comrades dead on the ground behind them, their colonel included. Not a single Frenchman had been wounded in the action.

Once reunited with the division, considerable praise was heaped on the detachment. Of course the hussars and the general who had wanted to escape naturally claimed the lion's share of the glory; but Meunier saw to it that all the voltigeur officers were rewarded too, all except for Girod. Meunier took the young man to one side and said he wanted to put him forward for a cross of honour, but he was only recently arrived in the regiment. Girod accepted this disappointment with good grace.

Meanwhile, Marshal Bernadotte was beginning to grow anxious. Since beginning the retreat he had not received any news from the emperor and was uncertain if he should carry on retreating westwards or make a halt. In danger of moving too far away from the Grand Army, he resolved to make a stand and await the Russian army. He therefore spent the remainder of 29 January passing among his soldiers, encouraging them.[16] Presuming he would be attacked at dawn he had his corps form line of battle at 2am. Dupont was brought southwards from Rozenthal to Löbau where the infantry divisions of Drouet and Rivaud were already in position with three regiments of dragoons. The Ninth and the light cavalry were left at a midpoint between the two places at Bischwalde (Byszwald) as an advanced guard.

The sun rose over the snowy panorama, but there was no indication the Russians wished to attack. While the French waited, a division of cuirassiers under General d'Hautpoul arrived from Strasburg (Brodnica). The sun set and rose again, still without news of the Russians or from the emperor. They spent a jittery night in the same positions. There were a number of alerts and Bernadotte still fretted over the lack of instructions. With the countryside devoid of inhabitants the marshal was unable to procure spies who might inform him of the Russians' movements and intentions. He began to fear he was too far away from the Grand Army for them to come in support of him should he be attacked. Perhaps the Russians were encircling him as he spoke? His corps would be surrounded and swallowed up by the Russians without the emperor even knowing it. At the end of these deliberations Bernadotte decided he should continue his retreat towards Thorn and by doing so, if nothing else, he would at least cover the army's lines of communication.[17]

On 31 January the retreat commenced at midday. The Ninth acted as the army's rearguard and burned several wooden bridges to slow down the Russian pursuit. That evening they arrived at Neumarck (Nowe Miasto Lubawskie) but any chance of a dry night in a billet was dashed when the regiment was ordered to press on through the night. Further along the road they ran into a veritable jam of guns, horses, wagons and noisy infantrymen as the whole of Bernadotte's corps tried to pass through a bottleneck in the road. It was absolute chaos and it took a further 12 hours to cover a distance of just two leagues (8km). That night the temperature really plummeted. The men were suffering badly from fatigue. They were tormented by hunger and above all else, desperate for sleep. Growing ever colder in the dark of night men fell asleep while marching and slumped into the snow by the side of the road. A rearguard of officers and sub-officers was formed to wake these poor wretches up and keep them marching any way they could. That night was one of the worst Girod experienced in his life.

In the morning they halted at a forlorn, deserted village. A score of officers lodged themselves in a building recently used as a stable. The floor was covered with manure a foot deep, but the officers lay down on it and slept anyway. When they awoke they learned that the last of their supplies had finally run out. They were hungry all night and hungry all the next day, marching on empty bellies as far as Strasburg.

At Strasburg Colonel Meunier summoned Girod to his quarters. The plucky young officer was finding his first campaign extremely hard-going. Surgeon-Major Vanderbach was called to examine him. A combination of dysentery and fever had left him exhausted and his feet were in tatters. Vanderbach's prescription was a three-month break to restore his strength and allow his feet to heal properly. Girod was naturally disappointed to drop out, but he had the consolation of not being alone. There were a considerable number of sick and wounded; many had frostbitten feet from marching barefoot in knee-deep snow. Girod was put in command of these unfortunate wretches and sent off to the rear. Given Girod's inexperience, Meunier put him under the care of an old sapper who did not leave his side for a moment.

As Girod left the regiment, Bernadotte was still without news. He later learned that all the messengers the emperor had sent to him had been intercepted by Cossacks. While Bernadotte had been ignorant of Napoleon's intentions, Bennigsen had been reading the captured dispatches and understood them all too well. He saw Napoleon had set a trap for him with Bernadotte's withdrawal as the bait. Bennigsen turned tail and marched with all haste in the opposite direction to Bernadotte, trying to reach Königsberg. It was not until 3 February that a messenger finally got through to Strasburg, ordering Bernadotte to retrace his steps and rejoin the army as quickly as possible. It was approximately 100km back to Mohrungen. The corps set off on the morning of 4 February and arrived there on 7 February, marching through the same barren and devastated countryside they had already exhausted of resources.

On 11 February they finally rejoined the Grand Army at Eylau. An epic battle had been fought at this place on 8 February, one which remains known as one of the bloodiest of all of Napoleon's battles. The soldiers of Dupont's division saw the field of battle choked with the remains of men and horses, slowly being covered over by the snow. Field hospitals had been set up in the farmhouses and scores of amputees sat around freezing to death, unable to eat their rations because the soup froze before reaching them.

The Russian army had fallen back on Königsberg after the battle so Napoleon decided to allow his soldiers some respite. It had been a harrowing winter campaign; his men were starving and frozen through. They needed to rest and regroup before the campaign was brought to a resolution in the spring. The Ninth was sent north-west from Eylau to Kreutzbourg (Slavskoye) on 12 February, then moved further westwards and formed cantonments around Braunsberg (Braniewo) on the River Passarge a week or so later. During this time Dupont's division was reinforced by the arrival of the 24th Line, which was brigaded with the Ninth and placed under the command of General André-Adrien-Joseph Labruyère. Being paired with a line regiment was something of a novelty for the Ninth, which had thus far been brigaded with the light cavalry of the divisions it served in. This was perhaps an indication that Napoleon saw little difference between his fusiliers and chasseurs and also indicated the growing importance of the voltigeur companies in each battalion. It emphasized the voltigeurs were now the only true light infantry France possessed.

Any hope of a quiet end to the winter quickly faded. On 26 February a large Russian force came out to occupy Braunsberg. Dupont gathered his division together and marched off to intercept. It was a sharp action, made all the more confusing by dense fog. At one point the 32nd Line were nearly overwhelmed by Russians whose silhouettes were mistaken for those of the Ninth. At this time French line infantry were still issued with the same felt bicorne hats that they had worn at Marengo and the battles of the Revolution. The Ninth had adopted the cylindrical shako as its headdress and when the men wore greatcoats there was little to tell them apart from the Russians, except for the colour of the cockade. The 32nd were lucky to realize their mistake in time.

From the point of view of the Ninth, the battle of Braunsberg was remarkable for two acts of courage. At the head of a detachment of a dozen men, Lieutenant Jean-Pierre Malgontier forced a company of Russians and their officer to surrender, a feat for which he received the Legion of Honour. The other feat of daring was performed by Surgeon-Major Vanderbach. In order to retrieve the wounded, Vanderbach led forward a chasseur company from the 1st Battalion. Vanderbach was riding with the company when he spied through the fog a battalion of Russians advancing with several guns. With their inferior number concealed in the fog, Vanderbach put himself at the head of the company and charged the Russian battalion. His horse was killed beneath him in the charge, but the shock of the attack repulsed the Russian battalion and allowed the chasseurs to seize two guns.

This action proved the last major action of a long winter. It marked the end of a difficult campaign which had begun with the battle of Jena, continued into deep midwinter, and remained without a conclusion. After the battle the Ninth took up residence in the villages in front of Braunsberg and remained there until the first days of April. As the weather improved the men built huts from wood in a settlement they called the Camp of Ponte-Corvo, in honour of Bernadotte's ducal title. The Ninth was a few kilometres in front of this camp with the order to protect it. On 14 April the regiment was awarded 18 crosses of the Legion of Honour, eight to officers, ten to the troops. On the surface all appeared good with the regiment and its illustrious reputation. In the 64th bulletin of Grand Army, which contained a description of the action at Braunsberg, it was written Colonel Meunier 'deserved particular eulogies'.[18] Clearly Napoleon had not yet learned what had really happened at Mohrungen.

TO THE RESCUE
AT FRIEDLAND

We left poor Sub-Lieutenant Girod with his frozen, blistered feet heading for safety at the end of January 1807. Given the distance from the main depot at Landau to Poland, the regiment had formed a forward depot behind the Vistula to act as a halfway house.[1] Here Girod was billeted on a Polish baron with several sub-officers for company. Within three weeks of eating and sleeping normally, he was back on his feet and visiting the regiment's cobblers to see about some new shoes. He restored his fitness by going for walks and maintained his spirits by going out with other officers, getting drunk and singing his way through the evenings. Before long he declared himself fit for service and indicated that he wished to return to the regiment. A detachment was formed which Girod thought he would lead back to the regiment. Alas it was not to be. The day before the detachment was due to leave, Girod held a review of the men and, perhaps with ideas a little above his station, he decided to conduct the review from horseback. Prancing around on the ice, his horse slipped and fell. Girod's left leg was trapped under the horse and his ankle badly sprained. The unlucky sub-lieutenant had the ignominy of being carried back to his quarters by his men.

After a time the forward depot was moved 30 leagues (120km) to the outskirts of Schwetz (Świecie), a town on the left bank of the Vistula, north-east of Bromberg (Bydgoszcz). Girod was transported in the back of a cart, still unable to march. Passing through Thorn, Girod was billeted in 'a hovel', which had served as a stable and was knee-deep in manure. If matters were not bad enough, he was woken up in the middle of the night by one of the regiment's cantineers who came to shelter in the room with her child, whom Girod looked upon as an unwashed scamp. We have no record of the cantineer's experience of this campaign, but it must have been a wretched state to be in, so far from France, with her husband up at the front and little news. They were hardy souls.

By May 1807 Girod was able to walk again and he rejoined the regiment at Braunsberg. Meunier was pleased to see him and congratulated him on his zealous return. In his absence Girod had been replaced in the first voltigeurs by another sub-lieutenant, but Meunier told Girod he would remain attached to his old company all the same. Although the fighting had ceased by mutual consent, service at Braunsberg was still demanding. The Ninth was posted on the outskirts of the city, across the River Passarge. The area was surrounded by ditches and redoubts, and the enemy's forward posts were barely a musket shot away, populated by the same Death Hussars they had faced at Grabaü. As the year drew on the nights became increasingly shorter. The voltigeurs would spend the time between twilight and sunrise standing in the advanced guard. At 2am the whole regiment would stand under arms waiting to see if the uneasy truce had faltered.

By the beginning of June the regiment was restored in strength. Columns of fresh-faced conscripts arrived from France, along with replacement uniforms, munitions, biscuit and wine. In addition to its usual stalwarts from the Vosges, the Ninth had begun to receive conscripts from farther afield. The regiment had never been fixed to a particular region. Even if one goes back to 1789 when the corps had the provincial name Cévennes and had been formed in the Languedoc, the battalion was in fact composed of men from all over France. Under the empire the regiment went a step further and actually ceased to be 'French'. Already in the early empire it was taking recruits from Holland. It then began taking large batches of recruits with German names from the Sarre Department on the right bank of the Rhine. It also received men from the annexed parts of Piedmont in north-eastern Italy. These recruits came from the Sesia Department (centred around Vercelli) and the Doire Department (centred on Ivrea and the Aosta Valley). It was a long march up to the depot, where they were given the rudiments of training in a foreign language that they were forced to learn quickly before being sent hither and thither.

In addition to the two field battalions, the elite companies of the third battalion had entered the theatre of war, although not with their parent regiment. In October 1806 Napoleon had ordered the creation of a reserve division, which was commanded by General Oudinot. The elite companies of the regiments of Dupont's division (9th, 32nd and 96th) were formed into a battalion, which was designated 1st Battalion 2nd Regiment in the brigade of General Ruffin. Although designated as a reserve, it was not long before Oudinot's division was marched into Poland where it assisted during the siege of Danzig, which lasted from 19 March 1807 until the garrison capitulated on 27 May. After this they joined the corps commanded by Marshal Lannes.

By the beginning of June it was clear that the Russians were ready for a rematch. As things began to heat up the Ninth made raids to round up enemy cattle. Skirmishes broke out all along the line. On 5 June Bernadotte was wounded in one such raid at Spanden and so was replaced by General Victor, who began concentrating his army corps around Eylau. In the early morning light of 14 June the officers of the Ninth visited the infamous battlefield. They were somewhat stunned to see that the battlefield contained lakes and a verdant plain, all of which had been frozen over and running with rivers of blood when they last passed through.[2] It appears to have been an emotional visit. They were shown a small mound upon which they found a plaque with the following words:

> Here are interred all the officers of the 14th Line with their colonel.[3]

This epitaph was true enough. During the battle, the 14th had been in advance of the main French position when it was exposed to a horrific Russian artillery bombardment. The survivors formed a square around a hillock and were assailed by cavalry and infantry attacks. In the end, there were too few men left to form an organized retreat. The major then commanding gave their eagle to a messenger with the words: 'I see no means of saving the regiment. Return to the emperor, bid him farewell from the 14th Line, which has faithfully executed his orders, and bear to him the eagle which he gave to us and which we can defend no longer.' Before the messenger could make off, Russian grenadiers broke into the square and the eagle fell.[4] The officers corps had fulfilled their solemn pledge to the full. Some of the Ninth's officers must have silently pondered their own performance at Mohrungen when hearing this story.

When the men were formed into ranks, they set off marching eastwards towards where the Russians were said to be engaged with Lannes' corps. At 8am the emperor came galloping past, easily recognizable in his grey overcoat. He appeared to be in a good mood and stopped to exchange pleasantries with Dupont. The emperor expressed his satisfaction at Dupont's 'fine division' which had been so distinguished since Ulm and said he looked forward to seeing it fight before his eyes.[5] Before parting, Napoleon urged Dupont to press his march and told him he was counting on his division's arrival before he committed to battle.

The French Imperial Guard was following close behind the emperor. In their haste to reach the battlefield Dupont's men did not give way to the Guard and so the two bodies of troops became mixed. Reaching a bridge, the Guard claimed it was their right to cross first. Dupont's men disagreed and the incident turned into something of a farce, with carts blocking the bridge and soldiers arguing with one another. Coming fresh from his meeting with Napoleon, Dupont exploded with rage when he saw the hold up. In the emperor's name he threatened the senior officers and had the carts blocking the bridge thrown into the river. Restoring order, he allowed the Guard to cross first and then advanced with his division. One wonders if old rivalries had resurfaced that morning?[6]

The Ninth passed through Domnau (Domnovo) at 2pm. The village was filled with wounded soldiers who told them about the morning's clash. As they continued on the road the number of wounded grew, leaving them in no doubt that the battle was a fierce affair. It was always disconcerting to see wounded men on the road; men who had been fit young specimens a few hours before but were now bludgeoned, bloodied and ruined. Girod noticed one group among them who were entirely naked and blackened head to foot. They walked with their arms outstretched as if blind, uttering pitiful cries. At first Girod could not guess what had happened, but his more experienced colleagues explained they were either gunners or members of the artillery train, burned by an exploding ammunition caisson. It was a sobering sight.

At 4pm they called a halt behind a thick wood that hid them from view of the battlefield. For the next hour the regiment prepared for action and waited for the stragglers to catch up. Girod's captain had been keeping hold of a bottle of brandy for a special occasion. The coming battle appeared to be as good an excuse as any, so he drew the bottle from his saddle. The four voltigeur officers each took a healthy swig in turn, then another, before preserving the rest in case one of them was wounded. Girod was not very afraid. Even the sight of the surgeons setting up the field hospitals did not unduly disturb him. His brother Marc had recently been killed in action and although Girod much regretted the loss, it did not occur to him that he might suffer the same fate.

While Girod drank his brandy and caught his breath, the remainder of Victor's 1st Corps deployed to the right of the Eylau road. The three infantry divisions were arrayed in two lines, with a third line formed by four dragoon regiments under General Lahoussaye. In total they formed a mass of over 20,000 men. With everything prepared, Colonel Meunier passed among the regiment offering encouragement. Seeing Girod he said, 'Well! You are going to see what a pitched battle is.' In a display of bravado Girod replied, 'I would have been really sorry to miss out on such a party.'[7]

Bennigsen had attacked Lannes in the early hours of the morning, but had been unable to put the French to flight. From noon there came a lull in the fighting. The battle had been raging for nearly ten hours and both sides were exhausted in the summer heat. The Russians had been marching long before the battle and were in no mood to press the French through the afternoon. This played into Napoleon's hands. He needed time for his reserves to arrive. Like Marengo, there would be a battle in the morning and another in the evening. The omens were good. Just behind the village of Posthenen there was a slight rise giving an uninterrupted panorama of the contested ground.[8] To the right of Posthenen was the Sortlack wood. The little town of Friedland was directly in front, across a gentle plain of wheat and rye, perfect ground for manoeuvring an army. To the left of Posthenen was a small stream, known locally as the Muhlosen (Millstream). It trickled its way towards Friedland, cutting the battlefield in two. Just before the Millstream reached the town, it passed between two steep banks before finally coming to a rest in a pond on the north side of the town. On the south side of Friedland was the River Alle, curving its way through the countryside. The combination of the Alle and the Millstream meant Friedland was situated on something of a peninsula, with pontoon bridges linking the town to the opposite bank. The Russians had drawn up on either side of the Millstream and soon realized the disadvantages of having done so. The two wings of their army were unable to act in unison. A handful of flying bridges were thrown across the Millstream, but not enough to permit the speedy lateral movement of troops.

Napoleon quickly guessed the key to the battle was Friedland itself. If the French could take the town, the Russian army would be cleaved in two and cut off from its escape route across the Alle. Napoleon summoned Marshal Ney and ordered him to capture the town. His instructions were to ignore anything occurring on his right and left, but to drive on and seize the bridges. If he could do this, Napoleon would annihilate the Russians. Ney understood his mission perfectly and returned to his corps with a lion-like expression of determination on his face.

At 5pm the signal for battle rang out. Twenty guns fired three salvoes in quick succession and Ney's corps advanced, each battalion forming a column of divisions.[9] Although the Russians were surprised by this late escalation in the battle, they responded quickly. As Ney's corps advanced towards Friedland it was exposed to a terrible enfilading artillery fire from the far bank of the Alle on their right. Ney ordered his corps to march obliquely to the left and deployed his columns into line to lessen the impact of the Russian artillery fire.

After reorganizing his troops, it took Ney's corps about an hour to advance one kilometre across the battlefield. Napoleon ordered Dupont's division to move forward in support. As the Ninth passed through the woods, Girod took in the great panorama before him. He had never seen so many soldiers gathered in one place. Formed in line, Ney's corps had a frontage of more than two kilometres. Beyond the line of advancing Frenchmen, over the rolling fields of crops, they could see the clock tower in the town of Friedland. As far as the eye could see, right and left, thick clouds of smoke billowed upwards marking the extent of the field in contention. Once clear of the trees, Dupont's division was formed into two lines. In the first line on the right, both battalions of the Ninth were formed in line of battle. On their left, the 24th Line adopted the same formation. Behind them was the brigade of General Barrois. The four battalions of the 32nd and 96th were formed in columns opposite the wings of the regiments in front. To the left of the division and slightly ahead of it, Dupont's artillery trundled forwards to support the attack.

Up ahead Ney's troops were engulfed in a dense fog of gunpowder smoke. Through the fog it appeared the French soldiers were turning back. At first no one was sure if it was the wounded being evacuated, or if the troops were simply realigning themselves behind a fold in the ground. While Dupont was assessing the situation several cannon balls bounced their way towards him. He galloped off alone to find out the cause. Through the smoke it suddenly became clear what the trouble was. The Russian Imperial Guard had moved forward from a concealed position and was pushing Ney's infantry back. General Marchand's division was breaking up and falling back when the Russian cavalry suddenly charged. The plain was quickly dotted with stragglers running to avoid being cut down by Russian horsemen. Ney's corps was in danger of being broken in two. An erroneous cry went up that the marshal had fallen and been killed. A crisis had been reached.

Dupont seized the initiative. He sent a request back to Victor asking for the rest of the corps to come up in support and condensed the frontage of his division, with the Ninth remaining in line and supported by Barrois with the remaining six battalions in column close behind. They marched against the Russians in an oblique march to the right to allow space for the rest of Victor's corps to come up on their left. Ney's shaken troops were overjoyed to see Dupont's men advancing rapidly towards the Russian Guardsmen. Witnesses from Ney's corps claimed the division looked like a solid wall advancing towards them in support.[10]

Confidence was restored as Dupont urged the stragglers to rally and follow his division forwards. Arriving within musket range of the Russian Imperial Guard, the Ninth opened fire with a violent rolling fire. On the left, Dupont's artillery opened up, and before long the plain before Dupont's division was marked by spitting flames and billowing, sulphurous smoke. The Russian cavalry attempted a charge but Dupont's artillery commander Captain Ricci barked out the order to fire and mowed down the Russian cavalry with canister. On the right flank, the dragoons of Latour Maubourg charged forward with the light cavalry. Behind them, Ney's troops rallied and formed defensive squares bristling with bayonets. Faced with the hail of lead from the Ninth and the artillery, the Russians fell back in disorder. Ney raced to Dupont and shook his hand in gratitude. The attack allowed him to re-form his corps and resume the march on Friedland itself.

Another interested spectator was Victor's artillery commander, General Senarmont. He rode up to Captain Ricci to congratulate him, complimenting his gunners' calm and likening them to being on the drill ground. 'Yes, General, but look how many guns the Russians have to the right and in front of us!'[11] Senarmont looked, told the captain not to worry and galloped off looking for reinforcements. He went to Victor, explained the situation and asked for more guns. Although Dupont had asked Victor to send reinforcements, the reserve had not budged without a command from the emperor. Listening to Senarmont's request, this time Victor complied. Senarmont and Victor agreed there was little to be gained from deploying the guns piecemeal in separate batteries; what was required was a powerful concentration against the most important part of the enemy line. While Victor agreed, his divisional generals were less enthusiastic about handing over their guns, but Senarmont persisted. He was therefore able to reinforce Captain Ricci and formed two 15-gun batteries with six pieces in reserve.

When Senarmont gave the command for his 30 guns to open fire, the Russians were taken somewhat by surprise. The first firing position was 200 fathoms (390m) from the Russian line. After a dozen salvos, Senarmont ordered his gunners to close the distance by half. They began a devastating rolling fire, one gun firing after the other in quick succession. The 1st Battalion of the Ninth were sent to protect Senarmont's gunners. They formed square behind in case the Russian cavalry reappeared and watched intently as their comrades in the artillery took off their coats and rolled up their shirtsleeves in order to better serve their guns.[12]

Greatly disturbed by the hail of canister coming from these batteries, the Russians directed part of their fire on the battery in front of the 1st Battalion. Naturally enough, the balls aimed at the gunners and their cannons continued their flight towards the Ninth. Every now and then a cannon ball would strike, tearing down a file of men. There were a good number of conscripts seeing action for the first time. Girod thought they took it admirably. His curiosity was drawn towards one: a young conscript sitting on the ground in the middle of the square, calmly eating a piece of bread. Thinking the fellow was shirking his duty, Girod went over to him and ordered him to get up and rejoin the ranks. The conscript looked up at Girod then raised the corner of his greatcoat, revealing one of his legs had been half taken away by a cannon ball. With no change of expression the conscript went back to his bread.

Meanwhile, Napoleon had been watching the battle develop with a hawkish eye. Lannes and Mortier's corps had been in action since the morning and had suffered accordingly. Napoleon had intended Victor's corps to act as a reserve for these troops as well as Ney's and was concerned Senarmont had robbed all the reserve divisions of their artillery. He sent his aide-de-camp, General Mouton, to find out what Senarmont was up to. Senarmont's blood was up and he dismissed the aide. 'Leave me be with my gunners,' he replied. 'I will answer for everything.'[13] At that moment he was preparing to move his guns forward again. This time to just 60 fathoms (approximately 120m). Seeing an equal number of Russian guns ahead of him, he ordered his gunners to ignore them, but to concentrate on the masses of Russian infantry with canister. In total Senarmont's gunners fired 3,600 rounds, including 400 rounds of canister.[14] As the Russians retreated from this deadly onslaught their formations were compressed by the Alle on one side and the Millstream on the other. However, as each discharge tore shreds in the Russian lines, more came forward stoically to fill the gaps in the lines and suffer the fate of their comrades. The Russian cavalry reappeared on the right, looking to charge the guns, but Senarmont ordered a change of front and directed two discharges of canister from all his guns. No more was seen of the horsemen.

The Frenchmen could only admire the sacrifice made by their foes. As the Ninth advanced behind the battery, the ground was littered with dead and wounded Russians. Even the wounded had an inflexible sense of duty. Girod saw one badly wounded Russian struggling to end his own life by stabbing himself repeatedly with a bayonet. Girod was unsure if the Russian did not want to surrender, or if the pain of his wounds were too much for him to bear. Another wounded man had his thigh shot away. Despite this he continued to load and fire his musket at the Ninth. An adjutant went over to him and told him to stop, but the man would not surrender. In desperation he held the butt of his musket on his stomach and waved the bayonet at anyone who tried to approach him. Taking pity on the Russian, the adjutant left him alone, but no sooner had he left, than the Russian resumed shooting at them. Taking matters into his own hands, a chasseur broke ranks and walked up to the Russian, shooting him dead at point-blank range. This upset Girod, who felt they could have simply disarmed the Russian.[15]

While the Russians in front of Ney were being pushed back, those on the north bank of the Millstream were still holding their own. With his corps now firmly back on the offensive, the fiery marshal saw a new use for Dupont's troops. Ney galloped to the front of the Ninth's 2nd Battalion and with a cry of 'Vive l'Empereur!' ordered the whole battalion to deploy into skirmish formation and cross the Millstream on their left. They raced through the water and up the other bank arriving on the flank of the Russian centre, which was engaged against the troops of Marshal Lannes. Making a dash for high ground, the battalion occupied a hillock and began firing on the Russian gunners below them. Sub-Lieutenant Clopt put himself at the head of 30 men and raced down the hill to attack a Russian battery. They captured three guns but Clopt was seriously wounded in the process.

Once the Russians realized they were being attacked in the flank, they turned on the Ninth's 2nd Battalion and, according to Girod, gunned down around 300 men and 15 officers in a matter of moments with a hail of canister and musketry. It was a terrible ordeal, reminiscent of the losses at Marengo. However the 32nd and the 96th regiments crossed the stream and came up in support. At the same time the 24th Line crossed over the stream and inclined to the right. Passing behind the Ninth's skirmish line, and sheltering themselves on the blind side of the Millstream's steep banks, they followed the course to a large pond and arrived on the outskirts of Friedland almost without loss. They charged through the town towards the bridges over the Alle, but were stopped by Russian artillery placed on the far bank of the river. In the ensuing fire-fight several buildings were ignited and the flames spread to the bridges.

As Napoleon had predicted, once the Russians realized they were in danger of being cut off from the bridges at Friedland, panic set in. Towards the end of the evening the Ninth was involved in one last push. Although Senarmont's artillery bombardment had caused frightful casualties, the Russians still lingered on the west bank of the Alle. The French mounted a bayonet charge which pushed the Russians backwards and across the Alle.[16] With Friedland in French hands, the Russians north of the Millstream searched for an escape route. Unfortunately for Napoleon, they located some fords further up the Alle and were able to escape, but only after suffering heavy losses. The battle was won and Ney embraced Dupont amid a backdrop of flame and carnage. It had been a glorious day.

By 10pm the last of the firing had ceased. The Ninth set up a bivouac around Friedland. The men were famished after the battle so marauders were sent into the town to see what could be found. There was a general pillage of a store of groceries and the marauders of Girod's company returned laden with sacks. Jubilation turned to disappointment when it was found the sacks contained sugar and raisins. Such treats were all very nice, but Girod would have preferred a crust of bread.

Elsewhere on the field the elite soldiers of the 3rd Battalion were recovering from an exhausting day. Among them was carabineer Sergeant Jean-Baptiste Cardron, who we last encountered in hospital at Lübeck at the end of the 1806 campaign. After convalescing from the wound he suffered at Waren, Cardron was incorporated into the 3rd Battalion and became part of Oudinot's reserve formation. Cardron said Oudinot's command was nicknamed the 'Infernal Division'. Oudinot's men had been heavily engaged in the morning of the battle. In action since the early hours of the morning and outnumbered three to one, the Ninth's elite companies had spent much of their time contesting the Sortlack woods. Later in the year Cardron wrote about this action to his mother. The letter followed a letter by the captain of the 3rd Carabineers (identified only as 'Mr V...') to a sweetheart in which he indicated Cardron was seriously ill.[17] As was common, news from the front was passed around different families and so Cardron's mother was informed her son was ill. Naturally concerned, she wrote to her son. Although Cardron was indeed suffering from a fever at the time, he took great affront to his captain having written about him. His retort followed:

> You say to me that according to a letter he wrote to his darling, it is uncertain we would have gained a victory without his heroic deeds. I know nothing about these, but what I do know is that he runs like a real voltigeur, because in a chase we had with the Russians (we were skirmishing in a wood) I saw Mr V. beating a retreat at least 300 paces in front of us, jumping hedges and bushes like a little Billy goat. After this

we retook the ground which we had just lost by charging Mssrs the Russians in turn. I do not know where this so-called captain of carabineers got to, but I did not see him at our head. I cannot say if he distinguished himself somewhere else, but if agility gives one the right to Glory then he covered himself with it on this occasion.[18]

Reading between the lines of this sarcastic reply there are two very interesting points. Firstly is the insight into the skirmishing. The key difference between skirmishers and formed troops was skirmishers rarely stood their ground when attacked. They would always melt away, running back on their supports and then resume skirmishing once the danger had passed. In this instance the Russians appear to have sent a body of troops into the woods to drive the French skirmishers away. The French skirmishers fell back on their supports and by the time the Russians got anywhere near the supporting French troops they were so disordered by moving through the trees that they were vulnerable to a counter-attack. By the time the Russians would have re-formed outside the woods to try again, the French skirmishers would have had ample opportunity to resume their positions. By using the Sortlack Wood in this manner, the French were able to negate the Russian army's superior numbers and buy time for Napoleon to arrive. Perhaps of more interest is the way Cardron insulted his captain, writing he 'ran like a real voltigeur' – proving that rivalry existed between elite companies.

On the morning after the battle, Cardron went over to the main regiment and encountered his mentor, Battalion Commander Régeau. Cardron appears to have complained that being away from the regiment with Oudinot had hampered his promotional prospects. Régeau told him Colonel Meunier had not forgotten him and he would try to get Cardron appointed as sergeant-major of his 1st Battalion carabineer company. It was a fine gesture, but one which did not materialize. Cardron remained with the 'Infernal Division' and away from the regiment.

Elsewhere that morning Napoleon was in a jubilant mood. He wrote to the Empress Josephine: 'My children celebrated with dignity the anniversary of the battle of Marengo; the battle of Friedland will be just as famous and just as glorious for my people.'[19] The victory had come at a price for the Ninth. The French suffered something like 10,000 casualties in the battle, with the Russians losing at least double this number. In total Victor's I Corps had suffered 923 casualties (six officers killed, 38 wounded and 125 men killed, 756 wounded).

On its own the Ninth accounted for 46 per cent of the losses with one officer killed, 13 wounded and 38 men killed, 373 wounded.[20] In fact the regiment's loss was even greater as Oudinot's 'Infernal Division' had suffered heavily in the morning battle. The regimental history and rolls show a further nine officers were wounded and the full total of men killed in action was 46. Of these 30 had been killed in the 2nd Battalion, sent by Ney against the Russian centre in skirmish formation.

The regiment had played a full part in the victory, Napoleon awarding the regiment 36 crosses of the Legion of Honour and making good all the vacancies for promotion in the regiment.[21] However, Girod claimed Napoleon issued something of a snub while visiting the battlefield on 15 June. As the Emperor passed near to the Ninth, he allegedly complained that the 2nd Battalion had given way without his orders. Perhaps Girod misunderstood, or perhaps the heavy casualties the battalion suffered when skirmishing had indeed caused them to fall back. Then again, perhaps this complaint was a reference to Mohrungen, where the 2nd Battalion had lost its eagle. By now the Russian gazettes must surely have reached Napoleon's attention?

––––––––––

The morning after Friedland, at 11am, Napoleon set his army in pursuit of the Russians who were withdrawing towards the River Niemen and the safety of their homeland. On 19 June the Ninth passed through the town of Tilsit (Sovetsk) on the banks of the Niemen and were directed to a large village half a league from the town. When Napoleon arrived at Tilsit, some Russian officers arrived, sent by Tsar Alexander to ask for an armistice. The soldiers of the Ninth were filled with joy at the prospect of peace. They were far away from France and had no desire to go any further east. Much to their relief, Napoleon agreed to an armistice on 21 June and opened negotiations with Alexander for a lasting settlement.

Although they lived in hope, there was great anxiety that the negotiations might break up in acrimony. Knowing Napoleon's 'inflexible character' and 'enterprising genius', Girod says they feared the emperor might drive too hard a bargain with the Russian tsar. In this case they need not have feared. To destroy the Russian army in battle, Napoleon would have had to cross the Niemen and pursue it deep into Russia. Napoleon's army had been campaigning for ten months with only several short respites, and the emperor had been away from his capital for a long time. The last thing Napoleon privately wanted was an invasion of Russia.

While the negotiations commenced, the two armies sat either side of the Niemen watching one another. Girod said the Russian army offered them 'a most curious spectacle'. They were particularly interested in the religious ceremonies held by the Russian Orthodox priests. At this time the French army had yet to resuscitate the practice of employing regimental chaplains, a post which had been suppressed in 1794 by the republican government. The priests would give prayers in a loud voice with the soldiers gathered round chanting their responses in unison. The Russians were bivouacked in a large plain. The prairies extended far away along the Niemen and were covered with Cossack horses roaming in complete freedom. Girod noted how the Cossack sentinels promenaded up and down, carrying their lances horizontally, balanced on the pommels of their saddles. Rather than the French custom, where sentinels were assigned a fixed position, the Cossacks roamed far and wide, watching the French on the other bank. Girod also commented on the Kalmucks in the Russian army. These Asiatic fighters were armed with bows and were apparently a source of great amusement to the French.

On 25 June the peace conference opened in earnest. Napoleon met the Russian tsar on an elaborate raft moored in the middle of the Niemen. The Emperor's objectives were simple: an alliance between the two greatest European empires – France and Russia. Prussia would lose considerable territory and a Grand Duchy of Warsaw would be created for the Polish people. The most important objective was to secure Russia's support in blocking trade between continental Europe and Great Britain. Since the failure of the peace of Amiens in 1803 Britain and France had brought commercial sanctions against one another. In November 1806 this 'war of commerce' culminated in Napoleon's 'Berlin Decree', which forbade allied and conquered territories from trading with the British. Having given up on the idea of invading the British Isles, Napoleon hoped this 'Continental System' would hurt the British economy instead. If the Baltic was closed to the British this would be quite a coup for Napoleon. During the conference, Napoleon invited Alexander to come to Tilsit the following day. The tsar duly obliged and brought the King of Prussia with him.

Napoleon had his Imperial Guard parade in full dress, lining the streets from the riverbank to the conference building; Alexander brought a detachment of his own Imperial Guard with him.

The Ninth also made something of an impression that day. As Alexander came ashore he no doubt noticed the smoke from a huge fire outside the town. The Ninth had set fire to the village they had been resting in since arriving on the Niemen. Girod claims it was not started deliberately but was caused by an act of 'imprudence' by one of the men. The village was quite large and the closely packed houses were constructed entirely out of wood. The flames spread quickly and before long the whole village was consumed in a violent blaze. Fortunately for the Ninth they did not have to go back to make good the damage. Before the peace conference concluded, the regiment was sent to Insterburg (Chernyakhovsk), a pretty little town on the Pregel, where they arrived on 3 July. The staff and a few of the elite companies were billeted, while the rest of the division was ordered to make a camp. This was the scene of yet another disaster.

The regiment arrived at 10am and stacked their muskets. Before the ranks were dismissed the men were instructed to construct a camp before 4pm that same day.[22] Near the campsite was a small village which had been constructed by a Swiss colony three or four decades earlier. The residents still spoke French and might have believed themselves safe with their new neighbours. They were mistaken. The Ninth's working parties were sent into the town looking for wood and straw. Rather than go to the local burgomaster to ask for requisitions, the soldiers were ordered to take what they could find. It was a brainless order. Girod was one of the officers overseeing the operation. As soon as the ranks were dismissed the town was literally destroyed. First the interiors were ransacked, and then the houses were partially demolished for their timbers. The officers lost control of their men and were hard-pressed to save the local manor house from the same fate as its neighbours. They intervened when a woman's screams were heard from one of the houses. A group of soldiers had broken in and were about to relieve her of a pot of gold coins she kept under her mattress. The soldiers were driven away by their angry officers. While the building materials were carried back to the campsite, other soldiers gathered in the harvest. The poor villagers were left with nothing except a growing sense of resentment against Napoleon's army.

From Insterburg the regiment was sent back to Berlin. By now the treaty of Tilsit had been signed by Napoleon and Alexander, and a treaty had been concluded with Prussia. Although the conflict had ended, its impact was still felt. The lands they crossed were utterly devastated. The roadsides were still littered with the remains of men and horses left unburied for two months. Villages were deserted, their populations having succumbed to epidemics and famine. Death was etched on the faces of the survivors reduced to scouring the countryside for wild berries. The regiment crossed the Vistula at Thorn and went on to Bromberg where the scars of war were less evident. The temperature increased. The days were so hot they were forced to march through the night and were eaten alive by insects. Girod fell ill again. Having bought himself a horse to make the journey to Berlin, he could not even ride. He ended up in the back of a cart for the last stages of the voyage.

Once in the Prussian capital Girod was billeted with a family of French Huguenots. They spoke French as their mother tongue. He was able to rest properly at last. There were promenades, and Sunday visits to the Tiergarten where the ladies took coffee while the men drank beer and smoked pipes. There were visits to the Berlin orchestra conducted by August Wilhelm Iffland. Colonel Meunier's wife came to join him in Berlin. As a sub-lieutenant in an elite company, Girod enjoyed all the best postings. He mounted guard at the home of Marshal Victor, the governor general, or at the town hall.[23] A perk of these duties was that the officer of the guard was usually invited to dine and the dinners were nothing but sumptuous.

In October 1807 Dupont quit the division for an assignment rumoured to be in Spain. He was loved by his soldiers and they were sad to see him go after nearly four years at their head. In reward for his excellent service, Napoleon gave him the grand eagle of the Legion of Honour and domains in Poland valued at over half a million francs. He was given command of an army corps and, it was said, the promise of a marshal's baton if he was successful in his new endeavour. His replacement was newly promoted General of Division François Amable Ruffin, Count of the Empire.[24] Ruffin had commanded one of Oudinot's brigades at Friedland, which included the composite battalion of elite companies from Dupont's division. He was tall, dashing and handsome with long curling hair and a moustache and quickly proved himself popular among his subordinates. Ruffin was celebrated as one of the best dinner companions in the army and certainly enjoyed his drink.

With winter approaching, the regiment was assigned a series of cantonments on the road between Berlin and Frankfurt an der Oder. Girod was posted with half his voltigeur company at Seefeld around a large lake. With 50 men at his disposal, Girod enjoyed the trappings of semi-independent command. Each week he would submit a list of his requirements, stipulating quantities of wine, rum, sugar, coffee, meat and so on, and his host was obliged to provide them. Relations with the locals were cordial. There were hunts in the forests, carnivals, dances and masquerades. Girod was introduced to a flaming cocktail he called 'feu bleu' (blue fire) which was made by igniting the local firewater. Having been through the frozen hell of the previous campaign, this was a good time to be with the regiment.

Compare Girod's experiences as an officer with those of Cardron. The ambitious sub-officer of carabineers was still with the 'Infernal Division' and found himself at Danzig in 1807. In a letter to his mother on Christmas Day, he began to grumble about the conditions of service. The letter clearly shows the contrast between soldiers in barracks and those quartered on the civilian population:

> … for two months we have been in barracks, badly paid and what barracks they are. In the magazines, or better to say the sheds, we are three and four companies to a room, sleeping on straw bedding, almost rotten from damp; having nothing to eat but bread and a slender ration of meat. We still have a ration of vegetables. This ration consists of 30 peas (a grenadier took his to the home of the governor yesterday and there were just 30 well counted peas). You can see by this description how happy we are here. Ah! poor Frenchmen, what a reward for so much effort, fatigue and hardship. Sacrifice yourselves thus during the war and in the peace your reward will be hospital and even worse; and there you will find the end of all your troubles; here is your fate my fellow soldiers.[25]

Things were not all bad for Cardron. In the same letter he describes the arrival of a new commanding officer for the composite grenadier unit. Cardron explained when 'these sirs' arrived in a new corps they rarely found anything good in their predecessor's work. The colonel in question sacked the outgoing colonel's secretary and, having made enquiries for a suitable replacement, Cardron was given the task. Colonels were evidently far too busy to write letters of their own.

Although Cardron appears to be the classic French 'grumbler' and perhaps began his career with idealized expectations, the last point raised in his letter reveals a valid concern. A fear of hospitals was quite common in this era. People had the attitude that if there was nothing seriously wrong with you when you arrived, there soon would be. There was no concept of hygiene and the theory of the transmission of sickness through germs was unknown. It is no wonder more soldiers in the Ninth died in hospital than they did on the battlefield.

The losses experienced in the campaigns of 1805–07 are noted in an inspection made of the Ninth on 1 January 1808 by General Schauenburg. Since the last review of the regiment on 18 August 1805 the regiment had lost 1,503 men. The breakdown of losses was:

Dead	330
Deserted	171
Discharged	687
Struck off by judgements	20
Struck off by long absence	184
Transferred to other corps	83
Made officers	28

In the same period the regiment had received 2,463 recruits; three had transferred from other corps and 148 had returned having been previously struck off.[26]

Comparing this table to the regimental rolls over the same period (18 August 1805–1 January 1808) reveals some discrepancies. The 1808 report says 184 men were struck off from 'long absence', where in reality they had all died from wounds or sickness. By 1816 the records had been made good and we can see the mortality rate was actually higher than given by Schauenburg. The rolls give the names of 466 men who died in this period. Of these 112 were killed in action against 325 dying in hospital.[27] A further 29 are listed simply as having died from natural causes, wounds or sickness. Everywhere the regiment went, it left behind a trail of sick and wounded, stretching from Ulm and Günzburg to Vienna, then Augsburg, Heidelberg, Wesel, Worms, Landshut, Koblenz, Frankfurt, Cologne, Halle, Leipzig, Lübeck, Magdeburg, Kassel, Spandau, Berlin, Stettin, Frankfurt an der Oder, Küstrin, Thorn, Bromberg, Braunsberg, Elbling, Marienburg, Heilsberg, Danzig, Neustadt, Königsberg, Posen and so on.

Schauenburg's inspection contained the names of 251 men pensioned off or given the title of 'National Veteran'. Among the men are several names from past chapters. Among those granted a pension was Nicolas Huguin, the adjutant-major Godet had seen snoring off a hangover on the roadside in 1805. He was deaf in his right ear and had never properly recovered from the leg wound he received at Marengo. The least exertion caused him great pain and he had only withstood the last three campaigns because his rank permitted him to ride a horse. Two legionnaires were among those pensioned off. Thirty-year-old Sergeant Heckenroth had stopped a canister round at Waren, while Carabineer Camus, two years his senior and one of the heroes of Marengo, was shot in the left arm at the same action. The vast majority of men (198) had been wounded by musketry, with a dozen wounded by sabre or bayonet. One unfortunate, Chasseur Claudel, had suffered a wound from an axe and 21-year-old Chasseur Maxel had been wounded by a Cossack's lance at Friedland. Nine had been wounded by artillery fire and two more struck by shell-fire. Of the rest there were those suffering from hernias, rheumatism and other medical conditions. One had been burned in an accident (perhaps near Tilsit?) and some, like 21-year-old voltigeur Cornetist Daubigné, were so ravaged by sickness they were described as being no longer able to support the 'fatigues of war' despite their young age.

The loss of experienced men in the recent campaigns was a concern for the emperor. The men who had marched to glory with him at Marengo grew fewer every summer, and although Tilsit saw peace restored to central Europe, Napoleon needed to maintain a large army to police his empire. He set the Ministry of War the task of creating more battalions without significantly increasing the wage bill of officers and sub-officers.

The Imperial Decree of 18 February 1808 addressed this problem quite neatly. Each regiment of line and light infantry was increased from three to five battalions. The first four battalions were designated as 'field battalions' and the fifth as the regimental depot, which would have no elite companies. In order to balance the books, the number of centre companies in each battalion was reduced from seven to four. To compensate for this, the companies were made bigger. This reform made a great deal of sense. Quite often companies would often be well below strength on campaign, so the cadre of three officers, six sub-officers and eight corporals per company was perhaps somewhat top-heavy. The result of the reform was to give Napoleon more infantry battalions, for only a modest increase in the number of officers and sub-officers commanding them.[28]

At full strength the regiment would therefore consist of 3,970 officers and men, with two children permitted to join each company. The regimental staff would comprise one colonel, one major, one quartermaster treasurer, one payment officer, one eagle bearer, one surgeon-major, four assistant surgeons, five sub-assistant surgeons, ten adjutant sub-officers, two deputy eagle bearers, one drum-major, one drum-corporal, one chief musician, seven musicians and four master craftsmen (cobbler, tailor, gaiter-maker and armourer).

The four field battalions included a company of carabineers, one of voltigeurs and four companies of chasseurs. Each company would have an equal number of men and included one captain, one lieutenant, one sub-lieutenant, one sergeant-major, four sergeants, one quartermaster corporal, eight corporals, 121 carabineers, voltigeurs or chasseurs and two drummers or cornetists. Each field battalion would be commanded by a battalion commander, assisted by an adjutant-major and two adjutant sub-officers. The 5th Battalion would comprise four chasseur companies composed of the same strength as above. In lieu of a battalion commander, the fifth battalion would be commanded by one of the company captains with the assistance of an adjutant-major and two adjutant sub-officers. Another of the 5th Battalion's captains would also perform the role of clothing officer. The depot would be commanded by the major with the assistance of the quartermaster treasurer.

The reform of 18 February 1808 was not enacted immediately. The Ninth's two existing field battalions had to be recalled to Berlin from their winter cantonments first. Girod recalled how, on the eve of their departure for Berlin, the 1st Battalion threw a grand ball for all the local ladies they had socialized with over the winter. At first the officers groaned, thinking they would have to pick up the expense for the ball, but wiley old Régeau had taken care of everything. On the eve of the grand event he levied an emergency contribution on the locals invited to attend the ball. Already disapproving of their daughters dancing the night away with French officers, the fathers were now obliged to pay for the privilege! It is unlikely the regiment was much missed in that part of Germany.

The creation of the first three field battalions took place on 1 June 1808 in a grand parade before Marshal Victor and General Ruffin.[29] Colonel Meunier formed the regiment in line. His first act was to present Ruffin a list of sub-officers and soldiers proposed for the carabineer company in the new 3rd Battalion.[30] Previously, promising-looking recruits like Cardron could be posted straight into the carabineer companies, but in the new scheme carabineers had to have more than four years' service, or have participated in two out of the Ulm, Austerlitz, Jena or Friedland campaigns. Voltigeurs still qualified by height as set by the regulation of 1804. However, the new organization formally assigned the voltigeurs to the left of the battalion, the second place of honour.

Meunier then submitted the names of the regiment's sappers. As part of the reform, each battalion was required to nominate four sappers, each drawn from the carabineer companies. Although these men would remain attached to their parent companies they would be drawn together on active service and placed under the command of a corporal of sappers.

The next part of the ceremony is one of the most interesting parts of the reform. The new decree recognized each regiment as only having a single eagle. The eagle would follow the largest part of the regiment (i.e. with the colonel) and would be guarded by an officer with the title 'Eagle Bearer'. Previously the regimental standards had been carried by a sergeant-major with an escort of the battalion's quartermaster corporals. This was a practical measure as the company quartermasters had no formal place assigned to them in the platoon formation. However, one wonders whether, like cooks, they were deemed too useful to be exposed to enemy fire?[31]

The officer selected as eagle bearer would have the grade of lieutenant or sub-lieutenant, and would either have ten years' service, or would have been present at Ulm, Austerlitz, Jena and Friedland (none of the Ninth's officers would qualify this way). He would be supported by two brave, old soldiers unable to gain promotion due to illiteracy. These would be designated as second and third eagle bearers respectively and would have the rank of sergeant with the pay of a sergeant-major. To further distinguish them they would wear four chevrons on each sleeve and be armed with a spontoon and pistols in an 'oriental' holster worn across the chest. The three eagle bearers would be chosen by Napoleon himself and could only be discharged on the emperor's command. In this case the report on the ceremony records no proposals were made by Meunier for these ranks. The light infantry had been ordered to send their eagles to the depots during the lull between Eylau and Friedland, so we can assume the Ninth had complied with this, and at the beginning of 1808 at least, the surviving eagle was not carried by the regiment.

Lastly the regiment had to assign 12 companies of chasseurs to the new battalions. With 14 companies then in existence, the 6th Company of the 1st Battalion and the 8th Company of the 2nd Battalion were dissolved. The men from these companies were shared among the other companies to equalize their strength. The remaining companies were then each allocated to the three battalions in order of the captain's seniority (i.e. 1st captain to 1st Company 1st Battalion; 2nd captain, 1st Company 2nd Battalion and so on).

After the reform was completed, the Ninth prepared to go into summer camp where it could train and dust off the winter cobwebs (the creation of the fourth and fifth battalions at the regimental depot had yet to take place). As the regiment marched out of Berlin in the spring of 1808, the French Empire was arguably at its peak. In successive years Napoleon had defeated the Austro-Hungarian Empire, tamed the army created by Frederick the Great and bloodied the nose of the Russian tsar. Although the English were still a nuisance and there was talk of trouble brewing in far-away Spain and Portugal, confidence in the French army must have been at an all-time high. Time and time again, their self-belief and determination had seen them through and they were secure in the knowledge that they were led by the greatest military commander since Alexander the Great. What could possibly go wrong?

DISASTER AT
BAILEN

hile the regiment campaigned in Germany and Poland, the depot
had been commanded by Major Claude Marcel D'Eslon. He was
an old soldier, a former horse chasseur from the King's army who
had transferred to the light infantry in 1785. D'Eslon was a proud family man;
married with a son and daughter and as a Vosgian, he must have had an affinity
with the conscripts drawn from his native department. Like many of his
contemporaries, he had enjoyed rapid promotion in the 1790s, but since joining
the Ninth his opportunities for advancement had been limited. In 1807 he was
42 years old, five years Meunier's senior. If he was to progress beyond the rank
of major before retirement, he needed a spell of active service, and soon.

D'Eslon's chance came when the Ninth was asked to supply four companies
of chasseurs to form part of the 7th Provisional Regiment.[1] This new force was
to travel to south-western France to serve in a corps of observation under
Marshal Moncey. Its ultimate destination was secret, but when D'Eslon was
offered command of the regiment, he gladly accepted. Leaving Captain Paulet
in charge of the depot, D'Eslon quit Landau on 22 November 1807. The four
companies of chasseurs he took with him comprised 450 officers and men. The
rank and file were mostly new conscripts, a large proportion of them Italians.
While the physical quality of these recruits may have been good, one wonders
how much enthusiasm they had for fighting in the name of *Re Napoleone*?[2]

D'Eslon kept a journal of the expedition in which he speculated on his destination: a maritime expedition or more likely Spain or Portugal.[3] After the Berlin decree of November 1806, the Iberian peninsula had become something of a backdoor for British trade with Europe. A long-term ally of Britain, Portugal refused to join the Continental System, so Napoleon resolved to close Portuguese ports to British ships. The only practical way of achieving this was to send an army in to enforce the blockade. To facilitate the passage of troops to the Portuguese border, Spain and France signed the treaty of Fontainebleau on 27 October 1807. The Spanish agreed to let French soldiers pass through their territory in return for a share of the spoils when Portugal was carved up.

Once his troops entered Spain, Napoleon became embroiled in the country's internal politics. The labyrinthine nature of Spanish politics are beyond the scope of this work, but essentially the country was in such a state of confusion that Napoleon saw an opportunity to conquer the entire Iberian peninsula. With French troops all over Spain en route to Portugal, Napoleon quietly made sure he maintained garrisons in all key Spanish fortresses, waiting for the right moment to strike.

On 9 January 1808 D'Eslon's regiment arrived in Bayonne and rendezvoused with Marshal Moncey. Taking D'Eslon to one side Moncey confirmed their destination was indeed Spain. A few days later D'Eslon was sent over the border, arriving at Vitoria in the Basque country on 16 January. D'Eslon's first impressions of the native population were uncompromising, but fairly typical for the time: 'The inhabitants have something unpleasant about them which I cannot define. I see nobody working; the men gather together in the sun all day, wrapped in their coats; the women sit near their braziers, their arms folded; the riff-raff wallow on the ground, wrapped in rags, killing lice ...'[4] His views on the Spanish church were even more forthright: 'The Spaniards have many relics, many monks, much farce and hypocrisy, but no religion: it is totally foreign to them; they have only superstition!'[5] Napoleon had restored the Catholic Church in France and many Frenchmen saw themselves as believers. However, to the Spanish they were heretics. The Church held sway over the population in a manner alien to the French. This difference was one of many divisive points between the two countries, which bred an implacable hostility as long as a single Frenchman remained on Spanish soil. Even in early 1808 French soldiers walking the streets would be pelted with stones. Assassins were said to be at large and there was no opportunity to rest or lower one's guard. This mutual animosity would lead to a level of brutality unmatched elsewhere on the continent.

On 16 February the French coup began. Important cities were seized and Murat arrived to take charge. Before the Spanish knew what was happening, the French had 118,000 men in the country. The political situation was immensely complex. At first the Spanish king tried to flee; he then abdicated in favour of his son, only to withdraw the abdication, claiming it had been coerced from him. Napoleon offered to mediate between the different Spanish factions and invited the Spanish royal family to a summit in Bayonne towards the end of April 1808. Once the king was over the border, the jig was up for him. Napoleon appointed himself kingmaker and ultimately offered the crown of Spain to his own elder brother, Joseph Bonaparte.

On 2 May there was a dramatic uprising in Madrid when Murat tried to remove the last members of the Spanish royal family to France. Murat imposed martial law on the capital and on 5 May, King Joseph's accession to the throne was announced. By now D'Eslon's regiment had been stationed for some time north of Madrid at the Royal Palace of El Pardo. He was ordered into the capital in the aftermath of the uprising to maintain order.

The main resistance to Joseph Bonaparte came from a rival government or *Junta* in Seville. General Dupont was ordered south with 13,000 men and charged with the optimistic task of taking Córdoba and Seville and thereby putting an end to resistance. Alas, when Dupont arrived in Andalusia he found it in utter turmoil. His troops were not the same class as those he had led in the Grand Army. When Dupont entered Córdoba on 7 June his troops spent the next four days looting the city. It was a stark lesson in what to expect from the French and stiffened Spanish resolve accordingly.

The road from Córdoba to Madrid passed through the Sierra Morena mountains via a series of narrow, steep gorges. No sooner had Dupont crossed the Sierra Morena than the Spanish cut his communications by seizing the Despeñaperros Pass. There were a series of tit for tat engagements while Dupont struggled to keep a link with Madrid. In truth, he should have abandoned his mission and crossed back onto the Madrid side of the mountains waiting for reinforcements. Instead he dallied and allowed the Spanish forces to grow in strength.

On 2 July D'Eslon's regiment was ordered to march south with General Jacques Nicolas Gobert. With 4,000 men, their mission was to restore communications between Dupont and Madrid. Ahead of them General Vedel marched with another 6,000 men. Even before they reached the Sierra Morena the road was littered with signs of cruelty. The countryside was infested with insurgents and assassins. Three hundred wounded soldiers had been massacred in a hospital at Manazares. Their throats had been cut. At Valdepeñas more than 100 Frenchmen had been killed, including a war commissary with General Réné and his wife. They had been murdered in the most abominable fashion, D'Eslon recording: 'They claim the commissary was sawed in half between two planks while quite alive, and the general and his wife were killed with blows from an axe.'[6] Not only was the population against them but the very land seemed to despise them. The fields were empty and provisions hard to come by. D'Eslon's men were quickly reduced to a diet of grass supplemented by an occasional potato.

They crossed the Sierra Morena and marched into Andalusia. General Vedel had pushed the Spanish aside and pressed on to join Dupont at Andújar. Gobert's troops joined them on 7 July. With an additional 10,000 men brought to him by Vedel and Gobert, Dupont again had the chance to seize the initiative, but once more the Spanish outmanoeuvred him. Gobert was attacked on the morning of 16 July. Although D'Eslon was proud at how his conscripts stood up to the whistle of ball and shot for the first time, the Spanish were victorious. General Gobert was mortally wounded in the action and his troops pushed away from Dupont through Bailen and towards La Carolina. On 19 July there was a battle between Dupont and the Spanish General Castaños to the west of Bailen. Despite personally leading a last, desperate attack, Dupont could not break the Spanish line and was wounded in the action. He asked for a ceasefire and began negotiating a treaty.

On 21 July D'Eslon heard rumours that Dupont's corps had been destroyed. By now D'Eslon had retreated north of the Sierra Morena and was in a place of relative safety. However, he received written orders to travel south to Santa Elena. When he arrived at Venta de Cardenas, the entry of the steep gorges which passed through the mountain range, there were rumours that Dupont had capitulated at Bailen and included D'Eslon's regiment in the terms of surrender. D'Eslon saw the indignation painted on the faces of his officers and men when they heard the news. He halted his column for an hour and debated what to do. He was then 14 leagues (56km) from Dupont; not yet snared by the mountain chain. He could have made a run for Madrid, but he pondered the consequences of not carrying out his orders. What if news of the capitulation was a deception? What if Dupont was hanging on, desperate for reinforcements and D'Eslon turned tail and deserted him? It would be the end of his career. D'Eslon decided to fulfil his orders and share the fate of his chiefs, come what may. It was the worst decision of his life.

Arriving at Santa Elena, D'Eslon immediately regretted his decision. As part of the terms of capitulation most of the generals and senior officers had given their parole and had been sent back to Madrid.[7] It was now too late for D'Eslon to take advantage of this. However, the terms of the capitulation promised the French troops would be repatriated to France. It was a promise which would never be fulfilled. On 23 July D'Eslon arrived in Bailen and had his men hand over their weapons. They were then directed southwards to the coast of Andalusia, not in the direction of France as they'd hoped.

Passing through Andalusia, D'Eslon began to realize the full extent of Spanish hatred for the French invaders. He felt they were treated like dogs. They were jeered, insulted, robbed and pelted with stones. Even when he took a bath there would be a Spanish soldier sitting on the end of the tub making sure he did not escape. D'Eslon fell sick with diarrhoea then began suffering palpitations and fainting spells. He even began writing the names of particularly villainous or sadistic Spaniards in his journal so he might one day come back and take vengeance on them. As they marched on, his men became insubordinate. Morale plummeted when they were told the terms of capitulation would not be honoured. The British had warned the Spanish how Napoleon would send his soldiers straight back into Spain if they were released. As a final insult, more than 200 of D'Eslon's men joined the Spanish army. They could be seen, guarding their former officers, still wearing their French uniforms.[8] These turncoats were mostly Italians sent to the Ninth from the territories annexed to France by Napoleon. The redrawing of lines on a map turned out to be no guarantor of loyalty and the Italians felt little compunction about serving the Spanish instead. On 27 August they arrived at Puente-Real where the officers and men were divided. The officers were taken to Velez-Malaga under the guard of the local militia lest the local population got their hands on them. This was about the only favour they ever received. D'Eslon now faced five hellish years of imprisonment.[9]

Meanwhile, half-way across Europe, the Ninth's first three field battalions were still in summer camp at the end of August. The army's sojourn on the Channel coast in 1804/5 had demonstrated that there was nothing quite like a military camp to teach a soldier his trade. To this end Marshal Victor had his army corps form three camps in the outskirts of Berlin: Napoleonbourg, Louisbourg and Josephbourg.

Ruffin's division occupied Napoleonbourg, which was marked out on a barren height facing Berlin, resting against the Spree. The construction of the camp took 15 days and followed similar principles to that built at Montreuil four years before. The camp was surrounded by an enormous wooden abatis. There were broad streets along which they planted avenues of trees that were cut from a nearby forest and replanted with care to preserve their foliage. As the foliage withered, the trees were replaced with new ones. At the centre of each brigade the generals had their own huts. Dwarfing everyone, at the centre of the camp, General Ruffin was lodged in a veritable palace. Outside his 'hut' the stacks of arms were ranged along the front of the division. A lawn was created around the weapons and 'magnificent trophies' placed at the centre and on the wings of each battalion, formed from captured weapons, drums or other martial implements.

The soldiers' huts were constructed from planks nailed to wooden uprights and then covered with cob. Every Sunday the soldiers whitened the exterior of their huts with lime. Behind the soldiers' huts were the company kitchens. Each contained a stove and a brick chimney. The kitchens also doubled as a recreational space, offering a large covered area for lessons in dancing and fencing. Wells were dug to supply the soldiers with fresh water and every day the men were taken down to the river and taught how to swim.

The remainder of their week was filled with vigorous military exercises and manoeuvres which commenced at daybreak and continued until 6pm. Waking up at 2am each morning started to take a toll on Sergeant Cardron who had finally rejoined the regiment on 5 July. He was still feeling ill from the fever which he had contracted in Danzig (probably malaria) and was also suffering from the side effects of drinking quinine wine, which he believed had damaged his stomach. Having second thoughts about his career, Cardron began making enquiries about transferring to the Gendarmerie where the pay was better for less hardship.

Life in the camp was better for officers. They had their huts some distance behind the company kitchens. Sub-Lieutenant Girod shared a hut with the company lieutenant and divided the hut up so it had a small lounge and two sleeping alcoves. Used to the finer things in life, Girod and his companion travelled into Berlin and rented mahogany furniture, furnished beds and even some window-panes. They considered themselves exceptionally well lodged. Without hosts to feed them, they set up coffee shops and restaurants outside the camp by the edge of the forest. However, the table allowance granted to them was insufficient and all the officers quickly found themselves in debt. Although removed from Berlin, there was still the opportunity for some society as every Sunday the locals would walk up to visit. Of course, it was not all fun and games. Girod found himself placed under arrest for arriving a few minutes late at assembly one morning. He felt suitably chastised by the experience. In August a rumour circulated round the camp that there was to be a new war against Austria. The veterans of the 1805 campaign were eager to renew their acquaintance with the country, telling newcomers the countryside was a veritable land of milk and honey, abundant in every resource. The prospect of rich pickings appears to have excited the younger members of the regiment, who were obviously not told anything of the horrendous marches to Vienna.

The rumours of war appeared to be confirmed when the regiment was ordered to depart quickly on 15 August in the direction of Potsdam where the regiment was loaded onto carts. Covering more than 20 leagues (80km) a day they passed through Vittemberg, Leipzig and Ramberg, from where they unexpectedly took the road to Frankfurt and Mainz. Only then did they comprehend that they were not heading to Austria, but back in the direction of France. Until then they had been unaware of the disaster at Bailen and the fate of Dupont and his troops. Now their mission became clear.

The regiment arrived in Mainz and was given an itinerary to Bayonne near the Spanish border. The itinerary had been worked out so that each town on the route would only have to accommodate a single regiment each night. Leaving Mainz after a day's rest they passed through Bingen am Rhine, Alzey, Kaiserslautern and Saarbrücken without anything extraordinary to note. However, when they arrived at Metz they finally received the hero's welcome they had been expecting. The city authorities and population lined the streets and the regiment's entry was a triumph. A magnificent banquet was prepared for the officer corps at the town hall and there were enthusiastic toasts in honour of the Grand Army. After dinner the officers were taken to the theatre, which had thrown open its doors to the soldiers free of charge. It was a famous night.

After a day of rest at Metz, the regiment continued onwards. Of course, while passing through France everyone thought of obtaining leave. Given the urgency with which the regiment was required in Spain it is doubtful if leave was granted on the same scale as 1805. However, some of the officers obtained permission to race ahead of the regiment to visit their families on the understanding they would catch up on the march. Arriving at Verdun, Colonel Meunier granted Girod leave to visit his father in Paris. As the regiment would not pass through Paris, Meunier ordered Girod to rejoin it at Orléans. A colleague had been granted the same favour, so the two of them hired a seat on an uncomfortable, two-wheeled, open cart and raced from relay post to relay post, speeding towards the French capital. After 60 backbreaking hours on the road they arrived in Paris at midnight. Wanting to look their best before arriving at their respective homes, the two officers lodged at an inn on the Rue Saint-Denis. Rested and refreshed, Girod returned home the following day dressed in full uniform with shako and plume. One can imagine the joy he felt embracing his father.

Colonel Meunier also visited Paris to spend a few days with his wife who had left Berlin before him. When Girod's father learned that Meunier was in town he invited him and his in-laws to dinner. The young sub-lieutenant therefore found himself stuck on a table between his colonel and the most celebrated artist of the day, Jacques-Louis David. Things had come a long way since the terrifying welcome Girod had received from Meunier and the regiment's sergeant-majors in Berlin. The colonel was now all smiles, telling Girod's father that he had put forward his son for a promotion to lieutenant, and he well merited the promotion. These eulogies gave great pleasure to the father who had already lost one son in the war.

Girod finally rejoined the regiment at Tours, having missed it at Orléans by half a day. There was no great reception for the regiment as the weather was rotten and the inhabitants stayed indoors. The regiment was met by the civic authorities, sheltering under umbrellas. The officer corps was invited to a dinner, but everything was cold, even the coffee. It was something of a disappointment after the welcome at Metz. Marching onwards, the regiment passed through Poitiers and Angoulême in the direction of Bordeaux. The regiment passed through Bordeaux and finally arrived in Bayonne on 21 October. From there they were sent to Saint-Jean-de-Luz where they spent the night before crossing the Spanish border.

Girod's memoirs indicate that there had been a general decline in discipline and morale, caused by the relentless pressure of successive campaigns. In Girod's opinion the Napoleonic system of war was 'vicious'. It relied on fast marches that often outstripped the supply chain, forcing French soldiers to pillage in order to stay alive. Discipline had been relaxed to accommodate the systematic theft of food, and over time, the soldiers became progressively desensitized to the misery inflicted on civilians. There had not been enough time between campaigns to restore the army to the high level of discipline seen in 1805.[10] This ill-discipline manifested itself on the march to Angoulême. Several voltigeurs in Girod's company were billeted at the home of a peasant who was known to have fought with the Royalists in the Revolution and was still devoted to their cause. The voltigeurs used this as an excuse to rough up their host, who in turn went to Girod and complained. Girod reprimanded the soldiers and returned to his quarters. As soon as Girod was gone the voltigeurs began abusing their host again. When Girod was summoned a second time he lost his temper and began hitting his men with the flat of his sabre. One of them fell on the floor, so Girod trod on him while giving vent to his anger.

Reflecting on this incident, Girod knew assaults on soldiers were strictly forbidden. One of the grievances before the Revolution was the severity of punishment meted out to soldiers, in particular the humiliation they felt at being beaten. As we have seen with the trial of the rapist in Vienna, a strict process was in place for serious offences, but to bring a man before a court martial, one needed a very compelling motive. In garrison it was easy enough to confine a man to the guardhouse or prison, but while on campaign or while on the march, Girod explained, these punishments were not very practical. They already lost enough men to enemy fire and sickness, without having to lose more to military sentencing. The simplest and most expedient method of punishing minor infringements was to beat the soldier. Girod admitted it was surprising, but even soldiers of long service did not complain nor think it in any way dishonourable to be struck by the flat of the sabre. This incident demonstrates the extent to which egalitarian principles had fallen to expediency.

Following Dupont's capitulation at Bailen, King Joseph had quit Madrid and retired north to the River Ebro. Since Bailen things had taken a turn for the worse. The English had landed in Portugal and obliged Junot to surrender after the battle of Vimeiro on 21 August. Watching his schemes going up in smoke, Napoleon decided it was time he took control of the situation in Spain and returned his brother to Madrid with the crown. Bailen had been the first real defeat that Napoleonic France had suffered, so the emperor had to be seen to re-assert his authority.

On 27 October the Ninth passed into Spain over the bridge at Bidossa and went to Irun. Just a quarter of a league from the border, this was the first Spanish town they entered. Like Major D'Eslon before them, they were immediately struck by how different Spain was from anywhere else they had encountered. The language, the houses with their ground-floor windows barred, the women dressed entirely in black, with black mantillas over their heads, and the men looking like Capuchin monks in their thick brown woollen coats; everything appeared alien and hostile. Having heard horror stories of Spanish atrocities, the soldiers of the Ninth were wary and suspicious of their new environment. This would be a very different campaign to anything they had waged before; one without pity or quarter on either side. An officer in the same brigade as the Ninth, Jules Marnier of the 24th Line, made a frank admission about this mutual animosity:

> This southern war was a war of extermination. But if one had to blame the inhabitants of that unfortunate country for having become carried away by some bloody cruelties, it is fair to say these cruelties gave rise to wild reprisals. If a *dog of a Frenchman,* as these *fanatics* designated us, counted for little in their eyes, a *damned Spaniard* counted for very little at the end of a French bayonet. We killed them without reason, at random, in passing.[11]

In order to secure his brother's throne, Napoleon ordered an army of eight corps to assemble around the Basque city of Vitoria. Ranged against them was a Spanish army divided into four large corps. Buoyed by their victory over Dupont at Bailen, the Spanish strategy was to envelop the French army by advancing on it from different directions. It was a bold plan, which Napoleon quickly guessed and made provisions to deal with.

Napoleon planned to divide the Spanish forces in two and defeat each half in detail. One of the Spanish columns was commanded by General Blake and had 36,000 men advancing from the direction of the Biscay coast. Blake clashed with Marshal Lefebvre's IV Corps at Durango on 31 October so Victor's corps was sent up in support. The Ninth set out at 9pm in bad weather, passing through the mountains on detestable tracks. Girod lost his shoes in the mud and was forced to walk barefoot. In the morning they halted by a large, abandoned village. While the men set up bivouacs, Girod searched his voltigeurs' haversacks looking for a spare pair of shoes and gaiters.

At this time, the Ninth was in the brigade of General Labruyère with the 24th Line. On 1 November the brigade was sent towards Okondo to act as a link with the left flank of Villatte's division at Balmaseda. When the brigade reached a fork in the road, Labruyère decided to split his brigade in two. Labruyère put himself at the head of one column and went left, while Colonel Meunier took the track on the right. Girod was in the left column and was ordered to scout ahead with 18 voltigeurs. They set out fairly late and it was night before they reached the small village of Amurrio. On the far side of the village Girod found himself faced with a broken track twisting its way up a fairly tall mountain. Girod had been given a local guide, but the man refused to go any further, saying he did not know the way. Girod believed the man knew they were about to run into Spanish troops and was afraid of being caught in the crossfire. Girod forced him to continue, scouting the column's march.

The night was very dark and they continued to climb in the greatest silence when suddenly a voice called out in Spanish '*Quien vive?*' The challenge was followed by two or three musket shots. Without hesitation Girod and his voltigeurs ran forwards. They found themselves on a sort of plateau where there were four isolated houses. Although the place looked deserted, Girod guessed the Spanish were hiding inside the buildings. He led several of his men into one house and encountered an old man and two young women with fear written all over their faces. A Spanish soldier, evidently a musician, threw himself at Girod's feet and pleaded for his life. Girod questioned him and the Spaniard indicated his companions were hidden upstairs.

With several of his men behind him, Girod climbed a staircase leading up from the kitchen. Holding his sabre in his hand, he cautiously opened the door to the first room he encountered. In the corner of the room was a Spanish soldier. He aimed his musket at Girod and pulled the trigger only to suffer a misfire – a flash in the pan. The light from the priming charge illuminated the room for an instant in which time the voltigeur following Girod lunged forward and bayoneted the Spaniard through the body. It was a lucky escape.

Continuing the search Girod found a small staircase leading to the attic. One of the voltigeurs went up first, closely followed by Girod. Half-way up, a volley rang out and the leading voltigeur fell seriously wounded on top of Girod, sending them both tumbling to the foot of the stairs. The Spanish in the attic opened fire, leaving Girod in no doubt that they meant to resist. Girod's first thought was to set fire to the house and smoke the Spaniards out. Instead he took hold of the old man in the kitchen, and forced him to hold up a lantern and walk ahead of his men as a human shield. The Spanish soldiers would not fire at the old man, so most gave up. A few climbed out through a skylight and tried to make their escape over the roof-top. There were around 20 Spaniards remaining in the attic, all of whom were dressed in peasant clothing. Angry at the loss of their comrade, the voltigeurs began bayoneting the prisoners and killed several before Girod managed to stop them. As the surviving prisoners were led outside, several of them made a dash for safety, but in the darkness they ran into the head of the French column coming up behind Girod. The regiment's sappers were at the head of the column and dispatched the Spanish fugitives with their axes.

It was clear the Spanish forward posts were not far off. There were several exchanges of gunfire and so General Labruyère halted his column for the night. In the meantime Colonel Meunier had advanced with his column along the other track. Having not encountered a soul, Meunier ordered his column to halt at 11pm. His men were exhausted and threw themselves down on the floor to snatch a little sleep. Unknown to Meunier, the road ahead was barred by a large force of Spanish soldiers. Forewarned of Meunier's approach, the Spanish troops were formed in line with loaded muskets waiting for the Frenchmen to arrive. As the Frenchmen lay down to sleep the Spanish infantry opened fire blindly into the night. The musket balls whizzed over the sleeping Frenchmen's heads. Meunier turned on his local guide, accused him of treachery and ran the man through with his sabre. There was a moment of confusion and disorder as the sleeping soldiers leapt off the floor and fled, but Meunier was able to rally them and re-formed a short way down the track. With no idea of the forces ranged against him, Meunier decided to spend the rest of the night in the best position available.

When the sun rose on 2 November, Meunier saw the Spanish had decamped. It was the same story on the left. The brigade reunited and continued forwards. Girod's company formed the advanced guard and was reinforced by voltigeur companies from the 24th Line. They formed a strong skirmish line and shuffled around all day without receiving the order to advance. They found an officer and two men hiding in some hay. These were sent back to Labruyère for interrogation. Afterwards they were shot along with the remainder of the prisoners from the night before.

They drew up as night fell and spent a quiet night. On 3 November Labruyère feared he had been cut off from the rest of the division so ordered his brigade to retrace its steps. Towards the evening the column saw the heights around them full of Spanish soldiers. Their campfires lit up the night sky. Fearing he was surrounded, Labruyère ordered his brigade onto a plateau rising out of the middle of a gorge and forbade anyone from lighting a fire. He also ordered his men to lay down with their muskets between their legs so the barrels would not glint in the moonlight. Labruyère then asked Meunier for an officer and 25 determined volunteers to attempt to break through the enemy forward posts and to reach headquarters, informing Victor of his predicament. Carabineer Lieutenant Volsack was chosen to lead the detachment and he set out before daybreak on what was thought to be a perilous mission.

In the meantime the brigade waited for the first rays of light with great anxiety. As the sun came up it was clear the Spanish had retreated. They had left a few men behind to keep the campfires burning as a deception. It dawned on Labruyère his retreat had actually allowed room for the Spanish to escape. When headquarters realized what had occurred, Labruyère was blamed for everything.

Having not been made privy to Napoleon's plans, this seems somewhat unfair, but the emperor was furious that Blake had escaped. When he blamed Victor for the error, the marshal pointed the finger squarely at Labruyère.

After another day of seemingly pointless marches and counter-marches, on 5 November Victor decided his mission was accomplished and began retracing his steps towards Vitoria. It was a premature decision. On 7 November word arrived that Blake had rallied and attempted to attack Villatte. Victor was ordered to turn around and go to Orduna. While Victor was marching forwards Blake fell back on the town of Espinosa, an important junction where the roads between Bilbao, Santander, Burgos and Leon intersected. On 10 November Villatte attacked Blake without waiting for the rest of Victor's corps to arrive. After a series of inconclusive attacks a fog settled over the battlefield and brought the action to a close. The Spanish lit huge bonfires up and down their line and sang the night away, believing themselves to be triumphant. Meanwhile, under the cover of the fog, Ruffin's division arrived during the evening and was tasked with shoring up the French left flank. The Ninth and 24th Line formed the first line, with the 96th Line in support.[12] There were a few skirmishes overnight, but the main action came in the morning.

With his corps properly assembled, Victor was able to mount a coordinated attack against Blake on 11 November. The lion's share of the fighting fell on Villatte's division while the Ninth appear to have played a secondary role in the battle. Still, it was a hotly contested action during which Colonel Meunier was lightly wounded, although he remained at the head of his regiment throughout. Eventually Blake's troops were driven back against the River Trueba. Hemmed in, the Spanish forces eventually succumbed to panic and fled in disorder. After the battle the Ninth was sent west to occupy Reinosa, where they found considerable stores of English biscuit and Cheshire cheese. These were distributed among the French troops. Marauders were sent out to see what else could be found while the rest of the division made running repairs and cared for its wounded.

The day after Espinosa, an extremely unsavoury event was witnessed by Jules Marnier of the 24th Line. That morning, as the brigade was called to arms, a large group of marauders from the Ninth returned from their night's activities, bringing with them three young Spaniards. General Labruyère called out to the sergeant leading the marauders and asked: 'Who are these men?'[13]

'Some vile rascals we had all the trouble in the world bringing to you, my general,' the sergeant replied, continuing, 'Infamous bandits we have drawn by force from their hiding place, which is the mill at the foot of the mountain. We were very lucky to be so numerous, for they were going to butcher us like sheep.'

The sergeant was obviously trying to curry favour with the general. By the costume of the three Spaniards and the fact they were covered in flour, it should have been obvious that they were in fact millers and their only crime was not to have fled at the approach of the French. However, General Labruyère indulged the marauders' cruelty. He commanded: 'Very well, sergeant. Four soldiers with you and escort these Spaniards to the rocks over there.' Although there was no order to execute the three, the tone of the command left all the spectators in no doubt of the general's implication.

Outraged at what they were witnessing, several officers from the 24th Line went to get their colonel. However, one of them, Lieutenant Marnier, was so appalled at the injustice, about the lack of a trial and the obvious innocence of the millers, he went after the execution party. When he caught up with them, two of the Spanish were already lifeless on the ground pierced with balls. The third had only received a flesh wound and had darted off as fast as his legs would carry him before the soldiers had a chance to reload. Believing himself almost out of musket range, the Spaniard's hopes of salvation were dashed. One of the Ninth's musicians had sprinted after the Spaniard and being very agile, caught up with him. With a swipe of his sword he knocked the Spaniard off his feet and then messily finished him off despite the miller's loud pleas for mercy. Running behind the pair came Marnier. He was so sickened by what he saw he lost all self-control. He drew his own sword and began beating the musician with it and would have probably killed him, had not other officers seized his arms and pulled him away. Labruyère arrived 'boiling with anger' and confronted Marnier, asking him why he had dared strike a soldier who was carrying out his orders, concluding 'I will sentence you to a court martial. You will be shot.'

With nothing to lose, Marnier spoke the truth as he saw it. In front of 200 men from both regiments he said: 'General, I do not know the misdemeanours of these three victims murdered on your orders, but I have only one regret – to have arrived too late at the scene of this atrocity. It is not a soldier I struck, but a brigand who stabbed a wounded man on the ground as he called for mercy.

You threaten to have me shot: I grant my life to you; but my honour I will keep.'
At this point Colonel Jamin of the 24th arrived on the scene. Ignoring the general,
he said in a loud voice: 'Lieutenant Marnier, go back to your company right away
… and you sirs,' he said to the others, 'return to your ranks'. Labruyère said
nothing. He had been chastised by Victor and Ruffin, and now countermanded
by a colonel in as many days.

On 14 November Victor was directed on Burgos where imperial
headquarters was located. They arrived on 21 November and were inspected by
the emperor the next day. The division was drawn up in line outside the town.
Napoleon headed straight for Labruyère and reproached him for his conduct in
the mountains. Labruyère vainly tried to justify himself, but it was no use. After
the episode with the murder of the Spanish prisoners and now this dressing
down in front of his troops by the emperor, Labruyère's stock was running very
low. He would have to do something quite spectacular to restore his honour.
In the meantime Napoleon went to Meunier. The emperor announced he wanted
all vacancies in the regiment filled immediately. There was a vacancy for a
battalion commander and Meunier believed this was a good opportunity to
recall Captain Godet back to the regiment and therefore put his name forward.
Napoleon was unimpressed.

'Where is he?' asked the Emperor.

'Sire, he is on recruitment, but at the first notice he will travel post.'

'That's not what I need. Present me a captain who was at Marengo.'

'But Sire, the one I am presenting was there.'

'It is not enough, he has to be present now.'[14]

The promotion therefore went instead to Captain Simon Paul Bruyère, one
of the old Meuse Scouts. Bruyère had been wounded at Piacenza forcing
the river crossing against the Austrian bridgehead and then again at Marengo.
He had since commanded the second voltigeurs and had been wounded during
the Ulm campaign and again at Friedland. In fact, it was said Napoleon favoured
rewarding voltigeur officers with promotions at this review. There was therefore
a good case to have Girod promoted. Meunier and Battalion Commander
Régeau sang the young officer's praises, but in this case Napoleon was not
convinced. The emperor said Girod was too young; adding that a lieutenant
ought to have a beard on his chin. When Meunier said Girod was the most

senior sub-lieutenant in the regiment and had been on the campaign in Prussia and Poland, Napoleon countered by asking Girod if he had been at Austerlitz? Girod should have replied 'my regiment was not there'; instead he confessed to the emperor that he had been a cadet at that time. That was all Napoleon wanted to hear. He demanded another officer for the post. Girod then had the heartbreak of watching as eight sub-lieutenants junior to him were promoted over his head. Girod could not help but wonder if Napoleon had deliberately snubbed him because he believed Meunier and Régeau were trying to curry favour with his influential father. After the parade, Meunier sought out Girod and consoled him, repeating that he had already put him forward for promotion to the minister of war some time ago. Sure enough, a short time after this review, Girod received confirmation of his promotion, dated Burgos, 21 November. As the other lieutenancies had been granted during the review on 22 November, Girod reclaimed his seniority over them.

From Burgos, Victor's corps marched south towards Madrid with the Imperial Guard and part of the cavalry reserve. They did not encounter any resistance until they arrived at the pass of Somosierra on 29 November. Here the road to Madrid passed through a narrow gap in the Sierra de Guadarrama mountains. The Spanish had fortified the pass with 9,000 men and a succession of artillery batteries blocking the narrow road. If Napoleon wanted to get into Madrid with cavalry and artillery there was no way round the pass. He would need to attack head on.

Early next morning Ruffin was ordered to seize the pass. The Ninth was placed right of the road; the 24th to the left. The 96th Line formed up straddling the road and screened by the division's voltigeur companies formed into composite battalions. On the extreme right, Lapisse's division was ordered to attack the village of Sepulveda, while Villatte, the reserve cavalry and the Imperial Guard marched in reserve. The French advance was concealed by a heavy fog. Girod found himself in the 1st Voltigeur Battalion, forming the advanced guard on the road. As they marched up the pass Napoleon joined them for a time, riding in between the two sections of the company. There was a discharge of musketry on the left, so a detachment of voltigeurs was sent scurrying up the mountainside to flush the enemy out. They came across the remains of a bivouac, but there was no sign of enemy soldiers. As the column continued its climb up the pass they arrived at a wide ditch which the Spanish had dug across the road. While a portion of the voltigeurs began filling it with rubble, Girod was sent forward at the head of 50 voltigeurs and ordered to form a skirmish line on the left of the main road.

Girod advanced with his voltigeurs and quickly encountered the Spanish forward posts. Advancing boldly, Girod's men chased the Spaniards from rock to rock, until the fog lifted suddenly like a curtain and revealed the opposing army. Girod was no distance at all from the main Spanish position. At the sight of his voltigeurs, the first Spanish line fired a general discharge, felling nine of Girod's men and putting two musket balls through his uniform. His situation appeared critical and Girod was considering ordering his men to withdraw when the attention of the Spanish was suddenly drawn to the main road. Growing impatient at the slow progress, Napoleon had ordered his service squadron of Polish light horse to charge the Spanish batteries in the pass. The Poles advanced in the narrow space just four men abreast. The Spanish gunners did not panic, but remained at their pieces targeting the advancing column of horsemen with canister. The infantry on the heights poured volley after volley down onto the road, but the Poles pressed on and hacked at the Spanish gunners until the pass was clear. Behind the Polish horsemen the 96th Line scurried up the road to secure the pass and before long the road to Madrid was open.

On 1 December the Ninth reached Buitrago at nightfall. Napoleon and King Joseph were there with their staff, the Imperial Guard and Royal Guard. The rest of the army bivouacked around them. It was very cold and the Ninth lacked wood to cook their soup on. Marauders were sent into town to procure wood by any means. In the time-honoured way, they began dismantling the houses for their timbers. Unfortunately, these houses were already occupied by French soldiers who were keen to spend the night under a good solid roof. A veritable combat ensued between the 'hads' and 'had-nots'. Marshal Berthier put himself at the head of the Imperial Guard's cavalry pickets and chased off the marauders who were disturbing headquarters' sleep. The whole business appears to have been taken fairly light-heartedly; a story went round that Berthier had been sent out because a soldier had broken into Napoleon's quarters and made off with his camp bed.

The next day the Ninth set off for Madrid, expecting to enter the Spanish capital without a shot. As the regiment approached the city they heard the sound of artillery fire and naively supposed the inhabitants were firing the guns in celebration of the return of King Joseph. It was only when the regiment came within view of the city and found the army ranged around the city in battle formation that they suspected something had gone very wrong. They were quickly directed up into the first line from where the men could take their first proper glimpse of the city. There were countless dark towers jutting into the sky and everywhere they looked, the roof-tops and terraces were packed with the inhabitants of Madrid, shouting and obviously very angry at the reappearance of the French. The city walls had been fortified and bristled with artillery. The Spanish gunners were firing at anything that moved whether it was in range or not. Clearly they were not going to be offered the keys to the city on a silver platter.

On 2 December it was four years to the day since Austerlitz and five since the coronation. Napoleon placed great importance on making great events coincide. The idea of entering Madrid on the same day as his coronation would have appealed to his sense of destiny. Instead he had to make do with a reconnaissance of the city defences, postponing any assault until the following day. That night the soldiers of the Ninth bivouacked in the open. The night was very cold and there was a lack of firewood. It was so cold that many men went within range of the Spanish guns to dismantle houses for timber. As daylight broke, Napoleon summoned his generals and gave them their orders. From a political point of view, it was absolutely necessary to use minimum force against Madrid. The assault would commence at 10am and there would be no pillaging. Any man found entering the interior of a private house would face severe consequences.

Prior to the assault, Victor's corps formed battalions of voltigeurs. Each of these battalions provided an advanced guard of 100 men commanded by three officers chosen by seniority of rank. Girod's lieutenancy had still not been confirmed at this date, so he joined the advanced guard as the most senior sub-lieutenant. At the designated time the attack went in at various points covered by artillery fire. The Spanish artillery opened up in response, so the voltigeurs dispersed into skirmish formation and advanced at the run in order to reduce casualties. Girod's group ran towards a deserted building within close range of the city walls. They had hoped to use the building as cover from which they could fire on the Spanish gunners, but when they reached the building's perimeter wall, there were no gates on their side of the enclosure. In order to enter in the conventional sense, the voltigeurs would have to go round to the front of the enclosure where they would be in full view of the enemy guns. The French voltigeurs removed their bayonets and used them as picks to dig a hole through the back wall. Once the opening was made Girod was pushed through first. Quickly fanning out through the property the voltigeurs took position in the windows and opened fire on the Spanish gunners. The remaining voltigeurs stacked furniture alongside the enclosure wall facing the city and formed a fire-step.

Using the walls and windowsills to steady their aim, the voltigeurs targeted the gunners as they reloaded their pieces. In retaliation to this murderous fire, the Spanish artillerymen turned their guns against the house. At such close range the result was devastating. Cannon balls demolished walls and sent fragments of stone and timber flying through the air. Many voltigeurs were killed, but they held their nerve and maintained their fire on the gunners. Eventually the Spanish began to lose their courage and would not approach their guns to reload them. As the artillery fire began to slacken off the voltigeurs opened the enclosure gate and ran towards the city wall with a blood-curdling shout of '*Vive l'Empereur!*'

Meanwhile, the French artillery had battered several breaches in the city wall. When Girod reached it he had to climb on someone's shoulders to get in. Sword in hand, he jumped into one of the Spanish batteries and was confronted with a heap of dead gunners and abandoned artillery. With their entry uncontested, the voltigeurs pressed into the city and came into contact with some other advanced guard detachments which had broken in from the Retiro and Alcala gates. Together they advanced along the promenade of the Prado into the interior of the town. Every street leading off the Prado was blocked with barricades and artillery. The first and largest they came across was on Alcala Street. Every time a Frenchman poked his head round the corner to look at the barricade the defenders would fire off a deadly spray of canister. While the Spanish reloaded the pieces, small groups of voltigeurs were able to run across the street in relative safety. Entering San Hieronimo Street, the French found another strongly fortified barricade. Either side of the barricade, the houses had their doors barred or walled up to prevent the French breaking in. The windows were full of Spaniards sheltering behind mattresses and firing down on the Frenchmen. Just like a medieval siege, the balconies above were piled with cobblestones and cauldrons of boiling oil to drop down on the Frenchmen should they attempt to force one of the doors.

Maintaining their skirmish order, the voltigeurs slowly began making their way up the street, firing and loading as they went. After about 45m General Labruyère appeared as if from nowhere and made for the captain of the advanced guard. Having been so strongly rebuked by Napoleon, Labruyère had a death wish. To regain his honour and restore his family name, he would die gloriously leading a charge against the barricades. He rebuked the voltigeur captain for fighting in skirmish formation and ordered him to line his men up, in the middle of the street. Labruyère might have been suicidal, but the captain was in less of a hurry to meet his maker. Unfortunately for Labruyère the captain he encountered was Grandjean. Just as at Grabaü the year before, Grandjean ignored a superior officer to preserve the lives of his men. It wasn't a question of cowardice: deployed as skirmishers his men could fire aimed shots. If they were formed in ranks, not only would they have been slaughtered by the artillery, they would not have been able to aim properly firing volleys.[15] When Grandjean bluntly and firmly refused to follow this ludicrous order, Labruyère was enraged. He grabbed one of the sub-officers by the arm and dragged him into the middle of the street. However, when he ordered the men to form up on him, they ignored him and continued to load and fire from what little shelter they could find.

Labruyère ran off looking for someone 'more docile' to share his glorious death. He came across Lieutenant Marnier of the 24th, the officer he had fallen out with over the murder of the Spanish millers. Marnier's voltigeur company had already been decimated when Labruyère ordered it to attack a battery of ten guns. Marnier was quite surprised by the order: 'Please think about the order you have just given, my General. By halfway there will be none of us left.'

'What!' exclaimed Labruyère. 'You recoil in the face of danger?'[16]

Hearing his bravery challenged, Marnier formed his men as ordered and advanced with the general at their side. After 20 paces a score of men had fallen. A few paces further and Labruyère was mortally wounded with a shot in the throat from which he would die the following day. The voltigeurs reached the barricade but could not hold the position. They were forced back for no gain and several more were wounded retrieving Labruyère.

Meanwhile Girod's advanced guard had been forced back down the San Hieronimo Street with heavy losses. Girod was hit in the thigh by a ball and forced out of the line. Unable to advance down the street, the voltigeurs began climbing into the adjacent gardens and, despite Napoleon's orders to the contrary, some broke into the houses closest to the promenade. One of these houses was the palace of the duke of Medina Celi who had fled the city abandoning the family silver and jewels. It was too tempting to resist. Putting the battle to one side for a moment, the voltigeurs plundered the building. In the ensuing free-for-all, the soldiers stuffed their haversacks and pockets to the full. An officer of the 27th Light arrived late expecting to find all the valuables gone, but came out with a diamond diadem later valued at 50,000 francs. It had been thrown on the floor and discarded near some overturned furniture.

Meanwhile the inhabitants continued to resist and refused all summons to surrender. The French brought artillery into the city and began firing on the Spanish barricades and into the crowds of people in the streets. This was hardly the display of minimum force that Napoleon and King Joseph had hoped for. It was not until 5pm that the Spanish envoys finally came to parley.

While the negotiations were underway, the Ninth bedded down in Alcala Street. In the morning the Spanish had surrendered and so the regiment advanced into the interior of the city. The Spanish capital was treated with great tact. The Imperial Headquarters were set up outside the city with the Imperial Guard bivouacked around it. All the regiments not immediately marching off for other destinations were housed in large convents. The generals and senior officers found lodgings close to the convents, while the subalterns stayed with their men. The convents had been stripped bare and officers and men alike were forced to sleep on the stone floors. No rations were provided and so the officers found themselves forced to buy food from the locals at heavily inflated prices. This provoked a wave of discontent among the Frenchmen.

Madrid was obviously a very rich city. The time-honoured rules of war were very clear. The city had fallen to an assault and by rights the city should have been sacked. Several of the more mutinous voltigeurs in Girod's company openly preached sedition. The captain took one of them by the collar and threatened to have him arrested. At this the company revolted. They formed a menacing circle around the captain and presented their bayonets towards him. Seeing their captain in mortal danger, Girod and some of the sub-officers pushed their way through the angry mob of voltigeurs and rescued him. In the aftermath of the revolt the junior officers begged the senior officers to punish the ringleaders; however, wiser heads prevailed. The senior officers understood the men's frustration and played down the incident in order to prevent the disorder spreading through the regiment. This did not disguise the seriousness of the incident. The soldiers of the Ninth had never been angels and had plundered and brawled their way from one side of Europe to the other under Napoleon; but there had never been an example of the men turning on their officers as they had done on this occasion. There was something about Spain that brought out the worst in everyone.

On 5 December Ruffin's division took up arms and marched south-east on the road to Valencia. They had information that an enemy corps was coming up from Aragon not realizing Madrid had fallen. Napoleon rode with them two leagues (8km) from the city to an advantageous position where they waited several days in expectation. Eventually they realized the Spanish troops had taken a different route. New intelligence had the Spanish gathering in the Tagus Valley around Toledo and Aranjuez. Napoleon sent Victor in pursuit. The corps returned to Madrid and circled clockwise around the walls a short distance then marched southwards on Aranjuez. Victor split his forces directing Villatte on Toledo and Ruffin on Aranjuez.

Ruffin's troops arrived on the evening of 8 December and finally encountered the enemy, but it was too late in the day to begin operations. Around midnight the Ninth's advanced posts noticed the Spanish had retreated under the cover of night. Several plucky soldiers went into the town and found most of the houses there were abandoned. The marauders were let loose and before long there was a procession of light infantrymen going back and forth from the French camp to the town. The marauders discovered a considerable cache of sweet Malaga fortified wine stored in small barrels. Before long these were 'borrowed' in large quantities. Unused to this sort of wine, the light infantrymen overdid it. As the sun came up the whole regiment was suffering from a tremendous hangover and was unfit to resume the march. As they shook their heads clear, the rest of Ruffin's division passed them unaware of the previous night's revelry. At last at 10am the sore-headed regiment marched from Aranjuez southwards in the direction of Tembleque. From there they turned northwards again and marched to Toledo.

In their absence Napoleon had quit Madrid to join the pursuit of the British army under John Moore. Victor was recalled to guard the capital in his absence. The Ninth therefore spent Christmas and the New Year in the capital. It was a time of carnival and the theatres of de los Caños and del Principe were open. The Caños theatre had Italian opera featuring the singer Porto. There were also Spanish dancers performing the fandango. A number of restaurants were set up in Madrid, but were out of the price range of the men and most subaltern officers, however there were bargains at the Fontana de Oro. There were also sightseeing opportunities for the officers, such as visiting the royal palace, which reminded them of the Louvre. What made Madrid different from the other cities in which the Ninth had spent time, was the lack of contact with ordinary Spaniards. According to Girod the only Spanish they dealt with were waiters at the cafés and restaurants they frequented. This lack of integration did not bode well for the future. Although King Joseph had been restored to the capital and the English had been driven to the sea at Corunna, 1808 had not been a good year for the French. Despite Napoleon's successes in the second half of the year, the defeat at Bailen had shown Europe that Napoleon's armies were not invincible. The fallout from Dupont's capitulation was far from over.

THE HILL AT TALAVERA

C aptain Maurice Godet had become increasingly bored with army life. We bade him farewell as he quit Wesel in 1806 carrying a promise from Colonel Meunier that he would be recalled to the field battalions should war stir again. Since then Godet had been placed in charge of recruitment and had missed three campaigns without the least sign of a recall. However, the constant demand for new blood at least ensured the captain was kept busy.

During the empire the Ninth's primary recruitment area was the Vosges department in eastern France. Godet was therefore based at Épinal, the departmental capital. The previous incumbent of Godet's post had been Captain Pierre Gros, who had finally retired in 1806 and set himself up as a tobacco merchant in Épinal. Given Mortier's criticisms of Gros' limitations as a clothing officer, it is unsurprising that Godet found a number of irregularities in the recruitment system when he took over.

Below Godet were five officers and 40 men to cover the department, which was divided into five recruitment districts. Recruitment was very much a seasonal activity. There would be a mad rush to process the new recruits, a long hike to escort them to the depot and then a gentle amble back to the Vosges for a period of idleness, which Godet described as 'prejudicial to service'.[1] The 40 men were all sub-officers or corporals, but among them Godet could only identify two who were actually competent. It is surprising given their rank, but Godet found the others illiterate and unable to perform basic accounting. Under Gros these soldiers had been allowed to take things fairly easy, so Godet summoned the whole team to Épinal for a shake-up.

Godet told them he was going to form a school where they were going to be attentive and learn. The proposition was begrudgingly approved, with every effort made to sabotage this rude interruption of their otherwise trouble-free lives. The two competent sub-officers were appointed as tutors, the officers took turns to monitor the lessons and after six months there were signs of progress. As a reward Godet asked the five recruitment districts to chip in and buy his men some good-quality greatcoats. The ones delivered were dark blue and looked like those worn by sub-officers in the artillery. The men were genuinely delighted to receive them.[2]

While the men were being taught to read and write, the officers also required attention. Godet found one of them living in sin with a much younger woman. The Vosges was a fairly conservative place and this sort of scandalous conduct was unacceptable.[3] Two weeks after a showdown, the couple married. Another officer was crushed by debts. He had previously gone to Captain Gros who had helpfully suggested returning to the regiment where an enemy bullet might solve his financial problems. Godet counselled a wiser course. An officer in the field had much greater expenses, so he kept the officer with the recruitment party but made him submit to a strict budget until his debts were cleared.

As for the recruitment process itself, the government would set a quota of conscripts required from each department and the local authorities would draw up lists of the men eligible to serve. There was a ballot; if 50 men were required, those drawing numbers 1 to 50 were called to serve. Another portion were put on standby in case any of the first draw were exempted from service. Those with an unlucky number underwent a medical and interview at the local recruitment council. Other than being declared unfit through infirmity or illness, there were a number of cards the conscripts might play. Prize-winning painters, sculptors and architects were legally exempt from service, as were ecclesiastical students. Some professions were also exempt from army service, including arms manufacturing and marine trades.[4] Another means of avoiding service was for the conscript to purchase a replacement who would serve in their stead. This option was extremely costly and beyond the means of most. As the demand for conscripts increased, the price shot up from around 1,800 francs to 4,000 francs. At a time when a chasseur's basic annual wage was set at 164.25 francs, it is uncertain if any of these options applied to robust farm boys from the Vosges.[5]

Once declared fit the conscripts would be divided up between the various competing recruitment detachments. In the empire, selection was made on the basis of height. Those arms requiring the tallest men would have their quotas filled first. The men over 1.785m were offered to the heavy cavalry – the carabineers and cuirassiers. The artillery held claim to the next pick of the crop, selecting men over 1.69m, with a preference for men with experience in metal working trades. The dragoons came next, claiming its quota from the remainder over 1.649m. With the rest there was some attempt to match those with useful trades to the various supporting services; with boatmen going to the pontooneers and coachmen to the train. Then and only then, were the light cavalry and infantry assigned.[6]

The Vosges department was noted for its high yield of recruits and those going into the Ninth had a particularly strong sense of duty. Godet claimed he only ever posted one man as a deserter and even then the man turned up before the final deadline. The prefect overseeing conscription told Godet an anecdote about a voltigeur on leave in 1805 who had been asked to stay at home an extra day by his family. The voltigeur refused, saying 'that might do for another regiment, but it won't do for the Ninth.'[7]

This is not to say these conscripts were falling over themselves to join the army; quite the reverse. Godet recorded how the conscripts would initially attempt to evade service, but then submit to their fate with reasonably good humour: 'The Vosgians … leaving their baskets at the door of the prefect's office, were always admitted and heard with patience and perfect kindness … Every draftee wanted the honour of a personal hearing … [E]very man appeared to be affected by three or four diseases, all calling to be exempted. The piteous looks they gave would have been worth an exemption if they had been made before less experienced eyes. But the council considered only the realities and as soon as the prefect had pronounced the cabalistic word 'fit' then you would see the individual draw himself up and go back to his companions laughing.'[8]

Godet did come across examples of corruption. When he first arrived at Épinal in 1806 Godet was approached by the doctor who sat on the recruitment council. The doctor revealed how the two of them might work together and reap 'a respectable harvest', by which he meant financial bribes for issuing exemptions. Although Godet did nothing to stop this practice, he chose not to profit from it himself. He simply gave a stern warning for the doctor not to implicate him in his deals. On a separate occasion Godet was mortified to find his long-serving orderly arrested after being paid four sovereigns by a family to speak to Godet on their son's behalf. It was a stupid bribe to take and Godet imprisoned him. While the local authorities were lenient, Godet ruled that the only way the man would be released was if he went back to the field battalions.

Although Godet was proud of the job he was doing, his own absence from the field battalions pained him. He feared someone who had been a sergeant when he quit the field battalions in 1806 might end up as a captain and then be promoted over his head. He wrote to Meunier and set out his frustration, asking to be recalled to the regiment. This letter caught up with Meunier as the regiment was passing through France en route to Spain. Meunier went to visit the director general of conscription, General Lacuée. Nothing came of this, so Meunier appealed directly to the emperor during the review at Burgos in Spain, the result of which we have already seen. The rejection must have hurt.

Since D'Eslon's departure for Spain, the Ninth's depot had been commanded by Captain Paulet, the family man originally lined up for recruitment. It had been a busy time for Paulet, what with Schauenburg's review at Landau at the beginning of 1808 and the military reforms of February the same year. Paulet had attempted to form the new 4th and 5th battalions but had been hampered by a lack of men. The two new battalions were supposed to be formed from the old 3rd Battalion, but these troops were scattered far and wide. D'Eslon had taken 450 officers and men to Spain. The carabineers and voltigeurs were then still part of Oudinot's corps with 203 officers and men. In fact there were only 108 men still left in the depot.

In any case, on 1 May 1808 Paulet oversaw the formation of the two new battalions at Landau.[9] The fifth, 'depot' battalion was formed from the remainder of the old 3rd Battalion and a 19-man company cadre, which had arrived from the 20th Line.[10] The new 4th Battalion consisted only of the elite companies as there were no spare chasseurs to form the four centre companies. Just as more conscripts came in, several hundred were transferred to help form the new 31st Light in July 1808. For the remainder of 1808, the Ninth was unable to provide a fourth field battalion.

With D'Eslon taken prisoner at Bailen, in September 1808 Major Marc Obert arrived to take command of the depot.[11] On 16 January 1809 Godet was recalled to take command of a company in the 5th Battalion, while Paulet was sent to replace him as recruitment officer. Godet received a certificate of good conduct from the prefect, something of which he was very proud; then travelled up to the regimental depot which had taken station at Longwy nearly 200km to the north.

Even before the Industrial Revolution turned Longwy into a grim iron-smelting town, it was hardly picturesque. The town, encased by bleak, grey Vauban fortification, was stuck on top of a large rock guarding the road to Luxembourg. For young men used to the fields, woods and valleys of the Vosges, it must have seemed a depressing, claustrophobic place. Godet thought it a very unpleasant garrison, saying you could pass from one side of the town to the other in a pistol shot. The fortress of Longwy had already featured in the history of the Ninth. In 1791 the Chasseurs of Cévennes had been stripped of its regional title there and put on a war footing. Old Lieutenant-Colonel de Villionne had commanded the battalion with its noble officer corps still intact. Labassée had still been a sub-lieutenant, Kuhmann had yet to receive his epaulettes and men like Pierre Gros and Robert Marthe were still sub-officers with little inkling of what was to come. Nearly 20 years had passed since then; 20 years of harvesting recruits and schooling them into soldiers.

One old boy was around to remember this time; the Quartermaster Treasurer Etienne Saÿvé was still in the regiment counting his beans. Godet shared an apartment with him and Major Obert. By pooling their resources they attempted to bring a little joy to the world, throwing entertainments for their comrades and members of the civil authorities. Godet complained this 'little grandeur' cost four times the ordinary expense and was unsustainable for long.

The Ninth formed its own Masonic lodge at Longwy in April 1808. Masonry was well established in the empire, with Napoleon's elder brother Joseph holding the post of Grand Master and a number of marshals holding high office, including Massena and Murat. While other regimental lodges had martial names (the 4th Light's lodge was called 'The Pupils of Mars' and the 6th Light 'The Children of Marengo'), the Ninth's lodge was less bellicose in name: *les Amis Réunis* ('Friends Reunited'). Membership of the lodge fluctuated depending on the officers posted to the 5th Battalion or forming part of the regimental staff. The stalwarts were Major Obert, Saÿvé (and his eventual successor, Jules Saulnier) and Baudot, the voltigeur captain of long service who also took on the clothing officer role. At various times the lodge included the mayor of Longwy, a number of local bourgeois and several prominent merchants. In 1809 the lodge included a number of Swedish officers and in 1813 a pair of imprisoned British Royal Navy officers, captains Henry Stephenson and Thomas Parker.[12]

Despite the little distractions, Godet's memoirs indicate he was somewhat depressed at this time. When stationed at Wesel, Godet had become involved with the widow of a French noble. When Godet first encountered Madame de Stéphany, she was living with her brother-in-law, an émigré French noble. Godet was billeted on the family and after a frosty reception, his hosts warmed to him and began to socialize. The brother-in-law died suddenly and de Stéphany began to look to Godet as her protector. She entrusted him with her finances and took it upon herself to find him a wife. The motives of the widow might seem somewhat obscure today, but in essence she wished to build a surrogate family by finding a wife for Godet and having them live with her. In that era it was common for impoverished families to pass their daughters to wealthier families or individuals in the hope they would meet a husband. The first potential wife was Adelaide, a 17-year-old German aristocrat and relative of de Stéphany. Things looked promising, Godet booked some leave to travel to Germany to meet her, but the girl died before he left. Another potential spouse was found, but she became something of a tearaway and was sent back to her family.

Godet's life had entered a stalemate. He was unable to return to the field battalions; unable to gain promotion; unable to find a wife; and, to rub salt into the wounds, had been rejected for the Legion of Honour three times since the Austerlitz campaign. Godet attributed this as a snub for voting against the consulate for life in 1802.[13] Unable to rejoin the field battalions, Godet began filling out the papers requesting early retirement. Shortly after these had been presented to Major Obert, a nomination to the Imperial Guard came through. Obert asked Godet if he still wanted to go ahead with his resignation, or if he wanted to accept the post now on offer. Godet had always wanted to serve in the Guard. He reasoned service conditions would be better and there would be more opportunity to rest between campaigns. Sizing things up, Godet withdrew his request, packed his portmantle and bade farewell to Longwy and the regiment he had joined in difficult circumstances, but which he had come to admire enormously.

As one career waned, another was in the ascendancy. In the first quarter of 1809 Jean Baptiste Cardron arrived in Longwy. He had come to the end of his voluntary engagement and so went for an interview with Major Obert. Cardron described Obert as the 'best possible sort' and it is easy to see why. During their interview Obert asked Cardron to hand in his silver sergeant's stripes. In return, Obert offered Cardron a set of adjutant's epaulettes if he renewed his engagement. Cardron happily accepted, expecting he might become an officer. On 24 March 1809 Cardron wrote to his mother explaining his new uniform requirements. The letter demonstrates what slaves to fashion French soldiers could be.

> ... [A]n adjutant's uniform is something more than that of a poor sergeant. I am going to need many things – dress coat, fine linen, cravats, waistcoats of twill and dimity, quite a few and good quality and I need it as soon as possible. As you know I am here with almost nothing, therefore please send it to me in the big leather portmantle which I know has been around the house for a long time. It will not be too big especially on the march. Do not send me my bicorne as we wear officers' shakos, all brilliant with silver. Do not forget to insert my golden watch which my sister can clean and to which she can attach a chain with a fine golden winding key and it must have fashionable hands because it is an adjutant's watch.[14]

On 28 March Cardron drank a toast to his re-enlistment with his friend Michel Fleury, a fellow adjutant. The toasting appears to have prompted him to write home for more necessities the next day:

I do not know if in the list of effects which you have to send me I mentioned to you about nankin cloth.[15] In the fear of not having done so, I ask you not to forget it. Send some for Fleury and I, 6 pieces, it is so rare here we cannot find it. I forgot to say to you I am in the same battalion as Fleury and we expect to leave together in a while. Do not forget to send me stockings. Forget nothing.

p.s. Send me all my military books, theories, regulations, etc. I am to become a soldier again. I have to instruct more than 50 men.

Quite what Cardron's mother made of these expensive demands we can probably guess. In a letter to his sister on 7 April Cardron jokingly explained he had no intention of selling his gold watch and if his mother did not believe him she should not send it. However, Cardron went on to ask for 'fine stockings and also some silver shoe buckles', which he promised not to sell either.

A month later, on 10 May, Cardron was reporting how he had to 'pillage' the depot in order to provide for the 700 recruits who were descending on Longwy. True enough, depots all over France were awash with conscripts. At the beginning of 1809 a fifth coalition was formed against France, composed of Britain, Austria, Spain and Portugal. After Bailen Napoleon had anticipated trouble with Austria, so on 10 September 1808 he called for a levy of 80,000 extra conscripts. Under the conscription system, even if not called up at the age of 20, men remained eligible for future ballots until the age of 25. Taking advantage of this, Napoleon called up 20,000 men each from the classes of 1809 back to 1806. Just as people were coming to terms with this levy another 80,000 conscripts were called up one year early from the class of 1810.

One of the 1809 class was Nicolas Joseph Page from the village of Belrupt in the Vosges. Given the numbers of men being called up, being fit and aged 20, Page saw a spell in the army as inevitable, so chose to make his family some money by offering himself up as a replacement to a better-off family. On 2 March 1809 Page found himself in a crowd of 500 conscripts gathered at Épinal waiting to be cheered away by the townsfolk and local dignitaries. When everyone was gathered, they were marched off under escort to Longwy, six days' march away. Page arrived at Longwy on 8 March 1809 and was immediately entered into the rolls. He was one of the last to be processed in this batch and his details were recorded as follows:[16]

No. 5948 *Nicolas Jh. Page*

Son of *Claude Nicolas* and of *Elizabeth Obert*

born the *9 November 1788 at Belrupt*

Canton of *Darney*

Department of *the Vosges*

Height of *one metre 694 millimetres*

Face	*Full*	Forehead	*Round*
Eyes	*Grey*	Nose	*Pointed*
Mouth	*Medium*	Chin	*Short*
Hair	*Chestnut*	Eyebrows	*Chestnut*

Arrived at the Corps *8 March Year 1809*

Conscript of the year 1808

Substitute for Bertrand, Jean Claude, of the Commune of Senonges, Canton of Darney

No. 1

His place of residence, at the epoch of his entry into service, was at Belrupt,

Department of the Vosges

After his details were recorded, Page underwent a brief medical examination and with no obvious ailments, his military career commenced in earnest. With men immediately required by the 4th Battalion the contingent was processed very quickly. They were immediately put into squads, had the penal code read to them and given basic drill exercises such as the position of the soldier without arms. Three days on, they uniformed half of the contingent and marched them off to the Grand Army the day after, training them en route. 'There's well instructed soldiers!' mused Page.[17]

Page was kept back and given a longer period of training. He was quickly made a corporal. The absence of any experienced men for this job shows how stretched the regiment was to provide company cadres. The officers were hardly the most experienced group the Ninth had ever sent on campaign. Of 18 company officers, 12 had only received their grades in April or May 1809.[18]

While Page remained in the depot his comrades were marched towards Augsburg where the elite companies had been stationed since March. Training was given on the march. The conscripts practised forming platoons in the morning and breaking them during the halts. They marched in column through the day and formed line of battle on arrival. Once the men were billeted and the soup was on the boil, the men were taken into a nearby field to practise arms drill. This was not ideal, but after a few weeks of this regime the men started to look something like soldiers.[19]

Command of this new battalion was given to Battalion Commander Jean Prost. By early April it was composed of 10 officers and 407 men in four companies.[20] It formed part of 1st Battalion of the 1st Light Half-Brigade, a composite regiment in General Nicolas François Conroux's brigade in General Jean Victor Tharreau's division. The other two battalions in the half-brigade were formed by the 4th Battalion of the 6th Light and a battalion of Corsican sharpshooters.

Hostilities commenced with Austria on 10 April when Archduke Charles crossed the River Inn. On 19 April there was an engagement at Pfaffenhoffen and a second at Landshut on 21 April. Tharreau's division helped push the Austrians back, racing ahead to try and assist Marshal Davout at Eckmuhl. The next major encounter was at Ratisbon, after which the victorious French army marched on the Austrian capital. On the morning of 10 May, Conroux's brigade and the light cavalry of General Colbert entered the Viennese suburbs. They marched down the Schoenbrunn road and into the Mariahilf district where they found a roadblock. Forcing it aside, the light cavalry burst in followed by the light infantry. There was little resistance from the Austrian militia until the light infantrymen came within range of the guns mounted on the walls of the old city. Met by a hail of bullets and canister, Tharreau was wounded and the advance came to a halt. Realizing an assault would be fruitless, Napoleon instead ordered a bombardment which caused the Austrians to capitulate on 12 May.

Having taken Vienna, Napoleon's next objective was the destruction of the Austrian field army commanded by Archduke Charles. This army was concentrated on the other side of the Danube to the north of Vienna. On 21 May Massena opened the battle, crossing the Danube on a pontoon bridge via Lobau Island. He found himself in a bitter struggle against 80,000 Austrians between the villages of Aspern and Essling. That night Tharreau's division crossed over Lobau Island and formed the left of Lannes' corps. The battalions were drawn up in closed columns. Between Tharreau and Aspern was the massed cavalry of

Marshal Bessières. Towards the end of the morning Lannes' corps led the assault against the Austrian centre. The French columns groaned under the weight of Austrian shot and shell. There was no time or space for manoeuvre and the contest quickly developed into a battle of attrition between two obstinate foes. Just as it appeared that the Austrian line might be breaking, Lannes received unsettling news. The Austrians had been floating heavy debris down the Danube in order to smash the French pontoon bridge. Having repaired several small breaches the French pontooneers had run out of luck and the bridge was ruptured. Lannes' ammunition was running out and he had no way of receiving reserves. The marshal ordered a withdrawal. The Austrians sensed the French weakness and unleashed their reserves of men and artillery. Lannes fell mortally wounded when his knees were smashed by a cannon ball. The young conscripts kept huddled in their columns under heavy artillery fire. They were so inexperienced that their commanders did not dare deploy into line formation to reduce the terrible effect of the artillery fire.[21]

With all initiative lost, Napoleon ordered his army back onto Lobau Island as soon as the bridge was restored. Tharreau's men remained near Essling until halfway through the night. The division had lost over half its effective strength and 4th Battalion had suffered very heavy losses. Of the 19 officers who went into action, four were killed and 14 wounded. Among the wounded were Prost and all of the captains: Rebeaucourt, Méret, Bablon, Charton, Leroy and Etienne.[22] On 26 May the bridge was restored and the army crossed to the right bank to lick its wounds. Given the terrible losses, word was sent back to Longwy for reserves.

Nicolas Page suspected he would be sent to the front when a convoy of wounded men arrived in Longwy at the beginning of May. Page described how he recognized some of the wounded men from those he had left Épinal with two months before. The wounded were put into barracks and a detachment formed to take their place. Page was among those chosen and so wrote to his parents informing them he was setting out for the Grand Army.

The military postal system was advanced enough for a reply from his father to greet him at Munich. The letter showed how desperate the authorities had become to find recruits. To support his family Page had joined the army as a replacement for Jean Claude Bertrand. However, with Page now called up himself, the authorities ordered Bertrand to take Page's place. This of course meant the deal was off and Page's family would not receive any money. To add to the family's woes, the letter reported Page's younger brother was one of those called up early, leaving Page naturally concerned for his safety. Accepting his fate with a shrug, Page got on with the business at hand. From Munich he was sent to the Tyrol to fight Austrian insurgents. From there he was sent north to Vienna where he joined the Grand Army as it prepared to avenge the reverse of Aspern and Essling.

As final preparations were made for another great battle, Page saw his emperor for the first time at an inspection review at Vienna's Schönbrunn Palace. In Page's battalion all the chasseurs were recent conscripts and the only veterans were serving in the elite companies. Napoleon was in a generous mood when he inspected the battalion, taking time to single out veterans and offering encouragement to the newcomers. Every time Napoleon saw an 'old moustache' he would ask how long they had served and whether they had been at Marengo? When he came across one of these veterans he would give them rewards by way of annuities or promotions. When Napoleon came past Page he stopped and asked him, 'Have you tasted powder?'

'Sire, not much, but I hope to taste some more.'

'My friend, you must be a good soldier.'[23]

Napoleon brought the battalion to attention and called out to Battalion Commander Charles Planchet, who had replaced the injured Prost: 'Are these youngsters from the Vosges?' Planchet answered in the affirmative. 'They are brave,' Napoleon continued. 'They will make good soldiers. Take care of them.'[24] Such personal attention excited the passion of the French troops, and made them feel important and loved on the eve of battle.

Napoleon had suffered a reverse at Essling in May, but was determined to destroy the Austrian army in battle and draw the campaign to a close. Everything was set for the night of 4/5 July. Conroux's brigade was given the dubious honour of leading the first assault from Lobau. Just before dawn, 1,500 men chosen from the brigade were put into boats opposite Sachsengang and sent towards the Austrian lines. Paddling across the river, Conroux's men surprised the Austrians and captured a redoubt. Ropes were sent across to the other bank to permit passage of the remainder of Tharreau's division. A bridge was thrown across and the Austrian advanced guard pushed back towards Essling.

Daybreak revealed the French army deployed for one of the greatest battles history had yet known, with 300,000 men in combat for two days. Like many soldiers writing their memoirs, Page did not dwell on the trauma of battle. His description of the great battle of Wagram was limited to a remark that they marched out to the Isle of Lobau and suffered a lot. There is no clear picture of the number of casualties suffered by the 4th Battalion in the battle. A situation report from 8 August 1809 gives the 4th Battalion's strength and losses.[25] There were 25 officers present in August, two of whom were recovering from wounds; of the 659 men recorded, 439 were present, 159 having just arrived from the 5th Battalion. There were 61 men with the corps but convalescing from wounds or sickness. In addition there were 336 men in hospital, presumably from the early part of the campaign. The return then gives a number of figures, which when added together do not quite tally. It recorded 18 men had been killed in battle; with 11 officers and 152 men wounded. Among the wounded were 12 amputees. Of the officers wounded, nine had returned to their posts and one more was expected to make a full recovery. Of the wounded men, 102 troops had returned to the ranks and 40 more were expected back. In all, it appears the 4th Battalion lost about one-third of its number at Wagram.

The officer losses for this campaign were high. Eighteen had been killed or wounded at Essling, with 11 more at Wagram. Although some of those who fell at Wagram had been wounded previously at Essling, the toll was still heavy. Perhaps with the reduced quality of the soldiers, the officers had taken more risks in the battle, leading from the front more conspicuously? This was all well and good for the bulletin writers, but the ensuing loss of experienced officers must have been detrimental to the quality of the battalion. The problem was exacerbated further by sub-lieutenancies being offered to officer cadets, something that Cardron complained about in a letter dated 15 August 1809:

Upon my arrival here I found much had changed. Mr Ribeaucourt who is badly wounded has just retired and leaves for France in a few days. Quartermaster Corporal Dhoudaut, is now a sub-lieutenant and had his leg amputated. He has recovered and is also leaving. Sergeant-Major Any became sub-lieutenant two months ago. Huchat, the confidante of the house of Charlier, went from sub-lieutenant to lieutenant and captain in three months (he was my former sergeant-major) and many others who you do not know. Fleury missed out by being sent to the Tyrol and would now be sub-lieutenant. Despite his absence, the commandant, who has the most advantageous plans for him, had proposed him for a sub-lieutenancy. He would inevitably have been promoted if they had not sent us another heap of 'magazine officers'.[26]

Cardron wrote this letter on the emperor's 40th birthday. Every officer received a bonus of 12 francs and every soldier 2.50 francs with which to celebrate his birthday. Cardron boasted that every table was loaded with meat and wine, 'for wine is as common in this camp as water and they deliver two bottles to each soldier every day …'[27] With a sarcastic reference to the Austrian successes at Aspern-Essling, Cardron continued: 'The Viennese have less of the arrogance they had after the misfortune the army felt on the 22nd. They are now sweet as lambs [after Wagram].' Cardron speculated on the likelihood of peace, or further fighting: 'We know nothing of the peace or the war, some say peace is made, others the congress has only just opened. We do not know which to believe. Be that as it may, we work relentlessly strengthening all the bridgeheads established on the Danube. We supply 500 men every two days for the working parties.' His only complaint was having to pay for food, unlike in Prussia where they 'burned and plundered' everywhere they passed.

A few days after the fête all the Ninth's sick and wounded were gathered up and sent back to France. They also sent back a cadre to form new companies destined for Spain. Corporal Page was among this number. Arriving at Strasbourg, he asked the commander of the detachment for leave to visit his parents. The commander refused, but Page's officer told him to go anyway and he would not post him as a deserter provided he rejoined them at Metz. Page was naturally anxious to see his parents and tell them what he had seen on campaign and learn the fate of his younger brother. He need not have been concerned at all. He found the family safe. His brother had been declared unfit and discharged. Page spent two days with his parents before his father accompanied him part of the way to Metz. When they parted there were many tears. Page told his father he would soon be going to Spain and he had no idea if he would ever come back again.

While the 4th Battalion had been formed and blooded on the fields of Essling and Wagram, the remainder of the regiment had remained in Spain. We left Félix Girod and the regiment in Madrid at Christmas 1808, enjoying the theatres and cafés of the Spanish capital. Over the New Year period Girod's promotion to lieutenant finally came through. He quit the 1st Voltigeur Company and joined the 2nd Battalion's 2nd Company of chasseurs under Captain Nicolas.

The early part of the year had been eventful. On 13 January the regiment was in action near Uclés. With his captain absent, Girod commanded the company in action for the first time. It was not the most glorious affair. General Ruffin apparently got lost and blundered into the Spanish who were sheltering behind a range of hills. General Barrois had replaced the ill-fated Labruyère after Madrid and found himself at the head of the Ninth's 2nd Battalion who were the first to climb the hills. Without waiting for the remainder of his brigade to arrive, Barrois put himself at the head of the troops, raised a cry of 'Vive l'Empereur' and launched the 2nd Battalion straight at the mass of Spanish soldiers.

As the battalion advanced at a run, Barrois forbade them from firing their muskets. They quickly passed from one side of the valley to the other without becoming disordered. In the meantime the Spanish troops began lining up to deliver a volley. Nervous at the sight of the onrushing Frenchmen the volley was poorly delivered; the majority of the balls flew harmlessly over the heads of the onrushing battalion and it only caused a few casualties. When the Spanish realized their volley had missed and the French would be on them before they could reload, they threw their muskets on the floor and turned about in confusion. By the time the Ninth arrived, breathless from its charge, more than 7,000 Spanish soldiers were on their knees begging for mercy, crying out 'Viva el rey Jose y el gran Napoleon.' The action had lasted 15 minutes.

What Barrois had not realized when he launched his charge was that the Spanish troops had been pursued by Villatte's division from Uclés. When the Ninth appeared over the hill, the Spanish saw themselves surrounded, which explained their lack of stomach for a fight. Girod found himself slightly embarrassed by the whole thing. He realized he was standing on a Spanish flag discarded in the flight. He did not deign to pick it up and saw nothing honourable in possessing a trophy unless it had been seized in bloody hand-to-hand combat. Another officer, one 'less of a novice' than Girod, picked the flag up and ran off to present it to General

The military hospital at Marienburg, Poland.

The departure of French conscripts in 1807.

Officier des Grenadier du 9ᵐᵉ Regiment de chasseurs à pied.

Carabineer officer of the 9th Light Infantry.

Grenadier et Fusilier du 9ᵐᵉ Reg: des Chasseur à pié.

Carabineer and chasseur of the 9th.

Dupont surrenders at Bailen, 23 July 1808.

The battle of Somosierra, 30 November 1808.

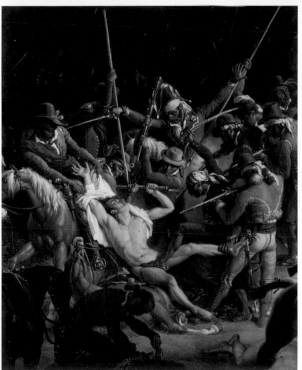

French brutality in Spain is pictured here (top) alongside an image depicting a guerrilla attack on a French convoy (bottom).

The battle of Chiclana, 5 March 1811. A French cantineer distributes brandy.

The defence of Badajoz, 6 April 1812.

Two light infantry battalion commanders, in the 1812 pattern uniform.

Count Gérard, as painted by Jacques-Louis David. He was wounded leading the 9th.

Barrois. The officer was mentioned in dispatches and recommended for the Legion of Honour. Girod could not believe it. He wanted nothing more than a cross of honour. In fact Girod had been recommended for one after Madrid, but he did not receive it. Speculating on the reasons for this, Girod believed Napoleon feared giving too much importance to the war in Spain and did not want the peoples of France or Europe to realize how serious the situation was there. He also thought there was a selfish element to the snub, claiming Napoleon was never lavish in his praise for battles at which he was not personally present. After the British were expelled at Corunna, on 17 January 1809, Napoleon quit Spain for France, fearing the war with Austria already described. In his absence the French soldiers in Spain became increasingly disillusioned and increasingly felt they were a forgotten army, fighting a forgotten war.

After the surrender of the Spanish at Ocaña the regiment turned eastwards and marched on Cuenca two days distant. On the first day they were assailed by bad weather. In the evening they were so wet, and the ground so damp, the regiment crammed itself into a church rather than bivouac in the open. The officers reserved themselves the choir and sacristy then laid the priests' robes and garments down for bedding in lieu of straw. No wonder they provoked such resentment among the locals.

The following day they found Cuenca abandoned by the enemy army and its inhabitants. Captain Nicolas was ordered to take his company to a small hermitage at the summit of a mountain overlooking Cuenca. Fearing there would be no provisions up at the hermitage, Nicolas asked Girod to take a few men and find some food. While the company marched up the mountain the foraging party broke into two houses where they retrieved a small quantity of bread, flour and some dry pork. Night had begun to fall so Girod ordered his party up the mountain track to rejoin the company. It was late when they arrived and they were somewhat surprised to find the hermitage had been full of food. The rest of the company had already dined, and the pile of debris on the table and contented faces of their comrades stood testimony to the quality of the feast consumed. The wine was also of a very good quality and Captain Nicolas displayed that common trait of the old timers in the Ninth of getting as drunk as a lord. When the company was ordered down from the hermitage the following evening, Nicolas was still in a stupefied state. His men tried getting him onto his horse, but he would not remain in the saddle. Somewhat exasperated by the situation, Girod had the company form a human chain along which the captain was passed man to man. Even then the captain appeared hell-bent on rolling down the mountain rather than walking.

For the next month the regiment found itself scouring the region of La Mancha where they saw the windmills at El Toboso made famous by Cervantes' *Don Quixote*. In this region the population had mostly stayed at home and so there was nothing like the pillage seen at Cuenca. Towards the end of February Victor was ordered westwards.

On 28 March the regiment found itself present, but not heavily engaged at the battle of Medellin, on the right bank of the river Guadiana. A Spanish army led by General Cuesta was arrayed in line of battle in a sort of natural amphitheatre formed by a hill which was separated from the town by an extended plain. The Spanish were slightly more numerous than the French in infantry so Colonel Meunier ordered his regiment to form a line of two rather than three ranks, thus increasing his frontage by a third and making the regiment appear more imposing. At one point the Spanish cavalry charged the Ninth, but Meunier had sufficient time to redeploy the regiment into square, which was enough to intimidate the Spanish horsemen who sped by taking fire from all faces of the formation. By the time night fell, the men in the regiment had little idea what had occurred elsewhere on the field.

The following morning a party of 600 men was sent to collect muskets from the battlefield. Only then did they realize what a bloody affair it had been. During the night it had rained and so the soil had been stained red by blood. Blood had trickled into little streams around piles of corpses, which were stacked one on top of the other a few paces from where piles of abandoned muskets were found. Many of the muskets were loaded and cocked, indicating their owners had not had the time or inclination to open fire before throwing them away. The French had not taken many prisoners. A few days before the battle the French advanced posts had found the bodies of some French horse chasseurs hanging from trees. The bodies had been horribly mutilated. The Spanish soldiers at Medellin had been shown no quarter and thousands had been slain. The French officers responsible for burying the Spanish dead said they interred 16,000 Spaniards, a task which took an entire battalion eight days to complete.

After Medellin there came a period of rest. Other than the occasional scorpion sting, it was a time to enjoy the warmth of a Spanish spring and rebuild their strength. Girod became acquainted with a Spanish girl. She took him home and embroidered her name in green silk on the lining of his epaulette. In turn Girod sent a portrait of her to his sister for approval, but as was so often the case, their courtship was terminated by more serious affairs.

As long as Portugal held out against Napoleon, the British had a gateway into Europe. A new British army under Sir Arthur Wellesley joined with Cuesta's Spaniards on 20 July 1809 and began advancing on Madrid. In response Victor moved his corps to Talavera de la Reina on the River Tagus, barring the road to the Spanish capital. After waiting a few days there, Victor realized he was outnumbered and so ordered his army corps to fall back on Toledo, where he joined Sebastiani's IV Corps, along with King Joseph's troops and staff. In total the French had 46,000 men covering the road to Madrid.

Learning the Anglo-Spanish forces had reached Talavera, King Joseph ordered his forces to take the offensive. Around 4pm on 27 July, the Ninth reached the banks of the Alberche River. The 16th Light Infantry had already forded the river and come to grips with the British advanced guard. Hidden by a forested and broken terrain, the soldiers of the Ninth could not see the engagement, but they certainly heard it. The veterans had fought all manner of European soldiers under Napoleon's reign. They had fought and vanquished men from the four corners of the Hapsburg Empire; they had fought the army built by Frederick the Great of Prussia; they had tilted bayonets with the giants of the Russian Imperial Guard; hunted Cossacks and Kalmucks on the outposts in Poland; and they had also vanquished the armies of Spain on numerous occasions. In all its history the Ninth had never encountered a British army in a pitched battle. The following words are how Girod described the sound of British musketry; a sound they would come to dread:

> It was the first time the noise of an English fusillade had reached our ears and I may say it was of a nature which made a certain impression on us. Indeed, never had we heard a rolling fire as well fed as that.[28]

The regiment advanced in support of their comrades in the advanced guard, fording the Alberche with water up to their armpits. The British had been surprised by the arrival of French troops on their flank and quickly fell back on a strong, prepared position. The Anglo-Spanish line stretched for two miles and was composed of 55,000 men. The bulk of the forces (34,000 men) were Cuesta's Spaniards, entrenched around Talavera. The redcoats were to the north and had their left flank anchored on the Cerro de Medellin, a steep hillock dominating the town. Between them and the French was the Portiña brook, which flowed north to south, intersecting the battlefield.

Marshal Victor was well acquainted with the local terrain and knew the key to the battlefield was the Medellin. Victor foresaw the difficulty his troops would have storming the Medellin in broad daylight and so formulated a daring but hazardous plan. If he could seize the Medellin overnight, the morrow's battle would already be half-won. Before sundown he had Ruffin's division take position on the Cascajal heights, due east of the Medellin, poised to seize the hill.

At dusk General Lapisse was ordered to mount a noisy diversionary attack on the centre of the British line. Although the attack soon petered out it achieved its objective, diverting attention away from the Cascajal heights. Shortly before 10pm Colonel Meunier ordered his men to load their muskets and then led them forward. The first two battalions were formed in columns marching level with each other, with the 3rd Battalion lingering some way behind as a reserve. As the last glimmers of sunlight disappeared behind the Medellin, the regiment picked its way down the ravine and stepped across the Portiña, unperceived by the British line. The brook was almost dry, a mere trickle coursing its way through a stony bed. The men quietly made their way over and began the ascent of the Medellin.

The gradient was gentle at first but soon became fairly steep. They were two-thirds the way up before they were challenged. Although Low's brigade of the King's German Legion was surprised by the attack, they were quick to respond. Drawn up in line, Low's infantrymen delivered a massive volley at close range which blew the head off the first two battalions. Several hundred Frenchmen fell, including Colonel Meunier who was struck by musket balls in the head and left leg. The 2nd Battalion's commander went down along with both adjutant-majors and both carabineer captains; in short, most of the command structure. Battalion Commander Régeau survived the volley and took command of the regiment. With their presence no longer hidden, the drummers beat the charge and the officers gave loud shouts of encouragement: 'Forwards Frenchmen, forwards my children!' A shout of *Vive l'Empereur* went up in response.[29]

Low's brigade was quickly swept aside in a rush of bayonets and a surge for the top of the hill ensued. In the race for the summit, Girod noticed a carabineer had broken ranks and begun walking back down the hill between the two columns. There didn't appear to be anything physically wrong with him, but he kept repeating, 'how is it possible men who have never met before can do so much harm …!'[30] Girod said this philosophical remark appeared so apt, no one thought of grabbing the carabineer by the collar and forcing him back into the ranks.

The Ninth arrived on the crest of the hillock as a single mass. As the ground narrowed both battalions became mixed up. It was absolute bedlam in the darkness, but the Ninth had done Victor's bidding – they had seized the Medellin. Régeau sent his voltigeurs left and right looking for the rest of the division supposedly coming up in support. These voltigeurs caused great mischief to the British scouts coming up from the far side of the hillock trying to discover what had occurred. As they came forward in the darkness the British scouts would call out, 'English …?' Several of the Ninth's soldiers responded mischievously to these challenges replying, 'Españoles, Españoles'. Believing the Frenchmen to be their allies, the British officers cried out, 'Don't fire on the Spaniards' and allowed the French troops to pass unmolested. In several cases British troops were pulled out of their ranks and taken prisoner.[31] Some of these drew the Frenchmen's curiosity – a number of Scots in kilts were captured, the first Highlanders that the men of the Ninth had ever seen. In one incident the aptly named British General Hill was almost captured while trying to discover the cause of the commotion. Somewhat annoyed by the musket balls whizzing round his head, he called out to a group of the nearby troops – which he assumed were British – and told them to cease fire. Hill was somewhat surprised when one of these fellows grabbed him by the arm and bade him to surrender. Hill spurred his horse forwards and broke free from his grip. The Frenchman levelled his musket and fired after Hill, wounding his horse.[32]

On top of the Medellin, Régeau was becoming impatient for the arrival of the rest of the division. In the darkness he could see the shadowy masses of enemy infantry manoeuvring round his flanks. With no sign of the reserves and fearing he was about to be surrounded, Régeau ordered the Ninth to about-face and withdraw. Having become completely disordered in the dark, the Ninth descended the Medellin in some disorder. The officer corps remained in the rear and tried to slow their men's descent with repeated shouts of 'Halt! Halt!'[33]

As the first two battalions fell back, the 3rd Battalion made a belated appearance coming round the side of the Medellin, marching diagonally across the British left. Having narrowly eluded capture, General Hill was leading the British 29th Regiment up from the bottom of the Medellin to attack the Ninth. The flank of the Ninth's 3rd Battalion was exposed to this regiment, so Hill ordered his men to open fire. Racked by rolling fire the battalion quickly withdrew back towards the Portiña ravine, their drummers beating the retreat.

The two other regiments of Ruffin's division were nowhere to be seen. The Ninth had crossed the ravine at a point where the ascent to the lower part of the Medellin was practicable. The 96th entered the ravine on the left and had enormous trouble climbing up the far slope. They became partially engaged with the 5th and 2nd battalions of the King's German Legion, but this action came to an end when the fighting on the hillock above them ceased. The 24th Line fared even worse. Entering the ravine to the right of the Ninth they became hopelessly lost and wandered up the valley between the hill and the northern mountains without coming into action at all.

Victor's gamble had failed to pay off. By 11pm the firing had ceased. The Ninth re-formed its ranks halfway down the hill. The attack had wrecked the regiment, with about 300 men falling killed or wounded. Although volunteers were sent back up the Medellin to search for the wounded, quite a number were missed, Meunier included. The wounded colonel spent the first of several unhappy nights as a guest of the British army.

The survivors were shattered. There was nothing to eat and their clothes were damp from wading through the river Alberche and the sweat from their exertions on the hill. It had been a fiercely hot day and it was a chilly night, but the close proximity of the British meant they could not light fires. Girod was told to scout a position on the left of the regiment. He only had 50 men left in his company so he formed a line of sentinels at 25-pace intervals along a section of the Portiña. With the chain created he allowed them to sit on their haversacks, resting their muskets between their legs.

Those men not posted as sentinels drifted off into a heavy sleep only to be woken suddenly by the sound of a fusillade. Girod jumped up and found himself shaking. A combination of the cold with physical and mental exhaustion following the battle had left him in a traumatized state, knees knocking together, teeth chattering. All around him, his men leapt up, cast their muskets aside, abandoned their packs and began fleeing in panic. Using the last of his will-power, Girod forced himself to snap out of his stupor and began rallying his men. He ran forwards to his chain of sentinels and asked what had been going on. His men were perfectly tranquil, they had also heard some gunfire and had seen muzzle flashes in the distance, but were unable to explain it. Once everything quietened down, Girod returned to the main body of his company and spent a quiet night. In the meantime a number of his men went beyond the sentinels to the Portiña with their canteens to draw water. The English troops did the same and both adversaries went about their business with an unspoken truce reigning between them.[34]

When the sun rose on 28 July Victor was determined to renew the attack on the Medellin. With such heavy losses the night before, the Ninth was in no condition to spearhead the attack. Instead Victor ordered the 24th Line to lead, with the 96th Line and the Ninth in support. There was a tremendous bombardment then the 24th Line advanced up the hillock with the 96th on their left and the Ninth a little way behind on the right. As the French approached the summit the British skirmishers opened fire and slowly retired. Just as the 24th thought they had reached the top, the redcoat line advanced forward from behind the brow of the hill from where it had sheltered from the artillery bombardment. Their skirmishers quickly melted away leaving an unbroken line of muskets waiting for the French. The British calmly allowed the 24th Line to approach even closer before delivering their volley. When it came, the 24th lost its front rank. Formed in battalion columns, the French could only bring a fraction of their muskets to bear, while the British line was able to use all their muskets. Victor had made a grave error in making this isolated attack. The British troops on the left of the 96th Line saw no threat in front of them, so wheeled round and began pouring volleys into the flank of this regiment. This stopped the advance dead in its tracks. Having delivered a succession of crippling volleys, the British charged with bayonets and swept the 24th Line down the hillside. Seeing their compatriots in a disorderly retreat, the Ninth advanced in line formation to cover the retreat.

With this second failure Ruffin's division retired onto the Cascajal heights to lick its wounds. Exposed to British musketry in broad daylight, the losses were even worse than the night before. The 24th lost 567 men and the 96th Line a further 606 men, a high proportion of whom were killed (93 and 39 respectively). The British line remained firmly planted on top of the Medellin and a lull descended over the field, during which the Frenchmen were allowed to prepare their breakfast. In a repeat of the night before, British and French soldiers met at the Portiña and collected water. There was a certain amount of fraternizing. Adversaries were seen to shake hands and an unofficial truce was negotiated for both sides to carry off their wounded. For two hours red and blue coats intermingled, going to the aid of fallen comrades.[35]

Around 10am Victor was joined by King Joseph and his chief of staff, Marshal Jourdan, for a council of war. There was an acrimonious debate with Jourdan urging caution and Victor demanding a renewed assault. Jourdan agreed with Victor's initial assessment: the key to the position was the Medellin, but the British were now also aware of this and were reinforcing their left flank as they spoke. Further attacks on this position would be useless, he advised. Victor somewhat bullied King Joseph by pointing out the detrimental effect on the army's morale if they were seen to baulk after two probing attacks. Joseph preferred Jourdan's advice, but was fearful of what the emperor would say if he refused to give battle. In the end a decision to continue the battle was made. Having been bludgeoned by their earlier efforts Ruffin's division played no further part in the action. The division was sent to the extreme right and ordered to march around the Medellin towards the Sierra de Seguerllia to observe a corps of Spanish infantry seen on that side of the field. The Ninth therefore took no part in the ensuing battle and were instead reduced to the role of spectators.

Talavera was one of the bloodiest battles in the Spanish war. The British could not be budged from their position, but neither would they advance beyond it. In many respects the contest was a draw and might have gone on for a third day, had not news reached King Joseph that a Spanish column was threatening Madrid. The French were thus obliged to withdraw and leave the field in the hands of Wellesley, who was awarded a peerage and the title Viscount Wellington after the battle. Despite claiming a victory, news arrived that Marshal Soult was active on his left flank and rear, so Wellesley ordered his army to abandon its hospitals and retreat towards the Portuguese border on 4 August.

When the French reoccupied Talavera, they found many of their wounded comrades in the hospitals. Colonel Meunier was among those left behind and he was recovered enough to retake his position at the head of the regiment. The British surgeons had taken great care of the French wounded and protected them from the worst excesses of the Spanish. It is testimony to this care that Captain Martinet survived despite having received seven bayonet wounds during the night attack, two of which were declared life-threatening.[36] Even so, Talavera proved the costliest day for the Ninth since Marengo nine years before. The regiment had lost three officers (all captains) and 35 men killed, with 14 officers and 340 men wounded, plus 65 taken prisoner; a total of 457 losses in all. In addition to Meunier's wounds, two battalion commanders had gone down in the action. Although Battalion Commander Régeau had come out of the battle unharmed, he tragically lost two of the three sons who served with him in the battle. When combined with the losses at Wagram earlier that month, the regiment had truly suffered a bloody July.

The losses were not just counted in terms of killed and wounded. Unlike the conscripts thrown into action at Essling and Wagram, the men at Talavera were from the cream of the old Grand Army. These men were used to success and after the relative ease of their victories over the Spanish, had perhaps become complacent. To have been outgunned and outmuscled off the Medellin by the British must have dented their confidence. The truth was the attacks had been poorly coordinated by Victor and his generals. On the evening after the battle there were rumours that generals Ruffin and Villatte were drunk on Bordeaux during the battle. Ruffin certainly had a reputation. Girod claimed Ruffin drank copious amounts of wine with each meal, but never *appeared* to be drunk; while Villatte was sometimes so inebriated he was incapable of any activity at all.[37]

After the battle, Girod requested and received a fortnight's leave at a forward depot that had been established at Valdemoro, half way between Madrid and Aranjuez. He was joined by one of the battalion commanders and two or three of his comrades who were sick or wounded. The regiment was now so weak only two battalions could effectively be formed. Therefore the cadre of 3rd Battalion was sent back to Bayonne where a larger forward depot had been established while the soldiers of that battalion were shared out among the first two battalions.

Back at Longwy the call went out for replacements. By now Spain had achieved a certain notoriety among those at the regimental depot. Corporal Nicolas Page recalled how convoys frequently returned from Spain bearing the latest news from the peninsula. There were the usual rumours about the entire population being against the French, and how the women and priests were armed and woe betide anyone unlucky enough to be caught by them, as they would be chopped in half, or hung from a tree. Nothing like this had gone on in Austria.

Before Page was given his marching orders at the beginning of January 1810 much had been done to make good the earlier haste of the conscripts' training. Although Page and his colleagues may have considered themselves seasoned veterans after Wagram, in truth they were poorly schooled compared to the conscripts of previous years. Page had been one of the lucky ones, receiving three months' training before he went on campaign. For those sent from the depot after three days the level of training must have been rudimentary at best. By the time it took to reach Austria by foot, one imagines the conscripts had learned to march in step and fire their muskets; but the complex evolutions of line and column, the confidence to execute brigade- and divisional-level manoeuvres were beyond them. The last months of 1809 at least gave some time to re-address the balance and bring the men up to something nearer the required standard.

Of all the training Page received, target shooting appears to have been most popular. The sub-officers commanding the competition would offer cash prizes to the best shots – usually 3 francs to the winner, 2.50 for the runner up and 2 francs for the third. On one occasion no one could hit the bullseye, so the commanding sergeant-major offered a supplementary prize from his own purse. By the time Page stepped forward this prize had risen to 24 francs. Page took steady aim, fired and struck the bull. An adjutant went forward to verify the shot and called out 'it's in the black'. At this the sergeant-major paid up, asking Page to drink a toast in his honour. Page dutifully obliged.

The evening before Page set out for Spain, the other corporals in his company solemnly invited him for one last drink. Drinking the night before marching out was strictly forbidden, but Page agreed to go with them. After evening roll-call the corporals went to an inn and asked the landlady to put them in a quiet room at the back where no one would see them. They thought they had got away with it, but just as they were preparing to leave an adjutant and several sergeants arrived. The landlady indicated where the corporals were hiding and the ensuing exchange with the adjutant went like this:

'Messieurs, is this how you execute your orders? We are going to conduct you to the guardhouse.'

'Messieurs, some of us are leaving tomorrow so we had supper together and are now going straight back to barracks.'

'You will sleep in the guardhouse. Move now and don't answer back.'[38]

Page's last night in Longwy turned out to be extremely unpleasant. The corporals had gone out in their petty dress of linen trousers and jacket without greatcoats. It was too cold to lie down on the guardroom flagstones so they spent a miserable night stamping up and down, crying out about the cold. At 8am the following morning, the corporals were finally released and Page began the long journey to Spain without a wink of sleep. It was a cruel start to his campaign.

The beastly adjutant who locked Page up may well have been Cardron. By January 1810 he was also back in Longwy, still fussing over his uniform. He complained to his sister that he was without any linen and urgently required handkerchiefs, cravats, drawers and stockings. He needed his dress coat, but complained it was too long and needed to have the tails taken up by an inch at least. He also wanted a braid of his sister's hair, if she had time.

Cardron's obsession with fashion at last came to an end when he also received orders to travel to Spain himself. He had surely heard the horror stories coming out of Iberia, but when he wrote to his sister on 14 April 1810 he put on a brave face and played down the risks:

> I can see you with your mouth open pronouncing the terrible word 'Spain', and well yes, you are not wrong. On the 11th we received orders to start out on the 16th and after tomorrow the victors of the Danube will go to pick up new laurels on the banks of the Tagus. This news should not alarm you. Whatever they say about it, Spain is not unpleasant and I believe Poland offered us more misery than this country ever could.[39]

Time would tell for our adjutant beau. There was plenty of life left in the Spanish war.

THE BLOCKADE
OF CADIZ

t the beginning of 1810 the French had still not mastered Spain. In the south of the country, beyond the Sierra Morena, the province of Andalusia was as much a hotbed of resistance as when Dupont had been defeated at Bailen in 1808. King Joseph could hardly expect to keep order in his domain with a rival government sitting in Seville, so he decided to invade Andalusia in January 1810 with 60,000 men and bring a halt to the resistance. This was a fateful decision. King Joseph would have been better advised to rid himself of Wellington in Portugal first. As long as a British army was present in the peninsula, Spanish resistance had a beacon of hope.

In the first days of January 1810 the Ninth found itself at Ciudad Real with the remainder of Ruffin's division. Since Talavera, the regiment had been composed of the first two battalions and only the elite companies of the 3rd Battalion, the remainder of this battalion not yet having returned from Bayonne. When the movement order came on 13 January, the Ninth set of for Andalusia in Victor's corps. While the bulk of the army followed the route taken by Dupont over the Despeñaperros Pass, Victor's corps took a different route across the Sierra Morena, heading directly for Córdoba. Spanish resistance to this crossing was sporadic and no serious obstacles were put in their way.

Victor's troops arrived at Córdoba on 23 January and then pressed on towards Seville. On 31 January, Victor called for Seville to surrender or its inhabitants would be put to the sword. In response the church bells rang and the population mounted the walls in defiance. It was a noisy demonstration, but without much substance. The Andalusian capital was poorly protected, with a weak wall and small garrison. When the French opened fire with their artillery the following day, resistance swiftly came to an end. The gates of the town were thrown open and King Joseph made what he thought was a triumphant entry. In truth Joseph had placed too much importance on Seville. Although ample stores and great material wealth fell into Joseph's hands, the rebel government had evacuated the city and taken refuge in Cadiz before the arrival of the French. In the time it had taken Seville to fall, the rebels had been joined by an army of 18,000 men under General Alberquerque. The British also sent 4,000 men and supplies to Cadiz. Joseph should have closed off this bolt-hole first.

When Victor's corps arrived before Cadiz on 6 February it was too late. In 1810 the port of Cadiz was one of the greatest fortresses in the world. It sat at the end of a narrow, four-mile spit of sand extending from the Isla de Leon. The only bridge on to the island had been destroyed before the French arrived. Even if Victor had been able to establish a new crossing, he would still face several formidable obstacles. First was a line of entrenchments occupied by the Spanish outposts. Halfway along the sand spit, where the distance between the sea and the waters of the bay was no more than 200m, there was an impressive fortress called the Cortadura. This fortification was mounted with heavy-calibre guns and was further protected by a dozen Spanish warships in the harbour and four British ships of the line. Then came the defences of Cadiz itself, which took the form of a ditch and defensive wall. There was no army then alive which could hope to assail the place from the landward side. To attack Cadiz would require a fleet of ships and the French navy had bad memories of a certain cape just down the coast called Trafalgar.

Ever the optimist, Marshal Victor summoned the place to surrender. The Spanish angrily declined, so Victor commenced a blockade of Cadiz from the landward side. A great chain of redoubts was planned running 12 leagues (48km) from Chiclana, through Puerto Real and Puerto Santa Maria to Sanlucar de Barrameda. Victor ordered the arsenals at Seville to begin building heavy-calibre mortars capable of hitting Cadiz. The nearest piece of land to Cadiz was to the east where a peninsula extended out from Puerto Real. At the far end of this spit was the Trocadero Island and beyond this, Fort Matagorda, which was only accessible at low tide. After 12 days of bombardment Victor's men captured the fort on 23 March and then settled in for what was to prove a very long, frustrating siege.

While the British could supply Cadiz from the sea, Victor's lines of communication were precarious at the best of times. Victor relied on the local inhabitants paying 'contributions' to keep his corps fed and watered. When these demands for money and provisions were not met, mobile columns were sent into the interior of the country to collect them by force. This provoked widespread rebellion and disobedience, which meant increasing numbers of troops were required to make the collections.

While the actions around Cadiz had been underway, the Ninth's 2nd Battalion had been sent to the town of Medina Sidonia, occupied by General Latour-Maubourg who had requested infantry support for his force of dragoons. In early March the 2nd Battalion was charged with carrying out a punitive raid on Alcala, four leagues (16km) distant. Escorted by a squadron of dragoons, the Ninth entered Alcala meeting only with a few insurgents who retreated without firing a shot. The town was empty except a few elderly folk and religious nurses in the convent. The following morning a detachment of chasseurs went to round up the families hiding in the mountains. They were nowhere in sight and it began to pour with rain. Fed up with this thankless task, the soldiers returned to the town and enjoyed the comfort of the houses, while the residents hid who knows where. This particular day was Mardi Gras so the French decided to celebrate on their own.[1] In the house Girod was lodged in, they found a wardrobe full of fancy clothes, so the officers dressed up as ladies and gentlemen for fun, taking the precaution to hide their weapons in their costumes in case of a surprise attack.

After an amusing night the battalion set out for Medina Sidonia, brimming with loot, including a mule laden with candies found in a confectioner's boutique. While the battalion had been partying the night before, the elements had conspired against them. It had rained solidly for 24 hours and parts of the route were transformed into raging torrents. Despite the assistance of the dragoons and their horses, several men were drowned trying to cross the torrents and most of the loot was swept away, candies included. The march of four leagues (16km) back to Medina Sidonia was one of the worst they ever experienced. As night fell the ranks began to break up. Desperate not to get left behind, men threw away their loot, or had it torn from them while wading through the flood water. The head of the battalion arrived around midnight, but the last of the stragglers did not appear until sunrise the next day. What had seemed like a harmless mission left the battalion wrecked, requiring several days of rest and repair.

While at Medina Sidonia, the French were introduced to a Spanish tradition they could enjoy. General Latour-Maubourg presided over bull-fights in the town almost daily, sitting on the podium surrounded by his staff and a number of local ladies. At Girod's first bullfight a dozen bulls were killed, a few horses gored and two or three picadors wounded. It was an excellent source of meat for the butchers, but what the French officers most admired about the bullfight was the sangfroid of the matador. In the same way that they as soldiers would stand fast in the face of cannon balls bouncing towards them, they could identify with the bravery of the matador, being charged by a furious, wounded beast. The bull would only bow its head to present its horns at the last instant, which is when the matador stepped aside. To step away sooner would allow the bull to change course.

Every day the picadors would go up into the mountains to hunt more bulls. When they returned one of the picadors would ride into town to clear the streets and warn people to stay indoors as the bulls were driven through. A young quartermaster corporal of the Ninth was at the local abattoir when one of these bulls escaped. Backed up against a wall, it appeared the man would be gored and trampled, but, to everyone's astonishment, as the bull reared up on its hind legs to deliver the blow, the soldier seized the bull by its horns and wrestled it off-balance, giving the spectators time to come to his aid. The Spanish may have hated the French, but they admired this young man immensely and carried him in triumph through the town.[2]

After a time the battalion returned to the lines at Cadiz. It was the time of the spring equinox and there was a violent south-westerly wind which battered the coast from 7 to 10 March. Several Spanish warships and over 30 British merchantmen were blown in range of the French guns, or dashed against the coast. According to Napoleon's Berlin Decree, the contents of wrecked British ships had to be burned unless they contained hospital supplies. With Napoleon safely tucked away in Paris, the men took a pragmatic approach to this order. Once they had salvaged everything they could, the wrecks were burned. By this means Girod bought himself half a dozen new shirts at a bargain price.

Until he arrived at Cadiz, Girod had never seen a warship. One day, curiosity nearly got the better of him. He climbed out of the defence works and went for a better look. The British captain was not one to indulge spectators and did Girod the honour of firing a cannon at him. The ball landed very close by, covering Girod in silt. He took the hint and went back to his trench, thanking lady luck the British had not fired a musket at him as they would have had more chance of hitting him.[3]

Cadiz harbour contained a number of old Spanish warships which had had their masts and rigging removed. These hulks were used as prisons for the Frenchmen taken at Bailen. The Ninth's former major, Claude D'Eslon, had spent part of his captivity at Cadiz on a hulk. Since entering captivity in 1808, D'Eslon had become very depressed at his predicament. The night before being transferred to the hulks he sat in a corner 'crying like a baby', bordering on suicidal. Consoled by his comrades D'Eslon was transported onto a hulk called the *Castilla*. Conditions on board were difficult. He complained they were 'piled in like herrings'; many of the sick died on board. The worst aspect of incarceration was the utter boredom. D'Eslon wrote in his journal, 'Our days are very monotonous: always same things to do. Get up, make a tour of the deck, examine what was going on in the harbour, lunch, games, debate, dinner, lie down, go to sleep, be bored to death: this is our existence.'[4]

When the French arrived off Cadiz, the men on the hulks were naturally enthusiastic at the prospect of salvation. When the prisoners on the *Castilla* saw the great tempest blow so many merchantmen onto the coast, they realized they could take advantage of the next south-westerly gale to escape. The daring bid for freedom took place on the night of 15/16 May. The guards were overpowered and the moorings cut. As the wind began to blow the hulk towards the French-occupied shore several gunboats were sent to tow it back. The Spanish had not realized an escape was underway until they came alongside the *Castilla* and found themselves being fired at from captured muskets and having cannon balls thrown at them by the prisoners. As the *Castilla* came ashore the English and

Spanish gunboats opened fire and killed some of the prisoners. The French soldiers on shore, many of them from the Ninth, rushed down to the sea and waded in up to their waists, helping the escapees up onto the shore.[5] The intrepid Surgeon-Major Vanderbach swam out to the *Castilla* and got onboard the ship to assist with the evacuation. Despite coming under fire from the English, he helped several sailors of the Imperial Guard remove some of the prisoners' personal effects before the boat went up in flames.[6] As the escapees arrived on dry land the regimental cantineers were waiting for them, giving them tots of brandy for free to celebrate their release.[7] In this manner 600–700 prisoners were saved.

On the night of 26/27 May the prisoners on the *Argonauta* attempted the same trick. This time the vessel floundered on a mud bank several hundred metres from the shore. Boats were sent out to rescue the men, but many were killed when the enemy opened fire on the rescue operation. Despite the vessel catching fire, 700 did make it to shore safely. The escaped prisoners were fed and fêted, then sent back to Bayonne and from there to rejoin their main depots.

There was a single soldier from the Ninth on the *Castilla* (Chasseur Pierre Colson) and five more who survived from the *Argonauta*, including Drummer Laurent Vignot.[8] Several escaping officers were also assigned to the Ninth. Alas, D'Eslon was not one of them. He had been taken off the *Castilla* before the daring escape took place and transferred to the Balearic Islands. We will return to his unhappy story in due course.

Through the summer the Ninth alternated their stints of siege duty with the 24th Line. Each regiment would spend 15 days camped in a pinewood near Chiclana, then 15 days in Puerto Real itself. Their main work was constructing an enclosed redoubt with gun platforms for heavy-calibre artillery; but they also laboured on the construction of a flotilla of gunboats to blockade the local estuaries, creeks and ports between Sanlucar de Barrameda and Puerto Real. This work did not go unnoticed and there were several operations when the enemy fleet came out and stole the newly constructed gunboats from the mouth of the Guadalete.

Wary of attacks by the British navy, the French decided to bring their boats under the protection of their land batteries. The gunboats had to be dragged several hundred yards overland to the bay of Puerto Real while under fire from the guns of Fort Puntales. At the appointed time the gunboats were secured to drag ropes. Each boat required an entire battalion to drag it and place rollers under the hull as it went along. Once the boats reached the bay they were rigged and armed with an array of heavy-calibre guns, howitzers, carronades and so on. The work was overseen by naval officers who taught the men to haul the ropes in unison by crying out words like '*Charivari*'. When this word was called, the others would reply '*et pour qui*? [who for?]'. The caller would then reply with a name and something wittily offensive related to that person. For example, when General Leval came to encourage the troops with a lady at his arm, the men pulled the ropes to the call

Charivari! Who for?
For General Leval, and his whore!

The soldiers had nothing personal against the good lady, but in their vocabulary, Girod remarked, the words 'woman' and 'whore' were synonymous. Given the difficulty of the task, great licence was given to the men for these gibes.[9]

At this time the men were plagued by swarms of mosquitoes. They tried to smoke the mosquitoes out, burning pine and other green wood, but all they did was choke themselves, and to little effect. At the same time their clothes became infested with fleas; in the hot summer months they wore baggy trousers in the style of Egyptian Mamelukes and the seams became riddled with the creatures.

Then there was the constant shelling through the day which forced the French to work at night. Supplied by the British, the garrison in Cadiz had ample ammunition for their heavy guns. They even fired Congreve rockets at the French gunboats. The soldiers of the Ninth had never seen this type of weapon before and apparently made many jokes about them. A sort of routine developed: the defenders of Cadiz would come out each morning to see what the French had been up to overnight. Once an emplacement appeared finished the defenders would send over a hail of shot and mortar bombs. When the bombardment was over the French soldiers would run out of their trenches to recover the cannon balls, for which they were paid a prize by the artillery commanders.

On 26 October Victor's artillery commander, General Senarmont, made an inspection of the lines. When he asked why the artillery was not firing, the local artillery commander replied that for every ball he fired the enemy replied with a hundred. Senarmont ordered him to fire and sure enough the defenders of Cadiz replied. Girod saw what happened next. A shell landed next to Senarmont, but he noticed it too late and only just had time to turn his head away when the shell exploded. Senarmont was killed instantly and horribly mutilated by the blast.

Shells were a particular problem to the besiegers in their trenches. If the shell exploded in mid-air there was nothing the men could do to take shelter from the splinters thrown out by the explosion. When a shell landed in the mud it sent up a huge spout and showered everyone. When they landed in the water a bubble would come to the surface followed by a puff of smoke. When a shell landed in the middle of a detachment Girod was commanding, he ordered his men to lie down and remain still. The shell exploded and no one was hurt, much to Girod's relief.

Corporal Nicolas Page had arrived with the main regiment in the first half of 1810. On his first stint in the advanced posts, his shako was blown off by a shell fragment. They were constantly on their guard, musket at the ready, expecting attacks from the sea. Every night at high tide the regiment took up arms and remained in position for two or three hours until the tide receded. The boredom was oppressive and was interrupted only by the beating of drums to wake them in the middle of the night for guard duty. Page also had a three-week stint on the gunboats in the mouth of the Guadalquivir. One day it was so hot Page and his comrades decided to take a bath in the estuary. The sea was fairly calm and they spent an hour splashing around having fun. Meanwhile they did not notice the tide had begun to turn and the wind pick up. As they swam back to the boat, Page began to struggle. Reaching the boat each of the swimmers quickly descended into the hull of the gunboat to dress themselves. Page just reached the boat, but did not have the strength to climb onboard; he slipped and took a gulp of salty seawater. Luckily for Page a watchman was on deck and saw him struggling. He threw Page a rope and the corporal seized it with all his remaining strength and was dragged on board. If it hadn't been for the watchman, Page would have drowned.

Page complained about the lack of provisions, moaning that he had to work day and night on an empty stomach. Initially the French lived off rations and paid dearly for anything provided by the inhabitants. However, once the supply lines began coming under regular attack from the insurgents, the supply of rations was sporadic at best. Once the Frenchmen settled in, their diet changed to reflect the local produce. Being close to the sea, the light infantrymen learned to fish for prawns and crabs. They used their bayonets to prise small oysters from old pieces of submerged masonry. On land there was an abundance of fruit with delicious figs, oranges, melons, watermelons, peaches, apricots, apples and pears. It was only when the regiment was later posted inland that hunger truly set in.

While on route to Cadiz, Meunier had been promoted to brigade-general. Compared to men like Pierre Barrois, Meunier's promotion came comparatively late. Girod attributed this to the disaster at Mohrungen. When Napoleon finally realized the truth from the Russian gazettes he is said to have crossed Meunier's name from a list of men suitable for promotion, adding: 'This colonel lost an eagle at Mohrungen'.[10] Nonetheless, Meunier had been and remained an ardent supporter of the emperor all his life. He had been made an imperial baron in 1808 and could demonstrate his continued loyalty by the wounds he sustained at Talavera. Unlike Labassée, who was sent off to a different division, Meunier was destined to remain with the Ninth in the capacity of brigade-general. Meunier's close proximity proved somewhat uncomfortable for the new incumbent taking over the regiment.

Meunier's replacement was 40-year-old Guilhem Dauture, previously a major in the 47th Line. Dauture was the son of a Gascon tanner from Pontacq, a town at the foot of the Pyrenees in south-western France. He had been a National Guard Volunteer in 1791 and was quickly elected sergeant-major. Since then he had gained a reputation for fearless bravery and was covered in scars. He had been shot three times storming a redoubt near Mantua in 1796; he was shot in the leg at the bridge of Arcole the same year; then shot again at Marengo commanding the 40th Line. More recently he had led an assault against a redoubt at Oporto in Portugal. Conspicuous at the head of four voltigeur companies, Dauture had his face slashed by the sword of a British dragoon. Girod described Dauture as having all the 'qualities and defects' of the Gascon character: lively in spirit, mocking, strong-willed, occasionally imperious, gallant and a good dinner guest. His face was prematurely wrinkled from the 'abuse of pleasure'. Of his bravery, Girod acknowledged Dauture's reputation, but somewhat snobbishly remarked he was never sure if the Gascon was truly brave, or just very good at boasting.[11]

While the new colonel bedded down and found fault in his predecessor's administration, blockade service continued through the autumn of 1810 and into early 1811 without interrupting their boredom. On the evening of Christmas Day, the allies hoped to catch the French out and attempted to burn the French flotilla. The attack was repulsed and until the end of February there was nothing more than outpost skirmishes around the Isla de Leon. As the blockade moved into its second year, Victor was unable to contemplate any great offensive actions. He had fewer than 9,000 men to blockade Cadiz. This number was weakened by detachments guarding his supply line to Seville and his hospitals and magazines at Jerez. Another brigade was required to protect Medina Sidonia, all of which left the blockading force very weak. Sensing this weakness, the Anglo-Spanish decided to mount a foray onto the mainland.

A Spanish force 14,000–15,000 strong had collected near Tarifa under General La Peña. The British embarked 7,000 troops under General Graham at Cadiz and transported them to Algeçiras where they joined La Peña and began marching on the French lines. On 3 March the Spanish in Cadiz threw a boat bridge over the mouth of the Santi Pietri canal, which separated the Isla de Leon from the mainland. Villatte's division succeeded in repelling the sortie, but did not destroy the bridge. The following day Victor learned about the large Anglo-Spanish force coming up from Tarifa. Leaving a small force behind to guard the redoubts, Victor took 4,000 men up towards Chiclana to meet them.

On the morning of 5 March, learning the enemy was between the woods of Chiclana and the sea, Victor decided to attack the right flank of the Anglo-Spanish force and drive them into the sea. The Ninth and 24th turned the woods and marched to the Casa Blanca farm. They then climbed a section of high ground called the Cerro de Puerco. The hill was protected by five Spanish battalions and one British battalion. The allied forces had been split with disagreements over what action to take, the result being that the Spanish battalions evacuated the hill at the sight of Ruffin's men advancing towards them. The remaining British battalion remained on the hill for a time, but seeing themselves unsupported, they followed the Spanish down the hill. Meanwhile, General Leval attacked the British troops as they passed through the woods.

Initially surprised, General Graham attempted to recapture the initiative. He ordered a battalion to try and recapture the hill while the bulk of the British force met Leval though the woods. As the redcoat battalion came up the Cerro de Puerco into range, three French battalions and a battery of guns were able to rake it with fire. Several hundred redcoats fell and the advance stalled, with the British survivors taking what cover they could and returning fire. A brigade of British troops then advanced on Ruffin's left flank, screened by two companies of green-jacketed riflemen. As the redcoat line approached the summit it was charged by Ruffin's troops – two battalions from the 24th and two 'grenadier' battalions formed of the division's elite companies.

By attacking in column the French handed the initiative back to the British. The redcoats opened fire and shattered the 24th's columns, just as had occurred at Talavera. The grenadiers attacked and were met by the same withering fire. Ruffin ordered a battalion of the Ninth to come forward, but they were still engaged with the survivors of the first attack. There was a last surge and the two adversaries came to blows. In the thick of the fighting, General Ruffin's horse was wounded and carried him into the British ranks, throwing the general on the points of their bayonets. With their general mortally wounded and unable to break the British line, Ruffin's division retreated.

On their side the French lost 2,062 men killed, wounded and captured in the combat. A modest loss perhaps, but one Victor could ill afford. The Ninth lost 108 men in the battle including two officers killed and six wounded, including Surgeon-Major Vanderbach and Battalion Commander Régeau who was hit three times and had his leg broken.[12] Chiclana had been a strange battle. Until Ruffin rashly ordered his men to form columns and attack, the British had been at a disadvantage. If the French had met the British advance with musketry, perhaps the outcome of the battle would have been different. In some respects the battle could be billed as a draw. In the morning the Anglo-Spanish force crossed over to the Isla de Leon unmolested, but without achieving its objective of disrupting the French redoubts. However, the battle appears to have felt like a defeat for the French. Among the combatants was Nicolas Page. His assessment of the battle was fairly damning: 'We lost three generals, all our field artillery, the battle was lost for us and we beat a retreat.' Page thought it particularly odd how the officers kept saying, 'soldiers we do not surrender; we must conquer or die!' while leading them away from the battlefield back to the safety of the defensive works.[13]

After the battle, Ruffin was taken prisoner and was transported to England. Just before reaching England he passed away. Before his death he bought all the British officers on board a drink for the care he had received. It was a sad passing for a general whose many gallantries were perhaps only eclipsed by his legendary ability to consume alcohol. Commenting on the death of Ruffin, Girod lamented how his example was followed by the general's subordinates. As Godet had discovered before him, the old officers of the Revolution were particularly noted for their heavy drinking. They were rough diamonds torn from civilian life, not career soldiers. Girod noted how two senior captains died from 'the abuse of alcohol' during the siege of Cadiz. The first was Captain Nicolas, a long-serving officer who had been warned about his drinking back in Labassée's day, but who had apparently not heeded the concerns. Girod described him as very capable as long as he remained sober. When he was drunk he was prone to violence and had apparently tried to murder Girod a few days before his death. Every evening the captain would come back to his quarters drunk and the younger officers would play tricks on him. On this occasion Nicolas grabbed his épée and chased after Girod, who was preparing to go to bed and dressed only in his shirt. With nowhere to run Girod cowered behind his bed as Nicolas took swipes at him. Fortunately, the old man was so drunk Girod survived the encounter. The other was Captain Dongée, who had been a locksmith before joining the army and who had maintained a fascination for the trade. Girod volunteered to attend at his autopsy. He had witnessed all sorts of horror on the battlefield without the least trouble, but this proved too much and he fainted halfway through.[14]

Not everyone in the Ninth had fought at Chiclana. On the day of the battle a number of attacks were made against the French lines on Isla de Leon where Girod commanded one of the redoubts. Work on the redoubt had not been completed by 5 March, so when Girod saw enemy infantry massing for an attack he had his men fill the gaps in the defences with cactus plants. By 2pm the enemy demonstrations appeared more serious, so Girod ordered the gunners in the redoubt to lob a few shells in their direction. The enemy replied with superior firepower. In a 15-minute bombardment 93 cannon balls struck the breastworks and interior of the redoubt without causing a single casualty. Girod then got into an argument with an artillery captain commanding the guns in that sector. The captain reproached Girod for opening fire without orders and spoke in such an imperious tone, Girod lost his temper. He told the captain to get out of *his* redoubt and pointed out his orders were to defend the redoubt as *he* saw fit. The artillery captain was much larger than Girod and provoked a duel. The war with Spain was put aside for a moment while the two men climbed into the ditch to settle their matter with swords. Although the two men had their tempers up, their seconds pointed out that it was ridiculous for two Frenchmen to fight a duel in the middle of a battle. They urged Girod's adversary to adjourn his right for satisfaction until later. The artillery captain agreed and nothing more was ever said about the matter.

On the subject of duels, Girod had a hand in two other affairs of honour while at Cadiz. The first was between Girod and a good friend of his named Toullier. The two men kept playing practical jokes on one another, but one night Toullier went too far by putting a pot of water in Girod's bed. Girod got angry, heated words were exchanged and a provocation was made. Fortunately the seconds sorted things out on the duelling ground without either man losing face in front of their peers. On another occasion Captain Watt was insulted by an officer of the 24th Line who slapped him in public. The two men met at the duelling ground and Watt wounded his adversary. When the adversary returned to his corps, his brother officers decided the wound was too light and honour had not been satisfied. They gave the man an ultimatum – seek a rematch with Watt when his wound healed or they would drive him from the regiment. This was extremely unfair to Watt, who was a very distinguished officer and was well liked by his comrades. Two deputies were chosen to visit the 24th at their garrison at Puerto de Santa Maria. Girod was one of them. They went to a senior officer and explained the situation. He called several captains and lieutenants who listened to the appeal. Girod pointed out that they stood to lose one of their best officers in the rematch, while the 24th might only lose an officer no one liked. The rival officers saw sense in this and so agreed the matter was over. As a sign of good harmony between the two officer corps the negotiators drank a cup of punch together. Honour was seen to be done.

Not long after Chiclana the regiment was sent to garrison Puerto de Santa Maria, some 2.5 leagues (10km) north-east of Cadiz on the mouth of the Guadalete River. The port was a relatively safe haven for the French so there were opportunities to relax. Every evening the officers and townsfolk would promenade along the avenues and shows would be put on. The concert troupe was composed of a group of young sub-officers, mostly from Paris, who had put together some costumes and were backed by a very good orchestra. Their act aped Paris' vaudeville theatre, with songs like *La Femme Jalouse, le Déserteur, Le Secret,* and pieces of comic-opera from the Feydeau Theatre. The youngest would dress up and play the female roles and did so with 'the most complete illusion.'[15] Very few Spaniards took part in these productions, but occasionally a few ladies would come to watch.

Girod was captivated by the air of mystery surrounding the Andalusian girls. When they appeared in public they were dressed in their traditional black gowns and lace mantillas; but behind closed doors it was a different matter. Several Spanish families would admit French officers to evening parties. Here the ladies would appear in the latest French fashions without the slightest hint of Spanish costume. The house Girod frequented most belonged to a French ex-pat named Castera and his two daughters who spoke French as a first language. The eldest was Carmen, petite with dark eyes and an imperious manner. The younger was named Pauline and was by contrast blond and sweet. Girod enjoyed singing boleros and opera with the two. Although Pauline was more amiable, Girod was smitten with Carmen. Girod embarked upon a new campaign, taking guitar lessons so he might vie for Carmen's affections. Night after night he waited in vain for her to reciprocate his feelings. Eventually Girod plucked up courage and proposed, but Carmen rejected him. In time Girod could see why she refused. He was 22 years old, 500 leagues from home and without his family's blessing; but at the time, the feeling of being jilted hurt Girod considerably. He mused how falling in love was 'one of the greatest dangers of war I had ever faced.'[16]

Having demonstrated an interest in music, Girod was appointed 'captain of music' by Colonel Dauture. The Ninth's regimental band was led by the clarinettist Jacques Meynard, an old hand who had joined the army in 1770 at the age of 16 with the old Regiment of Brie. One of Meynard's contracts survives, showing the conditions of service the musicians signed up for:

I, the undersigned, declare the renewal of my engagement to serve in 9th Light Infantry regiment for the space of two years from this date with the following conditions.

I will fulfil the part of FIRST CLARINET.

I am obliged to train each year ONE musician or CLARINET pupil who will be appointed by the Colonel, or the officer in charge of music.

I will receive for my remuneration ONE HUNDRED FRANCS per month in wages, including the payment of a musician of the staff. The payment will be made to me regularly by the Paymaster gradually as the officers are paid their salaries.

The uniform will be provided for me by the regiment as that of the troop.

In the case of sickness and I am obliged to enter hospital, I will enjoy no lessening of my remuneration with the exception that for venereal disease I will receive only a third.

I will conform to all which concerns the policing and discipline, to regulations and all orders of the colonel.

The term of my commitment will count from 1st January 1812. In case it is my intention to leave the Regiment after two years, to recover my independence, or whatever motive decides me not to continue my service, I reserve the ability to retire in return that I give notice three months in advance. It will be the same for the Regiment in the case my services no longer suit it.[17]

While Meynard was responsible for the repertoire and conducting the band, the 'captain of music' was something like a manager, or agent, ensuring the musicians were properly uniformed and turned up on time. It was an unpopular appointment and caused Girod no end of trouble. The Castera ladies decided to throw a ball at their home and on the appointed day they badgered Girod to loan a few musicians to reinforce their own hired orchestra. Still vying for Carmen's attentions, Girod agreed, reasoning he would be in Carmen's good books and the musicians would earn a few extra shillings. Unfortunately he committed the cardinal error of not asking the colonel's permission in advance. When Dauture turned up to the ball he was somewhat surprised to find *his* musicians performing quadrilles in a private house. When the ball was over Dauture had Girod arrested. For his own part, Girod admitted he was at fault and accepted the charge without complaint.

For a short spell in 1811, all four battalions of the Ninth were united at Cadiz for the first and only time in the regiment's history. After Talavera the cadres of the 3rd Battalion had returned to France to take on conscripts.[18] These were sent down from Longwy and formed into companies at Bayonne where the Ninth had a forward depot. The battalion returned to Spain in November of 1809, but rather than rejoin the regiment, it was assigned to counter-insurgency operations and escort duties. They spent 11 months in the province of Segovia constantly harassed by partisans.

Before the battalion rejoined the regiment in June 1810 there was one operation of particular note. By now the former standard-bearer Fouquet was a lieutenant in the regiment. In the first half of December 1809, Fouquet was sent with a detachment of 150 men and a dozen hussars to guard the small town of Santa Maria la Real de la Nieva on the junction of the roads from Leon and Zamora to Madrid. A short time after arriving, a large band of insurgents descended on the town. When the insurgents saw Fouquet preparing for a defence, they called on him to surrender, threatening to put the whole detachment to the sword if he refused. Fouquet was too long in the tooth to trust the word of an insurgent, so continued fortifying the town, barricading the streets and loopholing the walls. On the morning of 15 December, 14 guerrilla bands attacked. One can only imagine the feelings of the conscripts holed up behind the barricades, surrounded, never having been in action before. Nonetheless the experienced soldiers cautioned them not to panic and take careful aim. Several hours later the Spanish were gone, leaving behind over 200 dead or badly wounded. Fouquet's detachment had just 11 casualties.

The 4th Battalion had a much more circuitous route to Andalusia and did not arrive until July 1811. The 4th Battalion's story can be told through the letters of Cardron who was finally promoted into the officer corps on 31 August 1810. The battalion had been held at Nantes for a time, before it marched down through western France to the Pyrenees and the Spanish border. Immediately thrown into counter-insurgency work, Cardron's first impressions of the country were expressed in a letter from Vitoria dated 21 October 1810:

> For fifteen days I tried to write to you. You will know that for a month, we have only run around the mountains after these accursed brigands, not content with marching all day, we march all night. Sometimes we are up in the heavens, sometimes on the plains. You will understand if one stops for a day, one does well to employ it all for resting.[19]

As a sub-lieutenant, Cardron had been placed in the second company of chasseurs in his battalion, but ultimately wanted to rejoin the regiment's carabineers. He concluded his letter confident of success in the current campaign:

> Don't worry about me, I am doing well, not lacking anything and armed to the teeth; that is to say, a heavy sabre, two pistols and a carbine. These are the weapons of all the officers who make war with these brigands ... I have received the order to go with sixty men to occupy (right away) a village four leagues [16km] from here, in the mountains where the brigands have to gone to take supplies. If I arrive early enough, I will give them some bayonets to chew on.

Just over a month later Cardron managed to snatch a few moments to update his mother and sister. Dated Salamanca, 26 November 1810, the letter emphasized the importance of wine to French soldiers and the sadness they experienced at witnessing uncultivated vines being choked by weeds. Cardron also complained their pay was sporadic and a lack of money was affecting everyone. The most important part of the letter concerned Cardron's next destination and his expected encounter with the British. Although Cardron clearly had gripes about Spain, judging by his letter, morale and confidence were still very high:

> ... The day after tomorrow we set off again to enter Portugal to join the army. Portugal is, they tell me, a desert, the residents having fallen back on Lisbon at the approach of French. Supplies there are very rare and often lacking; but we are used to privations and fatigue. We burn to join our brothers and share the honour of chasing these hated English from the continent. If they are stubborn, we will show them the cost of resisting the victors of the Danube reunited with those of Burgos.[20]

While King Joseph saw the subjugation of Andalusia as his first priority, Napoleon's objective was the ejection of Wellington's army from the Iberian Peninsula and the subjugation of Portugal. To that end Napoleon entrusted the conquest of Portugal to the stalwart Marshal Massena. As the French attacked, Wellington fell back to a defensive position around Lisbon, adopting a scorched-earth policy as he went, and leaving nothing for the French. Unable to live off the land Massena had to rely on supply lines that were under constant attack from insurgents. The 4th Battalion spent much of its energies trying to keep these supply lines open, but it was a useless task. Starved by the lack of supplies, Massena's army was forced to retreat back to Spain pursued by Wellington.

Cardron finally encountered the British when the 4th Battalion fought at the battle of Fuentes de Oñoro on 5 May 1811. There was heavy fighting over possession of the village. In the morning the French broke through the British barricades. Every street was choked with combatants; canister and roundshot smashed through the town killing and maiming indiscriminately. It was baking hot. In the churchyard at the top of the village French grenadiers and Highlanders fought across tombstones. The fate of the town hung in the balance, so Massena threw in another column to break the enemy's resistance. The Ninth's 4th Battalion led this new assault.

Watching the Ninth occupy the town, the British launched a regiment to counter-attack. The Irish 88th Foot (Connaught Rangers) ran through the narrow avenues to the cheers of their comrades who were already fighting. The Ninth saw the Irishmen coming and formed up by the chapel to meet the charge. Seeing the Ninth before them, the Irishmen let out a blood-curdling cheer and clattered into the Frenchmen. The ensuing mêlée was bloody and swift. The Irishmen had the momentum. Pushed back, the Ninth broke off and evacuated the village leaving a great number of casualties behind. Unable to gain control of the village, Massena saw the battle as lost and ordered his army to retreat on Salamanca.

The battalion went into action with 739 and 21 officers.[21] One officer was killed with six more wounded including Battalion Commander Charles Planchet. Cardron was among the wounded. From his earlier bragging about driving the English from the Continent, his next letter demonstrated a healthy regard for his new adversaries:

> … I cannot go without saying about an event which came a little too close for comfort. I mean the meeting I had with Messrs the English. It was the first time I had fought against them, and although many call them poor soldiers on dry land, they proved on this occasion, as in many others, they deserve the esteem of the French rather than their sarcasm and bad jokes. For my personal account, I have to be pitied in admiring them somewhat. The first time we had a full affair together, they wanted to deprive me of two limbs! Fortunately they succeeded poorly, because the first embrace was from

only a small bullet which hit me above right breast, near the shoulder and which, to my good fortune, having lost its force, did not penetrate at all, but rendered me all black and so swollen I was incapable of using the arm, which I had to carry in sling for a month. Another ball attacked my opposite extremity at the same moment. It cut the third phalanx of the little toe on my left foot. I want to believe this blow was sent with good intentions, because it relieved me of an ingrown nail which had made me suffer a lot. It was in this momentarily paralyzed state, mounted like Our Lord on an ass, because there was no other means of transportation, I arrived at Salamanca after four days of march. From there, after eight days of rest, it was on this mule, one arm in a sling and a foot over the shoulders of the animal, I made a journey lasting nearly three months. This delayed my recovery somewhat.[22]

The letter continued, telling of how he had been sent to the relief of the fortress of Badajoz – which was under siege – but the British had raised the siege before he arrived. The battalion had therefore rejoined the rest of the regiment. Cardron concluded his letter writing he was 'disgusted with Spain' and he could not wait to return back to France, but he would not push for a transfer as he did not want to be seen as too keen to go home. There was a postscript which showed he had the future on his mind: 'How are the young ladies of Philippeville for marrying?'

Five days after writing this letter Cardron received an invitation from General Meunier to a ball marking the emperor's birthday on 15 August. All the officers were invited to attend in full uniform, with breeches, silk stockings, shoes and buckles. The ball began early and continued well into the early hours of the morning. Just as the officers were beginning to think about retiring, they were confidentially told not to leave the party until dawn and to keep dancing. There had been trouble with the local insurgents and General Meunier had an expedition planned against them for the following day. There were so many spies about that Meunier feared the insurgents would be forewarned so he kept the officers dancing until it was time to take up arms. They just had time to run back to their quarters, swap breeches and shoes for trousers and boots, then assemble with their men. Alas the planned expedition was stalled and never took place. Girod was exhausted and rued his 'heroic efforts' dancing all night were for nothing.

The Ninth spent the autumn and early part of the winter in the trenches and camps raised around Cadiz. On 31 October 1811, the 3rd Battalion was sent to reinforce the fortress of Badajoz on the Portuguese border. Otherwise nothing out of the ordinary occurred. Cardron wrote to his sister on 24 November 1811 complaining the last letter he had received from her was dated 8 December 1810:

> We do not lack rations. We officers receive exactly three rations of all sorts and of good quality; besides bread and meat the soldiers receive wine every day: but we are not paid. I am naked, not having received my bonuses, the clothes which I had are worn out and I find it impossible to do anything but keep my backside covered. Cloth is a crazy price. My blue woollen pantaloons (our uniform) go for 60 francs, not even good quality ones. I have neither dress coat nor overcoat; in short, I am deprived of everything.[23]

In December the Ninth's 2nd Battalion returned to Puerto Real, leaving the 1st at Puerto Santa Maria with Colonel Dauture. In addition, Captain Perrin was sent with four companies of the 1st Battalion to guard the town of Sanlucar de Barrameda. Among those in the detachment was Corporal Page. At midnight on 19 December Page was sent out with a patrol of six men with orders to arrest anyone not carrying a lantern. They chased several civilians without success, but it was otherwise quiet. Two hours later Page returned to the convent overlooking the town where the detachment was quartered. No sooner had he arrived than shots were heard from the town. Captain Perrin was surprised by the sound of musketry and checked Page had not seen anything. Page shook his head and raced back into town with the rest of the men.

Unbeknown to Page, the civilians he had chased off had been scouts for a force of 800 mounted insurgents. Provided with intelligence by the inhabitants, the insurgents had crept up on the guard post and broken open the door. The sergeant commanding was killed, along with a corporal and several soldiers. There were insurgents everywhere and in the narrowness of the streets, the French could not properly assemble their platoons. Instead the men piled into the nearest houses, barricaded the doors and prepared for battle.

Captain Perrin found himself alone with just two soldiers. A great mob of Spanish attacked and surrounded the house. Perrin was an energetic officer.

He held his nerve and fought on for two hours until a company of men came to his relief. The Spanish panicked and fled leaving 200 casualties behind. Perrin is said to have killed five and wounded eight men on his own. Page was lucky not to have been butchered in the guardhouse, but did not escape unharmed. He received a nasty flesh wound that was enough to put him in hospital. He had good reason to dread such a place. Although his wound was not life threatening he quickly contracted a fever in hospital and was at the gates of death for some time. He did not recover for 45 days.

As 1811 drew to a close there was no great sense of optimism for the new year. There was a great deal of tension between Colonel Dauture and General Meunier. Having commanded the Ninth for so long, Meunier was finding it difficult not to involve himself in the internal affairs of the regiment. Every night officers and soldiers alike looked up into the sky watching a great comet blazing its path overhead. Comets had always been seen as portentous, but in this case 'Napoleon's comet' appeared to foretell nothing but woe and, so the rumours went, the very end of the world.

BADAJOZ

Two years after the invasion of Andalusia, Cadiz still held out. While the French became increasingly isolated and vulnerable in the south of Spain, the defenders of Cadiz were buoyed by the news of Wellington's successes against Massena in Portugal the previous year. By the end of 1811 the groups had become increasingly large and sophisticated and were united under the command of General Francisco Ballesteros. Their threat became so great by the middle of January 1812 that a significant number of troops were withdrawn from the lines in front of Cadiz and sent to guard the interior. As part of this strategy the Ninth was sent to Villamartin to guard the roads east towards Ronda.

After the demise of General Ruffin, command of 1st Division passed to General Conroux. As a brigadier general, Conroux had led the Ninth's 4th Battalion in the Wagram campaign and in Portugal. Although Conroux was as popular as his predecessor, towards the end of January 1812 he put his men's loyalty to the most extreme test. The division was extremely short on supplies, so Conroux formed a detachment from the division's elite companies and sent them to round up all provisions within three or four days' march of Villamartin. Several days later the detachment returned, driving a large herd of oxen and flocks of sheep before it. At the sight of these animals, the ravenous soldiers quit their posts and descended on the livestock. Before anyone could stop them, the men were running off with sheep over their shoulders back to their bivouacs and cook pots.

Conroux was furious. He paraded his division and asked if anyone had been arrested? Although pillage was technically illegal, the French officers had turned a blind eye to the practice for years. How could they punish their men for feeding themselves when the army could not provide rations? When Conroux learned no one had been apprehended he asked if there was anyone in the guardhouse who had been arrested for marauding over the preceding days. Of course there were, the officers replied. Conroux ordered one of these marauders, 'the worst subject among them',[1] to be brought before him. The adjutant-majors of the different regiments consulted one other and after some debate agreed the worst marauder was a soldier from the Ninth. The man's name was given to Conroux who replied, 'Bring him and shoot him this instant!'

The poor wretch was brought before Conroux and told he was going to be shot. The man was stupefied. When he was sentenced to a few days in the guardhouse for marauding he thought that would be the end of it. He could have had little idea his sentence would be commuted to the death penalty. Worse, he was in the guardhouse when the theft of the livestock took place and was therefore completely innocent of the crime he was being shot for. The man threw himself on his knees in front of Conroux crying 'Mercy! Mercy!', but the general was inflexible. A firing squad was formed and Conroux personally gave the command to fire. An instant later the man fell lifelessly to the ground, pierced by a dozen musket balls. Conroux then ordered the division to parade silently past the body so each man could see the consequences of breaking the penal code. Reflecting on this, Girod was extremely uneasy with Conroux's actions. Beating with a sword was one thing, but it was another thing altogether to shoot a man without the judgement of a council of war. Girod concluded the general had acted illegally and whatever justification may have been given, Conroux was very lucky his troops did not revolt. In fact the example served its purpose. A sense of discipline was restored and Conroux continued to retain the confidence of his men. However, it was not a decision Girod would have liked on his conscience.

There was little time to dwell on the execution. Several days later, on 2 February, Conroux learned Ballesteros was occupying a village just a few leagues from Villamartin. A surprise attack was planned to kill or capture the insurgent commander. An advanced guard was formed under General Meunier and Colonel Dauture, comprising of three voltigeur companies under Battalion Commander Bruyère and a body of 400 chasseurs. The advanced guard set out at 10pm and arrived at the village shortly before dawn.

Unusually the French gained the element of surprise. The voltigeurs burst into the village and the guerrilla leader only just had time to escape through a back door. The attack stirred up a veritable hornets' nest. The guerrillas were bivouacked behind the village and were quickly roused. Having missed their prize, the voltigeurs made an escape of their own before the guerrillas overwhelmed them. The advanced guard reverted to the role of rearguard. As an adjutant-major, Girod had to dismount and remain behind, rallying the scouts and skirmishers, ensuring they did not fall too far behind. The Spanish were quickly onto the French, and Girod was nearly captured clambering over rocks in his cumbersome, heavy overcoat. When he reached the rearguard he jumped up onto his horse and escaped down a narrow gorge hotly pursued by the Spanish. Finally they reached General Conroux at the head of the main column. At the sight of superior numbers the Spanish quickly broke off their pursuit and made off. The Ninth lost four killed and had 16 wounded in the action, but it taught Ballesteros not to be too overconfident.

This action was Girod's last with the regiment. As general of brigade, Meunier had asked Girod to become his aide-de-camp. Girod politely declined the offer. For one thing he would have to give up the rank of adjutant-major as a brigade-general was not allowed to have an aide-de-camp over the rank of lieutenant. There was another reason behind the request. Meunier's orderlies and aide-de-camp had said they suffered from his 'inner moods'. Girod did not want to fall out with Meunier, having enjoyed an excellent rapport with him. At the same time Girod did not want to remain in the Ninth under Dauture. The new colonel worked him to the bone, making him perform the role of adjutant-major for two battalions. When Girod complained, Dauture mocked him in front of everyone.

In February 1812 Girod was invited to become aide-de-camp to General Joseph Marie Dessaix who was with the Grand Army in East Prussia. Girod accepted the appointment and quickly left the regiment. As a scrawny 'magazine-officer', Girod had shown great determination and perseverance in his career thus far. He was not a natural soldier, but he had been a faithful servant. When it was time to leave he went round each of his comrades who showed their affection for him. It was a fine early spring day as he rode off to the forward depot at Jerez where he visited the paymaster and received eight months' back-pay. With that he was gone and off to new adventures.

At the beginning of 1812, Colonel Dauture's greatest concern was the breakdown in the supply chain from France. At this time the Ninth had three depots. The main one remained in Longwy under the command of Major Obert. A second depot had been formed at Bayonne to act as a staging post near the Spanish border. This was commanded by Captain Janin, the former voltigeur officer badly wounded at Haslach in 1805. Then there was the forward depot at Jerez where the paymaster, cobbler and other support services were concentrated.

Uniforms were being manufactured in France, but somewhere on the way to Andalusia they were going missing. As a result, the Ninth was in urgent need of replacement clothing. Since the beginning of 1808 the only articles of new uniform had come from captured British stores found after the battle of Ocaña late in 1809 and Seville in 1810. The British uniforms and equipment were used to the best advantage, but by 1812 the men of the first two battalions must have been dressed in rags.[2]

On 1 March 1812 Dauture wrote a series of letters from Villamartin which demonstrate the efforts he made to find his missing coats. The first was to Captain Janin at Bayonne:

> … In the two years I have been with the regiment, I have not received a single coat or greatcoat! Imagine the appearance. I have sent an officer to Madrid. Mr. Gobin has been ordered to go everywhere the items dispatched by you might have been stopped. Equally he must correspond with you, and with Captain Petit, who I have been informed remains at Burgos, in order to obtain any useful information. I am writing to this same captain, praying him to make all necessary enquiries with Messrs the finance officers, or commissaries and fortress commandants to try to discover where your consignments have been deposited. Write to him likewise and give him all the documents you believe suitable.

According to the advice I have had from the major, you ought to have recently received a very large quantity of uniforms. Take every measure to hasten their expedition to Seville and be exact in notifying me, as well as everything which remains in Bayonne for lack of transport … The items of linen and shoes you have sent us by order of His Excellency the Minister Director [of War Administration] are also held up …

The 12 shirts, 12 cravats, and 12 yards of flannel you returned to me by Mr Dauphin have been lost. On his arrival at Santa Maria this young man told me someone had stolen his portmantle near Toledo. I have put this one down to experience. It is a lesson not to be obliged to people without knowing them. In future when you have something to send to me, I pray you only confide them in men we can trust, or to officers of the regiment coming to rejoin me. Neither did I receive the six yards of flannel you sent me for which you paid almost a third over the ordinary price for their quality.

If my sister sends my epaulettes with my épée and some other personal things I have asked for, you will take care to confide them only to known persons.'[3]

The second letter continued in a similar vein:

Mr Captain Petit,

… Attached is a table of all the items of uniform and other objects which were sent to you from Bayonne by Captain Janin. As all these effects are late arriving and as I have not received any news, I am dying to hear all the information which you can get from Messrs the finance officers, commissaries, fortress commandants to try and discover where they could have been held up. You will correspond with Captain Janin who is in Bayonne, and with Sub-Lieutenant Gobin who I have sent to Madrid. You will give them and will take from them all the suitable information, and you will inform me of the result of the searches … Mr Dauphin with whom you left Bayonne brought me the news someone had stolen his portmantle in which were my shirts and the other objects with which he was in charged with bringing to me. If you receive any other articles for me I would be obliged if you gave them all your care.[4]

While the officers went looking for the missing supplies, counter-insurgency operations continued around Villamartin and Seville. Corporal Nicolas Page was part of a detachment of 50 troops sent to guard a large farm near Seville. The owner was of French extraction so was likely to be a target. Sure enough, eight days later a guerrilla band of 150 horsemen showed up. The French soldiers made ready and opened fire on the Spaniards as they approached. One of the riders came up at the gallop and circled round the French several times. The lieutenant commanding the detachment said, 'He's getting on my nerves. Who volunteers to go out and meet him?' No one volunteered, but the officer's gaze fixed firmly on Page. The meaning was clear. Page stepped forward and accepted the challenge. 'Off you go Page', said the lieutenant. 'Try and show him we are French.' As Page stepped forward to challenge the Spaniard man-to-man, he asked his comrades to step in if it looked like he was in trouble. With their assurance, Page stepped out of the ranks and motioned the Spaniard to come on. The Spaniard had no intention of fighting fairly. He approached Page then quickly raised his carbine, shot at the Frenchmen then galloped off. As the bullet whistled harmlessly past, Page took careful aim and shot the rider from his saddle.[5]

The French detachment then retired inside the farm and took up position around the walls. The Spanish adopted a new approach, running forward with burning torches trying to set the farm on fire. Around midday the ammunition started to run out. By 2pm things appeared to be desperate when a large dust cloud was sighted in the direction of Seville. There was an anxious wait to see who these newcomers were. Page contemplated being captured by the guerrillas, something he was very much afraid of. He need not have worried, the force turned out to be French. Three companies of infantry and a squadron of hussars had come to their relief. At the sight of this reinforcement the guerrillas made off and the farm was saved.

After a fortnight guarding the farm, Page went to Seville and was then sent off in the direction of Ronda. Their new mission was to collect unpaid 'contributions' from recalcitrant peasants. Page appears to have profited financially from this work. When they came across a house that had not paid its dues, the soldiers levied a supplementary fine of 5 francs an hour while they waited for payment. A week into this racketeering and Page had personally pocketed 100 francs, the equivalent of about seven months' pay. This profitable business soon came to an end when the guerrillas got wind of them and chased them off. The French knew when not to overstay their welcome.

With Massena ejected from Portugal, Wellington marched on King Joseph's capital. There were two main routes from Lisbon to Madrid; one was guarded by the fortresses of Almeida and Ciudad Rodrigo, the other by the fortress of Badajoz. By the end of January the first two fortresses had fallen, leaving Badajoz the sole obstacle to Wellington's plans.

Badajoz was on the left bank of the Guadiana and was protected by a strong belt of bastions and a castle. The Picurina lunette and several other outlying forts completed the defensive system. The French garrison was relatively small; just 5,000 men under the command of General Armand Philippon. This included the 15 officers and 580 men of the Ninth's 3rd Battalion under Battalion Commander Billon.

On 16 March 1812 the Anglo-Portuguese army arrived and invested the city with 27,000 troops. Badajoz had survived two sieges in 1811, in both cases because a relieving force had driven the besieging troops away. Although the fortifications were strong, in 1812 the arrival of a relieving force was Philippon's only realistic chance of salvation. His troops would not be strong enough to break out. He held a council of war with his senior officers and decided on a defence plan. The Ninth was ordered to hold Bastions 1 and 2 on the west face of the city.[6]

On 26 March the British seized the Picurina redoubt south-east of the main works. They mounted a powerful battery there and began battering the city walls. On 29 March Philippon ordered Billon to mount a sortie with 400 men. Billon led his men racing towards the British trenches. Previous sorties had been successful in wrecking gun positions and stealing picks and shovels, but in this case the besiegers appear to have been pre-warned. As Billon arrived in musket range he realized the British were massed in force. There was a brief exchange of musketry in which Billon lost five men, after which he was driven back for no gain. No more sorties were attempted after this. There was nothing for it but to await the day of assault or the arrival of a relief column.

On 3 April the bombardment intensified, with 40 guns firing constantly. The bombardment played havoc, tearing down walls and breaching ramparts. The long-suffering citizens of Badajoz locked themselves in their cellars or trusted in the sanctity of their churches to avoid the perils of the bombardment. Before long it became clear a breach would soon become practicable. General Philippon called a council of war to discuss how to meet the inevitable assault. The first few minutes would be critical. The defenders would have to prevent the attackers gaining a foothold anywhere on the perimeter. Philippon decided to defend the breach with a 'sacred battalion' formed by the elite companies. Seven hundred strong, this battalion included the Ninth's carabineers and voltigeurs. Every man was given three loaded muskets so they would not have to pause to reload while meeting the attack. Behind the elite troops, a battalion of the 103rd Infantry was placed in an entrenchment as a reserve.

On 5 April two breaches were declared practicable around bastions 6 and 7. The one saving grace for the defenders was that the outer wall of the ditch, or counterscarp, was left intact by the British. Once the British entered the ditch they would find it very difficult to get back out again. Maximizing this fault, Philippon set about creating a killing ground in front of the breaches. Preparing for the attack, the French attempted to plug the breach as best they could, bringing up fascines, bags of earth, bales of cotton and a devilish cheval-de-frise constructed from cavalry sabre blades set into wooden planks and secured to the ground by chains. Artillery was placed on the flanks of the bastions and each gun loaded with canister. Explosive barrels and bombs were collected near the breach along with grenades to throw down on the enemy in the ditch below.

Wellington perhaps sensed the French preparations and so decided to put off the attack and open a third breach on 6 April. Similar efforts were made to plug this breach and a company of Hessian grenadiers were allocated to defend it. In truth, the opening of this third breach stretched Philippon's resources to breaking point. He realized there was very little chance of defending the fortress and perhaps would have capitulated if summoned to do so. Despite the conventions of war, Wellington did not call on the French to surrender. He reasoned the French could surrender any time they chose, but would probably decline if he asked them. For their part the defenders were fearful of capture, knowing they would probably end up on some decrepit prison hulk on the Thames, or worse. A steely resolve came over the garrison to make the British pay very dearly for Badajoz.

At 9.30pm the British artillery opened up with a hail of roundshot and exploding shells. The defenders realized the time had come, so took their positions and waited. Somewhat unexpectedly the first attack came against the castle in the north-east corner of the defences. This did enough to divert attention away from the troops advancing towards the breaches. It was an extremely dark night and the British managed to enter the ditch running parallel to the city wall without being seen. As they sped towards the breaches carrying their scaling ladders they were finally spotted. A cry of 'There they are!' went up along the ramparts.

Unbeknown to the British, in that same ditch French engineers had planted a line of 60 14-inch shells four feet below the surface at a distance of six feet apart. Lieutenant Mailhet of the miners had bravely volunteered to remain in the ditch to fire these bombs once the attackers reached the breach. The result was something akin to a volcanic eruption. The ground shook and the night turned momentarily into day. As the survivors staggered around, deafened and dazed by the catastrophe that had engulfed them, an avalanche of grenades, bombs, exploding barrels and sacks of gunpowder came rolling down into the ditch. The elite troops stationed at the breach jumped up and opened fire, quickly exchanging musket for musket to keep a rain of fire down on the assailants. It was absolute butchery. As more redcoats arrived, they stumbled over the bloody remains of their comrades and struggled to move forward. Their scaling ladders were too short. Their officers were cut down. As they reached the breach the leading men found themselves faced with the cheval-de-frise. Unable to shift it, the leading men were pushed onto the blades by those behind. It was hell on earth. The British lost around 3,000 men in the ditch. Over the same period the French lost just 20 men, including Lieutenant Mailhet, struck by a shell splinter in the inferno he initiated.

While the breach held, there was trouble elsewhere. Philippon was distracted by reports of British troops inside Bastion 6. He went from his command post to take a look and in his absence a crisis occurred in the castle. The defences had been judged unassailable at that point, but the British found a path and penetrated the castle. The redcoats quickly cleared the castle of its Hessian defenders and bolted the door shut so that the French could not enter.

The French were desperate to retake the castle, as they had planned to fall back on it as a last redoubt should the British assault succeed. Two companies of the Ninth were withdrawn from Bastion 1 and ordered to a side gate into the castle, which was believed to be unlocked. In the heat of battle the order became confused. The two companies rushed off not to the citadel, but to join the elite companies defending the breach instead. The error was compounded by the next British attack. Desperate to avoid the hell-hole in front of the breach the British probed for a weak point. Around midnight, just after the two companies of chasseurs set off on their wild goose chase, Bastion 1 came under a concerted attack from the British 5th Division under General Leith. With their number reduced by two-thirds, the defenders of Bastion 1 struggled to cope with the attack. Something like 100 chasseurs of the Ninth were faced with an entire British division. The Ninth's musketry caused terrible casualties, with as many as 600 redcoats falling in the attack, but by sheer weight of numbers the British were able to edge their way past the bastion and join up with those already in the castle. From that point on the night was lost. Bastion 1 fell and the British entered Badajoz in force. A chaotic street fight ensued as Frenchmen ran this way and that, with nowhere to retreat now the castle had fallen. The soldiers defending the breach could hear fighting behind them and without receiving any orders decided the game was up. They lowered their weapons and began contemplating life as prisoners of war. The British troops were drunk and enraged. The slaughter in the breaches was unparalleled in any other battle Wellington's troops had fought. In response the redcoats broke into houses and raped and looted the poor Spanish. During the fighting, General Philippon broke out of the town with a handful of men to Fort San Cristoval on the far bank of the Guadiana. In the morning Philippon hung a white flag outside Fort San Cristoval and surrendered along with the remainder of his men. Further resistance was pointless.

The French lost 1,500 men in the battle and 3,500 went into captivity with Philippon. The 3rd Battalion suffered heavily, losing about half its effective strength in the battle, with three officers killed and another six wounded. The survivors were taken captive and shipped off to England for the duration of the war. The loss of Badajoz opened the road to Madrid for Wellington and spelled the beginning of the end for the French occupation of Spain. For the Ninth it was an utter calamity. Never had the regiment lost an entire battalion in a single action. News of the disaster quickly spread to the rest of the regiment in Andalusia.

After Badajoz, morale in the Ninth declined significantly. On 14 April an officer deserted his post, the first reported case since the Dumouriez affair of 1793. On 28 April Dauture informed General Conroux of the episode:

Mr. Ogormann, lieutenant of the 9th Light Infantry has abandoned the regiment at Arcos, the 14th April, this present month at three o'clock in the evening. All the enquiries and information I have sought to obtain on his escape have not produced any result. I do not know if he has passed over to the enemy or which direction he has taken. According to some vague information, it appears he would have first directed himself on Jeres.

This officer who initially had served with the regiment, had been appointed ADC to General Meunier then passed to the 12th Light and returned to the 9th by the decision of His Excellency on 11 October 1811.

Since his return to the 9th Light he often gave signs of a disturbed spirit, he appeared to serve with lassitude and affected some pretensions. Furthermore, he was prone to pleasure-taking and independence. He spoke several languages, particularly Spanish and English.

I know of no other motives that have caused his desertion, other than a duel he had with a captain of the 96th regiment following a slap in the face he received from this captain in a café in Jeres in the presence of officers from both regiments.[7]

Later in the day the colonel elaborated on the case further, having interviewed Ogormann's commanding officers. The tone of the letter says as much about Dauture as it does about the deserter:

… The only merit I recognized in this officer was of speaking a few languages; without doubt fruit of a good education. He was held by the regiment as a liar, a fool and a joker, an attribute which he gave voice to perfectly everywhere he went. Finally he did not possess any soldierly qualities.

Mr Ogormann, prior to and since his return, was marked as constantly negligent of his duties, always late for service and without knowledge of his profession, having ceaseless excuses to display he was lacking in happiness. He has never even figured in any battle or combat where the regiment has been found. His taste and his principal habits were for games and pleasure.[8]

Further evidence of discontent came from a letter from Cardron dated 7 May 1812. French soldiers' post was normally opened and censored, so officers and men alike had to be careful what they wrote. In this case the letter was going to be carried by an aide-de-camp of General Meunier returning to France. At last Cardron could write freely of what was going on.

… My last letter was sent from Santa-Maria which we left on 1 February to drive into the mountains on the side of Gibraltar. Since that time we have not had eight days' rest, always on the march, always seeking out a cowardly enemy who knows only to escape on our approach and who, by this manner of making war in an equally disagreeable country, sometimes on mountains which menace the heavens, sometimes in hell, harasses us with fatigue and exhaustion.

Up until now, my health has not abandoned me, but now the hot weather is here, if we are not relieved by other troops and we continue the same campaign, I fear I could not hold on for much longer, nor anyone but the most robust.

Add to my fatigues the deprivations of every kind we experience, and the arrears of our pay which are due to us for 15 months, without one having a penny, you will have an idea of our sad situation; and if you believe we are reduced, officers as well as soldiers, to a half-ration of poor barley which we often have to wait for from the morning until the evening, and that it is impossible for us to obtain anything else because of a lack of money, then you will pity us with your whole heart …

As for political affairs, I am not in the habit of speaking to you of them. You will know before the reception of my letter, of the capture of Badajoz and the massacre of its garrison which our 3rd Battalion was part of and which no longer remains at all, other than very few who are prisoner.

In a word, everything is going badly. All our generals have asked to return to France. Several are there already and I profit from the departure of General Meunier who leaves us today with his aide de camp, to whom I will give my letter which he will carry until Bayonne where he will post it and reach you more surely.

It is also in the hope this letter will not be opened you will learn a few things of our sad situation, things I would be obliged to hush up if I did not profit this situation.

It is for this same reason I will tell you the morale of the army could not be more affected; that the soldiers frequently desert and I have to say, to the shame of the French name, the officers too. Judge by that the consequences.[9]

Cardron was a frequent grumbler in his letters, but the tone of desperation in this letter is palpable. Cardron was a committed soldier, a volunteer who had re-enlisted and wanted to make a career out of becoming an officer. If he was this troubled by the Spanish situation, imagine the feelings of the poor conscripts coerced into service.

At this time Napoleon was preparing to invade Russia with the Grand Army. While the soldiers gathering in Poland were refreshed, smartly uniformed and working under the loving gaze of their emperor, those in southern Spain could not have felt more ignored.

With their numbers dwindling, there was a reorganization of the forces in Andalusia. The three corps which had invaded Andalusia were amalgamated into a single one, under Marshal Soult. Victor was recalled to Poland and the siege of Cadiz put in the hands of Ruffin's old drinking companion Villatte. Conroux's division was placed on the Guadalete near the village of Bornos. A short way outside the village the Ninth began building an entrenched camp. One battalion would work on the camp while the other two remained in the village gathering supplies and mounting patrols. The 96th were half a league (2km) further on.

On the morning of 1 June, the 4th Battalion was in the camp with around 500 men. It was another fine day and the battalion set to work on the defences before the full intensity of the sun was on their backs. Shortly after sunrise, one of the sentries spotted movement ahead. Colonel Dauture took his telescope and scanned the area indicated between two mountain peaks. He dismissed the matter, saying it was a patrol coming back in and ordered the men to get back to work. Not long afterwards the familiar sound of musketry was heard in the direction of the forward posts. A second look at this 'returning patrol' revealed Dauture had made a grave mistake. It was in fact a column of Spanish infantry 10,000 strong led by Ballesteros.

There was a cry of 'to arms' at which the soldiers downed tools and ran to the stacks of arms. Outnumbered 20 to one, the men of the 4th Battalion knew they were in for the fight of their lives. Everyone went to the firestep and loaded their muskets; officers and drummers included. Ahead of them a Spanish battalion deployed and attacked. There was a murderous fusillade and a surge by the Spanish troops. There were four French field guns on the edge of the earthworks.

These managed just two shots apiece before the Spanish were on top of them, hacking the gunners to pieces.

Meanwhile the 1st and 2nd battalions came racing up from the village. They ran straight into the main body of the Spanish column and were greeted with a hail of lead. Realizing the odds were weighted too far against them, the two battalions broke off and made a disordered run for the safety of the entrenched camp. An epic bout of hand-to-hand combat ensued as the French tried to hold off the Spaniards and evict those who had broken in. Dauture's horse was shot from underneath him. Captain Etienne was badly wounded, but stayed at his post and refused all aid. Engulfed by a red mist, Lieutenant Barberis fought like a demon, throwing rocks at the assailants and grappling them with his bare hands. Nicolas Page took musket balls in his shako, backpack and through his greatcoat. His bunkmate was killed along with a fellow corporal, one of Page's best friends. Most seriously of all, Battalion Commander Planchet was mortally wounded. As he fell, Dauture rushed to his side to hear his last words.

At the point when it seemed the Ninth might be swamped by the tide, help arrived in the guise of the 96th Line. Believing the Ninth had been lost somewhere beneath the hordes of Spanish troops, dust and gunpowder smoke, the 96th opened fire on Ballesteros' men who were surprised by the newcomers. Under withering volleys, the Spanish troops began to hesitate. A charge by 120 troopers of the 5th Chasseurs caused panic and then a flight. Inside the camp, the Ninth saw the Spanish falling back. They seized the chance and counter-attacked. For the next hour they pursued the Spanish down the hill to the Guadalete River. There they bayoneted and shot the fugitives, turning the river red with blood.

When the dust settled, the grounds around the camp and hillside were littered with 400 Spanish dead and 1,500 wounded. The French took the trophy of two Spanish flags and four guns, in addition to recapturing the four they had lost at the beginning of the action. On the French side there had been 400 casualties. Dauture recorded the Ninth lost 27 killed, including Planchet and a further 185 wounded. The 4th Battalion had suffered the regiment's worst losses.

The aftermath of a battle was never a happy sight, but after Bornos, the soldiers of the Ninth witnessed a macabre phenomenon they had not seen before. Soon after the battle, masses of vultures began gliding down from the nearby mountains. Nicolas Page watched as they stripped the bodies clean until, a few days after the action, all that was left was a field full of human heads and piles of bones.

Bornos was Dauture's first serious action as commander of the Ninth. Given the loss of a battalion at Badajoz he was particularly keen to highlight the bravery of his men. Directly after the battle he wrote a list of men recommended for promotion. In a long note Conroux endorsed the recommendations, finishing with this eulogy: 'Each soldier was in this circumstance a hero and the two regiments 9th and 96th were reminiscent of the Spartans at Thermopylae.'[10]

Dauture mentioned the battle in several dispatches to his roving officers policing the supply lines. In a letter dated Bornos, 30 June 1812, Dauture alerted Captain Janin to an important shipment of silver heading his way:

> How is it my dear Captain I have not received news from you? What can be the reason for the long wait the regiment has experienced in receiving its uniforms, linens and shoes? This is what I am constantly occupied with …
>
> Mr Planchet had informed me some days previously to his death of two dispatches of silver he sent to his wife; they are quite consequential. Messrs General Meunier and Captain Fransquin have willingly offered to take it and give it to you on their arrival at Bayonne to then hold for his wife. I therefore recommend to you, my dear Captain, the interests of this widow and his children. I made certain commitments on the battlefield when receiving the last words and wishes of this brave commander …

Dauture then turned to the problem of supplying the field battalions with new uniforms. The letter indicates his roving officers had experienced some success with locating the missing uniforms, but that much was still lacking, particularly for the regiment's 'tête de colonne'.[11]

> … You will know Mr Gobin has been in Madrid for several months charged with waiting there to receive everything that is destined for the regiment. The uniform of the musicians, sappers, drummers, fifers and that of Messrs the officers all of whom experience the greatest need, is one of the first points I recommend to you as well as my equipment. Redouble your zeal my dear Captain and take every step …

> In the two years I have been with the regiment I have only received 760 coats and 515 greatcoats. Judge our needs for these two articles in particular. I would be obliged to you to let my sister know I am still doing well.[12]

In a second letter that day, Dauture tried to buoy Captain Gobin's waning confidence in the outcome of the war:

> … All the news they spread and circulate around Madrid should not worry you. Badajoz has fallen into the hands of the English it is true. This loss far from harming our operations augments them. Take Andalusia if you like, the Army of the South is strong enough to resist every enterprise and shock on the part of the enemy. It is unfortunate for the Spanish nation they cannot be convinced by our strength. They will however have to open their eyes and persuade themselves we will not be beaten.[13]

In fact Dauture was grossly over-optimistic in his forecast. While the Ninth was relatively cocooned from the outside world in Andalusia, those in Madrid had a clearer picture. Having reduced the border fortresses along the Portuguese border, Wellington advanced into Spain. Massena had been replaced by Marshal Marmont, but with little effect. The French were defeated at Salamanca on 22 July and Madrid opened its doors to Wellington on 6 August. King Joseph fled to Valencia and ordered the blockade of Cadiz to be raised and his remaining forces to concentrate. On 25 August the Ninth's bronzed veterans set out in the direction of Grenada, then passed through Murcia, Cartagena and Alicante before arriving at Valencia.

With the French armies united, the British evacuated Madrid and fell back towards Portugal. The Ninth formed part of the pursuit force, marching 200 leagues (800km) on half a ration of bread daily and whatever fruit and berries they could forage; but the French were used to marching on empty bellies. The lack of food was partly caused by the Spanish running off to the hills with all their food because the British had spread propaganda that the French would murder them. As a measure of revenge, the French pursued the English at a relentless pace, hardly giving the redcoats a chance to eat their supper and, on several occasions, surprising the English in their camps.

The pursuit continued until Rovigo, when both sides settled down for winter. Two companies of the Ninth were sent to the village of Salvatierra, three leagues (12km) from Villafranca near Salamanca. After 15 days' rest a detachment of 16 men was formed to collect supplies. It was then Sunday 20 December. Corporal Page had dressed in his best uniform to attend mass at the local church when his sergeant-major told him he was on the detachment. A colleague offered to go in Page's place for a bottle of wine, but Page decided he would go himself. He undressed and put on his marching clothes.[14] They were joined by a few peasants and their mules. Several of the soldiers took advantage of these mules, placing their haversacks on them, while they marched along gaily having a sing-song.

After passing through a village the detachment was confronted by 100 Spanish horsemen. They called on the Frenchmen to surrender, but Page's sergeant-major refused, instructing the detachment to load their muskets. The horsemen fanned out, surrounding the group, which remained formed in ranks to present a compact mass. The Spanish ran off with their mules, taking the haversacks with them, causing howls of consternation from those who lost their possessions. The sergeant-major scolded them for being lazy and not carrying their packs in the first place. A stand-off ensued for 15 minutes while both sides pondered what to do. The Frenchmen began edging their way towards a raised plateau that would have been easier to defend. The Spanish guessed their intention and opened fire. Reaching the plateau, Page climbed up and saw a Spaniard take aim at him. Expecting a bullet, Page dived for cover and the ball struck the leg of the man at the head of the file. Page returned fire breaking the Spaniard's leg and killing his horse with a single shot.

For a time it looked as if the French might make an escape; but then a company of Spanish infantry arrived on the scene, 80 strong. With three men wounded and cut off, Page's sergeant-major brokered a deal, offering to surrender if they could keep their haversacks. As soon as they surrendered, they regretted it. A mob of villagers turned up with picks and shovels calling for the 'dogs of Frenchmen' to be killed. On the second day of captivity the Spanish lined them up in front of a firing squad and appeared to be ready to execute them. Page had been in battle many times, but said facing a firing squad was 'as terrible as death itself'.[15] One of the younger Frenchmen began to cry, repeatedly asking the Spanish officer if they were going to be killed. In fact, the whole thing was staged to renegotiate the surrender terms, with the Spanish officer offering to spare their lives in return for their personal belongings.

Stripped of their packs and clothes, the unhappy Frenchmen were marched south through rain, snow and ice. At one place they encountered a British garrison. The English officers came to gloat over the Frenchmen, telling them their 'famous emperor' was losing an army in Russia. Of course Page had no idea of the news from Russia and took the whole episode as an insult. From there they were taken to Badajoz where they saw the damage inflicted when the 3rd Battalion was captured. They then marched full circle back to Seville, from where they had set off several months before. The local population would have torn them to pieces if they had not been under a heavy guard.

After crossing the Guadalquivir and passing through Puerto Santa-Maria, Page and his companions were thrown into a state prison with 600 common criminals intent on strangling them and inflicting every cruelty imaginable. Page refused to describe the barbarous suffering they endured in the place. After two weeks of this hell they were transferred to Cadiz, the fortress they had fruitlessly blockaded for two years. By now Page's strength had begun to fail. He had no recollection of arriving, only of waking up in a hospital bed with a priest from Strasbourg asking if he wanted to make his confession in French or German. Two thousand kilometres from home, the verdant fields and valleys of the Vosges must have seemed like a world away.

COLLAPSE

The path to Napoleon's abdication in 1814 was a painful one for men reared on two decades of martial success. While entrusting the subjugation of Iberia to subordinates, Napoleon's principal concern became the establishment of an imperial dynasty. In an attempt to produce a legitimate heir and in the hope of creating a blood alliance with Austria, Napoleon divorced Empress Josephine and married Marie-Louise, daughter of the Austrian emperor on 11 March 1810. Many had seen Josephine as Napoleon's 'lucky star' and were sceptical at the prospect of the emperor marrying the great-niece of Marie-Antoinette; but the new empress dutifully produced a male heir on 20 March 1811. Napoleon named the boy after himself and titled him the King of Rome.[1]

While the ulcerous war in Spain remained a persistent drain, Russia formed the object of the emperor's fixation. With tensions growing over France's influence in Poland and Russia's flouting of Napoleon's trade restrictions with Great Britain, the momentum for war began to build from late 1810. As the months went on, war became more certain and Napoleon began building a new Grand Army in the eastern reaches of the French empire. Finally, in June 1812, Napoleon launched half a million soldiers on the road to Moscow. By the end of the year this army was gone; consumed in combat or swallowed up in the ice and snow of a Russian winter.

As after Bailen, when Napoleon was seen to be down, his enemies rose up. A sixth coalition was formed against France, comprising Britain, Portugal, Spain, Russia, Austria, Prussia and Sweden. To meet this vast host, in 1813 Napoleon built a new army almost from scratch. Despite an optimistic start he met with disaster at Leipzig (16–19 October 1813) and from then on his fate was sealed. By March 1814 the coalition partners were over the Pyrenees in the south and knocking on the gates of Paris in the north. The Napoleonic adventure was snubbed out at Fontainebleau on 11 April 1814 when the Emperor abdicated and was exiled to Elba.

In this final phase of the empire, the French army struggled to meet the demands of a war on two fronts. At the end of 1812 the Ninth's depot did its best to make good the losses in Spain. The cadre of the 4th Battalion was returned to Longwy and an entirely new 3rd Battalion was formed at the depot on 1 December 1812, thus replacing the one lost at Badajoz. On 4 January 1813 Napoleon decreed that the regiments not annihilated in Russia should create a 6th Battalion. This was to be formed of conscripts from the class of 1814 who were called up one year early. Even that was not enough. Desperate for men after the Prussian declaration of war on 17 March 1813, Napoleon recalled the cadre of the first two battalions, instructing the officers, sub-officers and corporals to return post haste to France while the chasseurs and carabineers were distributed among the remaining regiments. This order was ignored. The situation in Spain was so bad the two battalions were required intact as they were.

The Ninth's new 3rd and 4th battalions were placed under the command of 43-year-old Major Jean-Baptiste Mourèze, a long-serving light infantryman, latterly a captain in the 1st Chasseurs of the Imperial Guard. While Dauture commanded in Spain, Mourèze would command in Germany. Mourèze was ordered first to Mainz and then Würzburg in northern Bavaria where he joined the 11th Division under General Étienne Pierre Sylvestre Ricard, in Ney's III Corps.

As part of 4th Battalion, Cardron's letters vividly portray service in the regiment on this campaign. On Cardon's return to Longwy from Spain, Captain Baudot offered him the role of paymaster. He turned this down and was instead nominated by Major Mourèze as captain of carabineers in 4th Battalion. His heart pounded with pride at the news:

I showed my gratitude to the major who answered that by my conduct in our various affairs I deserved the honour of commanding the Grenadiers and that he would have done me an injustice confiding the command of this company in another; you see we enjoy a certain reputation.

Some enemy parties came roaming two to three leagues [12km] from here; but they are only villains who try only to make off with some booty by plundering the unfortunate villages. There is no army to support them in spite of them saying they are an advanced guard. We are well disposed and we have nothing to fear from such brigands. Today they officially announced peace with Spain and the swift return of a French army 100,000 strong; so we shall soon be united with them and will make the enemy regret having dared to invade our lands. Our little soldiers sparkle with the desire to fight.[2]

While somewhat dismissive of the enemy, Cardron was not entirely happy with his own men either. He claimed the 4th Battalion was composed of 'the most villainous types' while 3rd Battalion was 'the finest battalion possible', being made up of conscripts from the Ardennes. In fact Cardron underestimated the foes ranged against him. The Russians would be the same unyielding and persistent opponents as before, but the real change came in the Prussians. This was not the rigid, 18th-century army shattered in 1806, but a new army, more flexible and dynamic, nationalistic and desperate for liberation from French influence.

The first major clash of the campaign came on 2 May 1814. Ney's corps encountered coalition forces south of Lützen. It was a hard day's fighting but with Napoleon and his Guard present, the victory went to the French. Cardron fought in the battle and described the outcome in a letter dated Torgau, 13 May:

This battle could not have been more fortunate for us. It has forced the enemy to re-cross the Elbe after having left the battlefield covered with dead and so much encouraged our youngsters, who for the first time fought against a hundred thousand of the best Russian and Prussian troops, who aspired for nothing but combat.

I could not have been more fortunate. I did not receive a single wound although exposed from morning until evening close to a battery which I protected with the company I command. I feel well enough and I hope to end the campaign lucky. There is the question of rewards: the cross, promotion; one might ask me if I have been proposed for one or the other, but I am certain the rank of captain has been asked for me to the emperor; as for the rest I cannot be sure … I cannot tell you any more, we are about to get underway and pay a visit to Berlin.[3]

Again Cardron was guilty of over-optimism. Although Lützen had been a victory, Napoleon's new army lacked cavalry. The retreating Prusso-Russian army was able to make good its escape and regroup for a second battle at Bautzen on 19–20 May. By the end of this engagement Cardron reported the Ninth had been reduced from 1,200 men at the outset of the campaign to just over 400. Cardron also had some bad news for his mother in a letter dated 25 May:

After the terrible event which has just taken place I cannot, nor would not, leave you worried after my fate, knowing how cruel it would be for both of us.

You will have heard before the arrival of my letter of the victory of Bautzen; a victory which has cost us dear. For two entire days death was vomited here and there, from 4 in the morning until 9 in the evening. Our army, numbering 250,000 men, all youngsters, covered itself in glory overthrowing the enemy and chasing them from a line of redoubts two leagues [8km] in length. The enemy is in full flight. The Emperor with three army corps which were not used in the action pursues them, hot on their heels …

I come now to my own account. I can guess your impatience to know if anything happened to me. Ah! How could one escape it; it would be a miracle. However, I still thank the gods for the wound I received on the first day; for the next day I could have been treated worse. The wound I received is up high in the flesh of my left arm. At the moment when the company of carabineers I commanded, with a company of voltigeurs, climbed a Prussian redoubt, bristling with bayonets and protected by four canons. At the moment we arrived on the breastwork, a ball came and struck me on the left arm, but fortunately did not break it, but flattened out on the skin. A doctor told me it has gone bad; all I know is all the muscles are cut and I am obliged to support the left forearm in my right hand. It could be some time before my use of it returns.

I am suffering, but that is inevitable after such a fresh wound; do not have a single worry. I am going to be evacuated to Dresden which is no more than 12 short leagues [48km] from here and there I will be restored to perfect health …

This new victory gives us rights for a reward. I notified you in my last letter I was proposed for the rank of captain and for the decoration and to give you certainty I enclose the letter my commander wrote to me relating to this.[4]

Cardron's battalion commander, Joseph Etienne, had also fallen in action and had written to Cardron from his bivouac on 26 May 1813.

I am very saddened, my dear Cardron, to learn your wound was so bad. We must hope you will not have any trouble and no unfortunate consequences. I have thought long on what you should do in these circumstances; it is only natural that you must heal before thinking of coming back. This is my advice to you. The campaign is finished for you and we must hope even the war.

As for what you asked me, I sent the note of recommendation for the Legion yesterday. Be assured you are not forgotten; it is enough to say it was me who made the recommendation …

As for my wound, it is a bad bruise which has made me suffer like the damned for two days. I have improved. It is in the left forearm. The ball pierced the cuff flap and sleeve of my greatcoat; you can judge it still had enough force so I will still have to carry my arm in a sling for a while. I still have my ear bandaged, but it is getting better.

Etienne, Battalion Commander.[5]

On 29 May Cardron arrived in the hospital at Dresden. He had begun worrying he might have his arm amputated, but the surgeons confirmed this was not the case. While convalescing he hoped for peace:

You would have learned before the reception of my letter that a two-month armistice was made. We are therefore certain to still be alive for another 60 days and perhaps more, for a congress will be held in Prague they say and they assure us we are going to see a general peace. God hope so and be praised![6]

True enough, Napoleon signed the armistice of Pleischwitz on 4 June, but there was little chance of peace. Both sides simply saw this as a pause in which to improve the strength of their forces. Cardron was not to know this and his optimism was buoyed by news that his promotion to captain had been confirmed. He was less hopeful about the Legion of Honour as Napoleon had returned to Paris after Bautzen without him being awarded the cross, but he was wrong to doubt his commander's words. Cardron had actually been admitted to the legion in February 1813, but an administrative error saw his confirmation posted to Spain. When he finally learned of the award he was justifiably proud. Reflecting on the suffering he had endured, on 8 July 1813 he wrote, 'I have in truth paid for these advantages with my blood. It is the fate of war; one must submit oneself to it.'[7]

With his wound taking time to heal, Cardron was evacuated to Metz. In addition to the wound he began to suffer from rheumatism, the result of ten years of wounds and sleeping rough. He was sent to take the waters at Bourbonne, a hot spring spa in the Champagne country. This treatment meant he was absent when hostilities resumed on 14 August and he missed the campaign which culminated in the epic battle of Leipzig on 16–19 October 1813. Here Napoleon amassed over 200,000 men to face a 400,000-strong coalition army, composed of Prussians, Russians, Swedes and Austrians. This 'Battle of Nations' was one of the largest ever fought, with the coalition forces ranged in an enormous arc around Leipzig. The Ninth was located in III Corps (Souham), which was part of the French left wing, commanded by Ney. By the time of the battle, Major Mourèze had received 6th Battalion as reinforcement. However, his three battalions could only muster 1,131 men on the day of battle, the 6th Battalion having been roughly handled at the battle of Kulm in northern Bohemia on 29–30 August.

For the first two days of battle the French stubbornly held on to their position. The Ninth fought at the village of Schönefeld, north-east of Leipzig. Here they took part in a desperate bayonet assault against the Russians and suffered heavy losses. By the evening of 18 October ammunition started to run low, so Napoleon ordered his army to retreat westwards. A great scrum of men, vehicles and beasts descended on the bridge over the River Elster. Although the retreat was well planned, a calamity ensued when an engineer panicked and blew the bridge while it was still crowded with troops. Although the Ninth had already passed the bridges, the regimental rolls show large numbers of native German conscripts from the Rhine and Moselle department in the 6th Battalion were captured on 19 October. It is unclear if 6th Battalion was marooned on the wrong side of the bridge, or if there was some mass defection by non-French soldiers.[8]

After Leipzig the French army headed westwards for the safety of the Rhine. The Ninth crossed the river at Mainz on 2 November. The losses on campaign had been so great that III Corps was reorganized into a single division. Likewise, the Ninth was only able to field a single, weak battalion. The cadre of 4th Battalion (19 officers and 101 men) was sent to Metz to re-form, while the 6th Battalion was completely written off on 17 November.[9] In the meantime 3rd Battalion was directed to Coblenz to help guard the passage over the Rhine. It had been a remarkable reversal of fortune. The empire had imploded spectacularly and now France faced the prospect of invasion on two fronts.

For his part Cardron had been lucky to miss this calamitous ending to French influence beyond the Rhine. In late October Cardron wrote to his sister from the spa at Bourbonne explaining he had taken advice not to return to duty until fully recovered. On something of a lighter note, the letter contains a reference to one of his colleagues, once a potential suitor to his sister, suffering from what appears to be a sexually transmitted disease:

The waters have had hardly any effect, especially for my rheumatisms, for I always feel rather lively pains in my knees and legs which prevent me even from resting. As for my arm, it is much better. I can extend it almost completely but it is without strength and takes hardly any nourishment. It is a limb from which I shall not draw any great service.

I am well enough here. I planned to rejoin the army, but Mr Baudot, who always takes a lot of interest in me, determined that I rest for a while; and the arrival of our major, to whom I am advantageously known, convinced me to wait for him. It might be that I can come to see you, because I can count on him enough to obtain leave. He should be here in about eight days.

I have found here some of my companions returned back from Spain who like me have received wounds or are sick. They gave me news of F… whose behaviour is always the same, which is he games and gets drunk as is his habit. He is even affected by a disease which we dare not name, which he has always hidden from us and which one of the regiment's medical officers considers incurable. Here is the monster who dared aspire to the hand of my poor sister!

I received my legionnaire's brevet and I now wear the famous ribbon in my buttonhole. You have to know the emperor did not make me a member of the Legion of Honour, but a Chevalier (Knight). I have nothing else to tell you. I still continue to be treated for my pains; they even ordered me flannel drawers and vests. I have aromatic baths every three days. I hope to get better.[10]

Things were equally perilous for the regiment in Spain. Towards the end of May 1813 Wellington launched an offensive which threatened to bypass the French right and cut King Joseph's principal line of communication. With no prospect of aid from France and his army weakened by Napoleon drawing off troops to help rebuild his own army, Joseph had no choice but to fall back towards the Pyrenees. The Ninth quit Salamanca on 24 May and retreated through Burgos and Vitoria, where it arrived on 20 June, closely pursued by Wellington's forces. The following morning a fateful battle was fought on the plain before Vitoria.

As part of the old Army of the South, the Ninth's first two battalions found themselves under the command of General Gazan in the French first line. The battle commenced with a probe by Wellington's right. A Spanish infantry division climbed up onto the Heights of Puebla from where they menaced Gazan's southern flank. The Ninth was among the troops sent to dislodge them, but they found the Spanish advantageously positioned on a precipitous slope, hidden behind rocks. There was fierce fighting as repeated attempts were fruitlessly made to dislodge the Spanish.

By midday fighting had developed across the French line without either side appearing to gain the upper hand. However Wellington had directed one of his columns round the north of the battlefield to fall behind Vitoria and cut the French army's escape route. When this force came into play, King Joseph realized the trap Wellington had set for him. He ordered a general retreat that descended into something of a stampede.

Having been one of the first regiments engaged, the Ninth had one of the longest distances to cover. The only road to safety was packed with thousands of baggage wagons and carriages containing the army's munitions and vast amounts of loot and art treasures plundered from the Spanish. It was all abandoned, along with the artillery and train. The Ninth was extremely lucky that General Reille's soldiers kept the road open long enough for them to escape. On several occasions the British cavalry charged and the regiment had to form square. King Joseph only narrowly avoided capture by British hussars who seized his carriage. If it had not been for the British becoming distracted by heaps of abandoned treasure, he may not have been so lucky. As it was, the battle effectively ended Joseph's reign and he raced off for the safety of the French border. It was an ignominious end to Bonapartist rule in Spain.

The Ninth followed the rest of the army back towards the Pyrenees. Badly weakened at Vitoria the regiment was harried all the way to the border. While passing through the mountains near Etxalar on 30 July 1813, the regiment was attacked by a large guerrilla band commanded by General Espoz y Mina. Almost within sight of the French border Dauture was badly wounded in the leg and had to relinquish command to Battalion Commander Perrin.

The remnants of the regiment occupied a camp christened 'Camp Bayonet' in front of Ascain. Marshal Soult was sent to take command of the army after Vitoria and, after a brief rest, on 31 August he attempted to take the offensive and go in relief of the French garrison at San Sebastian. This resulted in an action with the Spanish known as the battle of San Marcial. At daybreak on 31 August the Ninth formed the head of Taupin's division and marched on the River Bidassoa where they encountered the enemy forward posts. Wading through the water the two battalions breached the Spanish forward posts as planned. Unfortunately the remainder of the army ran into difficulty breaching the Spanish lines. Soult therefore cancelled the operation and ordered his army to return to camp.

In the afternoon the heavens opened, causing the Bidassoa to flood. The mountainous tracks were in a terrible condition and to make matters worse a dense fog descended over the region. When the Ninth reached the river it was found to be impassable. In the morning it had been knee-deep, but by the afternoon it had swollen to nearly 2m in depth. Perrin led the Ninth to the bridge at Vera which was defended by an artillery battery.[11] The obscurity of night and fog played into the Ninth's favour and they were able to force a crossing and regain the camp. Although Soult's planned offensive had failed, the Ninth was awarded 18 crosses of the Legion of Honour in reward for its efforts in the operation. The day was saddened by the death of Captain Régeau, whose two brothers had been killed at Talavera in 1809.

On 7 October the Anglo-Portuguese army attacked Camp Bayonet. Perrin occupied a redoubt which came under heavy attack and the intrepid battalion commander was shot in the thigh and through the chest. As the enemy poured into the redoubt, Perrin and a large number of men were taken captive. The next senior officer was Battalion Commander Nicolas Fouquet who led the regiment to safety, falling back to Ascain.

On 10 November Wellington renewed his attack and pushed the French back towards Biarritz. Five days later, Dauture returned to action, not as colonel, but a general of brigade. Fouquet was given provisional command of the regiment in Spain. It was less than nine years since Fouquet had stood in the Champ de Mars, shivering in the rain and slush, ready to take the eagle from Napoleon's hand. In those nine years he had risen from sergeant-major to acting commander. Any sense of pride the veteran may have felt at this accomplishment must have been tempered by the desperate plight of the army around him.

On 9 December Fouquet had his horse shot from underneath him in another murderous combat known as St-Pierre-d'Irube. After this the regiment fell back onto the outskirts of Bayonne where a reorganization took place. The forward depot was incorporated into 2nd Battalion, which in turn was incorporated into 1st Battalion giving it a strength of 19 officers and 819 men. The cadres of 2nd Battalion (11 officers, 50 men) were sent to Toulouse to form a new 6th Battalion made up of Basque conscripts.[12] To add to the confusion an entirely new 2nd Battalion was formed, officered by recently promoted men or those returning from captivity. Such was the shortage of proficient officers each company was reduced to just two officers.

On 24 March the regiment arrived at Toulouse for the final showdown of the Peninsular War. While the regiment prepared field fortifications, the new 6th Battalion arrived. It was a feeble reinforcement. Just 93 Basques had been recruited, giving the 'battalion' a grand strength of 11 officers and 143 men. However, spirits were buoyed somewhat by the arrival of the new colonel and old friend, Claude D'Eslon.[13]

We last heard of the Ninth's former major in 1810 when he had been held on the hulk *Castilla* in Cadiz harbour. From there he was taken to Palma in the Balearic Islands. Almost shipwrecked off the African coast, D'Eslon was herded into a lazaret for quarantine. Infested with fleas, D'Eslon was transferred to a Spanish prison where he lived in constant dread of being turned over to the local civilians. His biggest fear was the safety of the Spanish royal family held by Napoleon. If King Ferdinand died in captivity, D'Eslon and his colleagues predicted they would be burned at the stake in retaliation. They were frequently pelted with rocks and kept awake all night by their Spanish captors singing, or loudly calling out the challenge '*Sentinella alerta*' every 60 seconds. 'These villains, these blaggards!' he wrote in his journal, desperate for a peaceful night's sleep.

Finally in May 1811, D'Eslon learned he was going to be transferred to Britain. On the one hand he was overjoyed to escape his Spanish tormentors; but at the same time he was melancholic because the transfer showed there would be no quick end to his captivity. He was sent from Palma on 26 June and passed the nearby island of Cabrera to collect other French officers. What D'Eslon saw on this island deeply shocked him. It was a small, deserted rock on which thousands of French prisoners had been dumped and more or less forgotten. 'Good God! What misery we had before our eyes,' he wrote in his journal. 'Almost all our soldiers are naked; a large number came swimming near us to implore help ... We threw all that we could; these poor wretches were sorry to see their officers leaving them.'[14]

The captive French officers arrived off Gibraltar on 10 August 1811 and were transferred to the *Britannia* which set off on a 37-day voyage to Portsmouth. On arrival they were asked to give their word not to attempt escape in return for which the captain gave them money to buy a meal at a local inn. They enjoyed a feast and a walk through some gardens. D'Eslon was transferred to the market town of Chesterfield in Derbyshire and was then quartered in the village of Brampton.

Although their situation was infinitely more comfortable than in Spain, D'Eslon was under no illusion about this 'phantom freedom' he experienced. Although outwardly polite, the locals were intrinsically hostile. D'Eslon met some officers who had been captive for seven years already and had taken work as glove makers or language teachers. Despite a shortage of money, the idea of a civilian trade did not appeal to D'Eslon, so he wrote to his wife to petition the French minister of war for financial assistance. He also appealed to be exchanged for a British officer of similar rank. At one point in 1811 he believed he was going to be exchanged with a Captain Charles Otter, Royal Navy, but nothing came of this.

D'Eslon's journal abruptly ended on 18 April 1811 when he entrusted it to a colleague going home who passed it to D'Eslon's wife. The exact circumstances of D'Eslon's return from England remain something of a mystery. According to his service record D'Eslon returned to France on 23 June 1813 having 'escaped' on 9 June by 'weight of gold'.[15] It is unclear if this refers to bribery, or that he bought his freedom; but in any case, he returned without giving his parole and was therefore at liberty to renew hostilities. Returning to France he was given command of the 15th Light. He appears to have ignored, or petitioned against, this posting and instead travelled south to rejoin his old regiment. D'Eslon rejoined the Ninth as it arrived at Toulouse. By now he must have realized there would be no settling of scores against his Spanish tormentors. Wellington's army was approaching for the final battle of the conflict.

On 10 April the Ninth took part in the battle of Toulouse. It was an infamous affair. The regiment was stationed in the Calvinet redoubt under General Dauture's command. The regiment was doing well until General Taupin's division was routed and stampeded over the redoubt, carrying the Ninth along with them. After rallying, the survivors were forced to retire on Castelnaudry where they learned Napoleon had offered his abdication on 4 April. Toulouse had been fought in vain.

While the Ninth had struggled to prevent Wellington's troops breaking out through the Pyrenees, Napoleon had fought a desperate campaign to protect northern France. The 3rd Battalion was the only one to serve with the emperor as part of Marshal Marmont's VI Corps in Ricard's division. At the beginning of the year, the battalion found itself at Coblenz guarding the Rhine crossings. There was a serious outbreak of cholera in the city which weakened the battalion at the outset of the campaign. Their numbers were further weakened by a succession of gruelling marches and battles. On 30 March the battalion found itself at the gates of Paris, at Belleville defending the French capital from a Russian assault. By then Ricard's division struggled to form a single weak battalion. On 1 April 3rd Battalion's returns showed only nine officers and 37 men remaining. Of these, just 27 were capable of holding their place in the line.

When Marmont began negotiating with the coalition forces to surrender Paris, this handful of survivors were ushered out of the capital to Versailles. Seemingly blind to the hopelessness of their position, Marmont's troops were sickened at the thought of the marshal negotiating behind the emperor's back. Even after the disasters of the previous two years Napoleon's aura was such that the men retained the utmost faith in their emperor's ability to snatch victory from defeat. Marmont's soldiers revolted and made a bolt for Fontainebleau where the emperor was said to be with his Guard. It was to no avail. On 4 April Napoleon abdicated in favour of his son. The allies would not negotiate on this basis so Napoleon signed an unconditional abdication on 11 April and submitted himself to banishment on the Mediterranean island of Elba.

Throughout this last campaign Captain Cardron continued his recovery, moving to Arlon six leagues (24km) north of Longwy. Learning that coalition forces had taken his home town of Philippeville, Cardron wrote to his family on 26 March. Worried about their safety, Cardron was equally concerned with his rising debts:

> ... I have been in a mortal trance for 15 days. I saw in the local newspapers that Philippeville was taken. Since this moment I have not been well. I looked for 20 expedients to write you; but a lack of money has not permitted me to do this. I say the lack of money because besides them not paying us our arrears, they do not pay us currently, which means that until now we have lived on credit. The innkeepers today do not care to make advances and most do not know what will become of us. Moreover, my sickness caused me even more debt, which means I owe about 400 francs. It is true I am due more than 1,200 francs; but when shall we be paid?[16]

As the situation deteriorated further, Cardron donned his uniform and joined the last phases of the campaign. He picked up a slight wound which he reported in a letter dated Longwy, 29 April 1814:

> I hurry to write you to stop worrying about the rumours which are running around. They were not completely without foundations, but I was not in Paris. We did not pass Châlons and I cannot understand who said to you I had been wounded near Paris. We had several actions in the relief of Luxembourg, Thionville and Metz. Everywhere we fought an enemy three times our number. I was rather fortunate to get out of it except for a heavy bruise which I received on the flesh of the right thigh. I had a limp for a few days but at the moment it appears to have gone.[17]

On 17 May 1814 Cardron was complaining about the 'thankless French' abandoning Napoleon. Cardron shared the belief of many that Napoleon had been betrayed by his marshals. True enough, Ney and some of the other marshals had urged Napoleon to abdicate and allow France to live in peace. The Bourbon pretender, King Louis XVIII, arrived in Paris on 3 May and claimed the throne, restoring the old French white flag in place of the tricolour. Cardron was unimpressed and said of the French: 'They well deserve the fate which waits for them: slavery and poverty.'[18]

While waiting at the depot for events to settle down, his principal concerns were the prospect of unemployment and, with the country swarming with victorious allied troops, his sister's safety:

… How is your situation since the invasion of the barbarians? Did any harm come to you? Did you experience any humiliation? I know our enemies so well I dread from them all sorts of ill-treatment; they are capable of anything and I shall be absolutely reassured only when a letter from you assures me nothing of the kind was done to you.

The emperor by his abdication and departure has released us from our oaths towards him and we have sent our adhesion to the new government. There is the question of reorganizing the army, but we do not yet know how they will employ us all …

Meanwhile I have cause to hope for a company and here is the reason. Mr D'Eslon, our old major is now our colonel and although I am one of the least senior captains I will rely on him to employ me. I must not in truth count on a carabineer company because the regiments will never remain at four battalions and ours will be merged; but I have cause to hope for a centre company. If the worst comes to the worst, we will form some colonial regiments and I would prefer to emigrate than to go back to my family and become a burden to them; for I cannot hide from you or myself that I am at present unfit for any career; and which one could I devote myself to? Administration. Indeed, it would be necessary to start as a novice, which it is too late to begin at 29 years of age; and another reason still, and one no less valuable, is an officer with the character of his profession, could not, having commanded as a captain, servilely obey an office manager who, as they almost all are, is shaped by pride and vanity.

So my choice is made. I will remain a serviceman at whatever price and if I am forced to go overseas, I will embrace you for what could be the last time, a good mother and a sister, the only persons whom I value and ask their assent for a separation forced on me by necessity.

While writing this letter, Cardron received a letter from his family, which said his mother did not want to see him posted as a deserter. Cardron took umbrage at this suggestion and concluded his letter thus:

> … You have thus judged me poorly. Did you think me so cowardly to abandon the standards under which I have fought with honour for ten years? No, if it is the French who dishonour themselves, never shall the same criticism be made of your brother. He will know how to die, and he will die without a stain.[19]

By 5 June 1814 Cardron was still unclear as to his fate. The officers taken prisoner at Badajoz and elsewhere were returning home and as a consequence Cardron found himself one of the most junior captains. He still held out hope, writing home on 14 July, 'our colonel, Mr D'Eslon, has just arrived. I have been to visit him. He received me like a son. He has not promised me anything, but I think he will do something for me.'[20]

In fact, D'Eslon was fighting for his own job. On 1 August 1814 the regiment was merged with the 1st and 4th battalions of the 36th Light Infantry. When the Ninth returned from war they had 166 officers, 1,399 men and eight children.[21] For their part the 36th brought 47 officers and an additional 753 men. The new strength of the regiment called for 87 officers and 1,336 men. A number of grades were oversubscribed; for example there were 19 adjutant sub-officers, when the new formation called for three, two drum-majors, 31 sergeant-majors instead of 18, and 127 sergeants instead of 72.

There were also two colonels. Aged 50, Paul Hyppolite Alexandre Baume was the colonel of the 36th. Although a veteran of Napoleon's first Italian campaigns (1796–97) and an old 'Egyptian' wounded in Cairo, Baume had spent much of the war in Holland commanding various corps of observation. He was only called to the Grand Army in 1812 and served in the last campaigns of the war. He was apparently well thought of: 'Colonel Beaume is respectable through his services, his merit and wounds. He is very favourably noted by Count Durutte under whom he made these last campaigns.' D'Eslon was also given the inspector's seal of approval: 'Colonel D' Eslon is an officer of uncommon merit in every respect; his promotion was evidently delayed by the misfortune of being a prisoner of war for a long time. His zeal and dedication are exemplary and a regiment could not be entrusted to better hands.' But which regiment?

Alas for D'Eslon, Baume's promotion to colonel predated his by 20 months. Command of the Ninth was handed to Baume with D'Eslon temporarily remaining in place acting as a major. Cardron was not given a company, but was one of a number of officers provisionally assigned to a 4th Battalion. In 10 August he wrote home with the news and an unusual request:

> I am finally certain of my fate. I have been retained as a supernumerary with active appointments, but I lose 50 francs per month, being sent back to [captain] 3rd class. The carabineer companies were drawn by lottery and I was not fortunate enough to catch one.
>
> I had counted on coming to visit you, but the Duke de Berry has announced all leave will be refused until his departure. In order to obtain [leave] it is necessary to use a ruse. Write to me that mother is very ill and is crying out for me. I will present myself to the colonel who will give in this circumstance a 15-day vacation.[22]

In his next letter (undated) Cardron indicated he was not in the best of health and found walking very difficult. His earlier bravado about joining a colonial regiment had gone. His opportunities for promotion appeared negligible and his only ambition was to seek a military pension and retire. Again his biggest problem was money, presumably to pay off his debts before leaving. Yet again he asked his family to bail him out:

> Now it is no longer a question of having a grand motive but some money. The review takes place at the end of the month and everything is lost if I do not obtain my invalidity. You know the disgust which I have for the military and if I saw myself obliged to remain in this state I would die there. It is the last sacrifice. In the name of God make it and I shall prove to you afterwards my gratitude: the sum which they need from me it is considerable. It is 375 francs.[23]

Another person struggling to come to terms with the peace was one of the Ninth's cantineers, Catherine Campagne.[24] Born on 23 January 1767, she had served as a cantineer for 31 years. It had been a life fraught with heartbreak and difficulty.

Her father had been killed at sea in a previous war. Her first husband was killed, leaving her two children to mother while plodding along behind the regiment with her packhorse, brandy and tobacco. She married a second time, to Joseph Sabatier, a soldier in the Ninth who was killed near Saragossa in Spain. She was captured by the Spanish, deprived of her precious belongings and thrown onto a hulk in Cadiz harbour. Released with the other prisoners at the end of the war she reached Bayonne and set out her story and grievances in a letter addressed to the minister of war on 30 January 1815. In a somewhat rambling letter, she pleaded for his mercy and a widow's pension, concluding 'Now Sir, she is deprived of everything, having lost her belongings with the Army of Spain, she implores your mercy and hopes you take pity on her sad position by granting that which she asks.' Her plight won the attention of General Baron Baurot who added the following endorsement:

> I have the honour of addressing to Our Excellency the petition of the lady Campagne, Catherine whose father and two husbands have been killed in the army, and who still has two children in the service of His Majesty, a point worth taking into consideration by His Excellency if I can take the liberty to recommend her to his humanity.

Another returnee from Cadiz was Nicolas Page. We last saw the unlucky corporal in captivity, confined to a hospital bed in Cadiz early in 1813. After 45 days of sickness, Page was put to work dredging broken masonry from the harbour. His gang master was a fierce 'Barbary African' who worked them day and night. After a time Page secured work as a kitchen porter and as a water carrier. With regular meals his strength returned and with a little money he bought himself new clothes. He began passing himself off as Swiss, from near Grenoble. The British were seeking foreign auxiliaries and Page contemplated enlisting, reasoning anything was better than Spanish enslavement. He obtained a passport which took him to Gibraltar where his service should have begun, but Page could not bear to swear an oath to 'His Britannic Majesty'. Instead he threw his lot in with a motley assortment of deserters and displaced persons, becoming a fisherman for five weeks.

Together with four of his countrymen, Page hatched a plan to reach the French consulate in Tangiers. They duped a young, naive English merchant seaman who sailed them to the Moroccan port where they threw themselves at the mercy of the French consul. With reports of plague in Gibraltar, they waited six tedious months for a transport. When a ship finally arrived they spent a further 29 nervous nights at sea evading Algerian pirates and praying for favourable winds before ending up in Toulon where they were quarantined a further 25 days in case they had contracted the plague. Only then, in the spring of 1814, was Page finally allowed to set off on the long walk home.

At the end of this odyssey, Page knew exactly what he wanted to do. He went home to inform his family he was still alive. He had been away since the summer after Wagram and his father barely recognized him. Page then reported to the depot where he made it clear he was not interested in the army and was discharged on the pretext of 'his wounds'. At last free of military service, Page's first concern was finding a wife, married men being unlikely to be called up. A match was found; the engagement set; the banns read in the local church and everything set for the happy occasion. Alas his luck failed again.

WHERE IS
GROUCHY?

While Nicolas Page was looking forward to married life, Napoleon was also contemplating his future. The terms of his abdication should have provided him with a comfortable retirement on Elba. He was permitted a bodyguard of 800 men and an annual subsidy of two million francs from the French government. However, when this money failed to materialize, Napoleon began to suspect the Bourbons would renege on their commitment. There were rumours of Napoleon being exiled to some remote, godforsaken place and assassination remained a distinct possibility. Napoleon also wanted to be reunited with his wife and son, who had gone to Austria at the end of the war. None of Napoleon's problems could be solved while he remained on Elba.

In his absence, tens of thousands of soldiers had returned to France from fortress garrisons and coalition prisons. Some of these veterans were like Page and just wanted to go home and get on with their lives; but enough were like Cardron: fearful at the prospect of civilian life and unemployment and disgusted with the returning Bourbons and their lackeys. Ever the opportunist, Napoleon predicted the army would support him if he returned and reclaimed the throne. Landing on 1 March 1815, Napoleon marched on Paris. His little bodyguard was swelled by the jubilant defection of regiments sent to intercept him. The more regiments the king sent, the greater Napoleon's army became. On 19 March Louis XVIII fled for the safety of the Belgian border.

When news of Napoleon's return reached the village of Belrupt, Nicolas Page guessed it would spell trouble. It was the week of his wedding, so he went to the mayor and begged for the service to be brought forward to the Monday. The mayor dismissed Page's concern, saying he had not heard of any reason why the marriage could not go ahead. Come the Monday everything had changed. Page received an apologetic note from the mayor saying the local prefect had forbidden him from marrying any discharged soldiers. A few days later his recall arrived. He was ordered to Épinal to undertake a medical and before he knew it, Page was back on the road to Longwy and reporting for duty.

While Page was crestfallen, many of his former colleagues were ecstatic at the emperor's return. An incredible scene was recorded by Cardron in a letter dated Longwy, 9 April 1815:

As I had already written to you, my dear, we departed from here, two battalions, destined for Langres; but arriving at Saint Mihiel, we found a counter-order and after eight days' absence we re-entered our garrison. It appears they knew the spirit of the regiment well, because they feared that once we reached there, we would be turncoats to *Fat Louis* and join the emperor (which would undoubtedly have happened), so they marched us back; but thank God; Napoleon has not needed all the braves that went to meet him, in returning to his capital.

I cannot express the joy we felt when we learned of the news; you can judge how much for without doubt the garrison of Philippeville feels the same; who sees a regiment sees the whole army, it is a great family that has found the father that they had thought lost forever.

We were reviewed by the Prince of the Moskva [Ney] who, like all the marshals, generals, etc ... on seeing the regiment, said the most agreeable things to us; but his words were well chosen: 'Colonel, the emperor loves your regiment, he often recalls with pleasure its fine conduct at Marengo and its bravery in all the glorious affairs where it has been found. He wishes well to all your officers.'

... The day we raised the tricolour cockade, we took up arms. We were at the place where brave Colonel D'Eslon resides. Without knowing why, he formed us up and conducted us to beneath his windows.

Imagine seeing 80 officers in two ranks, asking one another what was going on? What was there? In the end we were filled with worry when we saw Colonel D'Eslon appear, holding in his hands, what? You would not guess what in a hundred years … Our eagle under which we had marched so many times to victory and which the brave colonel had hidden inside the mattress of his bed when *that rotten race of Bourbons* (an expression of the Prince of the Moskva) ascended to the throne and exchanged our cherished colours with those that reminded us of slavery.

At the sight of the cherished standard cries of '*Vive l'Empereur!*' could be heard; soldiers and officers, all overwhelmed, wanted not only to see, but to embrace and touch it; this incident made every eye flow with tears of emotion, and all, in a spontaneous motion; we have promised to die beneath our eagle for the country and Napoleon.[1]

This dramatic scene occurred on 26 March 1815.[2] The last mention of the Ninth's surviving eagle had been in 1807 when Napoleon ordered it returned to the depot. In 1808 the eagle remained at the depot and no new eagle-bearers were assigned in the reorganization of the regiment. However, there are indications that the eagle was taken to Spain. Among the list of wounded officers at Chiclana is eagle-bearer Lieutenant Mathieu. From the regimental rolls we find the second and third eagle-bearers were appointed on 1 May 1809.[3] However, these appointments may have been simply honorific, a way of favouring old soldiers with extra pay.

One of the Ninth's 'book of orders' was captured by Portuguese troops after an action on 7 September 1813. This book contains a specific order from Marshal Soult which said that regiments with two battalions in Spain, but with fewer than 1,000 men under arms, had to return their eagles to France. The eagles were to be wrapped in a case and sent to the director of post at Bayonne who would dispatch them to the relevant depot.[4] It may be no coincidence to see the third bearer, Piard pensioned off at the forward depot at Bayonne on 25 October 1813. Had he just escorted the eagle back to France as instructed? In any case the eagle was most likely at Longwy in 1814 and was hidden by D'Eslon on his return to the depot.[5]

A second standard went missing in 1814. When the remnants of the regiment returned to Longwy some of the older officers were pensioned off. One of these was Battalion Commander Fouquet, who retired on 30 July 1814. He was awarded a certificate with his service record and a message of the regiment's regrets and thanks for his long service. When Fouquet went into retirement at Verdun he was secretly entrusted with the surviving 1802 'Marengo' flag to avoid it falling into the hands of the Prussians. One can imagine Fouquet toasting his emperor's return with great delight.

Alas the great powers of Europe were not amused by Napoleon's reappearance, forming a seventh coalition even before he reached Paris. Declaring Napoleon an outlaw, Britain, Russia, Austria and Prussia each promised to put forward an army of 150,000 men to put a stop to Napoleon, once and for all. Of course, it would take time for these forces to assemble on the French border, particularly the Austrian and Russian armies, and this delay helped formulate Napoleon's strategy.

One option was to remain on the defensive; continue to rebuild the army, fortify Paris and Lyon, arm the peasants and train them for guerrilla warfare, then wage a mobile campaign as in 1814. With the army properly rested and re-equipped, this time Napoleon would have far more chance of defeating the coalition partners. Although there was merit in this approach, it meant Napoleon would have to surrender the initiative and this was not his style. He would take the war to his enemies.

The emperor's attention turned to Belgium where Wellington and Blücher's armies were camped. Although both armies screened the approaches to Brussels, their lines of communication went in opposite directions: Wellington's westwards to Ostend and the Channel; Blücher's eastwards towards Prussia. Combined, these armies were numerically superior to Napoleon's forces with 200,000 men; but if he could drive a wedge between them, Napoleon believed he could defeat each force in turn. The key to the campaign was surprise and speed. Wellington and Blücher could not be given time or opportunity to unite.

In the first days of June the Ninth was ordered to Philippeville, Cardron's home town. Just prior to leaving the depot the first two battalions were brought up to strength with men who had been earmarked for a new 3rd Battalion. This gave the regiment a field strength of 45 officers and 1,230 men under the command of Colonel Baume. Although the majority were veterans of former campaigns, a great many were like Nicolas Page and had only arrived back at the regiment two to four weeks before it set out. The condition of their uniform, equipment and fitness must have been somewhat questionable.[6]

At Philippeville the Ninth joined the brigade of General Hulot in the division of General Bourmont, a former émigré who had been a leader in the 1799 Chouan revolt which the Ninth had helped subjugate. A few old-timers in the Ninth like battalion commanders Billon and Parant would have been aware of the general's dubious pedigree.[7]

In total Napoleon managed to assemble 128,000 men in what was called the Army of the North. This was formed of five infantry corps, four cavalry corps and the Imperial Guard. The Ninth was in IV Corps under Count Etienne Gérard stationed on the right flank of the army. Napoleon's plan was to cross the Sambre at Charleroi and advance on Brussels, attacking the Prussians on the right with the bulk of the army, while Marshal Ney screened Wellington on the left. Once the Prussians were sent reeling eastwards, Napoleon would shift his reserves to the left and defeat Wellington. On paper it was a brilliant strategy and confidence in the army was high.

On 14 June Napoleon made a proclamation to his army: 'Soldiers, today is the anniversary of Marengo and Friedland, which twice decided the destiny of Europe. Then, as after Austerlitz, as after Wagram, we were too generous ...' It stirred up the soldiers' passions, reminding them they had been outnumbered by the Prussians at Jena in 1806 and in the campaigns of 1814. Napoleon invoked the anger of those who had suffered on the English prison hulks. The proclamation ended with a rallying cry: 'Soldiers, we have forced marches before us, battles to fight, perils to face. But, with perseverance, victory must be ours; right, honour and the happiness of our country will be regained. For every Frenchman who is good-hearted, the moment has come to conquer or die.'[8]

Having received the emperor's exhortation the Ninth was up early on 15 June, standing to arms at 3am and waiting for the signal to march. It did not arrive. The messenger bringing the order had fallen off his horse and broken a leg. Weary of waiting for orders, General of Brigade Hulot went looking for General Bourmont to find out what was causing the delay. Hulot was told Bourmont was already in the saddle and away from his headquarters. Hulot thought nothing of it, but shortly after 6am a party of horse chasseurs caught up with him bringing letters from Bourmont addressed to Count Gérard. Bourmont and his staff had quit the horse chasseurs near the Prussian forward posts, leaving a verbal instruction for Hulot that they were going to rejoin Louis XVIII and Hulot was to give Gérard the letters. This news caught Hulot completely off-guard. He informed Gérard immediately then summoned Baume and the colonel of the 111th Line, telling them to keep their men under arms and in ranks.[9]

Hulot was right to be alarmed. When the men heard the news there was uproar. Although morale among the soldiers appeared very good, it was also very brittle. It had only been a year since Napoleon had, in the eyes of his soldiers, been betrayed by generals. At the same time there could have been little surprise at being sold out by a former Chouan like Bourmont. In order to calm the situation Hulot rode up and down before his two regiments, sword in hand promising to 'fight with them against the enemies of France until his last breath.'[10] Gérard also quickly made an appearance, riding up and down the lines of men. Bourmont's desertion was extremely embarrassing for Gérard. The count had personally lobbied Napoleon to give a division to Bourmont. The emperor was initially against the idea of employing the royalist, but gave in, after which Gérard allegedly promised to answer for Bourmont's conduct with his own head. After the optimism of the day before, this was a very bad start to the campaign.[11]

When calm was eventually restored the Ninth crossed the Sambre at Châtelet, marching at the head of Gérard's corps. By nightfall only the lead division had crossed, now under Hulot's command. The Ninth camped at Cathelineau. Meanwhile the emperor had attacked the Prussians on the road to Namur and driven them back.

On 16 June Napoleon encountered the Prussians in strength beyond Fleurus, scene of a famous French victory in 1794. The Prussian commander, Blücher, had concentrated three army corps behind the bowed line of the Ligny brook, occupying the villages of St Amand, Ligny and Sombreffe. Delayed crossing the Châtelet bridge, Gérard did not arrive on the field until nearly 2pm. He took position on the right of Vandamme's corps, placing the divisions of Pécheux and Vichery in front of the Namur road facing Ligny while Hulot's division was at a right angle to this line, straddling the road opposite Potriaux and Tongrinelle, facing the Prussian left.

At 3pm three artillery shots rang out at regular intervals – Napoleon's signal to attack. All along the French line the bands struck up their military airs while the soldiers shouted the old battle cry: *Vive L'Empereur!* Vandamme opened the battle with an attack on the village of St Amand. After this attack was bludgeoned to a standstill, Gérard directed the divisions of Vichery and Pécheux in a frontal attack on Ligny. Step by step Gérard's men advanced, fighting for every ditch and tree with unyielding fury. When the soldiers broke into the villages the fighting was hand-to-hand with no quarter expected or received. The buildings caught fire as the Prussians threw in repeated counter-attacks to hold their line.

While these bloody attacks were made on St Amand and Ligny, Hulot's division began probing the Prussian left. At 4pm the Ninth's voltigeurs began advancing in skirmish formation followed by the remainder of the regiment in two columns, the first advancing eastwards towards Tongrinelle, the other northwards in the direction of Sombreffe. As this advance through fields of tall crops began, artillery fire opened from both sides with a number of enemy balls directed at the advancing light infantrymen. As the two adversaries came into musket range a series of heavy skirmishes developed. The French fought their way over the Ligny brook and fought over the hamlet of Tongrinne and the farm of Potriaux. Around 5pm the Prussians mounted a strong counter-attack and drove Hulot's men back across the brook, capturing a handful of voltigeurs as they went. The Prussians formed a chain of skirmishers along the edge of the brook and remained on the defence, waiting for the next French attack.

Around 7pm Hulot received reinforcements in the guise of a battalion of the 30th Line. This battalion had already been mauled in the fighting around Ligny village, so Hulot kept it in reserve. Half an hour later the Prussians finally advanced across the brook towards the French positions. The Ninth's skirmishers profited from the failing light and tall crops to fire on the approaching Prussians, popping up unexpectedly on the flanks and rear of the Prussian force and wreaking havoc. As this attack fizzled out the decisive moment of the battle was reached elsewhere on the field.

At 8.30pm the battlefield was plunged into darkness by a thunderstorm. Most of Ligny was in French hands and the Prussians were low on reserves. Napoleon judged this the moment to launch his reserve at the Prussian centre and bring the action to its close. As a monstrous barrage by 60 guns crashed down on the Prussians, the bearskins of the Imperial Guard were seen marching in two columns on either flank of Ligny. By now the Prussians were exhausted and unable to maintain their positions. As the last glimpses of sunlight broke through the darkening, cloudy sky Blücher's army finally began to retreat.

The French were equally exhausted and the troops bivouacked on the battlefield. The Ninth slept around Potriaux farm. Although it had been spared the slaughter of Ligny, the Ninth had suffered significant casualties. In total four officers were killed in action, including Battalion Commander Pierre Billon, who had commanded 3rd Battalion at Badajoz. A further ten officers were wounded in the battle and Colonel Baume had his horse shot from underneath him.[12] The regimental rolls record the names of 35 men killed at Ligny, with 230 wounded and three prisoners; a casualty rate exceeding 20 per cent.

On 17 June there was no vigorous pursuit. The Napoleon of old would have had them marching through the night on the Prussians' heels, just like after Jena; but this time the Prussians were allowed to make off relatively unmolested. The morning after battle the emperor instructed Marshal Emmanuel de Grouchy that he wished to make a tour of the battlefield at 8am. While the Prussians continued their retreat, Napoleon satisfied himself with talking to prisoners and encouraging his men. Only at 1pm was Napoleon shaken into action with news that the British were still in front of Ney and the left wing at Quatre Bras.

Racing after Wellington, Napoleon finally gave Grouchy his instructions. He was to take the corps of Vandamme and Gérard along with Teste's division and the cavalry of Pajol and Exelmans, a total of 30,000 men. They were ordered to Gembloux to reconnoitre the movement of the Prussians who were supposedly heading eastwards on their lines of communication in the direction of Namur and Liege.

While Napoleon toured the battlefield, the exhausted Frenchmen used the time to make soup and strip down their muskets for cleaning. When the order to march arrived the infantry were not ready for an immediate start. It was well into the afternoon before Grouchy's forces were ready to march. Vandamme's corps took the lead. Hulot rejoined Gérard's corps at Ligny and set out for Gembloux. Not long into the march the heavens opened; a deluge came down and the march slowed to a crawl. That night the Ninth attempted to bivouac behind Gembloux soaked to the skin. The weather was so bad, Grouchy ordered Gérard to issue his men with a double ration of brandy.[13]

On 18 June Gérard's troops were ready to march in the early hours, but the order to move out did not arrive until 10am.[14] It had first appeared that the Prussians were marching eastwards in the direction of Liege; however, the Prussians had in fact fallen back northwards to Wavre, a crossing point on the River Dyle on the road to Brussels. All the indications were that the Prussians were marching on the Belgian capital and were planning to join Wellington the following day.

Once the Prussian line of retreat had been established, Grouchy had Gérard follow Vandamme's corps. A further delay was caused by both army corps using the same churned-up road. Gérard's men were unable to move off until all of Vandamme's corps had passed. After marching a league in the direction of Wavre, at approximately 11am, Grouchy invited Gérard to dine with him at a farmhouse at Walhain. The count was frustrated at the snail-like pursuit. When he entered the farmhouse, Grouchy was eating strawberries. As the meal progressed, Gérard's aide-de-camp, de Rumigny, heard the sound of artillery to the west. He put his ear to a stone wall to amplify the sound and, sure enough, he could distinctly hear the detonation of guns of different calibre. The aide-de-camp went into the farmhouse and reported the sound of artillery to Grouchy.

The marshal appeared somewhat blasé at the news. He knew the emperor had encountered Wellington's army in front of the forest of Soignes the evening before. He expected the British to retreat in front of Napoleon and attempt a junction with the Prussians at Brussels. In fact he had only recently written to the emperor informing him he would be at Wavre by the evening, in a position to place himself between Wellington and Blücher the following day.[15] He dismissed the sound as nothing but a rearguard action.

De Rumigny persisted and asked Grouchy to come and hear for himself. The sound was indistinct, but this faint rumble of guns provoked one of the most famous arguments in military history. 'I think we should march to the guns,' advised Gérard. Grouchy stuck to his line about a rearguard action and became 'vexed' as the debate continued. The roads to the battlefield were poor and flooded by rain. Even if they did set off in that direction, he added, they would never arrive in time to be useful. Opinion was split. Gérard then overstepped his authority, saying to Grouchy, 'Marshal, it is your duty to march towards the guns.'

'My duty,' countered Grouchy, 'is to execute the orders of the emperor which prescribe me to follow Prussians: it would be to infringe his instructions to obey your advice.'[16]

They now received a report from General Excelmans, whose scouts reported the Prussians had crossed the River Dyle at Wavre and were marching to join

Wellington. Grouchy disagreed with the analysis. The Prussians were heading for Brussels, he believed, and would attempt to join Wellington's forces there. Gérard made a final plea, asking Grouchy to allow him to take just his corps to join Napoleon. Grouchy would not allow this. His forces would be split by the river Dyle, something he described as 'an unpardonable military fault'.[17] Gérard walked out disgusted, saying to his aide-de-camp, 'He's not going to do anything; it's terrible.'[18]

The Ninth's march continued towards Wavre, slowly plodding along behind Vandamme. On their left they could hear the thunder of guns intensify. Around 1pm, when Napoleon unleashed an 80-gun barrage on the British line, there was no mistaking the sound of a pitched battle. Then the murmuring began. It was obvious to everyone they were marching in the wrong direction. At Marengo they had famously turned round and arrived on the battlefield in the nick of time. Why was Grouchy being so stubborn?

In fact Grouchy was indeed concerned at the thundering barrage to the left. It had continued too long to be a simple rearguard action, but he received no word from Napoleon until shortly after 3.30pm. The letter had been written at 10am and ordered Grouchy to march on Wavre. Although the letter had been written before the battle commenced, Grouchy felt vindicated in ignoring Gérard's impertinent demands.

It was 4pm by the time the Ninth arrived at Wavre. The Prussians were firmly entrenched on the far side of the Dyle with the bridges in the town heavily barricaded and protected by artillery. Vandamme had dithered and no serious inroads had been made. He had tried outflanking the position by seizing a bridge on the left at Bierges but this attack had foundered.

At 5pm another message arrived for Grouchy timed at 1pm. Prior to sending the message Napoleon had seen a 'dark shadow' to the north-east of his position in the direction of Chapelle-Saint-Lambert. Cavalry had been sent to investigate and a Prussian officer captured. This officer confirmed the mass of infantry was the advanced guard of Bülow's corps, which had crossed the Dyle at Wavre the day before with no sign of Grouchy's forces.

Napoleon added a postscript to the message, which read: '… General Bülow has attacked our flank; we believe we can perceive this corps on the heights of Saint-Lambert; so do not lose a moment to move closer to us and join us, crushing Bülow, whom you will take in flagrante delicto.'[19] Grouchy must have felt sick reading this instruction. He had denied Gérard's request to march towards the emperor when there was still a slim chance of arriving.

With Vandamme struggling to find a way across the Dyle at Wavre, Grouchy needed to find another crossing point if he was to intercept the Prussians. So far only Hulot's division had arrived at Wavre. Grouchy ordered the remainder of Gérard's corps towards the bridge at Limale, which had been seized by light cavalry. To deter the Prussians from sending reinforcements to Limale, Grouchy ordered Hulot's division to make a diversionary attack on Bierges and pin down the Prussian reserves.

Grouchy and Gérard led Hulot's division towards Bierges where Lefol's division from Vandamme's corps had made several attempts to cross the Dyle. On arrival it soon became apparent why the previous attacks had failed. The Prussians had a division guarding the bridge and a nearby windmill and farm, which formed an excellent defensive stronghold. The Prussians had cut a section of the bridge and counter-attacked every time French engineers had gone forward to repair the damage.[20] To make matters worse, the ground either side of the bridge was extremely swampy and cut with ditches running parallel to the river.

Grouchy ordered the Ninth's 1st Battalion to renew the attack. Although the purpose of the attack was diversionary, if the Ninth could seize the crossing it would certainly be advantageous. Realizing the bridge was cut, Hulot directed the battalion to advance on the flanks of the bridge, over the broken ground. If Hulot could get enough skirmishers close to the bridge it might afford the engineers time to restore the bridge. The battalion's voltigeurs were sent forwards with orders to wade across the ditches if they were too wide to leap. As the first men jumped in they disappeared. The ditches were filled to the brim by rainwater and were up to six feet deep. The little voltigeurs were dragged down by the weight of their equipment and struggled to keep their heads above water. Several were hit by Prussian skirmishers on the opposite side of the river as they struggled to fish their comrades out of the ditches. The impetus of the attack was quickly snuffed out, so the battalion withdrew and regrouped.

At the sight of this check, Grouchy got off his horse and went to encourage the men for a second attack. Gérard did likewise, taking off his overcoat before advancing towards the Prussians. With his medals revealed, Gérard was an obvious target to Prussian sharpshooters. Men began falling either side of him and then Gérard was struck square in the chest. While Gérard was carried to the rear severely wounded, Grouchy turned to the artillery commander, General Baltus, and ordered him to take Gérard's place at the head of the Ninth's 2nd Battalion. Baltus refused. Grouchy became increasingly exasperated, so left Hulot in observation at Bierges and went to Limale to supervise the remainder of Gérard's division. With this, any hope the Ninth had of repeating their late arrival at Marengo vanished entirely.[21]

As the Ninth stood watching the Prussians on the other side of the Dyle, the curtain was falling on the Napoleonic era. As the sound of artillery fire petered out to the west, Grouchy's men had no inkling of the disaster at Waterloo. In fact there was some cause for optimism. Grouchy had secured the bridge at Limale. Shortly before midnight Grouchy ordered Vandamme to come to the bridge and in the morning they would go to rejoin the emperor outside Brussels.

The combat resumed at 3am. Grouchy advanced and seized Bierges joining up with Hulot's division. At 10.30am they were preparing to start out for Brussels when a dispatch rider arrived from Marshal Soult. One look at the man's miserable face revealed something was wrong. The officer did not carry any written orders for Grouchy, but gave an emotional account of the previous day's battle. Grouchy instinctively knew he would be blamed for not marching towards the sound of the guns. Nonetheless, Grouchy summoned his commanders and told them the news. It was scarcely believable, but Napoleon had been utterly defeated and the army was in headlong flight, streaming back to the French frontier as a disorganized mob. What were they to do?

Vandamme counselled marching on Brussels, a reckless piece of advice. Grouchy's 30,000 men were all that was left of the French army. The allies combined had five times that number. It was Grouchy's duty to get back to France and allow the remnants of the army to rally around him and defend Paris from the inevitable invasion. Grouchy chose a route through Namur, Dinant and Givet praying the Prussians had not already got ahead of them and taken Gembloux. The retreat began shortly before midday. The Ninth reached Gembloux at 9pm with the last of Vandamme's corps arriving two hours later. The road to France was open and despite the constant harrying by the Prussians, they finally crossed the frontier and arrived at Givet on the evening of 21 June.

Picking up the debris of Napoleon's army on the way, Grouchy steadily fell back on Paris. On 25 June Grouchy announced Napoleon had abdicated in favour of his son three days before. A new provisional government had been formed and recognized Napoleon II as emperor. Grouchy's proclamation called on the soldiers to remain faithful to the new emperor and to rally round their eagles while the politicians attempted to negotiate a peace which recognized French independence.

With the army already in a state of chaos, news of the abdication was a further blow to morale. Since Waterloo, desertion had steadily increased. The regimental rolls show 29 men deserted between 19 and 24 June. Before the end of the month 298 more had quit the colours for the last time. This rate is partly explained by the defection of large numbers of the Imperial Guard who, after the news of the abdication was made, encouraged their comrades to desert and rush to Paris to support Napoleon. In reality, many would have just decided to return home to help protect their farms and family.

On 29 June, the remnants of Gérard's IV Corps took up position at Vaugirard guarding the southern approach to Paris. Repeated peace overtures had come to nothing and the allies were not going to stop until Louis XVIII was restored to the throne. On 2 July the Prussians attacked near Issy. It was a fiasco which ended up in an unseemly French retreat. In the fighting Colonel D'Eslon's 19-year-old son, Sub-Lieutenant Joseph D'Eslon, was killed. He was the colonel's only son and his loss must have been devastating to a man who had already suffered so much. The loss was doubly cruel as it occurred on the last day of the war.[22]

On 3 July a treaty was signed. Napoleon's army was permitted to retire behind the river Loire while the Prussians occupied Paris.[23] The Ninth's depot had already been sent away from the frontier at the beginning of the campaign. Major Mourèze had been directed to the town of Niort in the department of Deux-Sèvres on 15 July. Having so readily served Napoleon, the army did not expect to be forgiven by the returning monarch.

Among those in the depot in those final days was Captain Cardron. His first concerns were for his family in Philippeville, as his home town had been under siege and bombardment. On 1 September he announced to his sister he would soon be coming home as the army was to be entirely broken up.

> [The army] is going to be dismissed, for it to be reorganized into departmental legions. All the officers, the non-commissioned officers and the soldiers of the same department will be directed on the departmental capital, thus expect to see me again soon. What a pleasure to squeeze you in my arms, but what a return and in what circumstances!
>
> And … what will become of us![24]

On 15 September the marshal of camps de Vittré passed the remnants of the 3rd, 4th and 5th battalions in review. There were just 35 officers, 327 men and another 22 in hospital at the time. The following day, the detachments went their separate ways to the four corners of France. Once they arrived in their respective departmental capitals, all the men with more than eight years' service were dismissed. The rest were kept on to form a new army.

On 18 September the two field battalions formed up for a final review by General Berthezène at Saint-Germain-Lembron (Puy-de-Dôme). The regiment had already been stripped of its eagle on 26 August. It was later sent to Paris and destroyed with the other flags of the Imperial army on 22 October 1815. There were just 36 officers and 380 men left. Following the same procedure as the depot, the 1st and 2nd battalions were broken up and formed into detachments. The following day they each said their farewells and marched off to an uncertain future.[25]

The last act was administrative: the formation of a five-man council of administration.[26] The president was Colonel Baume, of whom the inspector wrote: 'This officer does not appear well versed in administration; there are many complaints in his corps, however I do not believe that we can suspect his probity.' He was seconded by Battalion Commander Nicolas Parant, paymaster Louis Antoine Protin and captains Nicolas Coffin and Pierre Gros.[27] This caretaker council would remain in existence until October 1815, when the money and stores were handed over to the newly formed Legion of Ardennes.

It is fitting in this final phase of the regiment's history to find a man who had been present at the beginning of its story. Carabineer Captain Pierre Gros had been enrolled in the corps on 25 September 1784; the day after the chasseur battalion was formed in Carcassonne. His father was Captain Pierre Gros, the former clothing and then recruitment officer. Young Pierre Gros had literally been a babe in arms when he was signed up, barely two years old. His childhood had been spent in the depot, growing up listening to his father's tall stories and, at the age of 16, he followed him into uniform along with his younger brother Joseph. Reaching the lofty rank of carabineer captain, Gros shared his father's fate in being seriously wounded. He was shot through the leg by a Prussian in 1806, bayoneted in the face at Talavera and was left for dead on the field at Vitoria in 1813 and captured. On his return to France he would have drawn straws with Cardron for the right to command one of the two carabineer companies in the reorganization of 1814.

It is perhaps true that the men of the Ninth never again shone as brightly as they did at Marengo; but let us not forget the intensity of their brilliance that day. When given the opportunity to change the course of a lost battle, they seized it and will live long in the annals of military history for doing so. Marengo was unquestionably the platform on which the empire was built. Dark moments were to follow, such as Mohrungen and the many evils of the war in Spain; but the regiment's reputation lived on.

Had their luck been different at Talavera, perhaps the Ninth's daring night attack would have rivalled Marengo as their finest hour. How different history may have been if a defeated Sir Arthur Wellesley had not become Wellington? And what of Waterloo: what would have happened if Gérard had been granted the freedom to march westwards before noon? Marching at the head of Gérard's Corps, what if the Ninth had caught the Prussians on the march as Napoleon hoped? How different would Waterloo have been if Napoleon's reserves had not been used up at Plancenoit and if the Prussians had been delayed two or three hours longer?

EPILOGUE

Although the Ninth never reached the field at Waterloo, a few familiar faces were present that fateful day. Generals Barrois and Meunier were with the Young Guard, fighting the Prussians at Plancenoit. Barrois took a bullet in the shoulder, but lived to fight another day. As an imperial count he served in the army until 1848. He died on 19 October 1860 leaving two daughters. Meunier served the Bourbons, but remained a passionate supporter of Napoleon for the rest of his life. In 1842 he wrote a book describing Napoleon's military career for the benefit of his children. Meunier parted this world in 1846. His wife buried him in her father's plot in Paris' Montmartre cemetery, where he rests today.

Meunier and Barrois have their names carved onto the Arc de Triomphe in Paris along with Auguste Caffarelli. Caffarelli was made a peer of France in 1831 and died in 1849 after a long illness. His successor, Mathieu Labassée, was made a baron in 1808, but never progressed beyond the rank of brigadier general. He died on 25 August 1830 leaving a wife, daughter and a son, Frédéric, a lieutenant in the 5th Hussars. At the time of his death there were rumours he had been assassinated for supporting the 1830 July Revolution which overturned the reign of Charles X. His grave at Villecresnes is inscribed in French, with the epithet 'Colonel of the 9th Light at MARENGO.' The battle remained his crowning achievement.

General Dauture retired to Pau after the Napoleonic Wars. He was a bachelor without children and died after a sickness on 12 April 1820 aged just 50.

During the 1815 campaign, Colonel D'Eslon served as fortress commandant at Guise. Mourning the loss of his son, he retired from the army and went to Charmes where he died on 22 December 1832, aged 69. Colonel Baume also retired in 1815. He died on 23 July 1842 at Metz and was survived by a wife and four children.

Pierre Gros the elder lived to the ripe old age of 94, not passing away until 17 September 1844. His friend Christian Kuhmann died at St Cyr in 1811 aged 67. The Bavarian basket weaver's apprentice had risen to the rank of French imperial baron with an annual income of 2,000 francs.

The hero of Piacenza, Hippolyte Cazaux, commanded the 18th Light Infantry until he lost his left leg in Croatia. In 1811 he was named colonel-major of the Hôtel des Invalides, a post he retained until 1837. He passed away in 1846.

The heroic Surgeon-Major Charles Vanderbach made it through to the end of the wars and became a distinguished doctor, rising to surgeon-chief of the military hospital in Thionville. After retiring from the military in 1836 he continued in his grade at the civilian hospital in the same town and was noted for the way he helped the poor during outbreaks of cholera. He had a passion for the natural sciences and became an avid fossil collector in his spare time. One of the bravest men who ever served in the Ninth, he was described in his obituary as having a 'gay and amiable' nature. His passing on 21 July 1851 was regretted by his children and all who knew him.

Captain Cardron offered his resignation at the end of the war and returned to Philippeville. In 1817 he married Marie-Madeleine Picq and had three daughters. With Philippeville coming under Dutch control in 1815, Cardron was again pressed into military service. By 1820 his doctor recorded the former captain was suffering from 'chronic rheumatism' as a result of the hardships he had faced and his wounds. He died at the age of 59 on 25 July 1845.

Maurice Godet retired from the Imperial Guard and married Jeanne Suzanne on 15 June 1811. He became the manager of a tobacco bonding-house and wrote his memoirs for his grandchildren in 1846. He died in 1869 at the grand old age of 96.

Félix Girod had a long military career. After leaving the Ninth he went to Russia and fought at Borodino, one of the most epic battles of the era. He was fortunate to be spared the infamous retreat from Moscow, having returned to

Berlin with the wounded General Dessaix; but he fought in France during 1814 and had the ignominy of being in Paris when the coalition troops paraded through the streets. As an enthusiastic supporter of Napoleon's return, Girod was put on half pay after Waterloo until 1818. He remained in the army in a variety of staff positions and became chief of the Historical Section of the War Depot in 1839. He finally retired from the army in 1851. Girod married his first cousin Marie Fabry in 1814. She died in 1828 leaving Girod with five young children. Hi memoirs were published in 1873 so his family might know the events he witnessed as one of Napoleon's soldiers.

Of course many of the officers remained in touch, some through their membership of the Free Masons and others through correspondence. A focal point for their social network appears to have been the former standard-bearer, Battalion Commander Fouquet. At the end of the wars, the surviving officers came by to ask him for their own little portion of the 'Marengo' flag and so over the years the silk dwindled. When Captain Dubois corresponded with Fouquet for his 1839 history, all that remained of the 1802 flag was a small piece upon which were the letters 'RABLE'. Within a year Fouquet was gone, passing away on 16 May 1840 leaving his wife Charlotte and a single son, Théodore Achilles, a 'painter of history' residing in Paris.

As a mark of commemoration to his illustrious uncle, in 1857 the Emperor Napoleon III awarded the survivors of the campaigns from 1792–1815 with the 'Medal of St Helena'. Today the list of recipients is fragmented, but it is clear many former soldiers from the Ninth were around to toast their former emperor's memory. One of the recipients was Nicolas Page.

Page's memoirs are silent of what he witnessed on the 1815 campaign. He was actually posted as a deserter on 11 July after the regiment began its march behind the Loire. Having had his fill of soldiering, Page's life was modest and typical of those drawn from the Vosges. After the Waterloo campaign he returned home and married Marie-Josèphe Mouginé. He hired a farm in the commune of Bonvillet and worked the land – the only trade he knew outside of soldiering. In 1816 they had a daughter, Marie Page. As a father, Page toiled hard, meeting catastrophe when an epidemic wiped out most of his livestock in 1817. His wife was frail and needed medicines which Page could barely afford. His father-in-law was a miller, so Page gave up farming and took up this trade. In 1838 his wife died leaving Page with a broken heart. His family convinced him to marry again in 1840. After the privations experienced in his youth, Page's own health began to fail. He was unable to operate the mill. He retired to a poor house living with the children of his second wife, Agnès, and died in relative poverty during his 74th year in 1863. Before passing away, sometime between 1844 and 1848, Page set down into words his adventures with the Ninth for Napoleon.

APPENDICES

THE COMMANDERS 1784–1815

24 September 1784	Colonel Viscount François-Emmanuel de Toulongeon
1 May 1788	Lieutenant-Colonel Chevalier Joseph de Barroussel
1 April 1790	Lieutenant-Colonel Pierre Justin Marchand de Villionne
25 July 1791	Lieutenant-Colonel Jacques-Marie-Blaise Segond de Sederon
6 April 1793	Lieutenant-Colonel Mathieu Labassée
19 February 1794	Brigade Commander Michel Eirisch
4 June 1797	Brigade Commander Marie-François-Auguste de Caffarelli du Falga
4 January 1800	Brigade Commander Mathieu Labassée
19 July 1803	Colonel Claude-Marie Meunier
18 February 1810	Colonel Guilhem Dauture
25 November 1813	Colonel Claude-Marcel D'Eslon
1 August 1814	Colonel Paul Hyppolite Alexandre Baume

ORGANIZATIONAL SUMMARY 1758–1815

The Napoleonic 9th Light Infantry had its roots in the Seven Years War. In 1815 the Ninth's depot and material passed to the Legion of Ardennes, which became 1st Light Infantry in 1820; then 76th Line in 1855. After the Napoleonic Wars, a new 9th Light Infantry Regiment was created in 1820. This new regiment adopted the traditions of the Napoleonic regiment despite having no administrative link to the old regiment. The new 9th Light went on to form the 84th Line in 1855. On the eve of the Great War (1914–18) the 84th Line was carrying the battle honour 'Marengo' on its standard and had adopted the name *Incomparable*.

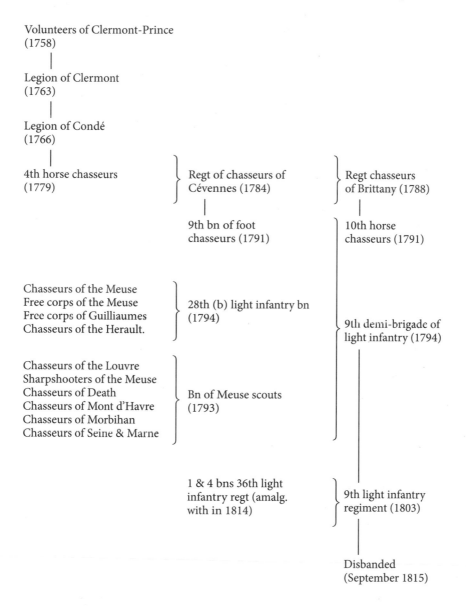

Volunteers of Clermont-Prince
(1758)

Legion of Clermont
(1763)

Legion of Condé
(1766)

4th horse chasseurs
(1779)

Regt of chasseurs of
Cévennes (1784)

Regt chasseurs
of Brittany (1788)

9th bn of foot
chasseurs (1791)

10th horse
chasseurs (1791)

Chasseurs of the Meuse
Free corps of the Meuse
Free corps of Guilliaumes
Chasseurs of the Herault.

28th (b) light infantry bn
(1794)

9th demi-brigade of
light infantry (1794)

Chasseurs of the Louvre
Sharpshooters of the Meuse
Chasseurs of Death
Chasseurs of Mont d'Havre
Chasseurs of Morbihan
Chasseurs of Seine & Marne

Bn of Meuse scouts
(1793)

1 & 4 bns 36th light
infantry regt (amalg.
with in 1814)

9th light infantry
regiment (1803)

Disbanded
(September 1815)

MUSKET OF HONOUR CITATIONS FOR THE MARENGO CAMPAIGN

Citizen Petit, sergeant-major in the 9th Light Demi-Brigade, at the action of Marengo, where this sub-officer advanced alone against the Austrian skirmishers, killing several and taking three prisoners.

Citizen Davion, sergeant-major in the 9th Light Demi-Brigade, at the action which took place on 25 Prairial Year 8, at Marengo, where this sub-officer penetrated the enemy ranks several times and took four prisoners.

Citizen Maquart, sergeant in the 9th Light Demi-Brigade, at the action of Marengo, where this sub-officer, at the head of a piquet of six men, gave proof of great firmness in successfully resisting a charge of twelve enemy cavalrymen.

Citizen Jacques, sergeant in the 9th Light Demi-Brigade, at the action of Marengo, where this sub-officer, at the head of some skirmishers, having been charged by the enemy cavalry, whose goal was to fall on the battalion, was held in respect by his intrepidity, dismounted several riders and forced the others to give up the project to advance further.

Citizen Benoist, sergeant in the 9th Demi-Brigade of Light Infantry, in the action at Marengo, where this sub-officer, detached as a skirmisher, having been charged by two Austrian cavaliers, dismounted one and made the other prisoner.

Citizen Bouvier, corporal of carabineers in the 9th Demi-Brigade of Light Infantry, in the action which took place on the 25 Prairial, Year 8, at Marengo, where this serviceman penetrated on diverse occasions the enemy ranks and killed several men with the bayonet.

Citizen Mahut, corporal of carabineers in the 9th Demi-Brigade of Light Infantry, in the action at Marengo, where this serviceman, seeing a dragoon officer on the point of falling into the hands of the enemy, flew to his aid, killed one of the Austrians who pursued him, put the others in flight and was shot at the moment he went to seize the horse of the cavalryman he had killed.

Citizen Camus, carabineer in the 9th Demi-Brigade of Light Infantry, in the action of 16 Prairial, in front of Piacenza, and notably at the battle of Marengo, where this serviceman dismounted two cavalrymen who he took prisoner.

Citizen Sallior, chasseur in the 9th Demi-Brigade of Light Infantry, in the action at Piacenza, and principally at the battle of Marengo, where this serviceman, detached as a skirmisher, was charged by two Austrian cavalrymen, killing one and dismounting the other.

Citizen Vinot, chasseur in the 9th Demi-Brigade of Light Infantry, at the action of Marengo, where this serviceman, having been assailed by two Austrian cavalrymen and a Hungarian grenadier, dismounted one of the cavaliers, put the grenadier out of action with a bayonet thrust and forced the other cavalryman to retire.

CAPTAIN CAZAUX'S SABRE OF HONOUR CITATION

CERTIFICATE OF HONOUR for **Citizen Cazeau [sic]. 4 Thermidor, Year 9 [23 July, 1801]**

Bonaparte, First Consul of the Republic, after the account which was given to him on the distinguished behaviour and of the stunning bravery of Citizen Cazeau, captain of the 9th Light Half-Brigade, in the affair of the bridgehead at Piacenza, 17 Prairial Year 8 [6 June 1800], when this officer hurried forward, followed by a sergeant who has since been killed, penetrated into the middle of the bridgehead, and made prisoner the enemy rearguard, consisting of 80 men: a moment later the enemy recovered from its surprise, and seeing that he had to deal only with two Frenchmen, did not want to surrender; but Citizen Cazeau who carried himself with so much valour and effrontery continued to impose himself and contained them by measures and a language as firm as it was audacious.

He is awarded, in national recognition, a sabre of honour.

He will enjoy the privileges attached to the aforementioned award, by the order of 4 Nivôse Year 8 [25 December 1799].

Source: *Journal militaire 23, 2 semestre, An 9,* p.573.

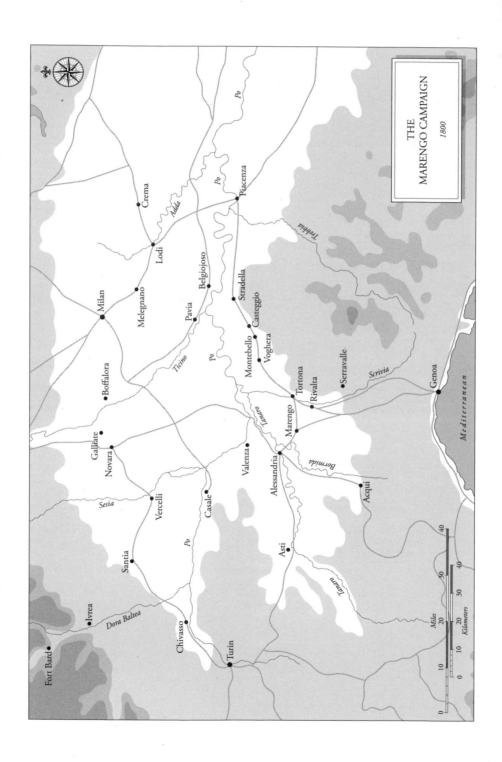

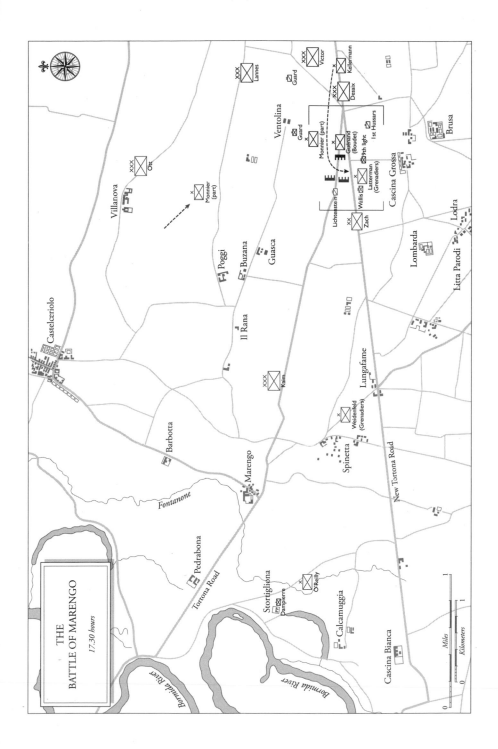

THE
BATTLE OF MARENGO

17.30 hours

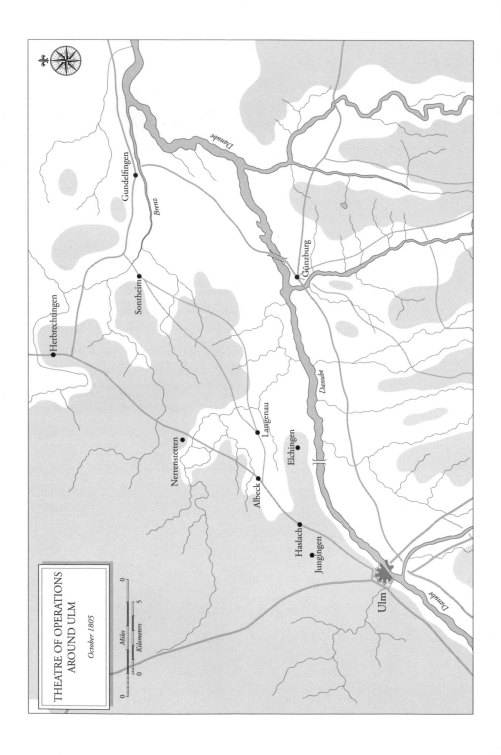

THEATRE OF OPERATIONS
AROUND ULM

October 1805

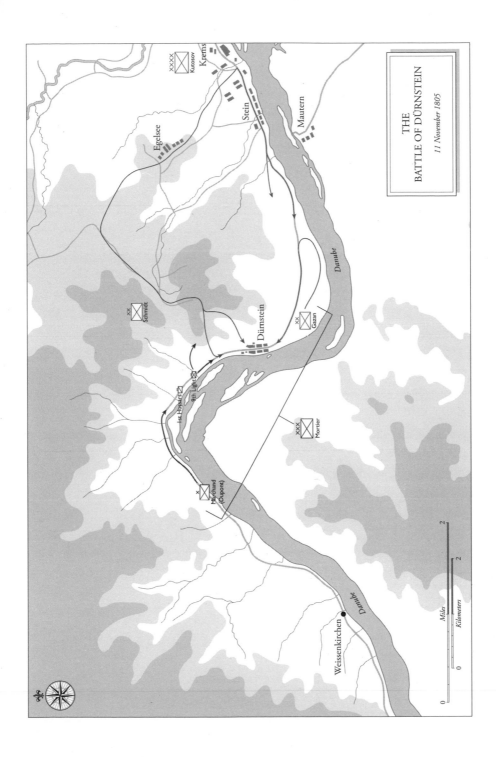

THE
BATTLE OF DÜRNSTEIN
11 November 1805

Kutosov

Krems

Stein

Mautern

Egelsee

Schmidt

Dürnstein

Gazan

Danube

9th Light

1st Hussars

Mortier

Marchand
(Dupont)

Danube

Weissenkirchen

Miles

Kilometers

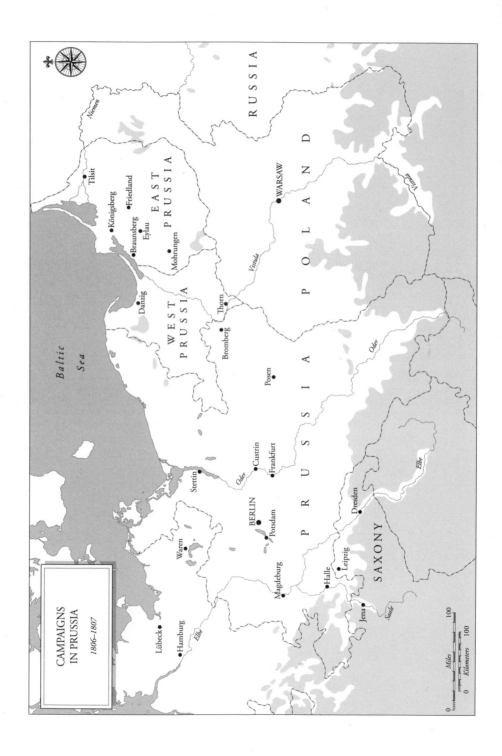

CAMPAIGNS
IN PRUSSIA

1806–1807

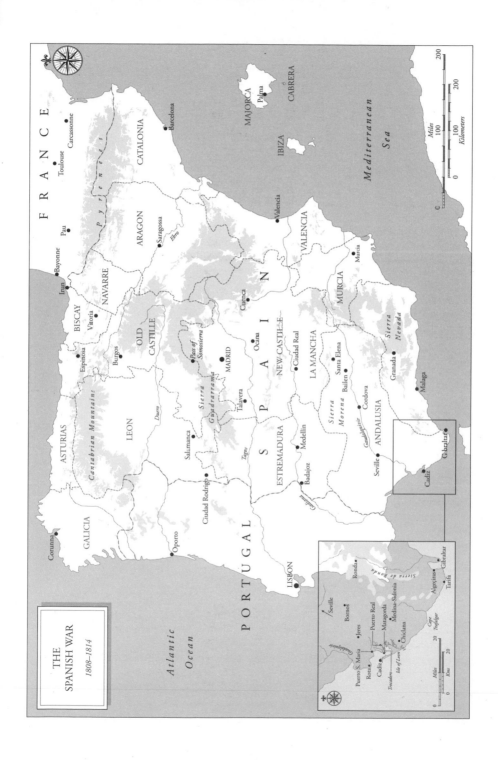

ENDNOTES

CHAPTER 1

1. *Résumé de corps*. Inspection Year VI; (Service Historique de la Défense, Vincennes [SHD] Xb327).
2. See the law of 11 September 1797; *L'organisation des conseils d'administration des troupes de la République.*
3. *Résumé de corps*. Inspection Year VI; (SHD Xb327).
4. Loÿ, L., *Historiques du 84e régiment d'infanterie de ligne 'Un Contre Dix'; du 9e régiment d'infanterie légère 'l'Incomparable'; et du 4e régiment de voltigeurs de la Garde 1684–1904* (Lille: L. Daniel, 1905), p.250.
5. With a sergeant husband and a boy as an 'infant' it is likely that Gros' wife, Jeanne, was a sutleress or cantineer. Each battalion was authorized to appoint four sutleresses.
6. Labassée, M., *Notice sur les batailles, combats, actions, Sièges et expéditions ou ces différents corps se sont trouvée depuis le mois de Septembre 1792 jusqu'è ce jour, 2 Messidor Year IX* (SHD MR1856).
7. The 1st of Vendémiaire was the beginning of the year in the Revolutionary Calendar. It usually corresponded with 22 September.
8. In 1799 the auxiliary companies came from the departments of Seine (15 August); Seine & Oise (29 August); Seine & Marne (3 September); Nord (4 September); Moselle (10 September) and Eure (29 September). A seventh company joined on 8 December from Eure & Loire.
9. A biography of Kuhmann entitled *Herr Christian Kuhmann, des Geneigten Lesers Landsmann* is found in: Hebel, Johann Peter, *Sämmtliche Werke – Erzählungen des Rheinländischen Hausfreundes* (Karlsruhe, 1838), p.210.
10. *Résumé de corps*. Inspection Year VI; (SHD Xb327).
11. The Legion of Clermont began service in 1759 under the title the Volunteers of Clermont-Prince, one of a number of irregular corps formed to counter the threat of newly raised German light troops. In 1766 the unit's proprietor, Clermont, gave the proprietorship of the legion to his nephew, the Prince de Condé, hence the change of title.
12. Labassée's birth certificate records his godfather was his uncle, Mathieu Delabassée de Falvy, Lord of Falvy and of Champagne, knight of the Royal and Military Order of St Louis, captain to the Regiment of Mestre de camp, general of the cavalry. (*Le fonds de la Légion d'honneur aux Archives Nationales 'Leonore'*, dossier LH/693/72).

13. An archaic description of 'major general'.
14. The site remains a barracks and is today named the Caserne Laperrine.
15. Report of 24 September 1784 (SHD Xc78).
16. Review of 24 September 1789 (SHD Xb124).
17. The colonel of the Cévennes regiment was Viscount François-Emmanuel de Toulongeon, a passionate writer who enjoyed a lengthy political career. See *Biographie nouvelle des contemporains ou dictionnaire historique de tous les hommes qui, depuis la Révolution Française, ont acquis de la célébrité* (Paris: la Librairie Historique, 1825), Vol.20.
18. De Barroussel's exploits over six campaigns are noted in *Memoire pour demander une pension sur l'ordre de Ste Louis*, dated July 1785 (SHD Xc78).
19. *Livre de Révue*, 18 December 1791. Throughout this period France was trying to destabilize British trade in India.
20. The first inspection was made on 18 July 1785 at Carcassonne. The regiment then moved to the north-eastern frontier, where it was inspected on 1 August 1785 at Huningue (SHD Xc78).
21. Susane, Louis, *Histoire de l'ancienne Infanterie française* (Paris: J. Corréard, 1853), Vol.7, p.377.
22. Inspections of 18 July 1785 and 1 August 1786 (SHD Xc78).
23. *Ordonnance du Roi, Portant règlement sur la formation & la solde de douze bataillons d'Infanterie Légère du 17 Mars 1788* (Paris, 1788).
24. The cavalry arm formed the Regiment of Brittany and was ranked tenth among the horse chasseurs.
25. *Ordonnance du Roi, Portant règlement sur la formation & la solde de douze bataillons d'Infanterie Légère du 17 Mars 1788* (Paris, 1788).
26. The battalion was increased in size to eight companies each containing a captain, lieutenant and sub-lieutenant, a sergeant-major, two sergeants, one quartermaster corporal, four corporals, four chosen men (appointés), a drummer, six carabineers and 40 chasseurs, in all 59 men. The battalion's staff composed of two lieutenant-colonels, one adjutant-major, one adjutant, one surgeon-major, one drum-major, four musicians, one master tailor, one master armourer and one master cobbler.
27. Bodinier, Gilbert, *Dictionnaire des officiers de l'armée royale qui ont combattu aux Etats-Unis pendant la guerre d'indépendance* (Château de Vincennes, 1982), p.430.
28. Segond took a pension from the Austrian government with the rank of general-major but remained unemployed. He re-entered France on 4 December 1810, where his offers to serve both Napoleon and Louis XVIII were refused. He died in 1832. A number of chasseurs followed their officers into exile. According to an inspection report by Citizen Poulet, dated 12 January 1794, in the previous two years the Ninth had lost 340 men to desertion. The fate of one appears on several genealogy websites listing victims of the guillotine: the baker from Clermont, Pierre Robert was a corporal in the Chasseurs of Cévennes, condemned to death as an émigré on 21 June 1794 by the military commission of Brussels.
29. The composition of the post-Dumouriez officer corps was detailed in *Bataillons d'infanterie légère de la Republique Francaise. Services des officiers de tous grades* (Paris, 1793). Apart from Labassée (who somewhat creatively withheld his age and listed himself as a former 'captain of corsairs'), of the remaining 26 officers, ten said they went to college, nine of whom then went straight into the army. Four listed themselves as having enjoyed being of 'independent means' while two were 'active citizens' – in other words taxpaying citizens aged over 25.The remaining 11 were apprentice merchants or carpenters, assistant locksmiths and weavers, a cloth manufacturer, a cloth-cutter, a wig maker, merchant, pharmacist and clerk. There was just a single manual labourer, the drum-major.
30. Each half-brigade consisted of one brigade commander, three battalion commanders, three adjutant-majors, three surgeon-majors, one drum-major and one drum-master (later termed drum-corporal). Each battalion had eight companies of chasseurs and one of carabineers; each

company comprising one captain, one lieutenant, one sub-lieutenant, one sergeant-major, four sergeants, one quartermaster corporal, eight corporals, two drummers and 103 chasseurs or 64 carabineers.

31. In French '28e bis bataillon de chasseurs' – bis meaning 'repeat'.
32. The 28th (b) chasseurs were formed on 14 February 1794; the Meuse Scouts on 12 September 1793.
33. Loÿ, *Historiques*, pp.237–8.
34. A second amalgamation in 1796 did not affect the Ninth. The only point to note is all the various corps drew their number by ballot. The Ninth drew the number 9 and thus did not change their title. In so doing, they were the only infantry unit in the French army to retain their 1791 identity.
35. SHD Xb327.
36. From the inspection of 12 January 1794.
   Poulet's overall opinion of the corps was good, describing it as composed of strong and robust men. At the previous inspection on 18 December 1791, the Ninth had an effective strength of 400 men. Since then 96 had died (in action or of natural causes), 340 had deserted, 17 discharged, 81 transferred to other corps, one was dismissed, 86 struck from the controls (mostly through invalidity), 22 had been made officer and two were foreigners sent to the interior.

CHAPTER 2

1. Loÿ, *Historiques*, p.250.
2. Cugnac, Gaspar de, *Campagne de l'armée de réserve en 1800* (Paris, Chapelot, 1900), Vol.1, p.271.
3. Loÿ gives a figure of 2,700 (p.257), while de Cugnac gives 2,542 for 30 April. See de Cugnac, *Campagne*, Vol.1, p.644.
4. Alexandre Berthier was the commander of the Reserve Army, not Bonaparte.
5. Loÿ, *Historiques*, p.257.
6. De Cugnac, *Campagne*, Vol.1, p.351.
7. The remaining battalion was part of the Army of Italy.
8. The formation and drill of infantry was set down in the *Réglement concernant l'exercise et les manoeuvres de l'infanterie* of 1 August 1791.
9. The evidence suggests the Ninth did not have flags in 1800.
10. De Cugnac, *Campagne*, Vol.1, p.422.

CHAPTER 3

1. In 1800 Napoleon's army corps system had yet to be formalized. The most experienced generals (Lannes, Murat, Victor, Duhesme and later Desaix) were given the appointment 'lieutenant-general' and entrusted with independent missions.
2. A 'flying bridge' was a raft attached to the riverbank by a cable. When the raft was released the flow of the river and the cable would combine, sending the raft from one bank to the other in an arcing motion. It would then be hauled back across the river by rope.
3. De Cugnac, *Campagne*, Vol.2, p.94.
4. De Cugnac, *Campagne*, Vol.2, p.95.
5. De Cugnac, *Campagne*, Vol.2, p.106.
6. De Cugnac, *Campagne*, Vol.2, p.105.
7. For a contemporary discussion of French 'petty war' tactics see Jarrey's *Instruction concernant le service de l'Infanterie Légère en Campagne* (London: Dulau & Nardini, 1801).
8. De Cugnac, *Campagne*, Vol.2, p.168.

9. De Cugnac, *Campagne,* Vol.2, p.200.

10. Both episodes are taken from the soldiers' biographies in Lievyns etc, *Fastes de la Légion d'Honneur. Biographie de tous les décorés, accompagnéede l'histoire législative et réglmentaire de l'ordre* (Paris, 1842), Vol.5.

11. De Cugnac, *Campagne,* Vol.2, p.201.

12. A return of 7 June 1800 gave the Ninth 2,000 present under arms. Until then only 109 casualties had been reported. At Ivrea there were 2,542 present. This leaves a discrepancy of 433 men unaccounted for. In his journal Boudet originally estimated his division's casualties as 500 on 5 June (de Cugnac, *Campagne,* Vol.2, p.167), stating more were killed than wounded due to the artillery fire. However, the official figures given by Brossier claim only 101 casualties. It is likely the casualty rate was far higher than admitted.

13. De Cugnac, *Campagne,* Vol.2, p.303.

14. In addition there were 26 gunners with an eight-pounder and a six-inch howitzer.

15. See Montaglas, Jean Pierre Galy, *Historique du 12me chasseurs à cheval depuis le 29 avril 1792 jusqu'au traité de Lunéville (9 fév. 1801)* (Paris: Chapelot, 1908).

16. Meat rations had been set at the beginning of the campaign as ½lb daily for each man.

CHAPTER 4

1. This story is outlined in David Hollins' *Marengo: Napoleon's Day of Fate* (Oxford: Osprey Publishing, 2000), p.53. The role of this spy has been underestimated despite being mentioned in a number of contemporary sources (e.g. Victor, *Extraits des mémoires inédits de feu Claude-Victor Perrin, Duc de Bellune* [Paris, 1846], p.158). An overview of the extent of espionage during the Napoleonic wars is given in the author's *The Enemy Within* (Oxford: Osprey Publishing, 2006).

2. The 3rd Cavalry's role on 13/14 June is given in their 1801 manuscript history (SHD MS1856).

3. Gioannini, Marco and Massobrio, Giulio, *Marengo: la Battaglia che greò il mito di Napoleone* (Milan: Rissoli, 2000), p.199.

4. De Cugnac, *Campagne,* Vol.2, p.394. Contrary to popular legend, Desaix did not march towards the sound of guns on his own initiative.

5. Popular legend has the message saying: 'I have always anticipated attacking the enemy. He has forestalled me. I had thought to attack Melas. He has attacked me first. In the name of God come back, if you are able to do so.' De Cugnac, *Campagne,* Vol.2, p.395. In the author's opinion, it is doubtful that Bonaparte would use such emotional language in a written order.

6. This 2.30pm timing is given in the manuscript history of 1st Dragoons (SHD MS1848 *Historique du 1er Dragoons*).

7. Timing of retreat: Victor, *Extraits des memoires,* pp.175–6.

8. For this phase of the battle see Joseph Petit's *Marengo* (Philadelphia: Aurora Office, 1808), pp.25–6. The terrain behind Marengo has changed dramatically since 1800. From older maps, the defile appears to have been located east of Spinetta, at the junctions of the modern SS10 and SP82 roads.

9. The timing of 4pm comes from Soult who viewed the battle from Alessandria. Soult, Nicolas-Jean de Dieu, *Mémoires du Maréchal Général Soult* (Paris, 1854), Vol.III, pp.275–7.

10. Perhaps the most balanced account of the Foot Guards in action appears in Victor, *Extraits des mémoires inédits de feu Claude-Victor Perrin, Duc de Bellune* (Paris: Dumaine, 1846), p.179: 'A few hundred men intended to stand in the way [of the Austrians]: it was the grenadier battalion of the Consular Guard; it was there, on the open ground, between Il Poggi and Villanouva [sic], formed in square, immobile. The enemy first tried to beat a breach with volleys of cannon balls, canister and shells; it did not move. Ott threw his cavalry against them; they did not move, and this cavalry fled and dispersed before its discharges and its bayonets; next came General Gattesheim [sic] with the Splény [sic] Infantry Regiment; our grenadiers deployed themselves on the centre and received

these new assailants with the most murderous fire; but at that moment they were charged in the rear by Frimont's hussars, who at last shook them, and the enemy continued its march forwards without encountering any resistance from then on.'

11. Foudras, Alexandre, *Campagne de Bonaparte en Italie en l'an VIII de la république; rédigée sur les mémoires d'un officier de l'état-major de l'armée de réserve* (Paris: Impr. des instructions décadaires, 1800), p.59.

12. Victor, *Extraits des memoires*, p.179.

13. Bell, Mrs. Arthur (trans.), *Memoirs of Baron Lejeune aide-de-camp to marshals Berthier, Davout, and Oudinot* (London: Longmans, 1897), Vol.1, p.21.

14. San Giuliano has become synonymous with the location of the evening battle. In fact, there is a distance of 6.5 km between the line held at Spinetta and San Giuliano – 1.5 hours' straight march. The French retreat was carried out slowly with numerous halts. If the Guard were engaged at 4pm and the retreat onto the plain did not commence until afterwards, it would have taken until at least 6pm to reach San Giuliano. The majority of sources indicate the Ninth was in action by 5pm. This puts the action level with Cascina Grossa, as shown in Lejeune's 1803 painting *La Bataille de Marengo*.

15. De Cugnac, *Campagne*, Vol.2, p.412.

16. Fleuriot de Langle, Paul (ed.), *Général Bertrand, Cahiers de Sainte-Hélène* (Paris, Albin Michel, 1959), p.436.

17. Guénand, Louis Charles, *Note pour le Général Dumas*, 30 Brumaire Year 10 (SHD MR610). It is surprising this account was not used by de Cugnac. Guénand was very critical of the lack of praise afforded his brigade.

18 Marmont, Auguste-Frédéric-Louis Viesse de, *Mémoires du Maréchal Marmont Duc de Raguse de 1792 a 1841* (Paris: Perrotin, 1857), Vol.2, p.132.

19. De Cugnac, *Campagne*, Vol.2, p.142.

20. De Cugnac, *Campagne*, Vol.2, p.429.

21. See Ogier d'Ivry, Vicomte Henri-Pierre-Georges-Marie, *Historique du 1er régiment de hussards* (Valence: impr. de J. Céas et fils, 1901), p.113.

22. Larchey, Lorédan (ed.) (trans. M. Carey), *The note-books of Captain Coignet: soldier of the Empire 1776–1850* (London: Chatto & Windus, 1897), p.78.

23. Larchey, *The note-books of Captain Coignet*, p.78. The freshly planted vines comes from an observation in Lejeune's painting. This field had been the sight of a battle the year before and may have been replanted with young vines. The length of 260m is calculated on 19 platoons (three carabineer and 16 chasseur), each with an average 23-man frontage, each man occupying 0.6m of the line.

24. Savary, Anne-Jean-Marie-René, *Mémoires du Duc de Rovigo, pour server a l'histoire de l'Empereur Napoléon* (Paris: A. Bossange, 1828), Vol.1, p.274.

25. Savary, *Mémoires*, Vol.1, p.274.

26. Victor, *Extraits des memoires*, p.183.

27. Accounts of Marengo often depict Desaix leading a charge in front of the Ninth. Captain Dubois' 1839 account (Dubois, L., *Historique du 9è Régiment d'Infanterie Légère* 1839 (SHD MR1842) suggests Desaix was making a reconnaissance from behind the skirmish line to direct the charge. Credence for this claim comes from Napoleon who later described Desaix being 'at the head of 200 scouts [*éclaireurs*] of the Ninth'. See Gourgaud, Général, *Mémoires pour servir à l'histoire de France sous Napoléon, écrits à sainte-helene, sous la dictée de l'empereur, par les généraux qui ont partage sa captivité et publiés sur les manuscrits entièrement corrigés de sa main* (London: Martin Bossange & Co and Henry Colburn & Co., 1823), Vol.I, p.292.

28. Victor, *Extraits des memoires*, p.185.

29. De Cugnac, *Campagne*, Vol.2, p.406.

30. De Cugnac, *Campagne,* Vol.2, pp.412–3.

31. Kellermann, Duc de Valmy, *Bataille de Marengo* (Paris, Bureau du Journal: Napoléon Journal Anecdotique et Biographique de l'Empire et de la Grande Armée: Neuvième livraison, 1834), p.530.

32. Guénand (SHD MR610).

33. The heroics of individual men from the Ninth were later recorded in award citations. A summary of these can be found in the appendices. De Cugnac, *Campagne,* Vol.2, p.568.

34. Boudet, Jean, *Journal des Marches et opérations de la division Boudet* (SHD MR610). Carabinier Michel anecdote from Lavallée, Joseph, *Annales Nécrologiques de la Légion d'Honner* (Paris: Chez F. Buisson, 1807) pp.258–9.
Michel joined Bonaparte's Guard in December 1800.

35. The Ninth forming square is only mentioned in Dubois.

CHAPTER 5

1. De Cugnac, *Campagne,* Vol.2, p.415.

2. De Cugnac, *Campagne,* Vol.2, p.420.

3. Dubois, *Historique du 9è.*

4. Unusually Boudet did not give any casualty figures. However, we can get some idea of the losses by looking at the returns made on 20 June:

Unit	14 June	20 June	Losses
9th Light	2,014	1,629	385
30th Line	1,430	1,030	400
59th Line	1,872	1,672	200

5. Funeral pyres from *Coignet* (see Larchey), p.80; brandy ration from de Cugnac, *Campagne,* Vol.2, p.469.

6. De Cugnac, *Campagne,* Vol.2, p.508.

7. Montaglas, *Historique du 12me chasseurs*, p.84.

8. Montaglas, *Historique du 12me chasseurs*, p.84.

9. Bonaparte's secretary, Louis de Bourienne, claimed Bonaparte learned this through mail censorship. Kellerman is alleged to have used the phrase in a letter to Lasalle. Bourrienne, Louis Antoine Fauvelet de, *Private Memoirs of Napoleon Bonaparte* (Philadelphia: Carey & Lea, 1831), Vol.I, p.347.

10. Savary, Vol.8, pp.343–4.

11. Crossard, Jean Baptiste Louis, *Mémoires militaires et historiques pour servir à l'histoire de la guerre depuis 1792 jusqu'en 1815 inclusivement* (Paris: Chez Migneret, 1829), Vol.2, p.308.

12. De Cugnac, *Campagne,* Vol.2, p.413

13. Guénand. (SHD MR610).

14. *Notice An IX – 2e cavalerie* (SHD MS1856); Fleuriot de Langle, Paul (ed.), *Général Bertrand, Cahiers de Sainte-Hélène de Bertrand* (Paris: Albin Michel, 1959), p.436.

15. De Cugnac, *Campagne,* Vol.2, p.573.

16. Dubois, *Historique du 9è.*

17. De Cugnac, *Campagne,* Vol.2, pp.568–9.

18. The figure of 500 comes from the Mortier inspection of Year 10 which shows 538 men had transferred to the Ninth from other corps after 23 September 1800.

19. *Procès Verbal de la réorganisation de la 9e ½ brigade légère* 22 Vendémiaire Year IX (SHD Xb327).

20. Labassée, *Notice An IX* (MS1856).

21. *Gazette Nationale ou le Moniteur Universel. 16 prairial an 9 No.256.*

22. *Mémoires de Madame la Duchesse d'Abrantes, Vol.4* (Paris: L. Mame, 1835), pp.151–2.

23. Labassée, *Notice An IX* (MS1856).

24. The sword is currently preserved at Musée de l'Armée, Paris.

25. Lannes, *Order of 23 Fructidor Year IX* (Carnet de la Sabretache, 1893), p.237–8.

26. Desbœufs, Marc, *Les étapes d'un soldat de l'Empire [1800–1815]: souvenirs du capitaine Desboeufs* (Paris: A. Picard, 1901), p.205.

27. *Gazette Nationale ou le Moniteur Universel Rapport de la Préfecture de Police du 4 brumaire an 10.*

28. Mortier, *Livret pour la revue d'inspection, 18 Nivose An 10* (SHD XB327).

29. Mortier's description of the uniform matches that portrayed in Lejeune's *Marengo*. Lejeune painted the carabineers in blue pantaloons with a red stripe down the outer seam of the leg.

30. *Gazette Nationale ou le Moniteur Universel. Samedi, 16 prairial an 10.*

31. *Gazette Nationale ou le Moniteur Universel. 16 prairial an 10 No.256.*

32. Dubois, *Historique du 9è.*

33. Croyet, Jérôme (ed.), *Lettres du capitaine Coudreux à son frère (1804–1815)* (Société d'Etudes Historiques Révolutionnaires et Impériales, 2010).

34. Napier, Sir Charles J. (ed.), *Lights and Shades of Military Life* (London: Henry Colburn, 1850), pp.235–6. The original French edition was Blaze, E., *La Vie Militaire sous l'Empire* (Paris, 1837), pp.19–21.

CHAPTER 6

1. Letter of 6 Vendemiaire Year XII (SHD Xb327).

2. Letter of 5 Brumaire Year XII (SHD Xb327).

3. Meunier was born on 4 August 1770.

4. Alombert, Paul Claude, *Campagne de l'an 14 [1805]: Le corps d'armée aux ordres du maréchal Mortier, combat de Dürrenstein* (Paris: Berger-Levrault & cie, 1897), pp.366–7.

5. The letter mentions the need to manufacture 'distribution sacks' for each man. These were large linen bags, approximately 1.5m deep which the soldiers used for collecting 'distributions'. The soldiers also used them as sleeping bags or mattresses.

6. Fezensac, *Souvenirs militaires de 1804 a 1814* (Paris: J. Dumaine, 1863), p.44; Vigo-Roussillon, F., *Journal de Campagne (1793–1837): François Vigo-Roussillon Grenadier de l'Empire* (Paris: Éditions France-Empire, 1981), pp.134–5.

7. A description of *soupe grasse* is given by a British author: 'They fill a large pot, or *marmite*, with water. When it begins to boil, they throw one or two handfuls of salt into it, according to the quantity of water, chop up some cabbage or herbs, which they also put in, and last of all, a ball of hog's-lard, kitchen-stuff, dripping, or any other grease they may have. They then allow it to boil until the materials are well done. It is afterwards served up in soup-plates or dishes, into which has previously put bread, cut into very thin slices.' O'Brien, Donat Hency, *My adventures during the Late War* (London: Henry Colburn Publisher, 1839), Vol.1, pp.64–5.

8. Fezensac, *Souvenirs militaires*, p.45.

9. Bardin, Etienne Alexandre. *Mémorial de l'officier d'infanterie*, Vol.1, p.39.

10. The calibre remained the same (17.5mm) as did the weight of the ball (24.45g).

11. The line infantry formed voltigeur companies in the same manner as the light infantry on 19 September 1805.

12. The concept of riding into battle was probably drawn from the example of *Velites* of the early Roman Republic, who were trained to ride pillion, quickly dismount and throw their javelins.

13. The law of 26 August 1805 would set the minimum at 1.544m (5ft).

14. Ney, Michel, *Mémoires du Maréchal Ney, duc d'Elchingen, Prince de la Moskowa* (Paris: H Fournier, 1833), *Vol. 2*, p.228.

15. Alombert. *Campagne de l'an 14*, pp.367–8.

16. If appointed, these fifers were never identified as such in official documents.

17. Ney, *Mémoires*, Vol.2, pp.206–7.

18. Dubois, *Historique du 9è*.

19. See Lievyns etc, *Fastes de la Légion d'Honneur, Vol.5*.

20. Ney, *Mémoires*, Vol.2, p.241.

21. Amey, *Rapport d'inspection* [12 Vendémiaire Year XIII] (SHD Xb581).

22. In a separate study for the Year XVIII (September 1804–September 1805) the Ninth received a total of 875 recruits and had 178 deserters – a rate of about 20 per cent. Alombert, Goget and Colin, *La Campagne de 1805 en Allemagne, Vol.1* (Librairie militaire R. Chapelot, 1902), p.148.

23. SHD Letter of 14 Vendemairie, Year XIII. The majority of first-time deserters were given an amnesty, although some were sentenced to 'public works'.

24. The inspector did not mention if there were too few or too many buttons, but a surviving coat worn by Captain Cardron shows eight buttons rather than seven. The Ninth's officers are also portrayed with a four-button cuff in the 1808 watercolour, attributed to Weiland.

25. Amey, *Etat Nominatif* [13 Vendémiaire Year XIII] (Xb327).

26. Lit. *The Emperor of the French to the 9th Regiment of light infantry/Valour and Discipline.*

27. Fouquet's attendance is confirmed in Dubois, *Historique du 9è*.

28. Nateuil, Luc de, *David* (New York: Harry N. Abrams, Inc., 1990), p.35.

29. David's other daughter, Pauline, married Jean-Baptiste Jeanin, who became colonel of the 12th Light. Meunier and Jeanin shared very similar career paths and were almost certainly acquainted before their respective marriages.

30. Ney, *Mémoires*, Vol.2, p.254.

31. Vigo-Roussillon, *Journal de Campagne*, p.136.

32. Maréchal Ney to Dupont 7 Messidor Year XIII (Carnet de la Sabretache, 1896), p.473–4.

33. Darricau to Dupont 19 Thermidor Year XIII (Carnet de la Sabretache, 1896), pp.474–5.

34. Ney to Dupont 20 Thermidor Year XIII (Carnet de la Sabretache, 1896), p.474.

35. Ney, *Mémoires*, Vol.2, p.230.

36. *Journal des opérations militaires de la Division Dupont, pendant la Campagne de l'An 14* (SHD 1M629).

CHAPTER 7

1. See Godet, M., *Mémoires de capitaine Godet* (Carnet de la Sabretache, Séries 3, 1927), p.248. Colonel Magnier was awarded the Legion of Honour at Boulogne and then quickly pensioned off. Also see Vigo-Roussillon; *Journal de Campagne*, for concerns about Napoleon's accession to the Imperial Throne, pp.133–4.

2. Adjutant-Major Antoine Reymond was transferred to the 21st Light at this time. This indicates a direct exchange of two unsettled officers. The identity of the unlucky duellist is indicated in a letter from Ney to the minister of war dated 4 August 1805. Ney records the arrival of 103 men from the Ninth's depot under the command of Lieutenant Andres. Colonel Meunier ordered Andres to remain with the field battalions taking the place of Lieutenant Collignon who died in the hospital of Étaples on 28 July. There is nothing to say Collignon died of a duelling wound, but the 34-year-old was an eager lieutenant of voltigeurs, not one of those of failing health sent back to the depot. His selection as a voltigeur officer implies he was in robust health, but perhaps of combative temper (SHD Xb327).

3. Godet, *Mémoires*, p.249.
4. Godet, *Mémoires*, p.249.
5. Godet, *Mémoires*, p.314.
6. Godet, *Mémoires*, p.251; Dupont's journal (SHD 1M629).
7. *Réglement concernant le service intérieur, la police et la discipline de l'infanterie du 24 juin 1792.* See Berriat, H., *Législation militaire* (Alexandrie: Louis Capriolo, 1812), Vol.1, p.378.
8. Godet, *Mémoires*, p.250.
9. Ney, *Mémoires*, Vol.2, pp.241–2.
10. Alombert, Goget and Colin, *La Campagne de 1805 en Allemagne* (Paris: Librairie militaire R. Chapelot, 1902), Vol.3, p.42.
11. Alombert etc., *1805,* Vol.3, p.47.
12. Six men were wounded from artillery fire in this action. Several more may have been killed outright (SHD 22Yc75 and 22Yc76).
13. Vigo-Roussillon, *Journal de Campagne*, p.151.
14. Godet, *Mémoires*, p.254.
15. Godet, *Mémoires*, p.254.
16. The French accounts indicate the village was lost and retaken five times; the Austrian accounts say three times.
17. Dubois, *Historique du 9è*.
18. Regimental rolls, (SHD 22Yc75 and 22Yc76).
19. For the loss of the medical supplies during the 1805 campaign see Paul Fouquart's *Campagne de Prusse (1806), d'après les archives de la guerre* (Paris: Berger-Levrault, 1887), p.50.
20. Loÿ, *Historiques*, p.280.
21. Martinien, Aristide, *Tableaux, par corps et par batailles, des officiers tués et blessés pendant les guerres de l'Empire (1805–1815)* (Paris: H. Charles-Lavauzelle, Paris, 1899), p.408. Loÿ claims the Ninth lost 15 officers wounded in this action. As a comparison the 96th had three wounded officers (p.312) and the 32nd four officers wounded, one mortally (p.192).
22. Seven prisoners were taken in the battle but escaped by the end of the day (SHD 22Yc75 [An 1–XII] and 22Yc76 [An XII–1809]).
23. Nothing is mentioned in Dupont's journal, but two carabineers and one chasseur were killed in action on 12 October; all three were from 1st Battalion.
24. Alombert etc, *1805*, Vol.1, pp.618–9.
25. Alombert etc, *1805*, Vol.1, p.687.
26. Vigo-Roussillon, *Journal de Campagne*, p.158.
27. Dupont's journal (SHD 1M629).
28. Godet, *Mémoires*, p.314.
29. Dupont's journal, 21 October 1805.
30. Vigo-Roussillion, *Journal de Campagne*, p.165.
31. Godet, *Mémoires*, p.317.
32. Godet, *Mémoires*, p.318.
33. Alombert, Paul Claude, *Campagne de l'an 14 [1805]: Le corps d'armée aux ordres du maréchal Mortier, combat de Dürrenstein* (Paris: Berger-Levrault & cie, 1897), p.128.
34. Vigo-Roussillon, *Journal de Campagne*, pp.168–9.
35. SHD 1M629.
36. Alombert gives the total as 56 wounded. There are 58 names in the regimental rolls. Dupont's initial assessment was 25 killed and 75 wounded. He gave the 32nd as losing two killed and 20 wounded, with the 1st Hussars having two wounded. Camille Reboulleau is believed to have been the younger

brother of Lieutenant Edme Reboulleau who had been wounded at Piacenza and had recently retired. According to local tradition, the Reboulleaus were Labassée's brothers-in-law by his first marriage.

37. The award was granted on 14 March 1806.
38. *22e bulletin de la Grande Armée, 13 novembre 1805; 23e bulletin de la Grande Armée, 14 novembre 1805; Ordre du jour14 novembre 1805.*
39. Vigo-Roussillon, *Journal de Campagne*, p.170.
    Dupont noted Napoleon said it verbally. The latter appears more likely.

CHAPTER 8

1. Loÿ, *Historiques*, p.286.
2. Vigo-Roussillon, *Journal de Campagne*, p.171.
3. Alombert, *Combat de Dürrenstein*, p.268.
4. When an officer was tried, the composition of the council altered so none of the judges was lower in rank than the accused.
5. The documents of this trial are published online by Robert Ouvrard at *Histoire du Consulat et du Premier Empire* (www.histoire-empire.org).
6. Alombert. *Combat de Dürrenstein*, pp.293–4.
7. SHD Xb327; Letters of 5 and 25 Frimaire Year XIV.
8. Loÿ, *Historiques*, pp.287–8. The reinforcements set out on 6 November 1805.
9. This letter was sourced online. It is now in private ownership.
10. Dominique Aubert was entered into the regimental rolls as No.2055, born on 12 July 1783, 1.676m tall, with black hair and grey eyes.
11. The longest surviving captain in each battalion was labelled 'first class' and had the right to command in the absence of a battalion commander.
12. Godet's transfer was formalized on 7 July 1806 (SHD Xb581).
13. Marneuf had replaced Portier as drum-major on 11 Thermidor XIII. Marneuf was 1.80m tall and had been a corporal in 1st Carabineers. He received the Legion of Honour on 14 April 1807 and was later killed in action on 7 October 1813.
14. Although annexed to France in 1659, Philippeville was in the Walloon region of Belgium. Cardron did not consider himself 'French' as such. In modern terms he was a French-speaking Belgian.
15. Couvreur, H., *Souvenirs d'un officier de Napoléon: Lettres du Capitaine Cardron, de Philippeville 1804–1815* (Annales de la Société Archéologique de Namur Tome XLII, 1937), p.155.
16. Foucart, Paul, *Campagne de Prusse (1806), d'après les archives de la guerre* (Paris: Berger-Levrault, 1887), p.50.
17. Foucart, *Campagne de Prusse*, p.312.
18. The situation report of 6 October gave the field battalions' strength as 2,010 men. *Marche du 1er Corps de las Grande Armée aux Ordres de le Maréchal Bernadotte Prince de Portecorvo, Années 1806 et 1807* (SHD 1M654).
19. See Chandler, David, *The Campaigns of Napoleon* (London: Scribner, 1973), pp.494–7.
20. Vigo-Roussillon, *Journal de Campagne*, p.156.
21. Loÿ, *Historiques*, p.291.
22. The 32nd Line formed their voltigeurs before the 1805 campaign, but the 96th waited until they reached Vienna.
23. Vigo-Roussillon, *Journal de Campagne*, p.186.
24. Couvreur, *Souvenirs d'un officier*, p.157.
25. Couvreur, *Souvenirs d'un officier*, pp.156–7.

CHAPTER 9

1. See Girod de l'Ain, Général, *Dix ans de mes souvenirs militaires de 1805 à 1815* (Paris: J. Dumaine, 1873).

2. Girod, *Dix ans*, p.3.

3. At this time 'la drogue' (the drug) was used as an adjective for a poor example of something. In effect, the loser was 'la drogue' and had to pay for this dishonour with a painful forfeit. A modern English translation would be 'the dope'.

4. Girod, *Dix ans*, p.43.

5. Loÿ, *Historiques*, p.296.

6. It is likely that this was the carriage Meunier had purchased in Vienna after Dürnstein.

7. The 55th Army Bulletin optimistically described this as the best temperature for soldiers.

8. In his history of the Ninth, Loÿ lists Lieutenant Donot as the eagle-bearer. This appears to be taken from Donot's biography in *Fastes de la legion d'honneur*. However, at this epoch the regimental colours were carried by a sergeant-major, only one of whom was killed.

9. Girod claimed 2nd Battalion fled having lost nearly 300 men. Although increasingly inaccurate, the regimental rolls do not support such high losses, showing 2nd Battalion lost ten killed in the action, with two posted as wounded, one of whom was left on the field and taken prisoner. In addition there are seven other men listed as captured in the battle. The inaccuracy in the rolls is exposed by a later inspection report (*Livret pour la revue d'inspection*, Landau 1 January 1808, Général de Division Schauenburg) which listed 11 men retired after receiving wounds at Mohrungen. Russian accounts indicate the Ninth did not wait to receive a charge. General Elmolov declared the Russians advanced 'without burning a cartridge, crossed the fences and exterminated all those who found themselves in the farm and in the gardens.' (Andolenko, C. R., *Aigles de Napoleon contre Drapeaux du Tsar* [Paris: Eurimprim, 1969], pp.128–9). With only ten killed, this indicates the Russians found very few Frenchmen remaining. Cuinat's incredible service history is available at 'Leonore', dossier LH/639/14.

10. Girod, *Dix ans*, pp.29–30, states three eagle-bearers were killed in succession, with a carabineer being the last to carry the flag and throwing it over a garden wall. If the last man to hold the flag was a carabineer, it is probable that the other bearers were also carabineers. According to the regimental rolls only two carabineers were killed in action: Corporal Antoine Toussaint and Carabineer Jean Louis Alondrel. This indicates the third carabineer who threw the eagle likely survived the battle and later reported his actions. When analysing the wounded later pensioned off, I came across the reference to 27-year-old Carabineer Etienne Lebassac, from Calvados, who was wounded by a sword and a musket shot in the battle and taken prisoner. This implies he came into physical contact with a Russian officer and was injured by his sabre. The fact Lebassac was unable to get away suggests he may have received the gunshot wound prior to the sword wound.

11. Anon. *Campagne de la Grande Armée en Saxe, en Prusse et en Pologne en l'an 1806 et l'an 1807* (Paris: Chez Pougin, 1807), p.294.

12. See the order of 26 March 1807: 'His Majesty orders that the regiments of light infantry will have no eagles with the army, and that the eagles of these regiments will be sent to the depots. This arm must not have an eagle in front of the enemy.'

13. Andolenko, C. R., *Aigles de Napoleon contre Drapeaux du Tsar* (Paris: Eurimprim, 1969), p.128.

14. Command of the Grabaü post was given to Valdec Boudinhon, supernumerary colonel of 4th Hussars. He later attained the rank of brigade-general so Girod likely referred to him by this title when writing his memoirs. *Précis historique des campagnes du 1er Corps de la Grande Armée 1806 et 1807* (SHD 1M654).

15. Girod, *Dix ans*, p.37.

16. *Précis historique des campagnes du 1er Corps de la Grande Armée 1806 et 1807* (SHD 1M654).

17. *Précis historique des campagnes du 1er Corps de la Grande Armée 1806 et 1807* (SHD 1M654).

18. *64e bulletin de la Grande Armée, Osterode, 2 mars 1807.*

CHAPTER 10

1. The location of the forward depot is uncertain. Towards the end of 1806 it was at Stettin (Szczecin), but it had moved closer to Thorn by the time Girod arrived.

2. Vigo-Roussillon, *Journal de Campagne*, p.203.

3. Girod, *Dix ans*, p.54.

4. Marbot, J. B. A. Marcellin de (trans. A. J. Butler), *The Memoirs of the Baron de Marbot* (London: Longmans, 1893), pp.214–5.

5. Girod, *Dix ans*, p.54; Vigo-Roussillon, *Journal de Campagne*, p.203.

6. Derode, M., *Nouvelle Relation de la Bataille de Friedland* (Paris: Anselin & Laguionie etc., 1839), p.38.

7. Girod, *Dix ans*, p.55.

8. Posthenen has merged with the town of Pravdinsk, the name Friedland bears today.

9. In a 'column of divisions' each battalion had a frontage of two platoons, in this case 60–80 bayonets.

10. Derode, *Nouvelle Relation*, p.58.

11. Derode, *Nouvelle Relation*, p.60.

12. At Friedland Senarmont gave one of the most celebrated artillery actions in history. However from Girod's memoirs it is obvious the artillery did not act independently as commonly described, but enjoyed the protection of the Ninth's square. Would the gunners have been so bold advancing if they did not have the safety of this infantry square in support? Victor should also be given great credit for authorizing Senarmont to proceed.

13. Derode, *Nouvelle Relation*, p.62.

14. Derode, *Nouvelle Relation*, p.65.

15. Girod, *Dix ans*, p.58.

16. Dubois, *Historique du 9è*: 'Towards the evening a bayonet charge vigorously supported by other forces decided the victory.'

17. 'Mr V.' was possibly 35-year-old Captain Nicolas Vadel. He was actually wounded in the battle which is why Cardron may not have seen him in the later stages.

18. Letter dated 27 November 1807. Couvreur, *Souvenirs d'un officier*, pp.160–1.

19. Napoleon I (ed. Keizer van Frankrijk), *Correspondance de Napoléon Ier.* (Paris: Imprimerie Impériale, 1867), Vol.15, p.418.

20. Derode, p.79. One of the wounded officers was Captain Balson, the hero of Halle. Having recovered from multiple wounds in 1806, he had the misfortune at Friedland to have a musket ball pass through his testicles into his left leg, shattering the bone.

21. Dubois, *Historique du 9è*.

22. Girod, *Dix ans*, p.63.

23. Victor had been promoted to the marshalate on 13 July 1807 and governor of Berlin on 9 August the same year.

24. Ruffin was a brigadier general in Oudinot's 'Infernal Division'.

25. Couvreur, *Souvenirs d'un officier*, p.161.

26. Schauenburg, Général de Division, *Livret pour la revue d'inspection*, Landau, 1 January 1808 (SHD Xb581).

27. Of those killed in action: nine were at Haslach (11.10.05); three near Albeck (12.10.05); two at Albeck (14.10.05); 19 at Dürnstein (11.11.05); one on 25 August 1806 on the Jena campaign; eight

at Halle (17.10.06); eight at Waren (1.11.06); ten at Mohrungen (25.01.07); two on 15.02.07 near Eylau; five at Braunsburg (26.02.07); 45 at Friedland (14 June 1807) (SHD 22Yc75 and 22Yc76).

28. Before this reform, a three-battalion regiment required 81 company officers, 162 sub-officers and 216 corporals; post reform a five-battalion regiment required 84 company officers, 168 sub-officers and 224 corporals. In effect, for the addition of an extra company's cadre per regiment (three officers, six sub-officers and eight corporals) Napoleon gained two extra field battalions per regiment.

29. *Procès Verbal d'Organisation en exécution du Décret Impérial du 18 février 1808* (SHD Xb581).

30. The old 3rd Battalion was broken up to form the new 4th and 5th battalions. See chapter 12.

31. The regimental rolls show no quartermaster corporals were killed in the period 1805–07. Remember also Mortier's criticism from the 1802 inspection, that they were not even armed with muskets. For the record, it appears at least one quartermaster corporal had a horse in 1807. Witness Cardron's letter of 27 November 1807, in which he discussed a quartermaster corporal he was acquainted with: 'The famous B. is still the same and by means of some thefts that he made on campaign he is mounted like Saint George [i.e. well-mounted], but he is still a quartermaster corporal and hardly knows how to read.' Couvreur, *Souvenirs d'un officier*, p.161.

CHAPTER 11

1. Contingents for this provisional regiment were sent from the 6th, 9th, 25th and 28th Light Infantry.

2. Napoleon adopted the title 'King of Italy' in 1805.

3. Metzger, Paul, *La capitulation de Baylen et le sort des prisonniers français, d'après le journal du colonel d'Eslon (1807–1811).* (Limoges et Paris: Charles-Lavauzelle, 15 novembre 1908).

4. Metzger, *La capitulation de Baylen*, pp.7–8.

5. Metzger, *La capitulation de Baylen*, p.17.

6. Metzger, *La capitulation de Baylen*, p.10.

7. Parole was when a soldier gave his word of honour they would not to bear arms against their captor for the duration of the war.

8. Metzger, *La capitulation de Baylen*, p.16.

9. Dupont returned to France in disgrace and was never forgiven for Bailen. Napoleon stripped him of his titles and ostracized him. It was a sad end to a previously glittering career.

10. Girod, *Dix ans*, pp.63–4.

11. Marnier, Jules, *Souvenirs de guerre en temps de paix, 1793, 1806, 1823, 1862: récits historiques et anecdotiques* (Paris: Ch. Tanera, 1868), pp.83–6.

12. The 32nd Line had been transferred to Villatte's division by this time.

13. Marnier, *Souvenirs de guerre*, pp.83–6.

14. Godet, *Mémoires*, pp.484–5.

15. Girod, *Dix ans*, p.107.

16. Marnier, *Souvenirs de guerre*, p.41.

CHAPTER 12

1. Godet, *Mémoires*, p.446.

2. From surviving comments in the inspection reports, the greatcoats issued to the Ninth were either a beige natural colour, or even off-white.

3. The culprit here is likely Parisian Lieutenant Alexis Jean Baptiste Goisez, born 1761. He had been a soldier since 1781 and had a sabre scar over his left eyebrow.

4. Berriat, *Législation militaire*, Vol.1, pp.34–5.

5. Bardin, Étienne-Alexandre, *Mémorial de l'officier d'infanterie* (Paris: Magimel, 1813), Vol.2, p.806.

6. Berriat, Vol.1, p.52. See *Instruction Général sur la Conscription 1er Novembre 1811*. There was nothing to say that infantry recruits could not be tall, only that light cavalry had to be under 1.649m, presumably because of the size of their mounts. The Tirailleurs (light infantry) and Grenadiers of the Young Guard would draw their recruits from the taller men. Half the contingent would be over 1.731m tall, with the other half at least 1.677m tall. The men all had to be literate and numerate. Although this no doubt made the Young Guard an excellent corps, it robbed regular infantry regiments of the most promising recruits.

7. Godet, *Mémoires*, p.446.

8. Godet, *Mémoires*, p.484.

9. *Organisation des 4 et 5e bataillons ordonnée par le Décret Imperial du 18 février 1809* (SHD Xb581).

10. The cadre included the officers, sub-officers, corporals and drummers.

11. Obert was 34 years old at the end of 1808 and had been in service since 1792 having volunteered at the age of 18. Obert had first risen to prominence when Bonaparte promoted him to battalion commander in Italy. After a spell as a prisoner of war between October 1799 and April 1800 he served in a succession of light infantry regiments.

12. Bibliothèque Nationale, Fond Maçonnique, dossier FM2-28: Premier Empire, *Régiments d'infanterie légère 4e au 9e*. Research courtesy of Pierre Yves Chauvin. See also Rebold, E., *Histoire des Trois Grandes Loges de Francs-Maçons en France* (Paris, Collignon: 1864). The origins of Masonry in the Ninth begin when the Légion de Condé formed a lodge on 15 June 1771 called Saint-Louis de l'Union. This lodge was resurrected on 19 August 1784 when the old Condé officers regrouped to form the Chasseurs des Cévennes. When the cavalry arm of this regiment was separated in 1788 the lodge followed the colonel and ended up as the 10th Horse Chasseurs in 1791. Prior to this, several infantry officers were members of the lodge. This Masonic past may also explain how Hubert de la Bassée secured his son's posting from the navy.

13. An undated letter by Meunier recommending Godet survives. In it the colonel wrote 'this officer is full of intelligence, serves with zeal and maintained a distinguished conduct during the war.' See 'Leonore', dossier LH/1160/67.

14. Couvreur, *Souvenirs d'un officier*, p.163.

15. Nankin was an Indian cotton used to make summer breeches.

16. Regimental rolls, (SHD 22Yc76).

17. Michel, Marie-Françoise and Jean-François, *Nicolas de Belrupt: Entre Wagram et Waterloo souvenirs d'Espagne du Caporal Nicolas Page* (Éditions Saône Lorraine, 1997), p.12.

18. *Etat nominative de Messieurs les officiers du régiment à l'époque du 1er Julliet 1809* (SHD Xb581).

19. Godet, *Mémoires*, pp.487–8.

20. The battalion would not reach full strength until May 1809 when the last two companies of chasseurs finally arrived.

21. Loÿ, *Historiques*, p.331.

22. Loÿ, *Historiques*, p.332.

23. Michel, *Nicolas de Belrupt*, p.13.

24. Michel, *Nicolas de Belrupt*, p.13.

25. *9e Régiment d'infanterie légère 4e Bataillon. Situation sommaire du bataillon en 8 Aout 1809* (SHD Xb581).

26. Couvreur, *Souvenirs d'un officier*, p.164.
    Magazine officers were inexperienced – lit. 'straight from the store'.

27. Couvreur, *Souvenirs d'un officier*, p.165.

28. Girod, *Dix ans*, p.139.

29. These exhortations were heard by Lieutenant Charles Leslie in the 29th Regiment. Cited in length on the website of the Worcestershire Regiment (www.worcestershireregiment.com).

30. Girod, *Dix ans*, p.140.

31. From the diary of Sergeant Daniel Nicol, published in MacBride, Mackenzie (ed.), *With Napoleon at Waterloo and other unpublished documents of the Waterloo and Peninsular Campaigns* (London: Francis Griffiths, 1911), pp.98–9.

32. Oman, C., *A History of the Peninsular War* (London: Greenhill Books, 1995), Vol.2, p.518.

33. Girod, *Dix ans*, p.141.

34. The British historian Oman was very critical of Victor's decision to make a night attack: 'Thus ended, in well-deserved failure, Victor's night attack. To attack in the dark across rugged and difficult ground was to court disaster. The wonder is not that two-thirds of the division went astray, but that the other third almost succeeded in the hazardous enterprise to which it was committed. Great credit is due to the 9th Léger for all that it did, and no blame whatever rests upon the regiment for its ultimate failure. The marshal must take all the responsibility.' Oman, *A History of the Peninsular War*, Vol.2, p.509.

35. Oman, *A History of the Peninsular War*, Vol.2, p.526.

36. Forty-six-year-old Nicolas Martinet had joined the Ninth from the 28th (b) Light Infantry Battalion in 1794. He was returned by the British on 5 August 1809 and pensioned off due to the severity of his wounds.

37. Girod, *Dix ans*, p.187; Vigo-Roussillon, p.247.

38. Michel, *Nicolas de Belrupt*, p.23.

39. Couvreur, *Souvenirs d'un officier*, p.167.

CHAPTER 13

1. Shrove Tuesday.

2. Girod, *Dix ans*, p.171.

3. Girod, *Dix ans*, pp.161–2.

4. Metzger, *La capitulation de Baylen*, p.22–3.

5. 'Biographie de M. De Vanderbach', *Société des études historiques: L'Investigateur: journal de l'Institut historique* (Paris: E. Thorin, 1851), p.217.

6. C****, Capitaine en non activité. *Evasion des prisonniers français détenus à bord du ponton la Vièille-Castille, en rade de Cadix, Le 15 Mai 1810* (Paris, Delaunay & Pélicier, 1818), p.44.

7. *Prisonniers de guerre français et étrangers, 1792–1874.*
   Prisonniers de guerre echaper du Ponton le Aronaute 27 Mai 1810' Echappes du Ponton La Vielle Castille (SHD Yj10).

8. SHD Yj10.

9. Girod, *Dix ans*, pp.177–8.

10. Girod, *Dix ans*, p.30.

11. Dauture was appointed to the Ninth on 18 February 1810, but did not arrive immediately.

12. This appears to have been Régeau's final action with the Ninth. He was later made major of the 26th Light and then became colonel of the 46th Line. Unlike his sons, he survived the war.

13. Michel, *Nicolas de Belrupt*, p.26.

14. Girod, *Dix ans*, p.187.
    Nicolas died on 1 November 1811, Dongée on 25 November. Letter from Dauture to the minister of war dated 25 January 1812 (SHD Xb582).

15. Girod, *Dix ans*, p.199.

16. Girod, *Dix ans*, p.191.
17. This contract was dated 1 January 1812 (SHD Xb583).
18. The elite companies of 3rd Battalion had remained with the regiment.
19. Couvreur, *Souvenirs d'un officier*, p.169.
20. Couvreur, *Souvenirs d'un officier*, p.170.
21. Oman, *A History of the Peninsular War*, Vol.4, p.27.
22. This letter is dated Puerta-Santa-Maria, 10 August 1811. Couvreur, *Souvenirs d'un officier*, pp.170–2.
23. Couvreur, *Souvenirs d'un officier*, p.173.

CHAPTER 14

1. Girod, *Dix ans*, p.202.
2. Girod, *Dix ans*, pp.153, 157.
3. Dauture letters (SHD Xb583).
4. Dauture letters (SHD Xb583).
5. Michel, *Nicolas de Belrupt*, p.31.
6. Bastions 1 and 2 are sometimes described as 'San Vincente' and 'San Jose' respectively.
7. Dauture letters: *Rapport à M le Géneral de Division Courroux de Pepinville, sur le désertion de M. Ogormann lieutenant au 9è Infanterie légère* (SHD Xb583).
8. Dauture letters (SHD Xb583).
9. Dauture letters (SHD Xb583).
10. *Etat nominative de M.M. les officiers et sous officiers du 9e Régiment d'Infanterie Légère qui sont particulièrement distingues à Bornos dans l'affaire glorieuse du 1er Juin 1812 et pour lesquels le colonel sollicite de l'avancement* (SHD Xb582).
11. Lit. 'head of the column'. This designates the musicians, standard-bearer, sappers and drum corps who formed the ceremonial head of the regiment on the march.
12. Colonel Dauture: letter dated Bornos le 30 June 1812 (SHD Xb583).
13. Dauture letters (SHD Xb583).
14. Page probably wore linen or cotton trousers on the march with a greatcoat.
15. Michel, *Nicolas de Belrupt*, p.48.

CHAPTER 15

1. On the subject of the divorce of Josephine, and Napoleon's marriage to Marie-Louise, Nicolas Page wrote: 'This did not bother the army too much; but the old ones said 'France is lost, here we are being screwed by the Austrians', Michel, *Nicolas de Belrupt*, pp.13–14.
2. Couvreur, *Souvenirs d'un officier*, pp.176–7.
3. Couvreur, *Souvenirs d'un officier*, pp.178–9.
4. Couvreur, *Souvenirs d'un officier*, pp.179–80.
5. Couvreur, *Souvenirs d'un officier*, pp.180–1.
6. Couvreur, *Souvenirs d'un officier*, p.182.
7. Couvreur, *Souvenirs d'un officier*, p.182.
8. Notes courtesy of Pierre-Yves Chauvin. SHD 22Yc78.
9. Loÿ, *Historiques*, p.375.
   Presumably any 6th Battalion survivors were incorporated into 3rd Battalion.
10. Couvreur, *Souvenirs d'un officier*, p.183.

11. Other accounts mention a detachment of British 95th Rifles holding the bridge until morning. Dubois mentions the Ninth encountering only artillery.
12. This 6th Battalion bore no relation to the battalion that had fought in the Leipzig campaign.
13. D'Eslon arrived in theatre on 12 March 1814.
14. Metzger, *La capitulation de Baylen*, p.40.
15. '*Échappé de ce pays au poids de l'or*' (SHD Xb583), 9e léger 1814.
16. Couvreur, *Souvenirs d'un officier*, p.184.
17. Couvreur, *Souvenirs d'un officier*, p.185.
18. Couvreur, *Souvenirs d'un officier*, pp.186–7.
19. Couvreur, *Souvenirs d'un officier*, pp.186–7.
20. Couvreur, *Souvenirs d'un officier*, p.187.
21. The inspection contained several interesting comments on the 1814 corps. The sub-officers and soldiers were 'animated by a good spirit' but the men were described as 'generally small' in stature. Half of their uniforms needed replacing and many were without greatcoats, pantaloons, drawers, shakos and forage caps. They were also lacking cartridge boxes, belts and musket slings. The cloth in stores for making greatcoats was described as 'beige'. There was no indication of the number of losses since the previous inspection in 1808, but from a study of the available regimental rolls, the Ninth received something like 15,000 recruits between 1800 and 1814. Given the effective strengths remained similar in 1800 and 1814 (1,629 officers and men after Marengo; against 1,565 in 1814), it is sobering to see the regiment lost as many men as it gained during this period.
22. Couvreur, *Souvenirs d'un officier*, p.187.
23. Couvreur, *Souvenirs d'un officier*, p.189.
24. Campagne was 1.62m tall, with a dark complexion, brown hair, black eyes, a long nose and pointed chin. She was authorized to follow the army with a 'beast of burden'. SHD Xs12 *Cantinières, vivandiers et bancheuses 1793–1939*.

CHAPTER 16

1. Couvreur, *Souvenirs d'un officier*, p.191.
2. Couderc de Saint-Chamant, (Capitaine) Henri, *Napoléon, ses dernières armées* (Paris, E. Flammarion, 1902), p.123.
3. These were (2nd bearer) Chasseur Jacques Galois, 1.788m tall and a soldier since 1793; and (3rd bearer) Carabineer Jean Piard, 1.768m, another veteran of the campaigns of the French Revolution.
4. Hollander, O., *Nos drapeaux et étendards de 1812 à 1815* (Nancy and Paris: Berger-Levrault et Cie. 1903), p.65.
5. It is unclear if the Ninth was issued with a new pattern standard on 25 December 1811. This new flag carried battle honours for the first time. Those awarded to the Ninth were Ulm, Friedland, Essling, Wagram. It is interesting the emperor chose not to recognize Marengo. Loÿ, pp.273–4.
6. Page was entered onto the rolls on 2 May 1815 as No. 2534. Another 298 names were recorded after his.
7. Jean Nicolas Parant had joined the Ninth in 1791.
8. Guillon, E., *Napoléon: Textes choisis et commentés* (Paris: Plon-Nourrit et Cie, 1913), pp.145–6.
9. For Hulot's report and other interesting documents relating to this episode see Wit, Pierre de, *The campaign of 1815: a study* (www.waterloo-campaign.nl).
10. Houssaye, Henry, *1815: Waterloo* (Paris: Perrin & Cie., 1908), p.113.
11. Bourmont told the Prussians that Gérard was going to march on Charleroi that day with 20,000 men. Learning of the defection Blücher famously dismissed the report saying 'Hundsfott bleibt Hundsfott', in other words, once a cur, always a cur.

12. Loÿ, *Historiques*, p.386. See also Baume's service record at 'Leonore' reference LH/145/57. His name is spelt 'Baume' in these records, while in the Ninth's correspondence he signed 'Beaume'.

13. Grouchy, E., *Relation succincte de la Campagne de 1815 en Belgique* (Paris: Delanchy, 1843), 3rd series, p.20.

14. De Rumigny, Marie-Théodore Gueullon de, *Le Général Gérard et la Bataille de Waterloo* (Carnet de la Sabretache, 1920), p.177.

15. Grouchy, *Relation succincte*, 2nd Series, p.6.

16. Houssaye, *1815: Waterloo*, p.307.

17. Houssaye, *1815: Waterloo*, p.304.

18. De Rumigny, *Le Général Gérard*, p.179.

19. Houssaye, *1815: Waterloo*, pp.465–6.

20. Hofschröer, Peter, *1815 The Waterloo Campaign: The German Victory* (London: Greenhill Books, 1999), p.162.

21. In these attacks the Ninth lost two carabineers killed, with four carabineers and three voltigeurs wounded, along with four chasseurs and a sergeant. Grouchy's aide-de-camp, Commandant Bella, did not blame the Ninth for failure at Bierges. He later wrote: 'I do not remember myself the number of the regiment which attacked the mill at Bierges; but I well know that a very-wide ditch and a muddy swamp rendered the approaches very difficult and that it was almost impossible to surmount obstacles of this kind. No criticism was thus merited by this regiment.' Grouchy, 4th series, p.55.

22. At Issy the regiment lost two men wounded and one killed other than D'Eslon's son. The last non-commissioned soldier in the regiment to be killed was 28-year-old Chasseur Pierre Sagnole from Chavanne in the Loire department. He had served with the regiment since September 1808.

23. The march to the Loire appears to have begun on or around 10 July. Having settled down after the armistice, the desertion rated spiked on 10 July at 91 men, with another 153 over the next five days. The desertion rate is so high one suspects the officers were doing little to discourage men from going home.

24. Couvreur, *Souvenirs d'un officier*, p.194.

25. The regimental rolls were completed over the next year by Nicolas Baudot and several former officers of the Ninth. The rolls show 468 men were released on 12 September and 19 on 20 September. The vast majority (799 men) were posted as deserters. This does not tally with the inspection records.

26. *État nominatif de MM les officiers qui composent le conseil d'administration. Ardennes, départment où ils se retirent, c.* September 1815 (SHD Xb583).

27. According to Cardron, the previous paymaster, Saulnier, had 'blown his brains out' around the time of Napoleon's return from Elba. Couvreur, p.192.

SELECT
BIBLIOGRAPHY

MANUSCRIPT SOURCES

The following dossiers were consulted at the Service Historiques de la Défense (SHD), Vincennes.

Archives administratives des corps de troupe:

Xc78 *Chasseurs des Cévennes 1784–1788*
Xb124 *Chasseurs des Cévennes 1788–1790*
Xb201 *Formation de 1791 (9è–12è legs.)*
Xb222 *Formation de 1793*
Xb327 *Ans IV, V à XI, XII. XIII*
Xb581 *9è regt. Consulat et Empire 1806–1809*
Xb582 *9è regt. Consulat et Empire 1810–1812*
Xb583 *9è regt. Consulat et Empire 1813–1815*

Contrôles des officiers:

Yb486 *Chasseurs Royaux des Cévennes (9è leg.)*
Yb487 *Chasseurs Royaux des Cévennes (9è leg.)*
2Yb560 *Officiers 9è leg. an VII–1811*
2Yb561 *Officiers 9è leg. an X–1811*

Contrôles de troupes:

9Yc3 *Chasseurs à Cheval des Cévennes 1776–1786*
9Yc3 *(2è registre) Chasseurs des Cévennes (a pied)*
16Yc640 *9è bataillon (Volontaires Nationaux 1791–93)*
16YC641 *9è bataillon (Volontaires Nationaux 1791–93)*
18Yc324 *3è bataillon 9è*

22Yc75 *9è leg. an I–XII*

22Yc76 *9è leg. an XII–1809*

22Yc77 *9è leg. 1809–1810*

22Yc78 *9è leg. 1812–1813*

22Yc79 *9è leg. 1813–1814*

22Yc80 *9è leg. organisation 1814*

22Yc81 *9è leg. 1814–1815*

Miscellaneous documents:

B5138 *Situation 18 janvier 1800. Armée d'Ouest*

1M629 *Journal des opérations militaires de la division du général upont pendant la campagne de l'an XIV*

1M654 *Grande Armée, 1806–1807: Tome II. – 1er corps. – Feuillets 1 à 127*

1M654 *Marche du 1er Corps de las Grande Armée aux Ordres de le Maréchal Bernadotte Prince de Portecorvo, Années 1806 et 1807*

1M654 *Precis historique des campagnes du 1er Corps de la Grande Armée 1806 et 1807*

MR610 *Journal des Marches et opérations de la division Boudet*

MR610 *Général Guénand. Note pour le Général Dumas, 30 Brumaire An 10*

MS1848 *Historique du 1er Dragons*

MS1856 *Historiques des corps de troupe, an IX (2e cavalerie)*

Xs12 *Cantinières, vivandiers et bancheuses*

Ya159 *Compagnie des cadets du roi de Pologne. (Écoles, diverses pages A. régime)*

Ya409 *Dossiers par régiment 1740–1792 Bretagne (Cévennes)*

REGIMENTAL HISTORIES

Dubois, L., *Historique du 9è Régiment d'Infanterie Légère 1839* (SHD MR1842)

Labassée, M., *Notice sur les Batailles, Combats, Actions, Sièges et expéditions ou ces différents corps se sont trouvée depuis le mois de Septembre 1792 jusqu'è ce jour*. 2 Messidor Year IX (SHD MR1856)

Loÿ, L., *Historiques du 84e régiment d'infanterie de ligne 'Un Contre Dix'; du 9e régiment d'infanterie légère 'l'Incomparable'; et du 4e régiment de voltigeurs de la Garde 1684–1904* (Lille: L. Daniel, 1905)

ORAL HISTORY AND BIOGRAPHY

André, Eugène, *Le Général Comte Barrois: Grand-Croix de la Légion d'Honneur 1774–1860* (Bar-le-Duc: Imprimerie Comte-Jacquet, 1901).

Couvreur, H. *Souvenirs d'un officier de Napoléon: d'après les lettres du Capitaine Cardron, de Philippeville (1804–1815)* (Namur, Imprimerie Jaques Godenne, 1938) Note: this account first appeared in the *Annales de la Société Archéolgique de Namur* Tome XLII, 1937.

Girod de l'Ain, Général, *Dix ans de mes souvenirs militaires de 1805 à 1815* (Paris: J. Dumaine, 1873).

Godet, M., *Mémoires de capitaine Godet*; Carnet de la Sabretache. Séries 3 (1927). Note: Certain details on Godet's private life were withheld at the family's request. The unedited memoirs were published online in 2010 by the Société d'Etudes Historiques Révolutionnaires et Impériales.

Metzger, P., *La capitulation de Baylen et le sort des prisonniers français, d'après le journal du colonel d'Eslon (1807–1811)* (Limoges et Paris: Charles-Lavauzelle, 15 novembre 1908). Note: D'Eslon's original journal can be found at the Bibliothèque Nationale de France; département des manuscrits; code NAF 13007: Colonel d'Eslon. Journal, 10 novembre 1807–18 avril 1811.

Michel, Marie-Françoise & Jean-François, *Nicolas de Belrupt: Entre Wagram et Waterloo souvenirs d'Espagne du Caporal Nicolas Page* (Éditions Saône Lorraine, 1997). Note: the memoirs of Page can be found in the Archives Départementales des Vosges; code FR AD 88, ms 112: *Souvenirs de Nicolas Page, ancien soldat de l'Empereur, 1788–1863*.

Meunier, C., *L'Histoire populaire de Napoléon, suivie de la translation de ses restes mortels à Paris* (Paris, B. Renaud, 1842).

INDEX

INDEX

Tavazzano 62
Tennis Court Oath 136
'Terror, The' (1793–94) 26–27
Tesson, Sub-Lieutenant 54
Thalfingen 151
Tharreau, General Jean Victor 267
Thionville, Marc 132
Thirry, Lieutenant 99
Thorn (Toruń) 196, 213, 227
Ticino, River 59, 60, 67, 157
Tilly, General 147
Tilsit (Sovetsk) 224, 225–226
Tilsit, treaty of (1807) 227, 230
Toledo 275
Toullier (Girod's friend) 296
Toulouse 332, 334
Toulouse, battle of (1814) 334
Tours 241–242
Toussaint, Sergeant 128
training 25, 110, 114, 131–132, 137, 266–267, 282
Trebbia, River 70–71
Treviso 104
Trueba, River 247
Turbigo 59
Tuscany 106

Uclés 272–273
Ulm 150, 151, 156, 160, 163
uniforms 20–21, 22, 40, 46, 110, 121, 126, 130, 132, 138, 139–140, 186, 210, 264, 303, 308, 309, 319–320

'V, Mr' (3rd Carabineers captain) 222, 223
Vadel, Lieutenant 156
Valais region 41, 45
Valance, Marie 178
Valdemoro depot 281
Valdepeñas massacre 237
Valenciennes 34, 35
Vandamme (corps commander) 346–347, 350, 351, 352
Vanderbach, Surgeon-Major Charles 59–60, 99, 127, 157, 182, 209, 210–211, 289, 294, 357
Vannes 27
Vedel, General 237
Velez-Malaga 239
Vendée, the 27
Venta de Cardenas 237
Vercelli 58–59
Verger, Battalion Commander Jean-Baptiste 37, 43, 51, 112
Verona 104–105
Vevey 41–43
Victor, Marshal Claude 42, 73, 75, 78, 79, 80, 81, 89, 95, 214, 219, 227, 232, 239, 247, 249, 256, 274, 275, 276, 278, 279, 280, 281, 284–285, 286, 293, 294, 317
Vienna 172, 174, 177, 178, 267, 269
　Alstergasse, No 107: 175
　Kempandorf barracks 172
　Schönbrunn Palace review 269
Vignot, Drummer Laurent 289
Vildier, Chasseur François 134
Villamartin 305–306

Villatte, General Eugene-Casimir 247, 250, 281, 317
Villemer, Mr 179
Villeneuve 43, 44
Villionne, Lieutenant-Colonel Pierre Justin Marchand de 30–31, 33, 262
Vimeiro, battle of (1808) 243
Vinot, Chasseur Jean 93, 103, 106
Virey, Corporal 128
Vistula, River 212, 227
Vistula Lagoon (Frisches Haff) 197–198, 200
Vitoria 235, 244, 330
Vitoria, battle of (1813) 330–331
Vittemburg 197
Vittré, marshal of camps de 354
Vivenot, Sub-Lieutenant Paul 58
Voeglin, Sub-Lieutenant 66, 67
Voghera 72, 100
Volsack, Lieutenant 128, 246
voltigeurs 123–124, 197, 198, 204, 205–207, 210, 232, 252–255
　revolt by 255–256
Vosges region 145–146, 258–259, 260–261

Wagram, battle of (1809) 269–270
Walhain farmhouse 349
War of the Fifth Coalition (1809) 267–271
War of the First Coalition (1792–97) 20, 23, 26, 33, 34, 46
War of the Fourth Coalition (1806–07) 183–190, 195–211, 212–227
War of the Second Coalition (1798–1802) 19, 20, 25–26, 39–40, 53, 54–56, 57–73, 74–96, 97–100, 104
War of the Seventh Coalition (1815) 344–353
War of the Sixth Coalition (1812–14) 324–327, 328, 334–335
War of the Third Coalition (1803–06) 141, 145–171, 172–179
Waren 186–188
Waterloo, battle of (1815) 350, 352, 355, 356
Watrin, General François 41, 54, 55, 56, 81
Watt, Captain 296
Wavre, battle of (1815) 349, 350, 351–352
weapons *see also* French army: artillery
　'arms of honour' 103, 105–106, 107, 127–128
　bayonets 50–51
　cartridges, deficiency in 62, 71, 72, 75
　guns, four-pounder 44, 46
　howitzers, six-inch 44, 46
　musket, dragoon model 124
　muskets, flintlock 17, 48, 111
　'muskets of honour' 103, 105–106
　sabres 111, 130
　'sabres of honour' 107
　shells 290–291, 313
Weissenkirchen 165, 166
Wellesley, Sir Arthur (later Viscount Wellington) 275, 280–281, 301, 305, 311, 312, 314, 320, 330, 332, 344, 355
Werneck, General 158, 161
Wesel 179, 263
Württemberg, Prince of 184, 185
Würzburg 324, 325

Zach, General Anton 74, 79, 84, 85, 90

400